JEWS IN NEVADA

Wilbur S. Shepperson Series in Nevada History

JEWS *A History*
IN NEVADA

JOHN P. MARSCHALL

▲▲ UNIVERSITY OF NEVADA PRESS
RENO & LAS VEGAS

The University of Nevada Press thanks John Farahi
for his generous assistance in the publication of
this book.

Wilbur S. Shepperson Series in Nevada History
Series Editor: Michael Green

University of Nevada Press, Reno, Nevada 89557 USA
Copyright © 2008 by University of Nevada Press
All rights reserved

Manufactured in the United States of America
Design by Omega Clay

Library of Congress Cataloging-in-Publication Data
Marschall, John P.
  Jews in Nevada : a history / John P. Marschall.
    p. cm.
  Includes bibliographical references and index.
  ISBN 978-0-87417-737-4 (hardcover : alk. paper)
1. Jews—Nevada—History. I. Title.
  F850.J5M37 2008
  979.3′004924—dc22
2007040990

17 16 15 14 13 12 11 10 09 08   5 4 3 2

Frontispiece: Detail of Michelson family photograph.
Courtesy of the Nevada Historical Society.

To the Jewish people of Nevada,
for whom preserving the memory is tradition

CONTENTS

CONTENTS

ILLUSTRATIONS AND TABLES

FIGURES

Photographs following pages 84 and 178

Stereotypical caricature of a Nevada Jewish peddler

Abraham Klauber and Theresa (Epstein) Klauber, 1861

The 1862 Fleishhacker Carson City store

Mark Twain with members of the Nevada Territorial Legislature, 1864

Rabbi Herman Bien

Malvina and Joseph Platt, ca. 1864

Olcovich Brothers Dry Goods and Clothing Store

Haas Brothers' 1862 advertisement

Jacob W. Davis

Jacob W. Davis's patent for "Improvement in Fastening Pocket-Openings"

Canvas stores in Elko, 1869

E. Reinhart store, Winnemucca, 1915

Morris and Lina Posener Badt, ca. 1880

Abraham Mooser in Confederate uniform, 1861

Solomon Ashim's Eureka general store

Regina Moch advertised a new start

Max Oberfelder advertisement

Eureka, 1870s

Hamilton, Nevada, 1869

Carson City Brewery

Leah and Adolph Sutro

Mark Strouse

Elizabeth Rosenstock, Essie Rosenstock Reinhart, and Milton Reinhart, 1894

Nevada Jewish history has been so well hidden that even natives are unaware of its presence. The present volume is an offering to both the Jewish and general readership about this people's place in the state's development from mining camps to a premier tourist destination.

Were Jews in Nevada any different from Jews elsewhere in the West or the United States to warrant an account of their history? Because Nevada's early Jewish settlers came from somewhere else and so many left the state before they died, it might be said that they were no different from their counterparts elsewhere. In its first fifteen to twenty years, Nevada was largely an extension and cross-section of California Jewry, and for many, San Francisco was the home to which they would return when the economy began to slide after 1878.

Nevada Jews shared similarities of birth and occupation with other western Jews, but they could boast some significant "firsts." The state's first legislative assembly included three Jews, one of whom was a rabbi. One of Nevada's several Jewish tailors invented the copper-riveted jeans in Reno. The Sutro Tunnel on the Comstock was an engineering feat unparalleled in its time. Jewish clothing and dry-goods merchants dominated the business districts of Virginia City and the state capital for almost thirty years. And the more than one hundred Jewish citizens of Eureka formed the first official Reform congregation in the Far West in 1876.

Jews who came West thrived in urban environments such as San Francisco, Denver, and Portland. Nevada had no comparable large city for almost a century. Nevada was a rural state with many isolated camps and small towns whose Jewish presence may have been limited to a single store. Unlike their urban coreligionists, many Nevada Jews had little opportunity for regular communal worship. Likely, more Nevada male Jews than their western or eastern fellows married Gentile women, contributing to a lack of family Sabbath observance. In spite of severe obstacles, many maintained a level of religious observance to keep them in the faith. The pressures to assimilate ran high in this rural state. Formal congregational affiliation ran as high as 100 percent in Eureka in 1876 but evaporated to less than 10 percent statewide in 2000. In this latter respect, contemporary Nevada Jewry ranked well below the national average.

Although Jews played prominent roles elsewhere in the Far West and Southwest, few could measure up to their part in the development of Las Vegas as a gambling mecca and tourist designation. The imprint of Jewish gamblers, builders, bankers, merchants, lawyers, educators, and civil servants on modern Nevada is unmistakable and unique.

Occupationally, Nevada Jews in the nineteenth and early twentieth centuries were—like their counterparts elsewhere—heavily invested in merchandising, particularly in textile businesses. They were also significantly represented as jewelers and purveyors of tobacco and alcohol. One occupational difference from the national profile is that more Nevada Jews were engaged in the mining business. Although only a minority actually worked in a mine or panned a stream, many merchants accepted mining stock as payment for goods and also speculated in mining stock based on the best local knowledge. Nevada Jewish women, like most in the West, played some role in the merchandising ventures of their husbands. But there is evidence that Nevada (particularly in Virginia City and Eureka) had a higher percentage of Jewish women working independently than elsewhere.

Nineteenth-century Jews in the Far West may have felt an antisemitic barb from eastern visitors or competitors, but there was little evidence of hostility from Nevada locals receiving their services. The acceptance of Jews in Nevada society was due to several factors. Nevada had the highest percentage of foreign-born population of any western state through 1930. The early Jewish population was almost entirely foreign-born, and approximately 40 percent were from Polish Prussia and Slavic Europe—well before the mass migration from Eastern Europe after 1880. Their place of nativity was no obstacle to social and civic involvement. Second, most Jews were assumed to be "white," espousing a Germanic ethos that was already endemic to American culture. Third, Nevada Jewish males, like many in the West, were charter members of Masonic and fraternal organizations, whose eastern lodges often banned Jewish membership. Nevada Jews also held public office well beyond their percentage of the population. Although Jewish civic activism was common elsewhere in the West, the Jewish leadership in small-town Nevada was arguably more significant than elsewhere in the nation. One long-term legacy was that overt anti-Jewish bias was particularly quiescent in northern Nevada. Finally, most Jewish merchants earned a reputation—noted in the press—as hardworking, honest, and law-abiding people.

Although the Nevada Jewish population in the last quarter of the nineteenth century peaked about 1880 at less than nine hundred, it was larger than that of Maine, New Hampshire, or Vermont. The Jewish population in Nevada declined along with the general exodus from the state after 1878. It recovered in modern times. Las Vegas now has, by some counts, about one hundred thousand Jewish citizens. It is arguably the fastest-growing "Jewish city" in the country.

Why this Gentile wrote a history of Jews in Nevada was the result of several coincidences. I intended to write a critical history of religion and politics in Nevada. To acquaint myself with primary sources, I decided to use one of the smallest religious groups in any state, Jews, as a manageable preliminary guide to the subject. An initial bibliographical search revealed, however, that with the exception of a few short articles, virtually nothing had been written about Nevada Judaism or Jewry.

My initial task was to uncover identities, and I began with Jewish cemeteries. This first step was most productive, though headstone names such as Harris, Rice, McCreadie, and Shannon sent me on peripheral adventures that proved valuable. It became evident immediately that the Jews were not going to be a "manageable" group. Name changes were common, and addresses changed quickly. Transiency in search of a better market for goods was a hallmark of merchants and the bane of later historians attempting to corral their subjects.

The religious practice of Jews in Nevada was a controlling focus in this research. What emerged was the widest disparity of belief and practice—with the exception of those who chose to reject or hide their ancestry altogether. Those who embraced the traditions of their religion at one level or another structured their lives accordingly. One observant family, for example, after twenty-five years in Carson City, moved to Denver shortly before their second youngest son was to marry a Gentile. Religious practice was not, however, the primary goal for most Nevada Jews.

The Jews who came to Nevada—like the tens-of-thousands of Gentiles from all over the world—did so because there was economic opportunity. Jewish numbers were minuscule compared to the general population, but their positions as first arrivals in many Nevada camps and towns assured them of an acceptance unequaled in the Old Country or in the nation's eastern cities. They found themselves in the midst of an international polyglot population, from Chinese laborers to Irish miners and Canadian lumbermen, who patronized the Jewish stores. Economic security and the pressures of cultural accommodation proved to be the most significant agents affecting Jewish life. As the twentieth century ended, southern Nevada's explosive growth produced a surge in the Jewish population and a concomitant increase in the number of religious and cultural opportunities.

Writing about the past fifty years of Jewish activities in the state has proved to be a special challenge. A Las Vegas physician attending a presentation on Reno Jewry several years ago advised that if I took my research to southern Nevada, I should wear a "bulletproof vest." Much of the work for recent history has been drawn from interviews and newspaper reports—sources about which professors correctly advise students to be cautious, lest the outcome prove fabulous. "Welcome to Fabulous Las Vegas Nevada," reads Betty Willis's 1959 neon greeting on the Strip. "Fabulous," of course, can mean "resembling a fable" or simply "marvelous." Much of contemporary history is a product of memoirs, which often contain conflicting accounts and interpretations of the facts. What follows is a sampling of paraphrases from persons interviewed for this work over the past decade. Most are from Las Vegas:

> Publish the book and then I'll tell you what really happened.
> You don't want to print that, do you?
> Some of your sources have axes to grind, so beware!
> Am I talking to the priest here? Under the seal of confession?
> What I've said is all you need to know about that person!
> Please do not quote me on this, but . . .
> Don't tell me *that* was in the newspaper!
> Are we off the record here?

These comments reflected pride and fear—protecting personal reputations or that of Jews in general. So the historian in me had to move with trepidation, trying to uncover the facts while protecting confidences and maintaining the rigors of historical discipline. Every effort has been made to corroborate information from several sources. Dozens of unattributable "stories" could have added to the tapestry of Nevada Jewish history and one day may become the burden of historians. Jewish readers are asked to be patient with the occasional but necessary explanation of Jewish terms for the wider audience. Documentation abounds in the hope that scholars will critique this effort and be moved to include and expand on Nevada's rich Jewish history in future works. The record is far from complete, but this is a place from which others may begin.

It is now a pleasant task—a mitzvah (as Jews would put it)—to remember and acknowledge those who provided me with information, assistance, and encouragement to complete this work. The staffs of libraries, archives, and museums were invaluable. Many thanks to Guy Rocha and Christopher Driggs of the Nevada State Library and Archives; state historic preservation officer Ron James; curator of manuscripts Eric Moody, curator of photography Lee Brumbaugh, Michael Maher, and Phillip Earl of the Nevada Historical Society; and Nevada State Museum director Robert Nylen. Also, I am grateful to the staffs of the Western Jewish History Center and the Blumenthal Library at the Judah Magnes Museum in Berkeley and at the Jacob Rader Marcus Center of the American Jewish Archives in Cincinnati, whose generous one-month fellowship allowed me to mine its resources. Jacquelyn Sundstrand of the University of Nevada, Reno's Department of Special Collections and Su Kim Chung in Special Collections at the University of Nevada, Las Vegas, were ever on the lookout for materials related to Jews in Nevada. Likewise, the staffs of the Northeastern Nevada Museum and Ely State Museum generously provided photographs.

Dr. Barbara Zarrzewska-Nikipoczk kept me out of jail and served as my invaluable guide and translator in accessing records at state archives in Poznàn, Poland, which positively established the Polish origins of many Nevada Jews. The staff of Poznàn's Archivum Panstwowe were most helpful, as were Feliks Gruszka, a local Kepno historian, and Jozef Adamski, a Kepno museum curator who had salvaged headstones from a bulldozed Jewish cemetery. Walter Cucine was my Eureka guide extraordinaire. Among those providing tangible support for research and travel were Nevada Humanities, the Charles H. Stout Foundation, Myra and Barry Hanish, Henry Garell, and John Farahi.

I am most in debt to those who provided me with background information concerning Jewry in Nevada over the past fifty years. More than sixty people agreed to be interviewed for this book and almost all generously released their statements for publication. They, along with many correspondents, are appreciatively recognized in the footnotes and bibliography. Readers and others who provided materials, assistance, or advice on the manuscript were Professor Alan Balboni, Richard Beeman, Dr. Leroy Bernstein, Patricia Blanchard (Feinberg), Dr. Alvin Blumberg, Meyer L. Bodoff, George and Eileen Brookman, Bea Brown, Betty Akert Brown, Marilyn Burson, Eileen Cohen, Robert Dickens, William Douglass, Nancy Badt Drake, Dorothy Eisenberg, Chana Feinhandler, Rabbi Harvey Fields, Kenneth Fliess, Jean Ford, Abraham Kep Freedman, Jack Friedenthal, Georgia Fulstone, Professor Michael Green, Judith Greenspan, Shawn Hall, Mella Harmon, Ben Harrison, Professor James Hulse, Ray Izen, Jim and Linda Jaffe, Ron and Susan James, Arthur Johnson, Dee Kille, Dwayne Kling, Shel Kolner, Karen Laramore, Ron and Judy Mack, Dr. Leslie Malkin, Art Marshall, Steve Matles, Bonnie Matton, Mary McKain, Jerome Morrissy, Heather Nobles-Altman, Eugene Nudelman, Brian and Sherrie O'Callaghan, Irwin and Sylvia Olcott, Jennifer Olcovich, Patsy Olmstead, Susan Paslov, Fran Pettite, William Pettite, Harriet Rochlin, Israel Rogers, Doris Rosenburg, Professor Hal Rothman, Professor William Rowley, Hynda Rudd, Jaclyn Rusch, Elmer Rusco, Reba Gordon Saiger, Doug Samuelson, Joyce Scheinman, Katherine Selinsky, Marion Sieber, Professor Richard Siegel, Allan Silver, Dr. Anton Sohn, the Honorable Charles E. Springer, Cindy Sutherland, Frances and Mervin Tarlow, Christine Hilp Tweet, Douglas Unger, Anita Watson, Barbara Weinberg, Thomas R. C. Wilson, Gil and Edythe Katz Yarchever, and Pamela Zohar. I apologize to anyone I may have missed. Finally, I thank my son, Peter, daughter, Sarah, and wife, Rita, who unstintingly read draft copies and listened with encouragement to my latest breakthrough or misstep. Although I am beholden to these and many others, any errors of fact are my full responsibility.

Celebrating Tradition and Resisting Assimilation

Nevada Jewry would not have existed without millions of its ancestors maintaining Judaism. Comprehending its history requires some understanding of the milestones remembered for more than two millennia and the struggle for acceptance in a Christian world. There were also the lures of accommodation or assimilation, especially in the isolation of Nevada's desert, where Torah study and kosher diets were among the 613 religious duties (mitzvoth) fondly remembered but rarely observed.

Sabbath observance was a sign of the covenant of Yahweh with Moses on Sinai. Passover marked the angel of death "passing over" Egyptian Jewish households and the subsequent Exodus toward a promised land. The Jews celebrated their redemption from extermination in a later dispersion, as described in the book of Esther, as the Feast of Purim and observed it with gusto even in Nevada's most depressing years.

By the time Jews suffered the Jerusalem temple destruction in 72 CE, they were no longer exclusively agrarian. They were artisans, traders, and more. Religiously, Jews retained some visionary relationship to a homeland without a temple and evolved into a "People of the Book"—not unlike Christians and Muslims. They remained, however, strangers in many countries, and anti-semitism was a constant companion.

Christian Antisemitism

The cultural and religious bias against Jews was born in the first century of the Common Era. Many early Christians considered themselves one of several Jewish sects. An early dispute in the primitive church was between "Judaizers," who thought it necessary for Christians to observe Jewish law, and those, like Paul, who treated Jesus' teaching as a new revelation freeing Gentiles from any allegiance to the "old" Testament (Gal. 2). Elsewhere, Peter twice condemned the Jews for not accepting Jesus as the Messiah and blamed them for his death (Acts 3:14–16, 5:30). In the Gospel according to Matthew, Jews are recorded as having said of Jesus: "His blood be on us and on our children" (27:25). Christians now had a scriptural basis for blaming Jews as "Christ-killers," but there was more to come.

It took several hundred years for Christianity to sort out the issue of Jesus' relationship to God. The Council of Nicea (325 CE) defined the ambiguous attribution of Jesus as "Son of God" to mean he was both human and equal to Yahweh. Arian Christians, the majority in some quarters of Christendom, considered Jesus divine but not equal to God. For these Arians as well as all practicing Jews, the notion that the God of Abraham, Isaac, and Jacob could in any way be human was unthinkable. Nevertheless, the Nicene Creed emerging from the council cemented the identity of Jesus and Yahweh and opened Jews to vilification and charges of deicide. Constantinople's Archbishop John Chrysostom (ca. 347–407 CE) characterized Jews as having "all the vices of beasts and are good for nothing but slaughter. . . . They behave no better than pigs in their lewd vulgarities."[1]

Throughout the Middle Ages, zealous Christians extended their ideological differences with Judaism by making Jews scapegoats for many disasters and killed thousands of them without cause or remorse. However, some Christians tolerated Jews for their mercantile skills and as lenders of money—a usurious practice that non-Jews considered sinful. Roman Catholic liturgy, however, kept alive the common reference to the Jews as faithless. Popes, monks, and kings organized crusades to capture the Holy Land with orders that "infidels"—whether Islamic or Jewish—choose between Christian baptism and the sword.

Theologians like Thomas Aquinas justified these "holy wars," arguing that anyone who heard the Gospel and refused to accept it lost the right to property and freedom. Later, English Reformer John Wycliffe (1330–1384) stated that such a refusal deprived one of the right to life itself. Martin Luther reminded Christians in 1542 that "you have no enemy more cruel, more venomous and virulent, than a true Jew." As Luther's recent biographers have noted, such unbridled attacks on Jews reflected contemporary thought and polemic. Shakespeare's depiction of Shylock as "stiff-necked" had its basis in Yahweh's many such characterizations of his chosen people. The notion that Shylock was consumed with exacting his usurious "pound of [Christian] flesh" easily became a stereotype of all Jews.[2] More important, on the eve of European migration to the New World, both Catholics and Protestants were united—if only in a common anti-Jewish prejudice.

Jews of the European Diaspora remained isolated by law and often by choice. They were routinely ineligible for citizenship in any European duchy, town, or city. The dilemma for Jews was the extent to which they should accommodate their religious beliefs and practices to the norms of a hostile environment. The New World was the next crucible to test Jewish religious commitment amid temptations to assimilate.

Jews in Colonial America

Virtually every religious group in the American colonies tried to enforce a uniformity of practice that often was as burdensome on a minority as it had been on the new enforcers. When twenty-three Jews fled Portuguese-controlled Brazil for New Amsterdam in 1654, they expected a warm welcome from the relatively tolerant Dutch. But Governor Peter Stuyvesant regarded the presence of Jews as disruptive to the colony's otherwise Reformed Christian ecumenical peace. Dutch Reformed minister Johannes Megapolensis complained to his religious superiors in Amsterdam that the Jews from Brazil and, most recently, from Holland worshiped mammon and had "no other aim than to get possession of Christian property, to win other merchants by drawing all trade to themselves." He requested that religious leaders pressure Dutch West India Company directors to authorize deportation of "these godless rascals, who are no benefit to the country." Having acknowledged the presence of papists, Mennonites, Lutherans, Puritans, atheists, and others "who conceal themselves under the name of Christians," Megapolensis further pleaded that "it would create a still greater confusion, if the obstinate and immovable Jews came to settle here." Unmoved by his argument, the Dutch West India Company ordered that the Jews be free to carry on their business, lest a reputation for intolerance jeopardize the advancement of colonization and trade.[3]

Jews in New Amsterdam remained amid laws restricting certain civil rights. They were unable to hold public office, worship publicly, trade with the natives, or—for a time—purchase real estate. Maryland's Catholic proprietors—fearing a future intolerant Protestant majority—proclaimed an "Act of Toleration for All Christians." A Protestant majority repealed the act in 1654, and Catholics became political pariahs. When Maryland became a crown colony in 1692, Anglicanism was made the established church. Consequently, Maryland Jews and Catholics lived for almost a century in a hostile political environment but became essential to the colony's economic well-being and won general, though unofficial, respect for their contributions.

In other colonies such as Rhode Island, South Carolina, and Pennsylvania, small groups of Jews managed to avoid open persecution but were routinely encouraged to convert to the "true faith" and repent of their sins. The pressure to accommodate to the dominant Protestant culture was enormous. Leonard Dinnerstein, a historian of antisemitism in America, notes that "every Jew who settled and remained in colonial Connecticut before the Revolution married a Christian."[4] Intermarriage became the preferred ticket for Jews seeking respect and acceptance even after the revolutionary First Amendment began the process of disestablishing religion in the United States. Many patriots, such as Patrick Henry of Virginia, lobbied strongly to establish Christianity as a generic state religion. Although unsuccessful, the notion that the new United States had a special relationship to Christianity was already embedded in the Protestant majority's ethos. The individual states did not all adopt the federal position on separation of church and state. Congregationalism, for example, remained the Massachusetts state religion until 1820. The United States, in short, had yet to demonstrate a track record of tolerance for religious pluralism, and Jews needed to be circumspect.

Nineteenth-Century Immigrants from Where and Why

Historians have traditionally designated the earliest migration of Jews to America as the "Sephardic" period because most had roots in the Iberian Peninsula. The larger wave of immigrant Jews to the United States, often dated from 1820 to 1880, has been commonly characterized as the "Germanic" phase. Because Prussia was increasing its control over portions of central Europe in the mid-nineteenth century, almost half the "Germanic" migration included large numbers of Bohemians, Moravians, Latvians, and Russians and a significant minority from the Duchy of Poznán in western Poland.

The Jews of expanding Prussia generally clustered in their own neighborhoods and interacted with Gentiles only for business and legal reasons. For the most part, the men earned their living as small-time merchants—often of dry goods and household necessities. Others, with an uncanny skill for determining relative values, engaged in bartering between farmers and governmental agencies. Hasia R. Diner has noted that this unique and necessary role in German society raised the respectability of Jews among neither the peasants nor the middle class.[5] The role of the Jewish merchant in Nevada, however, created an altogether different outcome.

Europeans generally considered Jews a separate people without citizenship rights. They operated legally under self-rule through an organization called a *kahal*. The leaders of local *kahals* met regionally and shared information on subjects ranging from mercantile opportunities to marital alliances, the experiences of emigrants, and the status of Jewish civil liberties. In 1833, the Prussian government promised full citizenship to those Jews who became culturally, socially, and linguistically assimilated. For all practical purposes, this often meant conversion to Christianity.

In some places, Jews could not move from rural to urban areas, and those in the towns had limited civil rights. For example, Jews could not constitute more than one-third of the town council or own real estate, nor could they employ Christian servants or serve as judges. Prussian authorities lifted some restrictions in 1848, but the Polish authorities reimposed them in the Duchy of Poznán. Whereas western German Jews received citizenship in exchange for military service, the option was unavailable to Prussian Poles. Consequently, the out-migration of Prussian Jews was staggering. Three-quarters of the nineteen thousand Jews who left the Duchy of Poznán between 1835 and 1852 emigrated to the United States, Great Britain, or France.[6]

Pushed by political and economic disfranchisement and pulled by American opportunity, central European Jews streamed into eastern port cities and vied with Irish immigrants for jobs and respectability. Their acceptance by the entrenched Sephardic leaders in the major synagogues was another matter.[7] And even though Prussian Polish Jews arriving in the 1840s had been exposed to German language and culture as conditions for emancipation, language differences were—in many places—sufficient reason for two separate celebrations of High Holidays. Slavic Jews often faced hostility or intellectual snobbery at the hands of more "enlightened" native German and Sephardic Jews. Name-changing was common. Among future Nevadans, for example, "Placzek" changed to "Platt," "Opachinsky" to "Tarlow," and "Olcowicz" over several generations to "Olcott." Census records from this period reveal a majority of "Prussian" places of nativity. In 1860 and 1870, Nevada Jews who designated Prussia as their birthplace most often were from western Poland. One proud Pole in Carson City insisted that the census enumerator list him as from "Kempen in Poland in Prussia."[8] This detail in the original census rolls proved to be an important clue in establishing Nevada Jewry's heavy Polish ethnicity.

Chain migrations of relatives and friends to eastern California and Nevada originated from towns and cities like Kempen (Kepno) and Posen (Poznán). Families extended Old World neighborhood relationships through New World marriages and business liaisons. For most immigrants, the values of family and Jewish tradition were central. Some Jews certainly were secularized before leaving the Continent, but the isolation of Nevada's mining camps hastened the process of assimilation for others.

The Institutional Faces of Judaism

"Jewry" denotes a people who have or claim a genetic relationship to the Hebrews of old. "Judaism" is the religion of those Jews who choose to be observant. The basic forms of institutionalized Judaism have spawned offshoot movements. Not all groups recognize the legitimacy, integrity, or relevance of the others. All have their own complex history and schisms based on disagreements over doctrine or practice. Nevada's Jewish history includes the spectrum of Jews from those committed to Orthodoxy or one of its permutations to those who are ethnically Jewish but not religious. Most of the latter, however, have at least a memory of relationship to one of Judaism's several movements or branches.

Orthodox Judaism is the oldest traditional form, which originally required observance of the 613 mitzvoth (duties and proscriptions identified in the Torah) and regulated every aspect of Jewish life, from maintaining a kosher kitchen to observing a family Sabbath meal and engaging in no work or travel on the Sabbath. Without a temple, prescribed ritual sacrifices no longer are observed. Its synagogues are affiliated with the Union of Orthodox Jewish Congregations (Orthodox Union or OU) and their rabbis customarily educated at Yeshiva University in New York. Of the several neo-Orthodox movements, two are prominent in Nevada. The Hasidic Lubavitch Chabad, founded in the eighteenth century, maintains international headquarters in Crown Heights, New York. Its most recent leader, Rabbi Menachem Mendel Schneerson, revered by many of his followers as the Messiah, died in 1994. The Young Israel Movement took form in 1913 in New York and is now part of an international organization centered in Israel.

Reform Judaism began as a mid-nineteenth-century movement to adapt Orthodox Judaism to modern times. Started in Germany, it was nurtured in the United States by, among others, Rabbi Isaac Mayer Wise (1819–1900), who had emigrated from Germany via Albany to Cincinnati. It adopted the English ritual *Minhag Amerika* and endured a number of changes in practice through the end of the nineteenth century. Whether to support the Zionist goal of an independent free state of Israel became a divisive issue at the turn of the century, and the Reform movement was anti-Zionist. The Union of American Hebrew Congregations (UAHC) early on abandoned separate seating of men and women at its services. Its Hebrew Union seminaries provided rabbinical education and were the first to open their doors to women, in 1972. Reno's Reform Temple Sinai, formed in 1962, and Las Vegas's Congregation Ner Tamid, established in 1974, were products of a schism from parent Conservative synagogues. A 1999 official statement from the Conference of Rabbis reflected support for the State of Israel as well as an embrace of more traditional observances that had been the hallmark of Orthodoxy.

Conservative Judaism was a late-nineteenth-century movement headed in the United States by Solomon Schechter (1847–1915), who assumed leadership of the Orthodox Jewish Theological Seminary in New York in 1902. He sought to bridge what he considered Reform's radicalism and Orthodoxy's exclusivity and immobility. The movement emphasized the use of English as well as modern theories of textual criticism. Its congregations often included a Jewish Community Center filled with social and religious activities to attract the swell of eastern European Jews who found Orthodoxy and Reform unappealing. Over time, the movement dissociated itself from Americanized Orthodoxy and established its own Rabbinical Assembly and congregational organization, the United Synagogue of Conservative Judaism. In its earliest days, Conservatism maintained the traditional separate seating of the sexes at services, and authorities did not open the rabbinate to women until 1983. This decision precipitated a schism leading to the Conservative offshoot that calls itself the Union for Traditional Judaism. Reno's Temple Emanu-El experienced a transition from Orthodox to Conservative between 1921 and 1946. An Orthodox rabbi occasionally led Las Vegas's premier congregation, the officially Conservative Temple Beth Sholom, until 1957.

Reconstructionist Judaism was founded by Mordecai M. Kaplan (1881–1983), who was raised in Conservative Judaism but believed in the need for even more sweeping changes to reclaim Jews from what he considered the bane of Orthodoxy. His redefinition of God as a process, his denial of the Jews' chosen status, and his willingness to discard what he saw as quaint

Jewish folkways immediately separated him and his followers from main-stream Judaism, while attracting those who would otherwise have become totally secular Jews. Kaplan emphasized Jewish art, dance, music, food, and customs over traditional mitzvoth. In 1968, the movement separated from Conservative Judaism to become an independent branch of Jewish religion. Valley Outreach Synagogue in Las Vegas is Nevada's sole Reconstructionist congregation.[9]

Peddlers and Merchants

1850–1863

Small-time trading had been the lot of about 85 percent of Prussian Jews in early-nineteenth-century Europe. Although many European countries banned trade with non-Jews before emancipation, peddlers became an indispensable link between isolated farmers and urban suppliers, often bartering manufactured goods for agricultural products. Some engaged in brokering the sale of horses to the army. Although the petty traders were part of a Jewish mercantile network, they lived a marginal existence and were often reduced to begging. The peddlers, or *Dorfjuden*, were at the lowest rung of German Jewish society. Prussian law forbade Jews to change residences within the Polish Duchy of Poznán, but they were permitted to leave the country. The Jewish establishment considered eastern European migrants into "old" Germany "unwelcome strangers," and they were among the first to depart for America in the 1840s.[1] The peddler quickly became a common figure throughout urban and rural America.

In the wake of the gold discovery in 1848 at Sutter's Mill at Coloma, California, Jews and Gentiles preferred to travel by ship for San Francisco via Cape Horn or the Isthmus of Panama, rather than overland. Although some Jews coming from Europe continued almost immediately by boat to California, many remained in eastern port cities or moved inland to save enough money for the next leg. The handful of Jews among the twenty-five thousand who went overland to California in 1849 likely passed through the area that later became Nevada.[2]

Peddling was an internship for young Jewish men who hoped one day to have their own store. Customarily, three stages of peddling characterized the fledgling immigrant: backpack, mule or horse pack, and, finally, horse and wagon. For these would-be merchants, the goal was usually San Francisco, first to connect with a supplier and then to head into the mining camps of the eastern Sierra Nevada or east into the desert to sell consumables to wagon

[9]

trains going to California. A military officer crossing the Nevada desert in 1850 recalled, "There were several places on the Humboldt and Carson Rivers where whisky and flour were sold from a canvas tent or cloth house, but these traders packed their house on a mule and left when the emigration for that season was over."[3] Such was the custom of the itinerant Jewish peddler.

Successful peddlers had a San Francisco supplier, but their geographical focus was wherever good business opportunities could be found. During the 1850s, they appeared in virtually every mining camp, and Jewish peddlers in the Sierra Nevada may have numbered more than a hundred. Their occupation was dangerous: accounts of an attack on a peddler were common. For example, in 1857, near Grass Valley, California, two masked robbers accosted "Mr. Jacobson a peddler," relieved him of $380 and a pack worth about the same, tied him to a tree, and threatened to kill him if he tried to escape or hail the soon-to-arrive Marysville stage. Nevada had its own incidents. Twelve years later, Stencil and Louison, two peddlers from Prussia, were robbed, murdered, and thrown into the Humboldt River. Elko's few Jews collected money for the bodies to be forwarded for burial to San Francisco.[4]

Some Measures of California Intolerance

The gold discovery of 1848 attracted adventurers of all nations and creeds, and the Far West proved to be a relatively tolerant haven for Germanic and Slavic Jews. Moreover, it has become commonplace in recent historiography of Jews in the West to note the lack of blatant antisemitism both on the frontier and in San Francisco. Attorney Henry J. Labatt, writing in San Francisco's *Voice of Israel* of 1856, boasted, "Nowhere in America is the Jew so well understood and so readily appreciated as in this State [of California]."[5] Although his statement would be as applicable two decades later in Nevada, the California atmosphere was not free of anti-Jewish bias.

In the previous year, Labatt expressed outrage at state assembly speaker William W. Stow's effort to impose a special tax on Jewish merchants that was tantamount to a Jewish exclusion act for California. Stow hoped to bolster support for this legislation by pointing to the merchants' "desecration" of the Christian Sabbath with their open stores and markets. In the ensuing legislative debate, Stow's opponent noted that in many places Jews chose to close their stores on Saturday (the Jewish Sabbath) and therefore should not be penalized by having to close two days a week. In an open letter to Stow, Labatt offered an articulate defense of Jewish rights as well as support for legislation outlawing business on Sunday.[6] Although by all accounts an observant Jew, Labatt was willing to make an accommodation to the Christian Sabbath observance, knowing his coreligionists would likely stay open on Saturday to remain competitive.

The low level of antisemitism during gold rush days did not exclude the persistent use of the word *Jew* as an adjective to describe a peddler or store. Some used it as a national designation parallel to "Irish saloon," and it carried whatever stereotypical baggage the speaker or hearer imputed to it.[7] In a popular travel memoir, J. Ross Browne employed all of the exaggeration, understatement, and irreverence that would characterize the writings of Mark Twain and Bret Harte. He breezily referred to "Jew peddlers dripping wet," depicting one of them in a line drawing with a sharp hooked nose.[8] Doubtless, Browne expected no criticism from his East Coast readers, who, he assumed, shared his stereotype of the peddler.

Others criticized "the Jew store." In 1852, regarding competition with Jewish merchants in Sonora, California, William Perkins complained, "The Jews have built large numbers of small swindling shops in the broad bed of the *arroyo*, as the ground was unocupied [*sic*], and . . . belongs to every one. . . . The Jews receive very little sympathy from the community, for as their hand is against all men's pockets, their misfortunes only excite the mockery and risible faculties of the crowd."[9] Another complained of "Jew slop-shops" so small "that one half of the stock had to be displayed suspended from projecting sticks outside." The proprietors were "unwashed-looking, slobbery, slippery individuals." A Placerville chronicler remembered Jewish merchants as cheaters and "rascally traffickers." He expected his readers to understand that this was how "Jews became wealthy and prominent merchants in various California towns." Similar examples of Judeophobia were evident in the antebellum and Confederate South and in major midwestern and eastern cities in the 1850s. However, with few exceptions, such sentiments were not displayed in the relatively isolated desert camps east of the Sierra Nevada.[10]

Early Settlements in Western Utah Territory: Future Nevada

A popular trail to the California goldfields after 1849 followed the river named after Kit Carson and passed near what later became Nevada's capital. Except for the presence of a few hardy Mormon settlers, the valleys in this western portion of Utah Territory were dusty, forgettable way stations for peddlers and gold seekers heading for the latest California bonanza. A campsite, once called Nevada City and later named Dayton, grew up near an insignificant 1849 gold strike along the Carson River. The first identifiable Jewish resident in the area was Isaac Cohn. Born in Prussian Poland in 1823, he was packing freight from California to the area as early as 1850. Cohn was permanently settled at Dayton when he and Joseph Keller purchased the Old Pioneer Log Store in 1859 from Major William Ormsby. Cohn remained a fixture in Nevada until his death in 1897. Meanwhile, the settlement of Latter-day Saints at the foot of Kingsbury Grade in Carson Valley—first called Mormon Station and later Genoa—quickly overshadowed the Dayton tent city to the east.[11]

Genoa became the seat of the newly created and expanding Carson County, which by 1856 extended north to the Oregon border. Factions competed to align the county more closely to Utah authorities, while anti-Mormons agitated for annexation to California. Meanwhile, relations between Mormons in eastern Utah and the federal government became so strained that President James Buchanan sent a military force under Colonel Albert Sidney Johnston to establish order. In response, Brigham Young recalled all Mormons to Salt Lake City to defend Deseret against the advancing army. Over the course of 1857, hundreds of Mormons in the valleys of Carson County obediently returned to Salt Lake, and their neighbors of many ethnic backgrounds took over abandoned farms and homes at wholesale prices.

Genoa was the largest of the many stations on the way to the new gold discoveries along the American, Rubicon, and Yuba Rivers in the eastern Sierra Nevada. As county seat, it was the center not only of commercial activity but also of political action. On August 8, 1857, a group of citizens drafted a memorial to Congress requesting creation of a new territory separated from Utah. Pioneer Abram Curry crossed east over the Sierra Nevada and tried to speculate in property at Genoa. He found that the thousand-dollar selling price of a single lot was "firm" and, according to local lore, said, "I'll just go and build my own city." In fall 1858, he and three partners purchased the Mankin Ranch for five hundred dollars and a few horses several miles north in what was becoming known as Eagle Valley. Curry divided the lots with his partners, Benjamin F. Green, Frank M. Procter, and J. J. Musser, but as one commentator noted, "The population of the valley was so scant at the time that all of them gathered at a dance would not occupy more than three sets."[12]

That population included Bohemian-born Abraham Klauber. He had established roots as coproprietor of a store with fellow Jew Francis Mandelbaum at Volcano, a mining town in Amador County, California. When the nearby mines played out, he moved to Genoa in 1858 and soon earned an enviable reputation for liberality and fairness in a climate of high inflation. *San Francisco Herald* correspondent Richard N. Allen heralded the merchant's arrival. He noted that Klauber had brought in a large stock of goods and already reduced prices 75 percent but had quickly learned that not all gold ores taken in trade were of equal value. "Mr. Klauber, a trader here, has taken in a large amount of it at $12 per ounce, and finds himself taken in by the discovery that it is only worth eight or nine dollars." Experiences such as these encouraged Klauber and his partner to insist on "cash only" transactions for discounted goods. In two years, his real estate was worth five thousand dollars with other taxable assets estimated at twenty-five thousand dollars.[13] Klauber had gambled on the area's future, though the gold had been insignificant. That was soon to change.

The Rush to Washoe

The discovery of numerous but low-grade ore pockets in the high canyons thirty miles northeast of Genoa drew merchants and other adventurers to northern Nevada in what became known as "the rush to Washoe," or the Comstock Lode. Maps of the 1850s identified the area as "Washo" after its inhabitants, the Hokan-speaking Native Americans. By 1858, about 150 miners were working the canyon above Dayton. On January 28, 1859, James "Old Virginny" Finney and others struck gold-silver ore near what is now Virginia City. A frenzy of speculation on Comstock strikes in San Francisco prompted the first in a series of drops in stock prices. Undeterred, however, were those hoping to buy low and sell high on the next cyclic rise. Claims disputes attracted lawyers from California, and merchants abounded as scarce staple goods brought inflated prices.[14] The latter included relatives and friends of established Jewish businessmen in San Francisco, Nevada City, and Sacramento. A new rush was on, and the immigrant traffic from east to west was making a steady U-turn.

Thousands of gold seekers—soon to be silver seekers—poured into the valleys east of the Sierra Nevada and passed through Genoa and Carson City en route to the new bonanza. Right behind them were the peddlers, agents of established merchants, teamsters, carpenters, purveyors of distilled spirits, prostitutes, gamblers, and lawyers. One journalist described Carson City as "a mere accident; occupation of the inhabitants, waylaying strangers bound for Virginia [City]; business, selling whisky, and so dull at that, men fall asleep in the middle of the street going from one groggery to another; productions, grass and weeds on the Plaza."[15]

It was, in fact, a town in progress. All around the city and particularly in the fast-forming business district on Carson Street were the sounds of hammer on nail, neighing horses, and boisterous teamsters—to say nothing of the whoops and hollers from the plentiful saloons. Prevailing westerlies kicked up clouds of dust except when the occasional rain and snow turned the roads into slop. An 1860 line drawing of Carson City depicted a collection of wooden places of business—some of them two-storied along streets separated by large vacant spreads crisscrossed with trails for wagons and buggies.

The Comstock was a larger and more populated version of Carson. The adventurers who poured into the Virginia City area after the winter storms of 1860 created a surreal landscape over the sagebrush mountainside. Occasionally, a "boiled shirt" dandy with a stovepipe hat rose above the citizenry. J. Ross Browne described them as "keen speculators," "rough customers," "Jew clothing-men [who] were setting out their goods and chattels in front of wretched-looking tenements; monte-dealers, gamblers, thieves, cut-throats, and murders . . . mingling miscellaneously in the dense crowds around the bars of the drinking saloons."[16]

This was no place for families or the faint of heart. The *Weekly Gleaner*, edited by San Francisco rabbi Julius Eckman, carried under "Jewish News" advice from a Jew on the Comstock to future immigrants: "Those who can make a comfortable living in California had much better stay at home; those who cannot, will hardly do it here; but men of capital, who can make money anywhere, will find this a fair field. We want merchants, we want mills, we want ditches, and we want capital to work the mines."[17]

Abraham Klauber capitalized on the influx. His large inventories brought in from California allowed him to sell a hundredweight of flour at a fraction of his competitors. "His cargoes are no sooner unloaded than all is sold," wrote one journalist, "so that consumers have the alternative of paying twenty or thirty dollars a hundred to others, or waiting till more of Klauber's teams get in." In addition to his general store, Klauber, with his Sacramento-based partner, Mandelbaum, operated the Wells Fargo Express Agency in Genoa. The two apparently invested more than one hundred thousand dollars there before Nevada became a territory.[18]

The Comstock discovery was one of several western mineral attractions after the California mines began to play out. Discoveries of gold on the Fraser River in British Columbia, in Arizona's Gila River, and at Colorado's Pikes Peak, all in 1858, drew their own rush of old forty-niners and new adventurers, as did Montana, Idaho, and Wyoming in 1860. None of these booms had the staying power of the Comstock, whose mineral production continued to climb for almost twenty years.

David H. Cohen was a Jewish immigrant who arrived by steamer from Germany at San Francisco in 1852. Though he could speak no English, he eked out a living as a miner in Jackson and Rabbit Creek in the Sierra Nevada before spending a fruitless six months on the Fraser River in British Columbia. In 1862, he was unable to find his own productive claim in the Virginia City area and moved to Austin, Nevada, to sell liquor. In 1865, he was mining in Montana at Alder Gulch, Virginia City, and Ophir City. By 1867, he had earned enough in mining and speculation for a trip to Germany to seek a wife. The couple returned to Austin and then moved to Schellbourne in White Pine County, where they were in business for six years. The growing family moved to Butte, Montana, where Cohen prospered as a tailor and general merchandiser. He then invested in an Idaho claim and lost heavily. He returned to Butte and ended up selling fruit and tobacco. Cohen exemplified the transiency and bad luck of many western miners and speculators and, more important, the relative stability of staying aboveground as a merchant.[19]

Civil War, Territory Status, and the Wandering Jew

South Carolina had seceded from the Union in December 1860, and six other Southern states quickly followed. With Southerners absent, Northerners in Congress, especially Republicans, could create territories without dealing with the issue of slavery. On March 2, 1861, President James Buchanan signed a bill to create Nevada and two other territories. His successor, Abraham Lincoln, named Republican loyalist James Warren Nye of New York territorial governor. He also appointed three territorial judges and a territorial secretary, Orion Clemens. Two months earlier, the Utah authorities had moved the county seat of Carson County from Genoa to Carson City, helping to ensure its future designation as territorial capital. Nye arrived at Nevada on July 7, 1861, and soon authorized a territorial census, which yielded a total population of 16,374.[20]

Foreign-born Nevadans numbered approximately 30 percent in 1860. The Comstock's largely male population of more than 3,000 included immigrants from Ireland, the Germanies (including Prussian Poland), Britain, Canada, Latin America, Scandinavia, France, China, Switzerland, and Russia. The number of Jews was less than 1 percent of the total. Nye's installation as governor in July 1861 coincided with the arrival of a self-styled "wandering Jew" from Moldavia, Isaac Joseph Benjamin. He described Carson City as "a friendly little town," correctly estimated its population at about 2,000, and noted 20 Jews in the city. "They are occupied for the most part with trading and are well-off," he wrote, and "only one of them is married." Estimating the Virginia City Jewish population as "about thirty," he described them as "well-to-do" and mostly engaged in trade.[21] Benjamin's count of Jews was the kind of snapshot that changed by the time he got up the next day, as in-migration skyrocketed.

Klauber and Mandelbaum opened a new mercantile business in Carson City and built a huge warehouse. Klauber bought a sixteen hundred–acre ranch on which he raised mules and cattle about six miles southeast of Genoa, west of what is now Minden. Sufficiently established to bring his mother and sister to the United States, he sought out a girl he had met almost a decade earlier. He and Theresa Epstein married in Sacramento on October 31, 1861, and lived in a one-story house in Genoa. The Klaubers maintained a second residence in Carson City where their first child, Ella, was born. Theresa's brother, Henry Epstein, managed the ranch, played the piano for weddings and other festivities, and developed an interest in politics.[22]

Meanwhile, Isaac Cohn lost no time in expanding his interests from storekeeping to mining. In 1860, in partnership with Henry Hirschman and Joseph Keller, he built the Sweetapple Mill to service ore coming down from the Comstock. In the winter of 1862–1863, a sudden flood of the river due to thawing snow destroyed part of the mill. Cohn withdrew from his Dayton partnerships and went into ranching with Joseph Coleman about twenty-five miles south of Dayton. Within two years, he was back at Dayton selling wood and later ran an express-delivery wagon until his death in 1897. Coleman's agricultural property, commonly called the "Jew Ranch" or "Jews Ranch" as late as the end of the century, continued to flourish.[23]

Polish-Born California-Nevada Merchant and Miner

One man exemplified the European Jewish immigrant's highest hopes and aspirations. He bridged the California and Nevada bonanzas, was religiously active, was an affluent San Francisco merchant, and was the president of a promising mining venture. Morris B. Ashim (formerly Ascheim), born in 1818, was a Poznán native who made his way to London. There he met Rose Bartlett, who converted to marry him. They proceeded by covered wagon to Kentucky with their three children. Their daughter Harriet later remembered being temporarily lost as the family crossed the rugged Isthmus of Panama in 1850. Their granddaughter Janet Fleishhacker affirmed that the subsequent sea passage and land crossing at Panama was what "so many of the Jewish families did."[24] In San Francisco, Ashim founded and was first president of the city's Hebrew Benevolent Society, providing newly arriving Jews with needed financial assistance.

Ashim was a religious activist. Founding treasurer of Chebra Bikur Chdim Ukedisha in 1857 to assist the sick and president of San Francisco's International Order of B'nai B'rith, he was routinely called upon to speak at local High Holiday services.[25] He was part of an ad hoc committee that circulated a petition to San Francisco Jews to shore up Julius Eckman's failing *Weekly Gleaner.* As proprietor of the well-advertised Ashim and Brother Auction and Commission Merchants, he promised his customers reduced prices because his brother, Solomon Ashim of New York, supplied him.

During the summers, Ashim traveled to the latest Sierra boomtown. One such swing led him to open a store in Carson City in 1860. By 1862, he was buying and selling land to fellow Jews. Though he doubtless lived where he worked—as did most merchants in their early days—Ashim may have had a different plan: he purchased a residential lot in Carson City's new Procter and Green subdivision for one hundred dollars in 1863. That summer he was in Aurora long enough to be included in its city directory. The camp had an estimated population of five thousand, several newspapers, fire companies, a city government, and an eleven-piece brass band. "In common with all lively mining camps," wrote an early historian, "it was infested with bad characters; gamblers and thieves were numerous, and were incessantly getting drunk and killing each other."[26] A reign of terror existed for Aurora's first few years, because witnesses to assault or murder were afraid to testify.

Carson City, by comparison, was civilized and sophisticated. Ashim's wife,

Rose, stayed in San Francisco with their daughters, but their son, Simon, and his son, Baruch, were part of the Ashim Carson City adventure. Their store at 202 North Carson Street was duly noted as "Phillips & Ashim, clothing, etc." and located above the Aaron Fleishhacker general store. Ashim told his fellow miner and future son-in-law, Isidor Choynski, in May 1863 that he would not leave Aurora until he struck a rich claim.[27] But he never did. Death struck him down the following year. Like so many Jews who came to Nevada but considered San Francisco home, he was buried in Hills of Eternity Cemetery in Colma, California. Simon, his son, settled his father's estate in Carson City before moving his family to booming Eureka, Nevada. Morris Ashim was among the hundreds of Jews for whom Carson City was just one more stopping place on the way to something better. However, thanks to romances across Jewish families, his descendants figured prominently in Nevada's future.[28]

...

Abraham Klauber, Isaac Cohn, and Morris Ashim embraced the spectrum of Jewish arrivals to Carson Valley and the Comstock. Well fixed when he came to Genoa, Klauber leveraged his profits and was settled enough to marry and start a family. By contrast, Cohn moved from one business to another, ended up a teamster, never married, and died a lonely alcoholic. Ashim was a short-timer in the area who died relatively young but left a legacy of religious commitment for early Jewish settlers. A hundred more Jews were already in the hills, or in the streets and mines. Thousands more were on the way. How religious they were (or could be) was to be tested by the exigencies of geography and personal choice.

Obstacles to Religious Practice

A modern scholar of American Jewish history, Jacob Rader Marcus, concludes that in colonial times, "there were almost as many Judaisms as there were individuals."[29] This was equally true of Nevada Jewish immigrants for whom the complex rituals and mitzvoth that distinguished them in Europe were hard to replicate on the frontier in a Protestant nation, which expected cultural assimilation. The neighborhood Jewish clusters in New York and the old Sephardic (Spanish and Portuguese) congregations scattered along the East Coast managed to maintain the costly essentials of Orthodox observance: a *mikveh* (ritual bath), a *shochet* (kosher slaughterer), materials for Passover, rabbis, cantors, and a permanent synagogue. Jews who decided to move to the Far West must have known that their practice of Judaism would be reduced at least temporarily to what a family or a small group could sustain.

Many circumstances militated against regular or uniform religious observance—particularly in Nevada and the West. The vast distances between camps and emerging towns where Jews might seek work made it rare to have the minyan of ten adult Jews required for a formal religious service. The mining districts that attracted settlers were often boom and bust; prudent Jews avoided building expensive permanent structures and were ready to move on. Some immigrants sought to accommodate traditional Judaism to the exigencies of modernity, but even Reform leaders lacked a clear consensus about how much to depart from traditional observance. The freedom of religion in the United States, which led to the formation of numerous sects, encouraged religious change based on conscience and provided the option of converting to another accepted religion or simply "dropping out" of any affiliation. Finally, differences in native tongues and customs discouraged agreement on the language to be used in worship.

A few Jews adapted in different ways. Jacob Klein, a native of Alsace, France, came to Carson City in 1860. He immediately ingratiated himself with the thirsty population as cofounder of the Carson City Brewing Company. Fr. Hugh Gallagher struck up a friendship with Klein, who helped him build St. Teresa of Avila Church. Klein was a better brewer than carpenter: the church blew down in less than two years. He married French-born Marie "Nettie" Antoinette in 1865. A ceremony that may have been kept secret for a while was the baptism of Jacob, Marie, and their daughter, Maria Eugenia, on October 29, 1865. Though in a town as small as Carson City Klein's conversion should have been common knowledge, a San Francisco Jewish newspaper continued to acknowledge him as a Jew for the next five years—after which the editor finally got the message.[30] He was the first known Nevada Jew to convert to Christianity. It was the ultimate act of assimilation. Although Klein was no longer a member of the Jewish worshiping community, the second floor of his brewery became the regular meeting place for Jewish organizations and for High Holiday services.

. . .

Cohn, Klauber, Ashim, and Klein are representative of the Jews who first tested the Nevada economic potential. They were among the minority who chose to leave settled areas farther east, following trails, canals, and later railroads from East to West.[31] Why Jews came to northern Nevada by the hundreds over the next few years is not difficult to discern. The interrelated reasons came down to these: economic opportunity and a kinship relationship. Charles H. Meyer, who became a partner with Aaron Fleishhacker in 1863, wrote to the prominent rabbi and editor of the *Occident*, Isaac Leeser, in Philadelphia: "There exists too much wealth in the silver mines of the territory to deny the expectation of a very rapid increase of our population, for it is a known fact that our people are found to reside where 'money can be made.'"[32] Meyer may have facetiously been alluding to the stereotype of the acquisitive Jewish merchant, but his remark would have been just as applicable to Nevada settlers of every ethnic background.

From Territory to Statehood

Whereas miners moved from one place to another, depending on their luck, merchants had to decide whether to rent a firetrap or take a chance and build in stone. Jewish entrepreneurs were as cagey as the next person, but attempting to assess the most profitable location was a gamble, given the uncertainties of mining. Impossible winters in Virginia City, the difficulty of bringing goods up the mountain, and the rise and fall of mining stock prices all affected a decision whether to stay put or leave.

Settlement and Itinerancy

In its earliest settlement days, northern Nevada appeared, like Oregon, to be a California colony. The Jews who came to Carson City and the Comstock towns of Virginia City, Silver City, and Gold Hill often had clear connections to San Francisco, Sacramento, and Nevada City suppliers. The relative proximity of these providers gave Nevada merchants an edge rarely found among early settlers in the Southwest or the Mountain West. Nevada's first directory identified these California affiliations in lavish advertisements. Samuel Haas of the Pioneer Auction and Commission House announced stores in Virginia City and Gold Hill managed by his two sons. Samuel Wasserman and Company of San Francisco had a location at Union and C Streets, selling Havana cigars, glassware, alcohol, playing cards, and musical instruments. The Joseph Barnert (later changed to "Barnett") San Francisco Clothing Store was centrally located next to the Virginia Hotel. At the corner of Union and C Streets was Gold and Philippson's dealership in cigars, coal oil, and liquor in competition with Wasserman's emporium across the street.[1] In Carson City, Aaron Fleishhacker added one more store to his string of ventures that had peppered California's mother lode. Joseph Rosenstock and Samuel Price's satellite clothing store was in the center of the business district next to Fleishhacker's. Samuel Witgenstein ran his mining office out of Adolph

Rosenfeld's cigar store on Carson Street opposite the capital plaza. Henry L. Joachimsen established a law practice, and others plied additional trades from grocer to tailor.

Although fewer than half of Nevada's enumerated population in 1860 listed occupations, the most common were miner, lumberman, teamster, carpenter, blacksmith, merchant, and laborer. Saloon keepers outnumbered engineers; speculators and hustlers outnumbered butchers. In Carson City, of the twenty-nine listed as merchants, tailors, or clerks, a quarter were Jewish, and most lived where they worked. A few, like Rosenstock and Klauber, could afford separate residences in what became the fashionable Procter and Green subdivision.[2] Five other Jewish bachelor merchants and clerks appeared in the census: the young Serenthal brothers from Poland, Jacob Kempner from Poland, David Zerker from Prussia, and Adolph Lindauer from New York. All engaged in mercantile activity on the main street, Carson, across from the future site of capital buildings.

But Nevada's Jewish community was as mobile as the miners it served. By 1862, Lindauer had sold out to Fleishhacker, who already had another thriving store in Virginia City. Klauber purchased the prime property across from Fleishhacker. In 1865, Rosenstock and Price bought property from San Franciscan Hermann Bloomingdale, one of many absentee speculators, and built a "new stone store" across the street on the southwest corner of Musser and Carson—advertising a full array of men's and boy's custom-made clothing. A stone store was the sign of prosperity and insurability, for boom towns were frequently torched by their own kerosene lamps.[3] Clerk Jacob Kempner was gone, as was his boss, Rosenfeld, who owned a cigar and stationery store at the corner of Carson and King before selling to other new arrivals. The Serenthal brothers also moved on.

The itinerancy continued. Mendelson and Armer were selling "cigars etc" a block south of them all, directly across from competitor Rosenfeld. They, too, soon moved up the mountain to Virginia City. One block farther south on Carson Street stood the popular Ormsby House, which rented space to tradesmen such as clothier Morris Weinberger. Samuel Cohen opened a grocery store near the Ormsby and showed taxable assets of sixty-seven hundred dollars in just a few months.[4] Separately listed in the 1862 city directory were clerks who would soon be proprietors themselves, including Abraham Katzenberg (with Rosenstock and Price) and Joseph Mandelbaum (the son of Francis, who was tending his store in Sacramento).

Other Jewish boarders appeared as residents in nearby rooming houses, and the numbers kept growing. Early arrivals who became permanent residents included twenty-eight-year-old Baden-Baden native Jacob Tobriner, a clerk at Fleishhacker's and founding member and first president of the German Turnverein. Joseph Platt (originally Placzek) and his wife, Malvina Bash, both came from Kempen in Polish Prussia; they opened a clothing store at Carson near South Second with a silent partner, Koppel. Their son Samuel became a major political force in the twentieth century. Among the first set of siblings to arrive and last to leave northern Nevada were the Olcovich brothers from Kempen in Prussian Poznán. Bernhard, the first, avoided the Civil War by traveling to San Francisco via Panama and established a very profitable business in the heart of Carson City. His brothers, Hyman, Hermann, and Joseph, followed. Some ran the main store, while others traveled to purchase large quantities of goods. The Olcovich brothers' several businesses and real estate properties soon placed them among the county's heaviest taxpayers.

Most Jewish merchants became indirectly involved in mining by accepting shares of stock in exchange for merchandise. An informal study of Jewish employment between 1860 and 1870 in northern Nevada produced a statistical profile representative of Jewish occupations generally in the state until the turn of the twentieth century. About 35 percent sold dry goods and clothing, with 13 percent as grocers; 12 percent in tobacco, stationery, and books; 11 percent in general merchandise, such as hardware and feed; and 6 percent in liquor and wine sales. The remaining 23 percent spread over a wide variety of occupations, including ranchers, farmers, tailors, bakers, miners, lawyers, boardinghouse keepers, and restaurateurs. By contrast, 43 percent of Virginia City's general male population in 1870 were miners, 12 percent were merchants, 9 percent were manufacturers, and 6 percent worked in the mills, with much of the remainder occupied in construction, service, and saloons and as teamsters.[5]

Missing from the data based on census and mercantile directory information was the informal activity of Jews in the volatile real estate and mining stock markets. The eighty members of the People's Stock Board in Virginia City included merchants Samuel Wasserman, Julius Rosenfeld, Nathan Solomon, A. Hecht, and Adolph Hirschman.[6] Clerk and rancher Henry Epstein was among the many buying and selling both land and mining stocks. The investment did not always pay off. He purchased thirty-five feet of a ledge in the Chollar Company mine for seven thousand dollars in June 1860 and sold it a few weeks later for half the price.[7]

Benevolent Societies and Cemeteries

Although economic opportunity was the primary catalyst for Jewish migration, once settlement took place, there were religious duties to be performed. As early as 1861, Carson City had the required minyan (ten adult males) for a formal religious service, and they strictly observed Yom Kippur, the Day of Atonement. The local Episcopal minister was so impressed that he announced that he would preach on the subject the following Sunday.[8] The next year, nine merchants advertised the closing of their stores from Friday evening until Saturday at sundown to observe the High Holidays. They set a precedent lasting more than thirty years.[9]

The first item of business for any self-respecting Jewish group in a town that had the promise of permanence was to establish a Hebrew Benevolent Society to help new coreligionists find work and lodging upon arrival. Such a society was formed at Carson City in 1862. The membership was small but needed no assistance, so they donated their first year's dues of $158 to the U.S. Sanitary Fund for the Civil War wounded.[10]

The establishment and care of a burial place were also primary duties. As Isaac J. Benjamin observed, "No matter how indifferent and cold in many places our fellow Jews are towards their religion, nevertheless they are never so completely estranged from all religious feeling that it is a matter of total indifference to them where they bury their dead."[11] On March 24, 1862, the Carson City Benevolent Society purchased ten lots north of town in a subdivision called Park Place. These properties served as collateral for the Jewish section in Lone Mountain Cemetery.[12]

The larger contingent of Jews in Virginia City identified a temporary synagogue to celebrate Yom Kippur and Rosh Hashanah in fall 1862. With no rabbi yet on the Comstock, laymen led the services. That year, they established B'nai B'rith Lodge no. 52 and also the Eureka Benevolent Association, which arranged for a cemetery site on public land more than a mile northwest of the city's other graveyards. A passer-by described it as a "very handsome plat of ground (nicely cleaned off and substantially fenced) about 100 feet square." Given the high infant mortality rate at this time, it came as no surprise that among the first of four to be buried in 1863 were four-month-old Adelia Adler and ten-month-old Aaron Korn.[13] Within a year, Virginia City Jews had established yet another benevolent society, the Hebrew Self-Protecting Association. Its formation was as much a sign of growth as an example of factionalism.

The first Jewish benevolent society had been formed in 1822 by members of New York's Temple Shearith Israel who wanted a charitable organization independent of the synagogue. In remote regions of the country that had no permanent congregations, Jews formed benevolent societies to dispatch some of the duties ordinarily left to the synagogue. The oldest national Jewish organization, which added insurance benefits and social life to its charitable work, was B'nai B'rith, or "Sons of the Covenant." Twelve recent arrivals from central Europe who were rejected by a New York Masonic lodge formed the organization in 1843.

The B'nai B'rith's stated purposes were to preserve a sense of Jewish peoplehood, contribute to the public morality, and provide medical and financial support for its members, widows, and orphans. The Jewish organization modeled itself in many ways after the fraternal lodges, including bell, book, and candle rituals and secret passwords with specific Jewish meanings. B'nai B'rith was no substitute for membership in the Elks, Odd Fellows, Knights of Pythias, or Masonic organizations, whose membership in Nevada was open to Jews. In some of the large eastern cities, the benevolent societies, or *landsmanschaftn,* and B'nai B'rith lodges were in competition with or alternatives to the local synagogues. In Nevada, they generally served as substitutes for organized congregations.[14]

Inside the Territorial Legislature

Lacking a suitable capitol building, Abe Curry offered his Warm Springs Hotel east of town to the new territorial legislature. An incident imbedded in the records of this body's first session—if its spirit of meanness had not been quashed—could have led to some prejudicial unpleasantness. According to *Sacramento Union* reporter Andrew Marsh, the house members had to sit on rough wooden benches when they first met in October 1861. The only store selling proper chairs was that of Mandelbaum and Klauber. Territorial secretary Orion Clemens wanted the chairs on credit—pending future payment by the federal government. Klauber declined, citing his "cash only" policy. Two weeks later, Margaret Ormsby and Hannah Clapp donated some "comfortable seats" to the legislature. A few minutes into unrelated deliberations, Representative John Mills of Gold Hill introduced a resolution "that the Sergeant-at-Arms confer with Mandelbaum & Klauber, and ascertain on what terms they would store the benches lately used by members, the understanding being that they must look to the United States Government for their pay. [This was supposed to be slightly ironical.]"[15]

It was, in fact, something more: a transparent attempt to put the Jewish merchants in the awkward position of having to provide free storage of fifteen benches for an unspecified period of time. The "irony" Marsh cited was that storage would be a "payback" for the merchants' refusal to provide chairs on credit. Representative Samuel Youngs sprang to the defense of the firm, which had been "misrepresented" as insolvent because it would extend no credit. He said he "knew these parties were worthy and patriotic citizens, and they had only refused to trust the Secretary of the Territory" in order to maintain a consistent cash-and-carry policy. William Teall, another representative, also condemned the Mills resolution as "one of contemptible meanness." Mills was put on the defensive, and two days later, the sergeant at arms submitted his report recommending that the matter be dropped.[16] The incident did not hurt the Jewish firm, which expanded its inventory over the next two years, showing assets in 1863 of eighty-one thousand dollars in property and goods and providing a solid contribution to the county's tax base.[17]

Another legislative event, this one involving Samuel Clemens and a Jewish boy, demonstrated that the legislature ultimately assessed performance without regard to ethnic or religious heritage. Clemens had followed his brother Orion to Nevada and immediately set out to test the latest gold discovery. Like most miners, Clemens struggled and within fifteen months of his arrival was broke. With limited journalistic experience, he was fortunate to land a position as a reporter for Virginia City's *Territorial Enterprise* in September 1862. Although he stayed for less than two years, during this time he began to use the name "Mark Twain" when authoring less serious articles or letters. Among other duties, he covered proceedings of Nevada's first constitutional convention at the end of 1863 and the territorial legislature's third session in January 1864. He found it impossible to keep up with the speakers and characterized his notes as "mysterious short-hand" and "interesting hieroglyphics."[18]

At about this time, Clemens visited William B. Lawlor's private school in Carson City, where he discovered a student proficient in shorthand. The young man, Baruch "Barry" Ashim, was Morris Ashim's grandson, and Clemens hired the boy as his transcriber. His efforts were so highly regarded that at the end of the legislative session, William M. Stewart resolved (and the house agreed) that each member give three dollars to the young reporter. Teenager Baruch Ashim appears to have been Nevada's first Jewish public employee, and he did not have to wait for payment from the U.S. government.

Twain had a less successful relationship with Adah Isaacs Menken, born near New Orleans about 1835 of uncertain ancestry. Menken was socially unconventional, personally complex, and nationally celebrated as an acrobatic actress when she appeared on Maguire's Opera House stage in Virginia City in February 1864. Menken, who had given a benefit performance for Sacramento's Jewish congregation in December, was an instant sensation on the Comstock. Her depiction of Mazeppa in skin-colored tights, riding a spirited horse up a staged mountain, was considered so risqué that some viewers were reluctant to admit being present at the performance. Few Gentiles likely knew she claimed conversion to Judaism and authored poetry published in Cincinnati's *Israelite*, unless they also read New York's *Jewish Messenger* exposing some blatant plagiarism. Over Menken's two-month stay on the Comstock, she was showered with silver by adoring miners, and *Territorial Enterprise* reporters Joseph Goodman and Dan De Quille competed in their lavish praise of her acting. Twain was more restrained. Menken shared some of her poetry with him, but he declined to submit it for publication. In a November column appearing in the *Californian*, he ridiculed her, even as she was thrilling London's theater crowd. After several marriages and alleged amorous relationships with international celebrities, she took sick in Paris in 1868, called for a rabbi, and was buried in the Jewish tradition. San Francisco's *Hebrew* weekly featured her in elaborate obituaries and biographies, several of which originated in Virginia City.[19]

A Unionist Rabbi on the Comstock

Whereas Nevada Territory was alive with profit seekers, the Civil War wreaked death on battlefields to the east. Union setbacks abounded during the spring and summer of 1864. The forthcoming election pitted Republican Abraham Lincoln against Democrat General George McClellan. Republicans in Congress recognized their need for additional support and passed an enabling act, paving the way for Nevada statehood before the November election. With an estimated Republican voting edge in Nevada of about three to two, Lincoln's party expected the new state to end up in its camp. Onto that scene walked a man espousing a super-Republican patriotism.

Herman Milton Bien had been no stranger to controversy when he arrived at Virginia City, Nevada Territory, early in 1864. Born April 26, 1831, in Naumburg, Germany, Bien trained with his father, a respected lithographer and rabbi, before coming to the United States in 1854. He received further instruction from Reform rabbi David Einhorn and traveled to San Francisco two years later to become a lecturer and leader of the High Holidays at Temple Emanu-El. Bien had been accepted as a rabbi, but his lack of ordination papers dogged him. He was one of many officially unordained rabbis who moved from congregation to congregation in search of a permanent position. After a brief stint in 1860 at Temple Beth Israel in Portland, he returned to San Francisco and published the first Jewish newspaper in the West, the *Voice of Israel*. His coeditor, Henry J. Labatt, was the attorney who had helped to quash the proposed tax on Jewish merchants. The newspaper failed, and Bien turned to writing musical extravaganzas, which played to packed houses but failed to show a profit. He eked out a living performing occasional religious services and in several short-lived ventures as a school headmaster. He was both hailed and criticized for his attempts to adapt Judaism to modernity, and a local rabbi opposed his support for flying the Union flag over synagogues as a violation of church and state, but others applauded his advocacy as an appropriate demonstration of Union patriotism. By 1863, Bien was penniless and decided to join some of his earlier Jewish supporters on the Comstock.[20]

The young rabbi's energy, idealism, and editorial, musical, and linguistic talents would have seemed a perfect fit in the Comstock's cosmopolitan and pluralistic atmosphere. Virginia City's Jewish community, however, was divided along religious, political, and ethnic lines. Furthermore, the Comstock area itself was almost exclusively focused on the local mining economy and not easily distracted by idealism or self-reflection.[21]

No sooner had he arrived than the press announced a public meeting of Virginia City Jews, who had unanimously passed a resolution to establish a formal congregation, and Bien's presence appears to have been its inspiration. *Hebrew* correspondent Jacob Kaplan wrote that Bien had assumed his presence would spark the formation of a congregation, but he miscalculated. If any of the Virginia City traditionalists had read or heard of Bien's substitution at Temple Emanu-El in San Francisco of his own paraphrase of the Haggadah (the Exodus account and reading) at the Passover seder, they would have automatically considered him too radical to serve their needs. Although Bien consistently used the *Minhag Ashkenaz* (German ritual) for High Holidays in San Francisco, many on the Comstock preferred the Polish version.[22]

The process of adapting Orthodox Judaism to the exigencies of modern times was called the Reform Movement. It began in Germany shortly before midcentury. Its chief leaders in the United States were Einhorn (Bien's mentor) and Isaac Mayer Wise (Bien's former critic). Every congregation engaged in wide-ranging discussion about exactly how far it should go in accommodating modernity. Some simply wanted to Anglicize the service, others to introduce organ music, still others to abolish gender-segregated seating, and a few favored moving the celebration of the Sabbath from Saturday to Sunday. Although Bien consistently observed the Sabbath on Saturday, he was known to light a cigar on that day—which was "work" to anyone with Orthodox sensibilities.[23]

Bien made his theatrical debut at the Virginia City Opera House with his five-act drama, *Leah the Forsaken*. The press immediately tested the newcomer with a less than enthusiastic review, deeming it "not of a character to suit the tastes of a Virginia [City] audience." The play "held the boards" for three performances and then ran to a full house two days after it officially closed. The newspaper ate crow.[24] In April, the rabbi announced the opening of an "academic seminary," including the study of Hebrew. He was soon active in the German Union Club (Verein) and published the territory's first German newspaper, the unabashedly Republican *Nevada Staats Zeitung*. This venture was no more successful than his previous publishing efforts, but Bien quickly made a name for himself as an articulate patriot.[25]

The Comstock observed the High Holidays that October more generally than anyone could remember. Jacob Kaplan, in his regular letter to the *Hebrew*, speculated, "Whether this fact was owing to the presence of a Rabbi or Reverend among us, or whether the Israelites hereabouts recovered from their bad ways and went heart and soul for reform, I know not." In reality, the city was divided by preferences for German or Polish traditional observance, leading to two packed services—one by Bien, the other by members of the Hebrew Self-Protecting Association. Kaplan concluded by noting that "Jews are fond of good and easy living, and for that reason, fast-day [Yom Kippur]

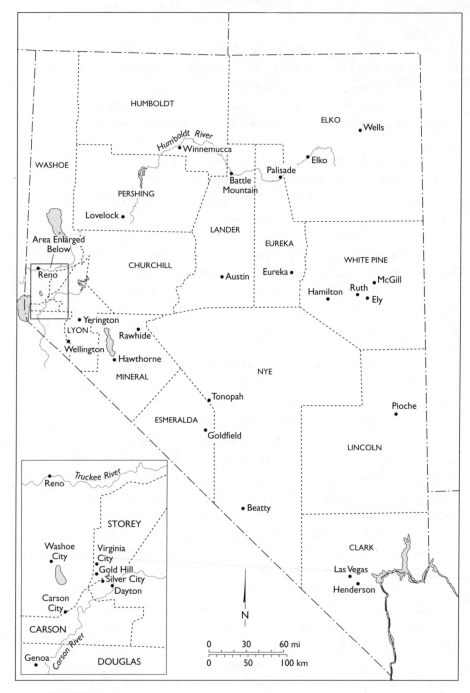

HUMBOLDT

ELKO

• Wells

WASHOE

Humboldt River

• Winnemucca

• Elko

Palisade

• Battle
Mountain

PERSHING

LANDER

EUREKA

• Lovelock

WHITE PINE

Area Enlarged
Below

CHURCHILL

• Austin

Eureka •

Hamilton

Ruth

• McGill

• Reno

• Ely

• Yerington

LYON

• Rawhide

• Wellington

• Hawthorne

MINERAL

NYE

Pioche

• Tonopah

ESMERALDA

LINCOLN

• Goldfield

Truckee River

• Beatty

• Reno

STOREY

CLARK

Washoe
City

Virginia
City

Las Vegas

Gold Hill
• Silver City

Henderson

• Dayton

Carson
City

N

CARSON

Carson River

0   30   60 mi

Genoa

DOUGLAS

0   50   100 km

State of Nevada

although occurring but once a year, pales many a face. Still, all seemed to bear it well, and but few left during the service[s]."²⁶

The unified congregation announced in April had obviously not materialized. The disputes over language, customs, and ritual that plagued San Francisco had migrated to the Comstock. Although these differences were not aired in the local press, they made their way into San Francisco's Jewish newspaper. Kaplan signed his dispatches to the *Hebrew* with the pen name "Nesop" ("Posen" spelled backward), clearly acknowledging the many Jews from this duchy of Poland among the *Hebrew*'s readers. Kaplan wrote tongue-in-cheek of the unanimity and fraternal feeling among Virginia City's Jewish organizations. It was a "harmony," he wrote, "seldom, if ever found, amongst a number of men from all climes and countries; for here we have not as yet learned that nice distinction which different dialects and birthplaces generally gives rise to." And in prose that was damaging with its exaggerated praise and emphasis, he exhorted: "We all have *one* ancestor . . . one common country, the United States of America! Poland and Bavaria, Hungary and Austria, France and England, walk arm in arm here, love and respect each other, know not these petty jealousies and party feelings, the curse of some communities. 'Brother' is the name for all; Bavaria shakes Poland's fraternal hand, and whispers words of eternal friendship into her ears. . . . All Israel is *one* family—*one*, eternally and inseparably!"²⁷

The reality gave the lie to this protestation of harmony. Astonishingly, a second B'nai B'rith lodge, King Solomon Lodge no. 64, with forty-two members emerged, signaling not only a sudden growth in the population but also further ideological and class divisions within the Jewish community. The two lodges in 1864–1865 listed 113 adult males and heads of household—a tripling of the Jewish population in two years, including a few families and small children.

Statehood and the First Jewish Legislators

When Abraham Lincoln proclaimed Nevada the Union's thirty-sixth state on October 31, 1864, Rabbi Bien was still running a small school, editing the *Nevada Staats Zeitung*, officiating at marriages and funerals, and serving as a member in good standing of B'nai B'rith Lodge no. 52. His popularity as a passionate Unionist elicited an invitation for him to deliver one of the speeches directed to "all loyal hearted men" celebrating Nevada's new statehood and encouragement to run for the first state legislature representing Storey County. He won the election.[28]

In the November election, 16,420 Nevadans placed in office virtually every Republican on the ballot by a margin of three to one. Although Nevadans were generally Republican, the state had its share of secessionists and antiwar Democrats. John W. North, Nevada's first surveyor general, called Virginia City a refuge for copperheads and secessionists.[29] Representing the latter were people such as William Clagett, who had vigorously opposed patriotic resolutions in the territorial legislature.[30] He would be obliged to endure the persistent introduction of such sentiments by the new assemblyman, Herman Bien.

Also among the fifty-four new legislators sworn into office were Henry Epstein, Abraham Klauber's brother-in-law, from Genoa; and Meyer A. Rosenblatt, a merchant from Austin in Lander County. They were the first in a long line of Jewish public officials whose relative numbers far exceeded the Jewish proportion of the population. Epstein was a "hail-fellow-well-met" rancher, musician, mining investor, and landowner who had been a Carson Valley notable for at least five years as a stand-in Pony Express rider in 1860–1861 and a member of Douglas County's first grand jury in 1862. When the senate and assembly could not agree on the language of a resolution to Congress urging it to provide a ten million–dollar incentive to the first company building a railroad from Sacramento to Nevada, Epstein's carefully crafted resolution finally carried both houses and was forwarded to Washington, D.C.[31]

Rosenblatt's credentials are less known, but he appears to have had legal training. While in Virginia City in 1863, he was secretary of Washoe Engine Company no. 4 and appointed to draft its bylaws and constitution. Most of his proposed legislation consisted of tidying up the new state's legal status—legitimating certain elections in November 1864, providing for a census, apportioning representation, and relieving insolvent debtors while protecting creditors.[32]

The assembly appointed Bien to the standing committees on education, federal relations, and trade and manufacture. He was among the first to introduce bills, such as that to prevent fraudulent use of the suffrage. The *Gold Hill Daily News* cheered Bien's first week in public office, referring to him as a solid "brick" and "creditable representative." Within days, however, editor Philip Lynch was skewering the rabbi. Lynch was one of five candidates for the office of state printer and had proposed printing rates to the assembly that Bien called exorbitant and outrageous. Bien, meanwhile, supported John Church for state printer. The bill containing Lynch's recommendations was killed—leading Lynch to attack "the *Reverend* Bien" as a "legislative blowhard" and "an Ass." "The Reverend Gas-pipe," wrote Lynch, "is fond of hearing himself talk."[33]

Bien rose to Lynch's bait as a matter of honor, holstering a revolver under his waistcoat. Gun-toting was common in lawless portions of the West, but less so in the legislative chambers. Lynch was unmerciful, caricaturing Bien first as a "monkey," then as a "burro" on the verge of kicking himself out of the community. If the beleaguered editor hoped to discredit one of the most vocal opponents of his candidacy for state printer, it backfired. Lynch's support evaporated, and Bien's favored candidate won by a landslide. The defeated editor retaliated by suggesting that Bien lacked uniform support in the Jewish community. The criticism was futile, which is not to say that intelligent Jews in any constituency necessarily agreed with a rabbi's politics.

Undeterred by the controversy, Bien continued to press for the adoption of postponed pro-Union resolutions. Lynch ridiculed even the latter as the work of "the sucking Melchisedec [*sic*] who pervades the Assembly . . . with the odor of his Rabbinical sanctity, [and] holds the uncircumcised of that body in mortal terror." Bien's colleagues in the assembly variously addressed Lynch's charge that he harangued the legislators "with the name of the Great Jehovah on his lips, and a loaded revolver on his ecclesiastical rump." One assemblyman expressed regret that Bien had, "from a meek follower of the lowly Jesus, become so demoralized as to carry a masked battery." Bien responded immediately to the misguided legislator that as a Jew, he had no such relationship to "lowly Jesus." Another colleague supported the "propriety of a clergyman or a gentleman with a white neck-tie carrying a weapon for the defense of his honor."[34]

In the end, Bien discontinued carrying the gun, his patriotic resolutions passed overwhelmingly, and the assembly authorized him to study Storey County's school system. His report proved to be a balanced but critical assessment of the educational facilities themselves, one of which he described as a "stable," "wholly unfit," and a proper "subject for the attention of a Grand Jury." The chairman of the Senate Education Committee endorsed the report despite its indictment of some highly placed Comstock constituents.[35]

Bien sought other reforms. He gave notice that he intended to introduce legislation to abolish the death penalty in Nevada. The final draft of Assembly Bill (AB) 299 was introduced just a day before the legislature was due to adjourn. The potentially controversial bill could have easily been buried in committee. Instead, Bien's colleagues on the Judiciary Committee recommended it for passage without amendment. Bien's idealistic hope for passage was never realized. Although it is extraordinary that he was respected enough to get the bill to the floor of the assembly with "do pass" status, time had expired, and the legislature never voted on the matter.

Bien's interest in abolishing the death penalty may have been out of step with the times and the frontier's lawless reputation, but his introduction of the issue was one more example of his reform and liberal inclinations. His Jewish colleagues in the assembly had allied interests concerning women's rights. Rosenblatt introduced a bill (AB 60) to authorize married women to execute powers of attorney, and Henry Epstein drafted a bill (AB 86) authorizing married women to transact business in their own names as sole traders. Both received scant notice or evidence of support.[36] Rosenblatt also introduced legislation prohibiting the carrying of concealed weapons. Though not directed explicitly at Bien, the matter was tabled indefinitely—due to its connection in some minds with the right to bear arms in defense of one's honor. Although all three Jewish assemblymen contributed to the new state's future, their efforts regarding women and the death penalty had to wait for others to advance.

Virginia City Jewry Mourning, Celebrating, and Disagreeing

Amid all of his aggressive legislative activity, Bien continued to serve the religious needs of the Virginia City Jews. When he officiated at a child's burial in February 1865, the *Hebrew*'s correspondent described how the solemn prayers deeply moved the many mourners. On the same day as the funeral, the new B'nai B'rith King Solomon lodge formally inducted officers. Jacob Kaplan described in detail the speeches, food, partying, and singing in the streets after the installation. Kaplan took the occasion to emphasize the camaraderie among members of both lodges and reminded readers that the scriptural paradise in which "the lamb shall peaceably graze and quench his thirst alongside the lion" was B'nai B'rith's guiding image. "In our midst we know of no dissension, the different nationalities to us are but the indications of geographical situations. Low prejudices can never be in unison with true B.B."[37] In all of Kaplan's heavy emphasis on unity and harmony, the sophisticated reader could easily detect that he protested too much.

[34]

Within three weeks, the dissension and spirit of competition erupted. Early in 1865, the Virginia City Jewish community began working to establish a library. B'nai B'rith Lodge no. 52, of which Bien and Kaplan were members, initiated the idea, and support poured in, allegedly from the "entire Jewish community." But by March, the newly formed B'nai B'rith King Solomon Lodge no. 64 had undermined the project. Kaplan identified "jealousy" over which lodge would get credit as jeopardizing the library cause. He publicly shamed the B'nai B'rith "Sons of the Covenant" in the *Hebrew*'s pages. The nonexistent "low prejudices" of three weeks before he now cited side by side with "mistaken notions of superiority, and also false pride of wealth," as the seeds of Jewish discord. He condemned the pettiness of those who withdrew their support. And in an attempt to encourage reconsideration by the intransigents, he hoped "they will not consider a man their inferior, because the country of his birth, of which he feels so justly proud, . . . is bounded by French, German, or Polish lines." In the end, the library venture completely failed. In this respect, Comstock Jewry reflected the turmoil found in any American city where new Jewish populations from German and Slavic regions adapted or held steadfast to their form of Judaism amid changing circumstances.[38]

Kaplan further criticized a misplaced attachment to wealth. He observed that most western Jews had left their European homes at an early age, and "our education has thereby been neglected, and most of us have become mere drudges." Wealth, he argued, was a blessing only in intelligent hands: "Let ignorance covet the coffers of avarice, the sensible man longs more for the inestimable treasures of the mind." Recognizing the vagaries of mining stock prices, he reminded that "a moment might deprive them of all their goods, but the refinement of manners, the culture of the mind, remains true to the last." In a final salutation to establishing a library, he wistfully likened it to "the appearance of a meteor, which flashes forth brilliantly for one moment, only to vanish in the next."[39] The library's demise could easily have been a metaphorical allusion to the brilliant Rabbi Bien, who had just left Virginia City for good. He traveled to New York where he started another short-lived Jewish newspaper, married, raised a family, produced more plays, and eventually became the head rabbi at Chicago's Temple Beth Shalom and later at Temple Anshe Chesed in Vicksburg, Mississippi.[40]

Jewish observations proceeded apace even after Bien left. Henry F. Lewitt —a sometime member of both Virginia City B'nai B'rith lodges—was called upon to officiate at marriages and funerals. In distant Salt Lake City, lay-men such as Frederick Auerbach spearheaded the successful formation of a temporary congregation complete with a *sefer* Torah, ceremonial robes, and special prayer books for the High Holidays. The *Hebrew*'s anonymous Utah correspondent could not resist favorably comparing the unanimity of the Salt Lake Jews to the climate of opposition to religious ventures "in every community where men have been away from their God and associated with idols." Although more than one hundred Jewish heads of Virginia City households were engaged in business, the local correspondent to the *Hebrew* reported in 1865 that only twenty-two merchants closed their shops for the High Holidays and hoped that "every respectable Jewish firm in this City" would follow suit.[41]

A Glimpse at Austin, 1864

One of several mineral booms outside the Comstock occurred in the remote Reese River Mining District, 175 miles east of Virginia City. A former Pony Express rider made the initial discovery of a complex silver ore at Pony Canyon in May 1862. A few California-bound travelers joined hundreds of Californians and miners from the Comstock by fall, resulting in the territorial legislature carving out a new county, Lander. Several camps and towns competed to be the county seat, and Austin was so designated in September 1863. San Francisco newspapers gave Austin and the Reese River area almost as much ink as the Comstock. The hype encouraged more adventurers, and the city was incorporated in February 1864. Although prospective miners were initially disappointed with the ore's quality, Austin became the hub of dozens of small mining camps and served as an important distribution center for future towns such as Eureka. Less than one month after its incorporation, Austin's Jews numbered an astounding 150. As usual, the vast majority were unmarried men; only three families were in the mix.[42]

Among the earliest Jewish arrivals were the Auerbach brothers: Frederick, Samuel, and Theodore. Their first American store was at Rabbit Creek in Sierra County, California. In 1864, they moved to Austin where, according to Frederick, they sustained "considerable losses and were largely in debt to creditors in San Francisco, whom we have paid in gold coin when we might have paid them in currency—Levi Strauss and others." The Auerbachs' experience was common. San Francisco supply houses often demanded payment in gold as a condition for a merchant maintaining credit with the company.

Local paper currencies could be 25 percent less valuable than the face value of gold coin.[43] Having satisfied their creditors, the Auerbachs left Austin in May 1864 for Salt Lake City, where they established one of Utah's most prominent mercantile institutions.[44]

Sixty Jewish males in Austin formed a Hebrew Benevolent Society as early as December 6, 1863. According to one insider, the society had already been active in alleviating the financial distress of Jewish miners and other migrants who needed relief, including the Auerbachs. The society procured a burial ground across the main road from the Catholic cemetery. An anonymous Jewish correspondent to San Francisco's *Hebrew* was understandably proud of the tangible evidence of Jewish faith and stated that the newspaper's masthead theme, "The Eternal Light He planted amongst us," was equally applicable to Austin.[45]

Jewish professionals also converged on Austin. Carson City attorney Henry L. Joachimsen was elected the first justice of the peace. San Francisco attorneys Labatt and Newmark organized mining companies in the Reese River District. One of the Austin Hebrew Benevolent Society's first officers, Alfred E. Shannon, New York–born of German and French parenthood, served as notary and Lander County commissioner of deeds and deputy collector for the Internal Revenue Service. Shannon was a founding member of the Reese River Pioneers (which may have been restricted to the American-born) and was elected grand vice chancellor of the Nevada Knights of Pythias in 1880.[46] Unlike many mining boom camps, Austin continued to survive, thanks to a more sophisticated means of processing its complex ore developed after 1870. Austin's regular correspondent to Jewish newspapers reported marriages, births, deaths, and even a murder. Within a decade, however, the number of Jewish residents had plummeted to eleven.[47]

Conclusion

Assemblyman Meyer A. Rosenblatt of Austin had left Nevada by 1870, as had Herman Milton Bien and Henry Epstein, who went to Hamburg to marry Jenny Solomon and then returned with her to San Francisco, where he became a prosperous broker of mining stocks.[48] The three Jewish legislators represented 8 percent of the state assembly, at a time when the Jewish population was hovering at about 1 percent of the total. Their movement out of Nevada also represented the volatile demographic changes based on boom and bust, affecting Jew and Gentile. Jewish merchants who prospered during the economic climb up to 1879, however, owed their success to a loyal Gentile clientele.

The early Nevadans were on the alert for more promising economic prospects—whether in towns of substantial population such as Virginia City in its heyday or at the site of a new bonanza. While Austin boomed, the Central Pacific Railroad was completed across northern Nevada, bringing life and permanence to beckoning new towns in its path. Jewish merchants and entrepreneurs were in all of them.

Riveted Jeans, Shopkeepers, and Ranchers in Railroad Towns

1868–1880

As the Comstock's ore production continued to giddy heights, the demand for a rail connection to Reno and San Francisco overcame years of bickering and competing proposals. Theodore Judah was the chief architect of the Central Pacific Railroad's route through the Sierra Nevada from Sacramento east through the Donner Lake pass and across northern Nevada to Utah.[1] The project began in January 1863, reached the Nevada border at Crystal Peak in December 1867, and five months later the track and the attendant telegraph line were completed to Reno. On May 9, 1868, Central Pacific auctioneers began selling 25-by-100-foot lots along the right-of-way to anxious bidders. The only visible structures in the area on that day were the shanties of railroad workers, tent saloons, and Myron C. Lake's hotel and gristmill near his bridge across the Truckee River. The first "through train" from the East arrived in Reno a year later, on May 15, 1869.[2] State officials recognized Reno's future commercial dominance and in 1870 moved the county seat from Washoe City to Reno, which became the crossroads handling freight and passengers between the Comstock and all points east and west. The railroad not only gave northern Nevada the most modern access to distant suppliers and customers but also proved to be one of the state's few lifelines during its long period of economic and demographic recession.

Jacob W. Davis and Copper-Riveted Jeans

One of Reno's earliest Jewish residents was Jacob W. Davis, born Jakov Youphes near the Baltic seaport of Riga in 1831. At age twenty-three, he emigrated to the United States, moving around as a journeyman tailor from New York City and Augusta, Maine, and then via the Panama crossing to San Francisco by September 1856. Gold discoveries on the Fraser River in British Columbia lured him and thousands more. There he moved from one job to another over the next eight years and even tried his hand in the brewery business. On January 3, 1865, he married his Prussian-born wife, Anna, in Canada, where their first two children, Marcus and Rose, were born. Soon he was back in San Francisco, where he invested in a coal business that failed.

In all these ventures, Davis was trying to be something other than a tailor. He dabbled with mechanical inventions and unsuccessfully applied to the U.S. Patent Office for rights to a steam-powered canal boat and a steam-powered ore crusher. Patent fees were sixty-eight dollars for each application, and to date he had nothing to show for his time and investment. In late spring of 1867, he moved his family to Virginia City, where Anna had relatives. Davis purchased a cigar shop and became an active member of B'nai B'rith Lodge no. 52. He kept the store for three months but could not make ends meet and regretfully returned to tailoring. Eight months at this old trade was enough, and he decided to be among the first doing business at the new town of Reno. He arrived in the middle of the land auctions and new construction in June 1868.[3]

Here Davis helped build the Reno Brewery on Commercial Row, and he established a partnership with proprietor Frederick Hertlein, which lasted about a year. Central Pacific Railroad surveyors, teamsters, and a rising permanent population abounded with a need for horse blankets, wagon covers, saddlebags, and tents, and Davis recognized a market niche. In 1870, he and his family of five were living a block south of the railroad tracks. From this Virginia Street address, Davis began to fabricate supplies from bolts of ten-ounce, off-white duck cloth—a durable, closely woven heavy cotton—that Samuel Packsher, Anna's relative, bought for him from Levi Strauss's dry-goods house in San Francisco.[4]

In late December 1870, the wife of a poor laborer suffering from dropsy came into Davis's shop and asked him to make a pair of pants from the heavy cloth for her husband. Due to his large size, she explained, he continually split the pockets and seams of regular sizes available in the stores. In addition, he could not come in for a measurement because he had no suitable clothes and was ill. Davis told the woman how to obtain his size using a knotted string for his waistline and outer seam. He delicately suggested that she use an old pair of pants to measure the inseam. When she returned with the strings, Davis asked her for three dollars in advance for the pants. As he testified several years later,

The woman asked me to make them strong and he generally tore off his clothes as she says. I was making horse blankets and covers for the teamsters at the time, and had used rivets for the snaps in the blankets—straps in front—and the crouper [covering for the rump of a horse]. These straps were not sewed with seams—but were just riveted together. So when the pants were done—the rivets were lying on the table—and the thought struck me to fasten the pockets with those rivets. I had never thought of it before.[5]

When he finished the pants early in January 1871, word spread immediately that someone had figured out a way to craft a durable pair of work pants. Davis fabricated ten pairs in February—mostly for teamsters and travelers—and another dozen for A. J. Hatche's surveyors in March. The material was Strauss's white ten-ounce duck twill or nine-ounce blue denim. Each customer became a walking advertisement, and the railroad multiplied its effectiveness. In eighteen months, Davis had sold more than two hundred pairs of pants and run up a bill of $350 to Levi Strauss and Company. Davis knew he was on to something and began to worry about possible competition. With no margin of profit to secure a patent for his riveted pants, he turned to his creditor for help. After paying off his bill in full, with the help of his pharmacist friend Will Frank, he wrote a letter to the Levi Strauss Company dated July 2, 1872. If the alleged copy is close to the original, the letter was a masterpiece of directness, naïveté and chutzpah. Davis sent two examples of his riveted pants to Strauss and asked him to apply for a patent in Davis's name in exchange for half the sales rights. Davis predicted the pants would sell for as high as three dollars a pair.[6]

A less scrupulous creditor might have taken Davis's sample and applied for a patent independent of the inventor. To their great honor, Levi Strauss officers acted with integrity and speed. Within a week of receiving the letter from Reno, lawyers for the firm forwarded the patent petition to Davis for his signature. The U.S. Patent Office rejected it, claiming that rivets had been used to bind seams in Civil War soldiers' boots. Undeterred, Davis began stamping each of his riveted pants or overalls as "Patent Applied For" and sold them "as fast as I could make them."[7]

His customers were no longer limited to individuals. Thirty miles east in Wadsworth, storekeeper James A. Ferguson ordered four pairs. Word of Davis's creation reached farther east along the railroad to Palisade, where a retailer ordered twenty pairs for sixty dollars in March 1873.[8] After several language modifications, the U.S. Patent and Trademark Office granted patent no. 139,121 to Jacob Davis and Levi Strauss and Company on May 20, 1873. Before the year ended, Davis introduced the orange linen stitching to match the color of the copper rivets, adding the double arc (arcuate) rear pocket design to distinguish Levi Strauss products from those of competitors.[9]

Anticipating the forthcoming patent approval, Davis closed his Virginia Street shop on April 26, 1873. He and Annie with their six children moved to San Francisco, where they purchased a comfortable residence in a prestigious neighborhood on Folsom Street below Market. Making this purchase possible, in part, was the sale of his Virginia Street store to Levi Strauss for one thousand dollars on April 27. The generous Strauss sold the property back to Davis for one dollar two years later. Davis, in turn, sold it for twelve hundred dollars.[10]

Potential competitors almost immediately challenged the patent granted to Davis and Strauss. The first major case involved a group of four San Francisco traders: Augustus Benjamin Elfelt, A. P. Elfelt, L. Goldsmith, and Albert A. Levi. It was an intra-Jewish affair. Over the next two years, Strauss Company lawyers and Davis personally provided testimony and secured witnesses concerning the date of the "invention." The concept was so simple and effective that tailors everywhere copied it, seeking a piece of the action, and claiming it was not a novelty at all. In the end, however, the case for Davis's invention of the riveted jeans was legally upheld. The U.S. commissioner of patents issued new letters of patent (no. 6335) on March 16, 1875, for the remainder of the unexpired term for which the patent was granted.[11]

The now successful Davis retained his dues-paying membership in Virginia City's B'nai B'rith Lodge no. 52 through 1886. By then, he was supervising 450 workers at Levi Strauss and Company, producing a variety of riveted denim work clothing that became a standard for the industry.[12] The man who had always wanted to have a profession other than as a tailor appeared in San Francisco's business directory as a "manufacturer." Davis's copper-riveted jeans became the most enduring Nevada-based creation in state history. In 2006, Reno memorialized the event with a plaque at the 211 North Virginia Street store location on the anniversary of the first patent.

David Lachman, Father of Reno Jewish Organizations

Born in Prussia in 1830, David Lachman was one of Jacob Davis's neighbors in the new city of Reno. He had been in the Virginia City area since 1861, where he and some Jewish cronies obtained a ruling from the territorial supreme court allowing them to establish a toll road up Seven Mile Canyon. The success of this venture is unknown, but by 1868 he was an established retail clothier and charter member with six Gentiles of Reno's Odd Fellows Lodge no. 14. His background was clearly that of an observant Jew. He married French-born Henrietta Bloch of Virginia City in Reno on November 15, 1870, in a ceremony witnessed by Samuel Cohen and solemnized by Rabbi Jacob Sheyer, who later circumcised the couple's son.[13]

Most Nevada Jewish merchants modified their business practices to remain open on the Jewish Sabbath while closing on Sunday. Lachman was one of the few in the West who resisted this accommodation. He brazenly proclaimed that because he lost business by observing his Sabbath and closing on Saturday, he intended to be open on Sunday. The *Reno Crescent* editorialized with sarcasm: "The merchants of Reno united in an agreement to close their stores on Sunday with the solitary exception of Lachman, and his refusal checked this step toward civilization and decency; and he was right—for by closing he might lose the sale of a pair of overalls, and the loss of a sale would certainly burst his gizzard wide open, and he might go into a decline, and die, and his estate be saddled with the expense of a cheap funeral." How long Lachman managed to defy the widely observed Sunday closing tradition is unknown, but he and his cohorts consistently closed their businesses for the fall High Holidays.[14]

Lachman was a principal in the formation of two Jewish organizations in Reno. The first was the Chebra B'rith Sholam society, whose chief purpose was to provide for proper burial. The founding members purchased two acres of ground from Wiltshire Sanders on May 25, 1877, for a Jewish cemetery a mile north of the business district. The Reno Hebrew Cemetery, dedicated by visiting rabbi Solomon Aragor, served Reno Jewry into the twenty-first century. And in Lachman's home, San Francisco rabbi Aron J. Messing dedicated a Sabbath school in December 1878.[15]

The fire of 1879 destroyed the Chebra B'rith Sholam group's meeting place, but it reorganized as the Reno Hebrew Benevolent Society later that August with thirty-two members. The society's officers over the next year looked like a page taken from Reno's city directory of dry-goods merchants: Morris Ash, David Pechner, E. Meyer, Thomas Barnett, Isaac Barnett, A. Prescott, J. Prescott, David Lachman, Benjamin Lachman, M. D. Levy, Isaac Frederick, and later Sol Jacobs. The benevolent society officers arranged for a visiting rabbi to lead High Holiday services except when the society's treasury was low. On such occasions, David Lachman led the services.[16] He was northern Nevada's conservator of Judaism until his death a quarter century later.

Winnemucca Cofounder Nathan Levy and His Jewish Neighbors

Winnemucca, 164 miles northeast of Reno, had been chosen as a stop on the Central Pacific because it afforded one of the best crossing points of the Little Humboldt River on an old emigrant trail. The area had early established a reputation among forty-niners as a useless desert filled with horned toads, crickets, rabbits, and game birds whose survival "passed the understanding of the average ox-driver who wended his weary, toilsome way" west to California. Few dreamed of returning to this desolate area, but after the Comstock Lode discovery in 1859, prospectors discovered silver in the northern Humboldt range.[17]

One of the dozen founding fathers of this small railroad town on the site of a hay ranch in 1868 was French-born Nathan Levy. Levy demonstrated organizational abilities and won election in 1872 as Humboldt County commissioner. His wife, Fanny, was also born in France. Together they had five children, all born in California. They did not join Nathan in Nevada until about 1876, when he had acquired a herd of cattle. The Levys were one of several "commuter marriages" the railroad made possible and remained in the area until at least 1885.[18]

Their next-door neighbors were the Prussian-born Openhime couple with three children, Harry, Ida, and Siegle. Frederika Openhime and her husband were grocers and had been moving around Nevada since 1862, when their first son was born. Fellow neighbors Simon and Delia Rosenthal also were in the "Grocery, Dry Goods, Boot and Shoe, Etc." business. Simon was part of Winnemucca's "invitation committee" for a social ball south on the railroad line at Oreana in 1868. Within a decade, they had moved several hundred miles south to Tybo in the remote Hot Creek Range of Nye County, where he became a charter member of the local Odd Fellows lodge in 1877. German-born John Roth had been a laborer for twenty years in Humboldt County before marrying Anna and moving to Winnemucca with their children, Samuel, Emma, and Frank, who had enough cattle to warrant a registered brand. M. J. Brandenstein—later of MJB Coffee fame—was an absentee owner of registered herds in Winnemucca from 1885 to 1891.[19] The Jewish presence in this railroad town was small and continuous, but there appears to have been no Jewish religious observance in Winnemucca, probably due to the lack of the ten-man minyan.

The Reinhart Families' Stores and Ranches

Another 125 miles northeast of Winnemucca, Central Pacific agents surveyed the town site of Elko in 1868 and sold lots for as low as three hundred dollars. The county around Elko was larger than Massachusetts, Connecticut, and Rhode Island combined and derived its economic stability from a dependable watershed and fertile valleys. The new town sported two thousand tents—including forty-five saloons, two brothels, a fashionable wooden hotel with eighty rooms, a flour mill, smelting furnaces, two semiweekly newspapers, and merchants' shops. One of these stores was owned by Maximo Reinhart.

Benjamin and Simon Reinhart left Oberlustadt, Germany, in 1844 and settled in Victoria, British Columbia. When the California Gold Rush began, they moved to Marysville, where their brother Eli joined them in 1865. The three operated a men's clothing store until 1867, when they decided to seek a new opportunity along the Central Pacific in northern Nevada. Their father, Maximo, was already there. Eli opened another store at Winnemucca in 1868. His first "Reliable Hardware Store" was a tent carrying basic foods and supplies. The venture prospered and warranted a proper building. Back in Elko, Simon had a tiff with his brother Benjamin and joined Eli early in 1872 in Winnemucca, where they announced their dual ownership of "Reinhart Brothers." Simon later patched things up with Benjamin and moved back and forth between Winnemucca and Elko, where the relatives also co-owned a store. By 1872, the Elko "Reinhart Brothers" store had become what the local newspaper called "one of the heaviest mercantile firms in Nevada." Their retail and wholesale prices were so competitive that they claimed it was unnecessary to travel farther west to save money.[20]

The Reinharts went an extra mile to satisfy customers and extend their own name recognition. They imported from the East a combination of molasses and maple syrup in gallon cans labeled as "made specifically for Reinhart's." The product was a big hit with the locals unaccustomed to the luxury.[21] The Elko community was looking for more than maple syrup. Whereas central Nevadans regarded it as the "Great East," western Nevadans saw it as a "cow county." Elko wanted respectability.

Gabriel Cohn and the Original Nevada University

One of those instrumental in achieving this goal was Gabriel Cohn. In 1867, he and his wife, Jane, were in Prussian Poland, where their daughter was born. A year later, in California, they had a son. In 1869, the family was likely on one of the first trains to Elko from San Francisco. By 1870, Cohn was an American citizen and an established clothing merchant with real estate and personal assets in excess of eleven thousand dollars. Soon he was in the middle of his town's instant claim to fame.

The Morrill Land Grant Act of 1862 included an endowment fund for public colleges that taught agriculture and the mechanical arts, and Nevada's constitution so provided. The state legislature dawdled over several sessions and succeeded only in naming a board of regents composed of the governor, secretary of state, and superintendent of public instruction. Reno, Carson City, and Washoe City competed to be the college's site. The regents could have chosen, but they deferred to the 1873 legislature.[22] Governor Lewis R. Bradley, an Elko County resident and an ex officio regent, was determined to give some state program to his home county. Those voting for Reno and Carson City neutralized each other, and Elko emerged the winner. The battle for small-town bragging rights had ended in a "cow county."

Elko citizens hoped for a future as a center of ranching, trade, and education that rivaled Denver and Sacramento. They now had to move quickly. It was April 23, 1873. Those elected to the building committee included banker and entrepreneur Merrill P. Freeman as chairman. The seven remaining members included Jewish merchants Cohn, Simon Reinhart, and Samuel Mooser. A day later, these commissioners met to form the seven-member "University Building Company." Its president was Cohn, with Mooser and Reinhart as members at large. Their task was to raise funds for the building and appoint men to canvass the northeastern Nevada camps and towns for six thousand dollars. One of their few instant successes was the donation of a building site by the Central Pacific Railroad.[23] The handsome building was quickly erected at a cost of about twenty thousand dollars.

Gabriel Cohn's involvement in the venture doubtless helped to ensure his election as state senator from Elko County in 1874. He was the first Nevada Jewish legislator elected on the Democratic ticket. His German accent was no bar to elected office in a state filled with the foreign-born. In its first year, the school attracted only a dozen students. The legislature sent a committee from its ranks to Elko to examine the first-year students' progress, and Cohn joined them. They expressed pleasure that the school had done so well in a short time, but despite its designation as a "university," the fledgling institution was little more than a college-preparatory school.[24] The *Reno Evening Gazette* editorialized that to call the Elko school a university was "as appropriate as to call a canoe a man-of-war. At present it is merely a good thing for the principal, who gets a University salary for primary school work." Although the *Gazette* editor's views may have reflected sour grapes, he was later vindicated. University historian James W. Hulse describes the debacle as "ten years of partly pathetic, partly noble, and partly comic efforts . . . before the school was moved to Reno."[25] Nevertheless, it is significant that almost half of the original university promoters were Jewish, though they composed a tiny proportion of the population.

Gabriel Cohn In and Out of Office

The 1875 state legislature was overwhelmingly Republican, and the Elko delegation was Democratic. Partisan politics were evident on most issues, and the Democrats took their lumps. A vigorous dispute over ceding part of Elko County to Eureka County marked Cohn's senate activity. In the end, Cohn and his colleagues failed to reverse the legislation. The debates between Cohn and his counterpart from Eureka County reached stentorian proportions and in one case nearly ended in a duel.[26] The *Gold Hill Daily News*, assessing the quality of senate oratory, damned Cohn's speaking ability with faint praise. But the local Elko newspaper congratulated him and his colleagues for "having survived the machinations and miasma at the State Capital."[27]

Cohn's first business venture with Morris Badt in 1869 was the Temple of Fashion, which provided a display of fine clothing and fancy goods but seemed out of place in Elko's rough environment. The partnership dissolved shortly thereafter, when Badt moved fifty miles northeast to Wells—another Central Pacific stop.[28] While Cohn was helping to build the Elko university campus and away on legislative duties in Carson City, his business began to go flat. He declared bankruptcy in December 1876. He liquidated, rallied, but finally sold what was once the largest fine clothing store in Elko at a U.S. Marshals sale in January 1880.[29] Cohn and Badt had a jointly registered cattle brand in 1874, but by 1880 they became separately involved in the ranching business. Cohn was one of the first to improve shorthorn cattle by breeding them with longhorns. He succeeded, as did others, in selling prize hybrids for

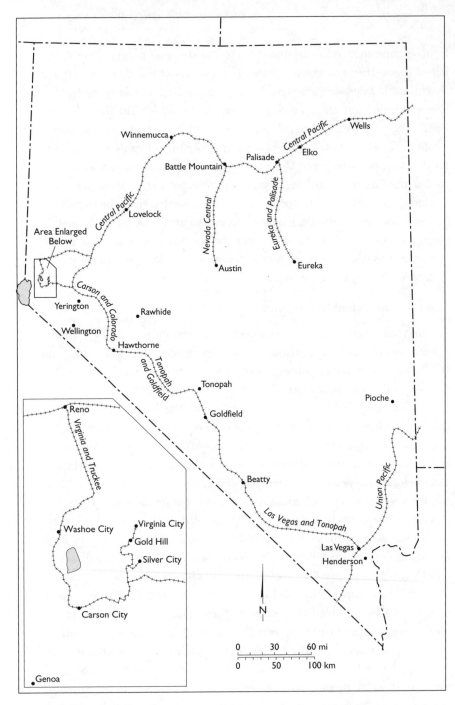

Early Nevada Railroads

as much as seven to ten thousand dollars per head. His family grew, as did his new business. Between 1870 and 1879, he and Jane had another daughter and three sons—the last in Virginia City, where several Cohn families to whom they may have been related resided.[30]

Eli Reinhart Truckles to the Railroad Magnates

In 1879, Eli Reinhart employed Eureka County state assemblyman F. E. Fisk to serve as the agent for his company's grain storage facility in Eureka. Fisk was committed to passing legislation to reduce the discriminatory freight rates levied against Nevadans. For example, a carload of dry goods transported in 1877 from New York to San Francisco cost $1,200. The same merchandise off-loaded in Winnemucca (475 miles closer) cost $1,616. In short, the freight charge from New York to Winnemucca was calculated as though the goods had been transported all the way to San Francisco and then back to Nevada. The "short haul" cost more than the "long haul."[31] Farmers in rural areas nationwide chaffed under unreasonably high in-state rates and their legislators being in railroad pockets.

Nevada was no exception. Candidates running for office predictably promised to fight discriminatory regulations imposed by the railroads. Once elected, however, they were heavily lobbied and paid by Henry M. Yerington, general manager of the Virginia and Truckee Railroad, to ensure that they would be favorably disposed to the railroad interests. Fisk was one of the 1879 Nevada assemblymen Yerington approached but remained adamant in his opposition to discriminatory rate practices.

After the legislature adjourned, the railroad moguls decided to make an example of Fisk. The Eureka and Palisade Railroad president notified Reinhart that unless he discharged Fisk and replaced him with a more cooperative legislator, the railroad would set up a grain business in Eureka to compete with the Reinharts.[32] Reinhart totally capitulated in the interest of the family business. It was one example of how big-business interests could checkmate the idealism of a firm whose local reputation was advertised as "integrity, goodwill and helpfulness to the people of Nevada."

The unmarried Eli Reinhart adopted five sons of another brother still in Germany. Between 1876 and 1882, Eli paid for nephews Amson, Edward, Simon, Louis, and Moses to come to Winnemucca, where they systematically apprenticed in the family's growing mercantile and ranching businesses. Their financial success—due, in part, to their acquisition of goods in huge volumes—would later prove in stark contrast to Nevada's depression years at the turn of the century.

Abraham Mooser and Samuel Mooser

On the heels of the Reinharts' arrival in Elko came Abraham Mooser. Born Abraham Schmuser in Ichenhausen, Bavaria, on June 19, 1842, he learned English and French in the gymnasium, spoke fluent Hebrew, and had an "uncanny ability to add up a column of figures rapidly." Concerned about rising antisemitism in Germany, his mother urged her children to immigrate to the United States. In 1858, he followed his brother, Isaac, to Corinth, Mississippi, where he worked as a bookkeeper for a Jewish merchant and Anglicized his name. He enlisted (reluctantly, say his children) in the Confederate army and was wounded four times at the April 1862 Battle of Shiloh. One bullet was so near his spinal cord that the field surgeons chose not to remove it. Mooser returned to Germany to visit his mother and consult with German specialists, who advised against tampering with the Civil War souvenir. Since he still was a German citizen and thus at risk of being conscripted into the army, he hastily returned to the United States; stayed briefly in Memphis (where he was a member of local B'nai B'rith Lodge no. 35); moved to San Jose, California; became an American citizen; and worked for a Jewish dry-goods merchant. Mooser likely passed through Elko en route to California and decided to return there in 1870 to open a jewelry store.[33]

Samuel, his elder brother by two years, also came to the area with his wife, Lucy, and settled first in Elko, where he was one of three Jewish merchants on the university's building committee in 1874. The family later moved to Tuscarora, fifty-two miles northeast of Elko, where they operated a grocery store that provided them enough money for a live-in Chinese cook. Samuel and Lucy had four children during their ten years in Nevada.[34]

Abraham, however, was twenty-eight and still unmarried. A friend, Jack Nathan from New York, visited him in Elko and asked about his single status. Abraham responded by pointing to the dearth of Jewish women in Elko. Nathan became a matchmaker and countered with the availability of a young Jewish orphan living with his relatives in New York. This began a correspondence with Henrietta Koshland, whom Mooser met in Salt Lake City rather than expose her to a smallpox outbreak in Elko.

Mooser spotted his future wife at the train station and walked up to kiss her before saying a word. They married on July 26, 1874, at Sacramento in the home of one of the bride's cousins, Sam Lavenson. The couple returned to Elko, where Abraham added a produce and deli market to his successful jewelry business. Celia and Joseph were born to the Moosers in Elko, and another pair, Minnie and Matilda, died in infancy.

Both Mooser families left Nevada for Sacramento near the peak of the state's prosperity cycle in 1879. Abraham's decade in Elko, without benefit of an organized Jewish community, dampened none of his enthusiasm for Jewish tradition. He moved on to Santa Monica, where his was the only Jewish family. When his marriageable children started dating non-Jews, he moved his entire family to the more Jewish-populated city of Los Angeles. There the family became active members of Congregation B'nai B'rith (now the Reform Wilshire Boulevard Temple).

Abraham Mooser was typical of young Jewish men who migrated from Europe to Nevada. They were usually single when they arrived but had family or friends in the area. Although Elko's economy was doing well, no place in Nevada had a promising future for someone concerned about maintaining Jewish traditions. Like many second-generation Nevada Jews, Mooser's children were attracted to relationships with non-Jews, and Mooser wanted to give them other options. All of them ended up marrying in the faith—outside Nevada.[35]

Morris and Lina Badt's Commuter Marriage

The Morris Badt family took a different course. Born in 1831 at Sverson (Schwerenz), a suburb of Poznán, the birthplace of many Nevada Jews from Prussian Poland, Badt came from Europe to New York and then to New Orleans between 1847 and 1851. From there he traveled around Cape Horn and arrived in San Francisco in 1861, where he remained for six years as a merchant. While in San Francisco, Morris married Lina Posener, from Poznán. They moved to Elko in 1868, where Morris immediately partnered with another Poznánite, Gabriel Cohn. He dissolved this relationship and, after a brief mercantile arrangement with his brother Alexander, moved with Lina to Wells in 1875.

When Badt sold his Elko branch store in 1875, he traded back to Governor Bradley a large cattle ranch, which he had taken in payment for the store. By the time he died, Morris Badt had added several cattle ranches to his already prosperous business.[36] In Wells, he built the town's first brick building, which sold everything from ranching equipment to oats, flour, and groceries. His

Table 3.1
Nineteenth-Century Nevada Jewish Populations

Unless otherwise noted, the figures are drawn from the author's database, which was built on census records, Jewish organization rosters, city directories, correspondence, and miscellaneous sources. The table is necessarily incomplete in several respects. The numbers are not perfectly accurate, and err on the side of being too low. Many children and spouses have been unaccounted. For example, they appear in 1880 with all children born in Nevada, but there is no evidence of them in prior census years. In 1870 alone, there were more than 240 separate populated camps and towns, many of which had a single Jewish place of business. Moreover, the census records for 1890 were lost in a fire, but statistical records remain. Consequently, the table is best viewed as a series of snapshots of a single year or period. The year 1878 is the best one to make comparisons across a number of cities.

City/Town	1860	1870	1880	1890	1900
Austin[a]	0	30	11	3	1
Carson City	7	52	86	89	33
Comstock: Virginia City/ Gold Hill/Silver City/ Dayton/Sutro	15	110	406[b]	123	17
Elko/Wells/Tuscarora	0	32	47	50	58
Eureka	0	100	113[c]	26	6
Genoa	4	4	4	4	3[d]
Hamilton	0	47	20	4	0
Pioche area	0	10	42	30	23
Reno	0	20	89	90	140
Wellington/Mammoth Eagle	1	—	—	—	27
Winnemucca/Lovelock/ Battle Mountain area	0	7	15	16	20
Miscellaneous camps and towns[e]	0	8	47	15	22
Estimated Totals	27	420	880	450	350

[a] Jews numbered 150 in 1864. *Western States Jewish Historical Quarterly* 9, no. 1 (October 1976): 87–90.

[b] At its peak in 1878, the Comstock Jewish population approached 500. Choynski (signed "Maftir"), San Francisco, August 8, 1882, *American Israelite,* August 25, 1882, 58:2.

[c] The Jewish population peaked at 172 in 1878. Norton B. Stern, "The Jewish Community of aNevada Mining Town."

[d] The number of Jews was 16 in 1898, when four families associated with the Wellington colony farmed the Haines ranch.

[e] The number of voting areas after 1860 ranged from 21 in 1870 to 240 in 1900

son Milton later remembered that twenty-horse teams freighted everything to and from the railroad on a jerk line.

The Badts reared four boys and four girls. When the first of them was of school age, the Badts purchased a home in San Francisco, where the children—under their mother's care—received a secular and religious education. They spent summers and holidays with their father in Nevada. According to Milton, Morris was depressed about being separated from his family, whom he visited several times a year. He died in 1898, a year after Milton and the rest of the family finally took up permanent residence in Wells.[37]

. . .

Jewish life was sparse along the 550 miles of Central Pacific Railroad from Reno to Wells, but its representatives had a substantial impact on ranching, politics, and commerce. The Levys, Badts, Reinharts, and Cohns were founding fathers and among the first to establish businesses in Winnemucca, Elko, and Wells. Being Jewish in the widely separated towns was a challenge met in several ways. Finding a Jewish mate was the first hurdle. After that was the issue of raising children in the faith. Morris Badt's solution was to have his family raised in San Francisco, whereas Abraham Mooser moved his family to southern California. Whether the five Nathan Levy children in Winnemucca maintained any Jewish tradition in Nevada after 1880 is unknown, as is the level of family observance in all of the smaller railroad towns.

A Gunfighter, a Physician, an Alleged Arsonist, and a Reform Congregation

By western standards, Virginia City and Carson City were law-abiding places. Pioche, however, was considered the wildest town in the West. Located in southeastern Nevada, Pioche was slow to boom and with no need to be on a railroad line. Mining discoveries drew more than five thousand treasure seekers to the area by 1872, including a small but influential group of Jewish merchants and professionals as well as several hundred ruffians who gave the town its reputation for lawlessness and mayhem.[1]

According to Myron Angel, on May 30, 1871, "Mike Casey was killed by James Levy, at Pioche, Lincoln County. Acquitted. Mike Casey is the man who killed Thomas Gorson, March 12th." Born in Ireland to Jewish parents in 1842, Levy was a miner in Pioche when he witnessed the Gorson shooting and publicly denied Casey's allegation that it was a matter of self-defense. Later, Casey met Levy at a local store and challenged him to a gunfight. They met in an alley where Levy called to Casey. His shot grazed Casey's head, but he lunged at Levy, who shot him again in the neck. As he keeled over, Levy administered a coup de grâce with the butt of his revolver. Casey's friend David Naegle then shot Levy in the jaw and took off. Peace officers soon arrived and arrested Levy. He was tried and acquitted and remained in the area to dig for silver.[2] More gunslinging was ahead for Jim Levy.

When Virginia-born Henry Bergstein arrived fresh from Medical College of the Pacific (later Cooper Medical College), booming Pioche boasted six attorneys, ten restaurants, seventy-two saloons, thirty-two houses of prostitution, and two breweries.[3] He later recalled that the local cemetery had 108 graves, and only three of the interred had died a natural death. "The crack of the revolver and knife-wounds were daily heard and seen," he wrote, "and to the sorrow of many surviving friends their companions frequently died 'with their boots on.' The average bravo had a great horror of dying with his boots on and, when wounded, before priest or surgeon were called, his boots were pulled off."[4] Evidence of violence could be found on almost every page of the *Pioche Record,* and Bergstein was one of six physicians qualified to handle the carnage.

A chief cause of bloodshed was mine owners hiring toughs to settle boundary disputes rather than calling for help from the understaffed constabulary. One such event was dubbed the "Raymond & Ely/Pioche Phoenix fight"—as if it were a boxing match. In fact, it was the all-night standoff between two mining companies whose tunnels intersected. The men were armed, and one bullet struck Thomas Ryan directly under the eye, killing him instantly. The assailant, identified as Jim Levy, was last seen heading north to Hamilton.

Within two weeks, Levy was extradited back to Lincoln County. It was January, and the return trip to Pioche gave the trussed-up Levy frozen feet. He was transferred to the county hospital and then to a jail cell. There he penned an open letter to the local newspaper detailing his version of the flight to Hamilton and emphasizing that he—"as innocent as the babe unborn"—was being pursued by a mob accusing him of Ryan's murder. Maybe he was right: no record exists of Levy being tried for killing Thomas Ryan.[5]

Levy left the mining business and the area. He worked as a professional gunslinger, gambler, and occasional merchant in towns as far east as Deadwood and as far southwest as Tombstone. He survived sixteen shoot-outs before he was gunned down in a gambling dispute. The Pioche newspaper recorded his death and remembered him only as Michael Casey's reputed killer in 1871.[6] If, as most local newspapers averred on the occasion of High Holidays, Jews were among "our best citizens," Jim Levy was one exception. He was also one of the few Jews in Nevada who chose mining as a career.

Jewish merchants had been among the first in the Pioche area when news spread about its silver strike. Prussian-born Louis Sultan came to Pioche in 1869 and established sufficient credibility as an educator and administrator to be elected Lincoln County superintendent of schools on the Democratic ticket in 1872.[7] Assuming that he had support of fellow Jews at the polls, his electors would have included the ubiquitous Solomon Ashim, who promised the cheapest prices for every miner's needs; Jacob, Jonas, and Benjamin Cohn and P. H. Felsenthal, purveyors of clothing and dry goods; Morris Cohn, selling Havana cigars and cutlery; J. Eisenman, hardware merchant; M. H. Lichtenstein, the local auctioneer; and A. B. Goldstein, the tailor who advertised that he worked "with neatness and dispatch."[8] Pioche had a minyan.

Religious Observances in Pioche and Its First Jewish Marriage

Pioche's newspaper made much of the town's first bris in 1873: the ritual circumcision of Jonas Cohn's son Hyman. The *Pioche Daily Record* noted that ordinarily this Jewish ritual was to be performed on the eighth day after birth. Henry Bergstein was available but lacked the proper religious credentials. Consequently, the Cohns delayed the ceremony for four months, and the Reverend Dr. Levinberg of San Francisco performed it. One can only imagine the size of the stipend that could entice an urban mohel (ritual circumciser) to travel by train to a northern Nevada railhead like Palisade and then rumble by stagecoach almost 250 miles to Pioche. For Jonas Cohn, the maintenance of this essential Jewish religious tradition could not be measured in dollars. Attending physician A. C. Bishop commented on Levinberg's skill, while the newspaper noted that "like all of his race," Cohn provided profuse hospitality and a "lavish" spread of food with the "choicest wines."[9]

Jules Abrahamson married Esther Davis in a civil ceremony in the middle of June 1874. The *Pioche Record* touted its religious solemnization two weeks later by Mr. Lichtenstein as the town's "first Jewish wedding." Others present at the gala were Dr. Bergstein, Mr. and Mrs. Jacobs, Louis Sultan, and Pioche notables. However, when it turned out a few months later that Esther was only fifteen years old, the marriage was annulled.[10] More circumspect was Louis Sultan, who married Ernestine Jacobs. Their son, born more than a year later, was circumcised by Rabbi H. L. Kalisher, who came at great expense. By 1876, a narrow-gauge railroad between Palisade and Eureka left only 186 uncomfortable miles by stagecoach to Pioche.[11]

Although the commitment of a few to preserve religious traditions was heroic, the general level of Jewish Sabbath observance was undocumented. Nevertheless, the small community of Pioche Hebrews celebrated Passover, Rosh Hashanah, and Yom Kippur at the Odd Fellows Hall and proudly extended an open invitation to Gentiles to witness the ceremonies. No one advertised store closings on these occasions, as was common in Carson City and Virginia City.[12]

But Pioche's Jews were active. Dr. Bergstein gathered seven of his medical colleagues from as far north as Austin to discuss Nevada's failure to regulate medical practice. The group recommended forming a state board of health and electing a physician to the legislature.[13] Bergstein was their Republican candidate for assemblyman in 1874. He won easily, departed for northwestern Nevada, and never returned to Pioche. As Bergstein explored Virginia City's possibilities, Pioche began its decline, with just enough mineral production to avoid becoming a ghost town. As Gentile merchants departed, a few Jewish merchants picked up the slack. Thanks to some new ore discoveries at nearby Delamar, Pioche had a second boom toward the century's end, and the Sultans and the extended Cohn family remained very much in the news—though announcements of Jewish holidays had long since ceased.

Hamilton: Alexander Cohn and the Great Fire of 1873

Hamilton—"made up chiefly of old Comstockers"—in the late 1860s was the center of a rich but short-lived strike of silver-lead in the White Pine Mountains about forty miles southeast of Eureka.[14] It became White Pine County seat in its boom days of 1868 when the newspapers wildly exaggerated its population as nearly twenty thousand. An 1870 list of Hamilton's twenty-four hundred registered voters included thirty-five Jewish merchants. One of these, Alexander Cohn, twenty-seven, was brother and partner in the tobacco store of Morris Cohn in 1875. Business had been better. Hamilton's best ore production was $2,137,801 in 1870, but it dropped steadily thereafter—as did the population. Jacob Cohn and Brother Clothiers was selling out, closing its doors, and promising to vacate the property by the Fourth of July, 1873.[15]

The *White Pine Daily News* reported that at 5:30 AM, June 27, 1873, a fire broke out "near the store of M. Cohen [*sic*] & Bro. on Main street." The fire was never under control. According to eyewitnesses, the White Pine Water Company was negligent in providing water to douse the flames. Within an hour, the firehouse itself had burned, and still no water had been applied to the fire. People were seen running half dressed in all directions. Water finally was forthcoming after two hours, but by then most of the business district was reduced to ashes.[16]

The loss in personal property at Hamilton was estimated in excess of $100,000, and the real estate loss computed at more than a half million. Victims of the blaze and the insurance companies called for swift justice. Within two weeks, the White Pine County Grand Jury issued a warrant for the arrest of Alexander Cohn, who was apprehended without incident and bail set at $3,000. According to the state law enacted in March 1873, a judge had the discretion of exempting anyone from jury duty whose distant residence was such that he could not be "conveniently summoned" by the sheriff. Presiding judge William Beatty had been instrumental in the law's passage, and he used it in this case to impanel a jury composed of persons who were victims of the fire. The result was predictable.

Because Cohn denied any complicity or wrongdoing, the prosecution tried to establish a motive based on Cohn having once expressed the belief that the tobacco shop was insured.[17] Although much of the evidence was circumstantial, the jury concluded that Cohn was the perpetrator and had acted "willfully and maliciously," and on October 23, 1873, it convicted him of arson. Judge Beatty sentenced him to seven years in the Nevada State Prison. Cohn never wavered in his protestation of innocence and reportedly "wept like a child upon hearing his sentence."[18] While in prison, Cohn became supervisor of the prison's new boot and shoe factory, where he earned high praise and helped create a revenue stream for the underfunded prison.

In May 1876, thirty-nine citizens signed a petition requesting that Cohn be pardoned. The first of the signers, Eureka businessman and future state governor Reinhold Sadler, had befriended Cohn with bail support. The petition failed in part because it indicted Judge Beatty's sentencing decision. Nor did it help that Beatty was a newly elected supreme court justice and an ex-officio member of the pardons board.[19] The petition was not granted.

Over the next eighteen months, a virtual "who's who" of northern Nevada rallied in support of Cohn's innocence. The new petition's first signer was Frederick Wadsworth Cole, Beatty's successor as county judge. Under Cole's signature were those of P. P. Canavan, former assemblyman; J. D. Patterson, White Pine County sheriff in 1873 (when the fire took place); and his successor, Edward Raum. Thirty-two other signatures followed, including county commissioners, state treasurers, educators, and legislators from two other counties. These prominent men of differing political persuasions had come to believe Cohn, who "still solemnly insists upon his entire innocence." Virtually all of the signers were Gentiles.[20] The June 11 petition took several months to make the rounds and was a day late being notarized. Thus, the pardons board did not consider it.

Although the pardon petition's rationale may have been factually correct, Judge Beatty and his colleagues on the supreme court were not about to grant a pardon based on judicial error. A new argument for pardon had to be the epitome of humility rather than a criticism of the legal process. The efforts paid off: Cohn was pardoned on November 9, 1878, and released from prison. He promptly disappeared from the written record.[21] One tantalizing piece of information appeared in the *Eureka Daily Sentinel,* which reported that on

July 24, 1880, Sadler left Eureka for San Francisco on the Eureka and Palisade Railroad with a person described only as "A. Cohn."[22] Whether Sadler provided temporary sanctuary for Cohn on one of his remote ranches near Eureka or Cohn remained in Nevada under an assumed name is open to speculation.

Although Cohn's alleged felony might have been expected to trigger some antisemitic backlash, there is no evidence of overt or even ambiguous anti-Jewish sentiment. On the contrary, those who rushed to support Cohn's innocence and petition for his pardon were mostly prominent non-Jewish men, including a judge, attorneys, sheriffs, congressmen, and educators from the scene of the fire. Cohn was a convenient scapegoat, satisfying the need to place blame for natural or human-caused calamities and find an example of how the young state planned to maintain law and order.[23] Hamilton never recovered from the fire or the continued decline in ore production, and many of its townspeople moved to nearby Eureka—a few hours on horseback to the west.

Eureka's Vibrant Jewish Community, 1875–1885

Silver and traces of gold were found 240 miles east of Virginia City as early as 1864 in Eureka. The metals were mixed with lead, and little progress was made in separating the profitable silver ore without a specialized smelter. This event coincided in 1869 with a rich discovery a few miles away at Ruby Hill, which precipitated the predictable rush. Over the next fifteen years, Eureka's high grade–ore production challenged that of the Comstock. The legislature designated Eureka the seat of a newly created county of the same name. By 1875, the area was prosperous enough to warrant a narrow-gauge railroad connecting it to the Central Pacific at Palisade. Eureka's population numbered about forty-two hundred, with a Jewish population of seventeen families and forty-three bachelors—slightly less than 3 percent of the surrounding neighbors. A correspondent tallied their country of nativity as "American, including all the children, forty-eight; Prussian, [which included a large contingent from the Polish Duchy of Poznán] forty-three; Bavarian, six; Bohemian, six; English, two; French, one; Russian, seven."[24]

Eureka Jews were not an island community composed solely of merchants. Many owned shares of stock in the local mines, which were as much assets as liabilities. Benjamin C. Levy was superintendent of K. K. Consolidated Mines and served as county recorder from 1878 to 1880. Max Oberfelder erected a gasworks and installed piping for illuminating homes, stores, and streets. Eureka Jews included a physician, miller, barber, gunsmith, fire insurance salesman, and pawnbroker. A remarkably high percentage of Jewish women were in business for themselves as milliners, restaurateurs, boardinghouse owners, and grocery specialists.[25]

A Religious Embarrassment

The existence of this thriving Jewish community of more than one hundred persons was made known to the readership of the *American Israelite* in the fall of 1875. Its articulate spokesperson, Samuel Goldstone, a native of Bavaria, described the unsatisfactory experiences of celebrating High Holidays with visiting clergy. One of the "self-styled 'Rabbis'" they hired was, wrote Goldstone, a "sleek Pollack, utterly ignorant of the German language, and speaking but a miserable English."[26] Goldstone's use of the term *Pollack* was a common Bavarian description of the presumably less literate Poles. What is noteworthy is that such a comment caused no rift with Eureka's Polish Jews.[27] The following year, a visiting rabbi publicly invited Christians to attend the Rosh Hashanah service at the local Masonic Hall. Several ministers, lawyers, and the *Eureka Sentinel* editor accepted. The rabbi's presentation proved to be a "rhapsody of unintelligible English, intermixed with Polish-German *(Yidish)* [sic], and Hebrew sentences, [which] never before assailed human understanding." The Jews were "utterly confounded with shame" and were glad the Christian contingent left the service. Goldstone went on to castigate such "pretenders" to the title of "rabbi" or *"shochet"* or *"mohel"*—nine out of ten of whom were "perfect frauds." The officiant at the High Holiday services also claimed to be a mohel and ended up permanently disfiguring six male children with his slovenly work.[28] Such were the risks run by isolated observant Jews without permanent religious leadership.

Nevada's First Reform Congregation

The Eureka Jewish community hoped to hire a trained rabbi from the Jewish College at Cincinnati and to affiliate with Rabbi Isaac Mayer Wise's Reform Union of American Hebrew Congregations. The congregation at Eureka officially organized on Sunday, August 13, 1876. The first elected officers were all merchants: J. Levin, president; O. Dunkel, vice president; Samuel Goldstone, secretary; and Solomon Ashim, treasurer.[29] Despite an offer of a $225 stipend in gold to lead High Holiday services that fall, a cantor from Nashville declined the invitation. In view of the enormous traveling inconvenience, his demur was understandable.

The congregation assembled at the new Odd Fellows Hall and settled for a lay-led service, including music by a quartet with a female soprano. The stipend money was used to fence the tiny Jewish cemetery tucked in a semisecluded glen off the main road south of town. It took another six months for the UAHC to formally accept the Eureka congregation. Not only did Eureka produce Nevada's first permanent Jewish congregation in Nevada, but the UAHC accepted it eight months before San Francisco's Congregation Emanu-El.[30]

The isolated Eureka congregation's affiliation with the fledgling Reform Movement was a remarkable achievement. American Judaism's adaptations to the exigencies of modernity were highly controversial. Despite standard-bearers such as David Einhorn in Baltimore and Isaac Mayer Wise in Cincinnati, Reformers lacked a set of common canons. In an 1863 editorial, Wise described the difficulty of reaching consensus to form an "American Synagogue" at St. Louis. Traditionalists such as *Occidental* editor Isaac Leeser opposed it. Additionally, Wise wrote, "There is the Polander, Bohemian, Englishman, Frenchman and, of course, Germans from all provinces, each of whom brought his own codex of religious observance from the old country, to be adopted by all. Then came the aristocratic atheists who consider this criminal folly a matter of style and fashion, and the let-me-alone infidels and others who used to be numerous in St. Louis."[31] Eureka also included Jews with diverse national backgrounds. They agreed to form a congregation, but they were not uniformly observant.

The catalyst for religious cohesion among Eureka Jews was Goldstone's strong leadership. He kept himself and others abreast of the development of Reform through the pages of Wise's *American Israelite.* He happened upon a few pages of the *Israelite* while at Shasta, California, in 1855. "I grasped at it with the eagerness of a hungry wolf, I devoured every word on these scraps, but my appetite is not satisfied," Goldstone wrote. He subscribed immediately and promised to stay in touch.[32] The newspaper followed him in his twenty-year odyssey to Nevada. Unlike some Reformers who wished to accommodate themselves to a Sunday worship observance of the Sabbath, Wise and Goldstone championed the traditional Friday-night-to-Saturday-night observance.

In a spring issue of the *American Israelite,* the regular New York correspondent, under the pen name "Phil Point," took the occasion to criticize

Dwight L. Moody's lively evangelism at the Hippodrome, adding that "American Israelites are too intelligent for paroxysmal religion." Phil Point also alluded to the Jewish Saturday Sabbath as "useless" and urged a change to Sunday worship. From two thousand miles away in tiny Eureka came an explosive repudiation of this accommodation to the Christian day of worship. Saturday "Shaboth," wrote Goldstone, was "Israel's majestic Queen," and faithful Jews should protect it at all costs. Goldstone's descriptions of Eureka Jewry in widely read newspapers and his passionate defense of tradition helped develop the necessary esprit de corps to form the Eureka congregation.[33]

Reform Judaism's Founder Visits Nevada

The stage was now set for Wise to visit the newly recognized group. Wise, regarded as a father of Reform Judaism in the United States, traveled west to enlist support for and allegiance to his recently formed UAHC. Considered so blunt, self-assured, and controversial that he was not invited to visit the large congregation in Los Angeles, Wise initiated his first correspondence from Salt Lake City, where he acknowledged the large mercantile houses of the Auerbach, Siegel, and Kahn brothers in contrast to the lack of any Jewish religious or fraternal organization.[34]

Leaving the Union Pacific Railroad for what he considered the more elegant and friendly Central Pacific, his first stop in mid-July 1877 was at Palisade, Nevada, "in a barren valley, where it has pleased the Creator to make a hole in the mountains just big enough for fifteen or twenty houses and a railroad station to be located and a hundred people to stir about." Even in this tiny rail town, Jews were to be found. In one of the shanties, Wise sought out a Jewish merchant eking out a living from a small stock of goods worth about five hundred dollars. Another, Mr. Baum, who ran a one-story hotel "surrounded by rough faces, hunters, miners, railroad laborers, Chinamen, flies, and sandstone," felt compelled to admit to the rabbi that his wife was a "shiksa" (an old-fashioned term for a Gentile woman) from Ireland.[35]

Wise had a six-hour wait at Baum's hotel before he could catch the narrow-gauge train to Eureka. His description of the landscape's barrenness was as negative as that of the short-haul rates from Palisade to Eureka. The ninety-mile trip cost him eight dollars in gold and took seven hours to complete at the snail's pace of thirteen miles per hour. The midnight welcoming committee included Dr. Morris Rockman (Eureka's first resident physician), mining executive Benjamin C. Levy, and Goldstone.[36]

Firecrackers and drumbeatings from a Chinese colony adjacent to the hotel awakened the rabbi in the morning. Eureka provided Wise with his first close observation of the Chinese, who favorably impressed him with their work ethic and frugality. In contrast, he judged the local Native Americans to be illiterate loafers and beggars. He was shortly squired off to the restaurant of Mrs. Regina Moch, where "to our surprise there was served a breakfast than which one could not find better at Delmonico's in New York."[37]

Wise lectured in the Methodist church, banqueted with old acquaintances from Cincinnati, characterized the Jews of Eureka as "neighborly, sociable and generous," and noted that they brought in a rabbi from San Francisco for High Holidays. Wise's visit elevated the religious consciousness not only of Eureka's Jews but also of some Gentiles. The Reverend John A. Gray, for example, eulogized Jews to his Methodist faithful the following Sunday.[38] The relationship of Protestants and the Jewish population in Eureka was clearly cordial.

Religious Celebrations

The Eureka Jews did not hire a rabbi for the High Holiday services of that year. Rather, the congregation's president, local watchmaker Pepi Steler, led the service with the assistance of Rockman, Goldstone, and a mixed choir. A few weeks later, the congregation celebrated the less known feast of Simchas Torah, which marked the completion of the yearlong reading of the entire Torah. The congregation held monthly meetings at one or another member's store and worshiped at the Masonic Lodge or Odd Fellows Hall.[39] They also hosted elaborate balls, open to the public. At the Simchas Torah ball on October 11, 1876, "our Christian townspeople demonstrated their appreciation of their Jewish neighbors by crowding the ballroom to its utmost capacity," Goldstone reported.[40] Festive suppers following a dance were usually served at midnight, and Eureka's Jewish cooks and suppliers were particularly up to the task. John and Regina Moch had been successful restaurateurs for more than fifteen years in Reno, Virginia City, and Hamilton. Bernhard Berg was Eureka's major green grocer and produce farmer. Mrs. Rachel Ashim's food market provided epicurean delicacies of fish and fowl, and Dave Rosenberg or Max Oberfelder supplied the spirituous beverages from an inventory exceeding forty thousand dollars.[41]

When Eureka's Jews held the "First Annual Purim Ball" in February 1877, the local press explained the holiday's biblical basis. The *Sentinel*'s editor headlined the 1879 Purim Ball as "An Event Never Equaled in the Social History of Nevada." He went on to elaborate: "Certainly, no one who attended last night's ball will ever say that the Hebrews do anything in a half-way manner, and there was but one sentiment expressed, namely, that never before has there been a social gathering in Eureka that surpassed or even equaled that of last evening." Purim Balls customarily were masked or costumed events, with prizes awarded for the best outfits. At this event, 109 Gentiles and Jews registered as entrants in the costume contest. Later that year, Eureka Jews formed B'nai B'rith Silver State Lodge no. 296—a further demonstration of its 23 members' commitment to the principles of Judaism. Together with a thriving Sabbath school, it capped three years' building a solid foundation for Judaism in this promising mining town.[42]

Jewish Fraternal and Business Affiliations

As elsewhere in Nevada, Jews were heavily involved with fraternal organizations. As early as 1875, a member of the local community noted that "there is scarcely a Jew in this place but what is a member of either the Masonic or Odd Fellows societies."[43] Levy was noble grand (president) of the Odd Fellows Mountain Lodge, and Goldstone was its deputy district grand master. In March 1879, Levy and Rockman were among the first officers of the Ancient Order of United Workmen, Alpha Lodge. The following year, Levy helped to organize and became chief ranger (president) of Eureka's International Order of Foresters lodge. Another officer was Alfred E. Shannon, former leader of the Austin Jewish community and future statewide grand master of the Knights of Pythias. Michael Borowsky, a charter member of Reno's Masonic Lodge in January 1869, was also a charter member of Eureka's Masonic Lodge, along with Goldstone, Marquis Levy, and treasurer Morris Calisher. Jews were clearly more than a token presence in Eureka's fraternal organizations.[44]

From its earliest days as a recognized religious community, Eureka Jewry could also claim an economic impact on the county. In the fall of 1877, the *Eureka Daily Sentinel* printed a list of taxpayers assessed at $5,000 or more. Considering that $5,000 equates to about $100,000 in current dollars, the inventories were staggering: Myers and Franklin (dry goods) assessed at $33,850; David Manheim (general merchandise), $27,185; O. Dunkel and Company (dry goods), $25,800; Ashim Brothers (general merchandise), $15,000; Samuel Goldstone (general merchandise), $10,875; Henry Kind (wholesale liquors), $5,025; and A. Berwin (clothing), $5,000.[45]

Bad economic news soon marred the rosy picture. In May 1877, Goldstone had been forced to foreclose on the purchasers of a boardinghouse he had sold. It had to be resold at a sheriff's auction, but he recovered his original investment for a pittance and was in and out of trouble again within months.[46] Matilda A. Ashim was less fortunate. A court ordered Sheriff James Siaff on June 1, 1878, to liquidate all of her assets the next Thursday. A local newspaper announced the impoundment of thousands of items to satisfy her indebtedness of $1,054 in gold coin. The inventory of the Ashims' mercantile assets ran four full columns, ranging from mirrors, chamber pots, spittoons, French dolls, kegs of Dutch herring, and a box of Limburger cheese to Jews harps and "boy pocket knives." No report followed on who purchased this inventory for a penny on the dollar, but the Jewish community itself probably rescued Ashim's assets.[47]

Within a year, both Mrs. Ashim and Samuel Goldstone were back on their feet. Assessment rolls for 1879 showed the combined capital of the Jews at $350,000, which after the usual debts and liabilities, according to the justly proud Sam Goldstone, left each man, woman, and child with an average net worth of $1,550—today, the equivalent of about $30,000. Goldstone attributed this abundance to "industry and frugality."[48] He failed to note that overextension of credit and unwise speculation in mining stocks were a Jewish liability. Two disastrous fires and a decline in mineral production were harbingers of bad times ahead.

The Great Fire of 1879

On the evening of April 18, 1879, the Eureka Volunteer Fire Department was on high alert due to a howling daylong wind. The fears were justified. The fire allegedly started at the rear of the Opera House at midnight and moved quickly, destroying three hundred residences and businesses and leaving 1,500 homeless. The casualties included John Moch, who operated the popular Epicurean Restaurant with his wife, Regina. He had been asleep when the fire began. When the flames hit the residence, he was pulled from his bed but died the following day. Josie Moch, their youngest child, had died in January. Moses, their only son, was attending private school in Placerville at the time and returned to Eureka to help his mother.[49] Despite her tragic personal losses, Regina Moch determined to stay on. "Again to the Front!" shouted her ad in the local newspaper. "Mrs. Moch's New Restaurant. Board Reduced to $9 per week. Single Meals 75 cents." Eureka's ore production was on the upswing, while the Comstock's was in decline. Consequently, many Eurekans chose to rebuild, and the population remained stable, but not for long.[50]

Jews and the Italian Charcoal Burners' War of 1879

Eureka was recovering from the fire when another cause for alarm was smoldering in the mountains around Eureka. Northern Italians constituted 14 percent of the area's 7,086 people and had perfected the art of producing *carbonari,* or charcoal, essential to smelt the peculiar mixture of silver ore mined in the area. The process involved cutting wood in the mountains, converting it to charcoal in earthen-mound ovens, and transporting it to Eureka smelters. As mountains became deforested, the Italian workers were forced to extend the perimeter of their harvest farther from Eureka. The smelter owners responded by passing on the increased transportation cost to the workers. The owners were prepared to pay twenty cents per bushel, but the workers refused to sell for less than thirty cents per bushel. Although the smelters had a year's stockpile of charcoal, they threatened to close the mines unless the charcoal burners capitulated. The workers organized against the owners (some of them Italians), and it led to the "Charcoal Burners' War" of 1879. The average burner's wage was ten dollars per week—half as much as a common mine worker, and Eurekans reportedly had "a good deal of sympathy for the plight of the burners and supported their efforts to improve the deplorable conditions of their life and labor."[51] The issue was social justice, and Eureka Jews figured prominently in the outcome.

On July 7, 1879, the workers elected officers: Joseph Maginni, president; Lambert Molinelli, vice president; Joseph Hausman, secretary; and Sol Ashim, treasurer. The organization, the Charcoal Burners Protective Association, was similar in name and purpose to the traditional Hebrew benevolent groups. The officers were well-known Eureka businessmen, and Ashim and Hausman were Jews. Their election was no accident. They were all friends, fraternal brothers, and business partners and had the organizational skills needed to empower the workers.[52]

Hausman publicized the newly formed association to boycott the sale of charcoal for any price less than thirty cents per bushel. Nine days later, the situation turned ugly. Thirty-five armed men—presumably Italian members of the association—rode into the camp of a nonmember, whom they stopped from making charcoal. The incident aroused the press and the populace. The fear was that the use of armed threats to force up the price would lead miners to shut down the smelters and send their ore to California for processing.[53] Ashim, Hausman, Molinelli, and Maginni immediately disclaimed the armed men's actions on behalf of the protective association. The near violence led the Jewish and Italian officers to tender their resignations—noting that they had done their best to bring about a peaceful solution to the problem.

The charcoal burners enforced their new leaders' plans with guerrilla-like forays against teamsters attempting to load charcoal. Rumors spread that the charcoal burners planned to march on Eureka itself. Consequently, the smelter owners asked Governor John Kinkead to send out the militia. While the militia kept the peace with the Italians, the militia's Jewish ranks debated whether this was a cause in which they should be involved. Major David Manheim, the Second Brigade's quartermaster, was found drinking with "Modoc Sam and Charcoal Bill, two violent thirty-cent-a-bushel men." Manheim, a Jewish clothing merchant and one of the county's leading tax-payers, was arrested for insubordination by fraternizing with the enemy.[54] On August 19, 1879, an aggressive sheriff's posse attacked a camp of charcoal burners at Fish Creek, thirty miles south of town, and killed five. The matter was investigated, but no one was brought to justice for the killings. Workers who had prevented the loading of charcoal for transportation were brought to trial. Justice was swift and benign. Max Oberfelder was secretary of the grand jury, which dismissed charges against the Italians.[55]

Ashim, Hausman, Manheim, and Oberfelder were leaders within the civic community and representative of the rank-and-file Eureka Jews who were on the sidelines in this Charcoal Burners' War. These merchants would have been unlikely to lend support to the Italian charcoal burners' demand for a fair price if a significant majority of the Jewish community felt differently. They opposed violence by the Italians but sympathized in the end with an ethnic group experiencing what Jews had endured for centuries as part of Europe's underclass.

Attrition and Departure

The threat of armed warfare was past, but the April fire left unhealed wounds. Goldstone lost his entire store and had no insurance. Sol and Bart Ashim, Dr. Julius Rockman, Aaron Berg, and Albert Rosenheim lost portions of their uninsured homes or businesses. Though some rebuilt, others planned to leave. Max Franklin and H. Myers sold out and left town in early 1880. J. H. Michel, Rosenheim, and the Elias brothers followed.[56] Most of the departing Jews settled in San Francisco. Samuel Goldstone, with his sons Edwin and Samuel, opened a cigar and tobacco stand at the prestigious Grand Hotel Café. His son Percy became a journalist and son Louis an attorney; Abraham worked for an uncle. Others settling in San Francisco were William Ash, the Henry Barman family, Meyer Davidson, J. D. Farmer, Max J. Franklin, Jacob Greenwood, and Max Oberfelder. Rockman had left Eureka to return to his practice in San Francisco but was back in 1880. He was a member of the Nevada State Medical Society and one of the Board of Censors while Henry Bergstein served as its president.[57]

Eureka's other Jews scattered. The David Lesser family opened a grocery store in Los Angeles, where Pepi Steler established a jewelry and watch-repair store. Julius Lesser moved to New York, and a few settled in Denver.[58] How much they debated "whether to leave" and "where to go" is unknown, but some of the advertisements provide a sense of their finality and urgency. Oberfelder (partner in Eureka's first store) proclaimed his liquidation of $42,000 in liquor and tobacco after the fire to be the "greatest inducements ever offered to the people of Eureka and vicinity." Five-year-old whiskey sold for $3.75 per gallon and cigars for $2.25 per hundred.[59]

Regina Moch sold her Epicurean Restaurant to Mrs. Matilda Ashim and purchased another site for a restaurant and boardinghouse in April 1880, but she resold it four months later. Eureka had proved unsafe for her family; in August, she left town for California.[60] It was not too soon. On August 17, 1880, another fire broke out at the rear of a fruit and vegetable store. It followed almost the same course as the 1879 conflagration. "Three hundred houses, many of them business establishments, and some of them the finest private residences in town were consumed. . . . Only half a dozen buildings remained to relieve the scene of desolation." One of these was the stone store of Jacob Cohn. Also destroyed in the second fire was the Odd Fellows Hall, used for Jewish celebration of the High Holidays and the biweekly meeting place of the local B'nai B'rith lodge.[61]

The fourth annual Purim Ball was held in 1880 with "our best society in attendance," but it was a shade of former glory. Shortly after the second fire, the local press simply noted the Jewish Holy Days with no indication of how they were being observed. Remnants of Eureka's Jewish community stayed on. Benjamin C. Levy was one of the few who remained until the mining company he supervised could no longer survive. The B'nai B'rith lodge limped along with eighteen members listed in 1885, "though some may have already left and retained their membership for reasons of nostalgia or the insurance benefits."[62] Bernhard Berg, Eureka's "green grocer," was one of the last Jewish heads of households to leave Eureka. His youngest daughter, Julia Berg, later remembered that the mines "had given out" and the town was "down and out" by 1900, when a fire destroyed the family store. The Bergs opened a market featuring "delicacies" on San Francisco's McAllister Street.[63] It was a sad end to an unusual story. For a short time, Eureka's Jewish community was more religiously focused and socially involved than any other nineteenth-century Nevada town.

Settling, Praying, Working, and Partying
in the Halcyon Years

1865–1880

All of Nevada's towns and mining camps had a cosmopolitan international population drawn to the United States by its economic opportunity.[1] Jews emigrating from Prussia and eastern Europe were also fleeing discriminatory laws, military service, and pressures to assimilate. Once here, they did not—like San Francisco Italians—wish eventually to return to the old country. And unlike English immigrants to Utah, Jews were not interested in establishing a refuge from religious persecution.[2] All of them, however, depended on the permanence and prosperity of their environment—neither of which was a certainty.

Mobility and Settlement

The mobility of Jews that was characteristic of the turbulent years before statehood continued through the 1870s. The early arrivals who rode out Nevada's economic cycles into the early 1880s did moderately well. Those who arrived on the Comstock or any mining camp at the peak of the ore production initially prospered, but they needed to move on before the best times passed them by. Jews chose to live in Virginia City for the same reason others left for Eureka or Hamilton: they were centers of mineral production and needed a mercantile support community. Virginia City also had culture, excitement, and a mystique long remembered after its decline.

Jews chose Carson City because it promised stability as the state capital and the permanent location for the Nevada Supreme Court, the U.S. Mint, the state prison, and other agencies. Also, the Virginia and Truckee Railroad conveniently connected Carson City to Virginia City in 1870 and Reno in 1872. Finally, the capital was tucked into the Sierra Nevada's protective lee side, providing it with a far more temperate climate, meteorologically and socially, than that of the mountainous mining towns.

As economic prospects waxed and waned, scores of Jewish single men and families changed their addresses. Gone from Carson City were the Armers, Ashims, Bloomingdales, Fleishhackers, Greenbaums, Klaubers, Mandelbaums, Rosentocks, and dozens of others for whom the capital provided a stepping-stone to even more successful businesses in the West. Almost all of those leaving Carson City sold their properties to incoming Jews. Many moved up to thriving Virginia City. The Simon Ashims, John A. Moch's family, some of the Wertheimers, and a host of early settlers left Virginia City for new bonanzas in Eureka and Hamilton. Joseph Rosenstock relocated his family to Elko, where he competed with the Reinharts in the general merchandise business. Soon the two families were joined by marriage. The Klaubers early abandoned what their son called northern Nevada's "primitive conditions." By 1880, the family of twelve children was in San Diego and Klauber had sold the Nevada property with one thousand tons of hay and a hundred cattle.[3] His gamble on Nevada had paid handsomely. He was one of those who left the state permanently before the peak of the party.

Virginia City's Jewish population neared five hundred in the late 1870s. In contrast, Carson City's much smaller Jewish population stabilized at about ninety in the same period. As elsewhere in Nevada, most were merchants, and their stores dotted Carson Street for eight blocks from Fourth Street, north past the plaza and state capital buildings to Robinson Street. On the Comstock, they popped up in the heart of the Gold Hill, Silver City, and Virginia City business districts.

Ethnic Living Clusters

Everywhere people lived in places they could afford—some in their stores, others in boardinghouses, and a few in well-appointed homes. The mostly unmarried French Canadians camped out in the forest during the cutting season and boarded around the French Hotel in the heart of Carson City during inclement weather. The Irish represented a full one-third of the population and concentrated in three areas in Virginia City. The tiny African American population had three small instances of residential proximity in Virginia City, though they spread out over time. The largest ethnic ghetto in many Nevada camps and cities was the ubiquitous Chinatown. In Carson City, the Chinese constituted 20 percent of the population and lived in uninsurable shacks on several square blocks east of the capitol building.[4]

Some people elected to settle in a particular place due to family or friendship ties going back to the old country. It was no coincidence that the Platts, Olcoviches, Morris and Solomon Cohn, and Amelia Sheyer, all from Kempen in the Duchy of Poznán, were related by marriage within a generation.[5] It was also common to find groups such as the Blumenthal, Abrahamson, Tobias, and Morris families—who shared a common East Prussian heritage—living side by side in Hamilton. Similar arrangements existed on the Comstock. Virginia City's Jews spread through the Germanic-European section of town, but in the 1870s, some began clustering on A Street. The Michelsons, for example, lived next door to the large Peyser family, adjacent to the Mandelbaums and two doors from the Rosenbrocks, Lowensteins, and Mayers.

In smaller Carson City, half of the Jewish population lived in a five hundred–yard square just west of the business district. Although this was an unmistakable Jewish neighborhood, it was not a ghetto. No one forced the Jewish merchants into the area or expected them to be "in their place," as were the Chinese. Nor was there any "Gentile flight" from the neighborhood, because the Jewish residents were part of Carson City's economic and political power structure. The area was an affluent mixed neighborhood of German, Irish, Polish, and American-born professionals, state officials, and businessmen who could afford it. The remaining half of the Jewish population continued to live at their work sites, as Charles and Elizabeth Schwartz did in their confectionery shop, or settled for a sparer dwelling, as the Sheyers did a few blocks north of Chinatown. The small Jewish neighborhood also encompassed the hall where the Jews observed High Holidays.[6]

Religious Observance with Rabbi Jacob Sheyer

Any Jew moving west knew that basic personal religious beliefs could remain relatively unaffected by even the most hostile environment. However, certain accommodations inevitably had to be made with traditional practices of Orthodox Judaism. Maintaining a kosher kitchen without a *shochet* was impossible. And although many Jewish families observed, at some level, the Sabbath's beginning on Friday evenings, it would have been ruinous for merchants not to do business on Saturdays, if they were forbidden to be open on Sunday. They generally observed the High Holidays with public notices of Jewish stores being closed—no matter the day.[7] In these early days, laymen led the services. Missing in most clusters of Jews in the western frontier towns was a rabbi. Bona fide rabbis were scarce and in great demand for ritual circumcisions, marriages, and High Holiday services. Rabbi Herman

Bien's brief tenure in Virginia City ended in 1865. Meanwhile, a less flamboyant man of the cloth was establishing a business and permanent residence in Carson City.

Born in Warsaw in 1834, Rabbi Jacob Sheyer married Amelia, a native of Kempen. Their children, Lizzie, Pauline, and Rose, were all born in Prussian Poland before 1861. They settled first with others from Kempen in Marysville, California, and moved to Carson City in 1863. Jacob purchased a store from fellow Pole Morris B. Ashim's estate, and he and a partner, Louis Morris, operated a "women's" clothing shop located in what is now the capitol complex.[8]

The Jewish community was prominent enough in 1865 for the *Carson Daily Appeal* to take note of their High Holiday services. In succeeding years, not only did advertisements appear announcing Jewish store closings for the High Holidays, but the newspaper staff editorialized on the nature of the services and their meaning in the Jewish tradition. In an 1868 advertisement, Rabbi Sheyer invited "the Israelites of Washoe, Genoa, and elsewhere in the vicinity" to observe Yom Kippur at the Masonic Hall. A rabbi trained in the Orthodox tradition but familiar with the early movement for reform in Germany and Prussian Poland, Sheyer had the ability to accommodate language and custom to satisfy the sensibilities of a multiethnic worshiping group. He also presided over marriages and served as mohel for the ritual circumcisions of male infants throughout northeastern Nevada.[9]

When he officiated at High Holiday services in Virginia City's Miner's Union Hall, the *Daily State Register* moaned that "yesterday our town seemed to be in mourning. The stores of all our Jewish merchants were closed, and *being the most prominent places of business,* made our city look like that old 'deserted village.' . . . Take the Israelites from our cities and towns and we could make but a sorry appearance."[10] On a similar occasion, the same newspaper commented on how "unusually dull" the streets looked. "The Israelites of this city are in good numbers and all engaged in some kind of business. Some of our largest establishments are owned by them, and when closed during week days, make the town look as though it was Sunday." The Jews enjoyed a respectability among Gentiles unheard of in the old country and elsewhere in the nation.[11]

In 1872, the *Daily State Register* adorned Sheyer with the title "Rabbi for the State of Nevada."[12] His popularity may have begun to burden him. Seeking better economic prospects or to be near Jewish friends at Marysville, he settled his accounts with Louis Morris and moved to that California mountain town on the Yuba River, fifty miles west. He had no sooner set up his shop there when a spring flood washed out his riverside store. "Looking healthy and vigorous," Sheyer and his family and his remaining inventory were back in Carson City in mid-March when he took ill and died at the age of forty-four. His widow, Amelia, reestablished the women's upscale fashion store under her own name and continued to raise her three daughters, while keeping an eye open for marriageable young men.[13]

Religious Leadership after Sheyer

Within a year of Sheyer's death in 1875, Carson City Jews formed a B'nai B'rith lodge with twenty-one charter members. Regional director David D'Ancona described the membership as representing "every dry goods store in the city." Almost all were married men with families on the way, and virtually all of the founding members were still affiliated with the lodge twelve years later. One of the defining purposes of the International Order of B'nai B'rith was to maintain a sense of peoplehood for all Jews, irrespective of ethnicity.[14]

Nevada Jews now lacked a rabbi. Joseph Kullman, B'nai B'rith member and president of the Carson City's Hebrew Benevolent Society, announced High Holiday services at the Masonic Hall. Kullman also noted that "all the leading dry goods and clothing houses will be closed." Replacing advertisements for the latest sales were unself-conscious notices of forthcoming religious observances, and again the newspapers noted the business district's "sombre appearance."[15]

At Virginia City, B'nai B'rith past president Louis Guggenheim announced the availability of tickets for High Holidays. Jews there hired Rabbi Feldman from San Francisco to lead the services, which were held for the first time in the district court. In a gesture that betokened the level of religious tolerance in this heavily Christian town and further demonstrated its cultural development and sophistication, the local authorities declared that "children of parents who observe these days will be allowed to absent themselves from our public schools without incurring any demerits therefor."[16]

Virginia City's leading newspaper, the *Territorial Enterprise*, extensively covered the Jewish services. The unsigned stories in 1875 contrasted Rosh Hashanah's feasting with Yom Kippur's grim fasting and sense of humiliation for sins of omission and commission. The reporter either received extraordinarily good coaching from a knowledgeable local Jew, or, more likely, he was Henry P. Cohen, the *Enterprise*'s bookkeeper and theatrical critic. Cohen was not a member of the local B'nai B'rith, nor was he mentioned in connection with the Jewish religious services he so carefully described. Cohen was one of the many Jews—on the Comstock and elsewhere—who may have lost the practice but not the memory of Judaism. "If those engaging therein did not have light consciences after the day of atonement passed, they at least had light stomachs," the reporter quipped, "and the fast was followed by the feast, which is always the more dangerous of the two."[17]

Virginia City's increasing Jewish population considered itself ready to establish a permanent congregation. The *Enterprise* reported that Rabbi Schwartz from San Francisco was in town to discuss a permanent organization. "There are many Israelites in this city, and we wonder that something of the kind has not been undertaken before." With what could be a mild criticism or simply a friendly incentive, the writer added: "People of almost every other religious belief have their places of meeting and worship, even though their numerical strength is much less than is that of the Jews in this city." Methodists, Catholics, Presbyterians, and Episcopalians had stable places of worship in Virginia City within a few years of statehood, and the Chinese had a joss house. African Americans numbered fewer than one hundred in 1870, and they had already formed a permanent African Methodist Episcopal congregation.[18] It was about time for a Jewish congregation.

This early initiative failed, but an encouraging sign of unity and consensus was the termination of King Solomon Lodge—established in the sixties as an ethnic or ideological alternative—and the subsequent merging of the two B'nai B'rith lodges back into the original Lodge no. 52. "A meeting of the Israelites of this city at the hall of the IOBB, Odd Fellows' Building, last Sunday for the purpose of organizing a Jewish congregation was a success," reported the *Enterprise* two years later. Established merchants Jackson, Hess, Schoenfeld, and Friedman were elected officers of the budding congregation and a committee of three appointed "to draft a form of permanent organization and report next Sunday. Steps will be taken for the erection of a synagogue at once."[19] A ball sponsored by the local Purim Club the following week may have distracted the committee. Nothing came of the permanent congregation or the building of a synagogue. The decision to form a new congregation and build a synagogue may have been postponed for Rabbi Isaac Wise's arrival. Rabbi Henry Loewenthal of Sacramento led High Holidays in 1876 with the aid of a *hazzan* (ritual cantor), who also happened to be a local miner.[20]

Adolph Sutro: Secular Jew on a Mission

Adolph Heinrich Joseph Sutro lived far from the Jewish residential areas and remained unaffiliated with any Jewish organization. And few were as closely connected as he to the Comstock during its heyday, although he lived at the base of the mines in a small town bearing his name. He was born of wealthy Jewish parents in Aachen, Prussia, in 1830, raised with his twelve siblings in a house of more than thirty rooms, and given the best education available up to the age of seventeen. When his father died, he took control of the family's clothing factory. With revolutions swirling about Europe, his mother urged their migration to the United States. The family landed in New York in October 1850, and within a week young Adolph was off to California via a harrowing journey across the Isthmus of Panama.[21]

After several false starts, he went into the tobacco business, with three stores in San Francisco. He married the devout Leah Harris in a traditional Jewish ceremony. He dabbled briefly in the Fraser River gold rush in 1858 and visited Virginia City two years later. There he envisioned building a tunnel from several miles below the Comstock mines, to provide drainage, ventilation, and a gravity-driven means of bringing ore to smelters below.[22] Just a few yards away from the mill of Isaac Cohn and Joseph Keller at Dayton, Sutro built a small processor in 1862. Unlike others, he focused on the ore tailings and found them extremely rich. For the first time, he could say that he made "a great deal of money." He traveled almost daily up the mountain to Virginia City on horseback, "exploring the country with a view to constructing a tunnel, which had been my idea from the very first."[23]

Sutro's plan initially met with stunning indifference. The Ophir Mine owners were more anxious to solve the problem of collapsing mine shafts and stopes' walls. They hired Philipp Deidesheimer, a young German who had invented a unique way of shoring up mining areas with wooden blocks: "square-set timbering." Deidesheimer then addressed himself to the issue of water in the mines at depths of only fifty feet. His system of Cornish pumps with rubber rather than leather washers temporarily quashed any enthusiasm for expensive tunneling.[24]

Deidesheimer's ingenuity, however, allowed the digging of deeper mines, which filled with water and became excessively hot. Sutro's tunnel promised to solve both problems, and he pursued the dream single-mindedly.[25] The Nevada legislature in 1865 and the U.S. Congress in 1866 granted Sutro legal authority to dig a tunnel from his mill on the Carson River almost four miles through the mountain to connect with the major mines below Virginia City. Sutro's payback was to be a fee of two dollars for each ton of ore extracted in the mines the tunnel served. He was also permitted to purchase 4,357 acres of land at the mouth of the tunnel.

Sutro incorporated the Sutro Tunnel Company on February 4, 1865. Its officers and trustees included prominent California Jews Michael Reese and Abraham Seligman. The mining companies pledged six hundred thousand dollars, with the prospect of raising millions more in San Francisco and New York. At this critical moment, the Bank of California, which effectively controlled the mines and mills, stepped in and opposed the project. The bank and its Nevada operator, William Sharon, feared that the tunnel would render unnecessary their planned railroad from the mountaintop to the mills on the river. Sutro likely contributed to their concerns by underemphasizing the Comstock's continued prominence in an 1866 pamphlet directed to New York financiers and suggesting that his town on the Carson River would eventually displace Virginia City and Gold Hill. The entire creative plan was now mired in controversy as quickly as it had demonstrated a promising start. The mining and banking interests ruthlessly attempted to discredit and destroy Sutro. Those who feared the bank treated Sutro like a pariah, but he remained as tenacious and focused as his adversaries.[26]

A disastrous fire in Gold Hill's Yellow Jacket Mine helped turn public sentiment in Sutro's favor. The upshot was that he secured fifty thousand dollars from the Miner's Union based on the potential safety escape features the tunnel would provide. On October 19, 1869, he posed for the camera swinging a pickax to start construction.[27] In Washington, D.C., however, the Nevada and California delegations had lined up behind the Bank of California to have Congress repeal that portion of the tunnel bill authorizing the royalty to Sutro and the venture's stockholders. Sutro raced to Washington, where he gained the support of the Ways and Means Committee, which submitted a report opposing the repeal. Sutro had dodged another bullet, and newspapers from Pioche to Elko fell in line to support miners' safety, while they encouraged the project opposed by the powerful. Sutro took advantage of the project's popularity, and in 1873 he ran for the U.S. Senate. Popular mine owner John P. Jones and Sharon, one of the power brokers opposing the tunnel venture, were equally interested. Jones gained the appointment in 1873, and Sharon bought the votes needed for the second senate seat in 1875.[28]

Sutro sailed to London to secure more capital and traveled again to Washington, D.C., to testify on congressional subsidization. Back on the Comstock, ore production was down, and mine owners encouraged their employees to oppose the tunnel, because the two-dollar-per-ton royalty would further erode profits. They held a mass meeting on Saturday, March 29, that *Gold Hill News* editor Alf Doten covered. His editorial characterized Sutro as a "Shylock" claiming his "pound of flesh."[29] Sutro's Jewish lineage was now an issue that Doten pursued. He labeled Sutro "this emigrant from Assyria . . . backed by certain foreign money lenders"—a not-so-subtle use of the stereotype of usurious Jews. Sutro was, wrote Doten, "a traitor to the people by whose sufferance he lives and urges his nefarious schemes in free America." His tunnel scheme was "a bold fraud from beginning to end." In August, Doten attended a Sutro lecture at the Gold Hill Miner's Union Hall and caricatured the inventor's German accent.

Others were more tolerant, or saw through the criticism. Mark Twain described the tunnel as a "prodigious enterprise" and Sutro as "one of the few men in the world who is gifted with the pluck and perseverance necessary to follow up and hound such an undertaking to its completion."[30] Isaac Mayer Wise labeled the opposition to Sutro's plans antisemitic: "As long as Mr. Sutro's grand scheme was incomprehensible to the masses, and he was obliged to fight the prejudices of the ignorant, the power of the politicians and nabobs, he was called the Syrian Jew, ridiculed by mobs and pelted with mud by the rich and mighty. Now as success is crowning his work, he is no longer called a Jew."[31] Workers completed the Sutro tunnel in September 1878.

In the fall of 1879, Mrs. Leah Sutro and a small party that included Mr. and Mrs. Philipp Deidesheimer hosted former president Ulysses S. Grant and his family at the mansion in Sutro.[32] Adolph avoided the event—doubtless because a breath of scandal had surfaced the previous evening. Leah had once suspected some indiscretion on Sutro's part while he was on business in Washington, D.C., and hired a lawyer to investigate. Reportedly, Adolph had been seen with a young woman on several occasions. When she learned that the same woman, Miss Hattie Trundle (using the alias of Mrs. George Allen), was staying at the International Hotel and Adolph was wining and dining her in her room, Leah became "judge, jury, and all but executioner." She sought out Trundle at the hotel and nearly killed her with a champagne bottle. This ended whatever relationship Adolph and Leah may have had. There was no divorce, but they permanently separated. He provided Leah with a large, comfortable house in San Francisco and a generous lifetime income for herself and the six children. There she was able to enjoy the religious activities and philanthropic opportunities provided by the presence of a large Jewish community.[33]

Meanwhile, mining stocks—always volatile—were not recovering from their highs in 1877. Sutro's technological marvel never made a profit. He sold his shares of the tunnel stock while prices were still relatively high and moved to San Francisco. He returned briefly to Nevada in 1880 to run again for the U.S. Senate. He took up residence at the Carson City Ormsby House, claiming enough money to capture the votes of his nearest competitor, Comstock millionaire James G. Fair. The cagey Fair neutralized Sutro's strategy with the legislature and won the Senate seat. Sutro retired in defeat but remained politically active in San Francisco. He increased his wealth through shrewd real estate deals, engaged in many philanthropic ventures, and was elected mayor in 1894.[34]

Throughout his life, Sutro avoided affiliation with organized religion, though he was by no means hostile to religious causes. While in Nevada, he never affiliated with any Jewish organization, and no evidence exists that he attended High Holiday services. In San Francisco, Sutro became friendly with religious leaders and supported both Jewish and Christian charitable causes. His children attended Catholic and Episcopalian schools. In an interview for Hubert H. Bancroft's history of California, he claimed that he "never was a very strong religionist" and that his liberal parents raised him to consider "charity and kindness" the "true religion of the world." As he said of his parents and siblings: "When it comes to religious rites and superstitions handed down in all directions, you find very little belief in our family."[35] Sutro never denied or disparaged his Jewish lineage. He remained a freethinking, charitable, secular Jew not interested in the Reform or the new Conservative attempts to reconcile Judaism with science and modernity, with which he so closely identified.

Is There a Doctor in the House? Yes, and More

A professional in a different scientific field, Dr. Henry Bergstein found political life, love, and a practice in Virginia City. Unlike Sutro, he remained in Nevada for the rest of his life. Bergstein was well known before he arrived in Virginia City in late 1874. The *Reno Crescent* had noticed his treatment of children suffering from spinal meningitis in Hiko Valley sixty miles southwest of Pioche. As an assemblyman, he introduced legislation to prohibit the practice of medicine to all but those with degrees from qualified institutions. Although this legislation was among the first statutes the 1875 legislature approved, Governor Lewis Rice Bradley wanted unlicensed medical practitioners with ten years of experience in the state to be exempt from the law. Bradley told Bergstein, "They were competent physicians and had endeared themselves to the people by years of practice among them, and he would veto any measure which would deprive them of the right to practice."[36] Provision was so made.

Legislative discussion focused on who would enforce the new legislation requiring appropriate degrees and licensing. Bergstein agreed to locate permanently in Virginia City and organize a state medical society.[37] A twentieth-century chronicler of Nevada medical practice, Silas Ross, called Bergstein the "Father of the State Medical Law" and founder of the Nevada State Medical Society in 1875.[38] Bergstein's account broadened the credit to include nineteen physicians. At the society's first meeting, papers were read and later printed. The society met irregularly over the next quarter century due to a declining economy and a widely spread population.[39]

At the age of thirty-one, Bergstein was one of the city's most eligible bachelors. Perhaps at one of the many dances, balls, and religious celebrations, he met the eldest daughter of Samuel Michelson, among Nevada's most influential merchants. Henry Bergstein and Pauline Michelson married in San Francisco in mid-January 1880, at his mother's residence, with Rabbi Elkan Cohn officiating. The couple moved into the large Michelson home at Virginia City, which also served other family members, servants, and boarders.[40]

Young Bergstein was outspoken, well connected, and capable, though he had his detractors. Virginia City's "spicily written" *Footlight* baited Bergstein when he was a candidate for Storey County physician in 1880. Initially, it appeared good-natured sarcasm. The paper facetiously suggested that no one shot through the heart "would think of dying" if attended by the next county physician. The following day, the *Footlight* questioned the competence of a person with Bergstein's "youth and limited experience" to distinguish between the symptoms of smallpox and chicken pox. Not amused, Bergstein had the *Footlight* editor arrested for libel. The case came to trial, and the matter was dismissed without closure.[41]

Bergstein was named "Storey County Physician" in 1881, but after he filed a report critical of local health facilities, the county commission terminated his contract after three months of service. He remained in private practice and as surgeon at St. Mary Louise Hospital in Virginia City until moving to Reno in 1883 with his wife. Bergstein remained an important and sometimes controversial figure in Nevada medical history through the turn of the century.[42]

Rabbi Isaac Mayer Wise Visits Virginia City and Carson City

Wise's impressions of Nevada contrasted sharply with those of his earlier trip from Palisade to Eureka. As the train crossed the Sierra Nevada, he found the night views magical before alighting at Reno and traveling up the "charming valleys" into Carson City. The arrangement was for him to proceed directly to the Comstock, which by summer of 1877 was home to about four hundred Jews.[43] He was met by five former presidents of B'nai B'rith Lodge no. 52 and delivered an afternoon lecture to a packed assembly at the Odd Fellows' Hall, followed by a formal reception attended by "sixty to eighty ladies and gentlemen." At this event, he apparently received a promise of five hundred dollars for seminary scholarships.[44]

Nevada, Wise observed, was "the back-bone of San Francisco. Here . . . are the gold, silver and lead, the gigantic enterprises . . . and down in Carson and San Francisco are the mints." He found the place "perfectly alive day and night," with everyone "going or rather running, it appears, after something." His assessment of religious observance in the city was less enthusiastic. Although Wise acknowledged observance of High Holidays, he detected no semblance of regular Sabbath worship. Most of the Jews were "young people," whom he found "generous, liberal, hospitable and social, but as for Judaism, they keep that down in San Francisco."[45]

This criticism, however accurately it might have applied to the Comstock's lack of regular Sabbath worship and disinclination for the Reform movement, was not entirely warranted. For most Jews leaving a Jewish neighborhood in the East, the prospect of observing Jewish dietary laws was reduced to becoming a vegetarian. However, a significant number of Jews in and around Virginia City longed for the mitzvah of eating kosher meat. One who recognized this niche, Mark Strouse, had driven five thousand sheep from California to Nevada in the summer of 1863. He became the city's leading butcher, with a five hundred–acre stock ranch north of Reno, and later served as Virginia City's chief of police and earned several terms as city treasurer. To meet the demand for kosher meat, Strouse announced in 1878 that he had hired

Rabbi Solomon Aragor as his *shochet.* The venture was short-lived, however. When Strouse left the city in 1881 to start a new business in the Bay Area, the kosher market went with him. Over the next fifty years, northern Nevadans traveled to Sacramento or San Francisco to buy kosher food for special occasions. In this respect, Wise's reference to San Francisco as a locus of Nevada Judaism was prophetic.[46]

While in Virginia City, Wise was a few miles from the Dayton-area home of Adolph Sutro, whom he considered one of the world's greatest mining engineers. Wise, perhaps tardily, invited Sutro to attend his afternoon lecture. Sutro's response was immediate:

> My dear Sir
>
> [T]he invitation to your lecture and reception has just reached me, for which many thanks. —I regret exceedingly that I cannot leave here this afternoon to attend and make your personal acquaintance, but it is quite impossible having [?] a number of people here who have called to see me. —If you could make it convenient [?] to come down here tomorrow I would be much delighted, and I have no doubt you will be pleased with your trip. —With many regards I am very truly yours Adolph Sutro.[47]

Wise claimed he was also unable to accept Sutro's offer because of a prior commitment in Carson City, though no speaking events were planned for the capital.[48] Two of the best-known secular and religious Jews in the United States were unable to meet.

Wise spent a few hours in Carson City, where Frank Boskowitz squired him around the city. In passing, he met several old acquaintances from Cincinnati and Albany. One of them, former assemblyman Emanuel L. Stern of Gold Hill, was on an inspection tour in his capacity as state grand master of the International Order of Odd Fellows. Wise made no comment on the level of religious observance in the capital, but he applied one telling observation to all of Nevada Jewry: its "ladies uphold Judaism."[49]

Humor and Partying

Jocularity was a part of life during Nevada's prosperous early years. Entertainment ran from lowbrow card parties to extravagant balls. Humor ranged from playful and tongue-in-cheek sarcasm to the sardonic and unkind. A savvy reader of advertisements could find a good bargain embedded in the occasional exaggerated claims of Jewish merchants for their goods.

One who laced his ads with wit was Frank Boskowitz, a New Yorker born of Polish parents. He came to Nevada in 1876, was married, and involved in civic affairs as well as in the B'nai B'rith lodge. Boskowitz purchased Joseph Rosenstock's leased space in the Ormsby County Building shortly after arriving in Carson City. The local newspaper saluted his luck in acquiring the best location in the building for half the rental price of inferior locations. Dubbed by the *Carson Daily Appeal* as "rotund and fascinating," he had a reputation for amusing oratory. Whereas most Jewish merchants advertised with large-type descriptions of their wares, Boskowitz appealed to his reader's literacy and appreciation of the comic.

One of his ads—a "Bosk-Oration"—began with a few lines from Thomas Hood's well-known poem "The Song of the Shirt." Little could Hood have imagined, wrote Boskowitz, that "You, my dressy friend, can procure for your adornment at Bosk's One Price Clothing Store, a boiled shirt, white as the driven snow, for the microscopical price of 25 cents . . . Here then is one of those rare chances which occur but once in a man's lifetime. To miss it, or treat it with indifference . . . is to do yourself an injustice." Boskowitz waxed eloquent for a half page on the comparable prices for hats, jewelry, shoes, and luggage. He challenged readers to visit his store at once "and buy yourselves rich."[50]

Boskowitz's interests soon began to turn. Wanting out of the clothing business, where his fellow Jews provided sharp competition, he showed interest in public service, though there was little money in that. He advertised for two years that he was "Selling Out for Cash Only," and eventually closed a sale to fellow Jew Alfred Lilienfeld. The *Nevada Tribune* reported that this "well known orator and jokist, is out of business and his delicate form will not wear out so many dry goods boxes. . . . A jolly native American is Bosko." The gifted wordsmith was encouraged to run for state assemblyman, and within weeks he set up his headquarters at Jacob Tobriner's cigar store.[51]

It was an obvious choice. Tobriner had won election to the state assembly in 1873, cofounded the Hebrew Benevolent Society, served as first president of the B'nai B'rith lodge, headed the local German Turnverein, and later won three terms as Ormsby County treasurer. He was an appropriate mentor—both as a tobacco merchant and as a political adviser. Boskowitz learned the tobacco trade as he waited for his chance at public office and won election for a single term to the assembly in 1882. Thereafter, he become a western regional distributor of tobacco products, which kept him in touch with Nevada customers over the next several decades.[52] There is virtually no written evidence of Jewish humor in Nevada's early days. Boskowitz was an exception.

Butt of Comstock Humor

Not all Jews were models of prosperity or propriety. One of the most quixotic figures on the Comstock was Morris Pinschower. When Mark Strouse announced his candidacy for Virginia City's chief of police in 1868, Pinschower threw his hat in the ring for county sheriff. That he received only a dozen votes did not dampen his interest. He ran again in 1870, riding a scrawny horse and using a soapbox as a pulpit. Pinschower railed in a German accent against the Bank of California, which invariably drew a raucous crowd that cheered every word but had no intention of voting for him. Scamps pulled the box from under his feet, sending him sprawling but undeterred. He ran unsuccessfully for sheriff a third time in 1872.

Pinschower tilted at windmills. He was convinced that a way could be found to bring water to Virginia City from Lake Bigler (Tahoe), Washoe Lake, and Mono Lake. The latter's salt and mineral contents were so high, however, that the result would have been less potable than the city's much derided well water. In 1871, he formed a waterworks company and identified potential investors. Coincidentally, the press came into possession of a large pocket memorandum book allegedly written by Pinschower, containing names of possible partners, including President Grant and local officials, and their expected share purchase. Morris Pinschower was an easy target for ridicule, and the news item probably was the product of an imaginative reporter or—as the newspaper mused—sent to the *Territorial Enterprise* as a joke.

On one occasion, it was reported that Morris Pinschower, "the Emperor Norton [a Jewish eccentric in San Francisco] of our city; was out in best raiment, mounted on a superb charger," trying to find anything resembling a procession he could lead. He bowed to the pedestrians on the street and eventually joined a funeral march into one of the local cemeteries. Pinschower was a pitiful case, but essentially harmless. At best, he was an idealistic eccentric; at worst, he was mentally ill and in need of help unavailable at this time or place. He was likely related to Jacob Pinschower, a respected merchant and former treasurer of the B'nai B'rith Lodge no. 52—an organization that never included Morris, who ended his days as a tailor mending clothes.[53]

The stereotypical caricature of a Nevada Jewish peddler by J. Ross Browne did not necessarily match the reality. Originally published by *Harper's Weekly* in 1860–1861.

Abraham Klauber and Theresa (Epstein) Klauber, 1861. A native of Bohemia, Abe Klauber moved his business from Volcano, California, to Genoa, Nevada Territory, in 1858. In addition to a warehouse of merchandise, Klauber ran the Wells Fargo Stage Line. (Courtesy of San Diego Historical Society)

The 1862 Fleishhacker Carson City store was in the same building as that of Morris Ashim, whose grandson Baruch was Mark Twain's stenographer. (J. Wells Kelly, *First Directory of Nevada Territory*)

Second from left: Mark Twain with members of the Nevada Territorial Legislature, 1864. Baruch Ashim, Twain's teenage stenographer, is likely the young man in front and center right. (Courtesy of Nevada Historical Society)

Rabbi Herman Bien—editor, composer, dramatist, and state assemblyman from Virginia City, 1864–1865. (Courtesy of Mary McKain)

Malvina and Joseph Platt, ca. 1864, Carson City. The Platts (originally Placzek) were among many Nevada Jews from Poznán in Polish Prussia. (Courtesy of Sylvia Olcott)

Olcovich Brothers Dry Goods and Clothing Store, across from the capital plaza, erected ca. 1866. The four Olcovich brothers (from Kempen in Prussian Poland) jointly owned more than fifteen major properties in Carson City from 1864 to 1891. (Photograph by author)

Haas Brothers' 1862 advertisement in Virginia City. Other members of the family had a store in Hamilton in 1870. (J. Wells Kelly, *First Directory of Nevada Territory*)

Jacob W. Davis, inventor of the copper-riveted jeans in Reno, 1870. Davis was from Riga (the present capital of Latvia). He helped to build Reno's first brewery before he turned to fabricating tents and saddlebags out of canvas and copper rivets. (Courtesy of Levi Strauss & Co. Archives, San Francisco)

Jacob W. Davis's patent for "Improvement in Fastening Pocket-Openings," 1873. The patent rights were shared with Levi Strauss. (Image courtesy of Levi Strauss & Co. Archives, San Francisco)

Canvas stores in Elko, 1869, site of the Morris Badt, Gabriel Cohn, Abraham and Samuel Mooser, and Reinhart family stores. (Courtesy of Northeastern Nevada Museum)

E. Reinhart store, Winnemucca, 1915. The several Reinhart families owned large general merchandise stores from Winnemucca to Elko for almost a century. (Courtesy of Northeastern Nevada Museum)

Morris and Lina Posener Badt, ca. 1880, had a commuter marriage after their children were born. Morris operated a ranch in Wells, Nevada, while Lina raised three boys and two girls in San Francisco, where they received a religious education. (Courtesy of Nancy Badt Drake)

Abraham Mooser in Confederate uniform, 1861, at Corinth, Mississippi. The picture is inscribed to his mother, Carolyn. German-born Abraham Mooser and his brother Samuel were among Elko's first merchants. Abraham also opened a jewelry store at Eureka in 1879. (Courtesy of *Western States Jewish History*)

Solomon Ashim's Eureka general store built about 1872 of local volcanic tuff survived Eureka's several fires. It is still in use as a restaurant. (Photograph by author)

Regina Moch advertised a new start five weeks after the Eureka fire that took the life of her husband. *Eureka Daily Sentinel,* 1879. (Courtesy of Tina Hubbard)

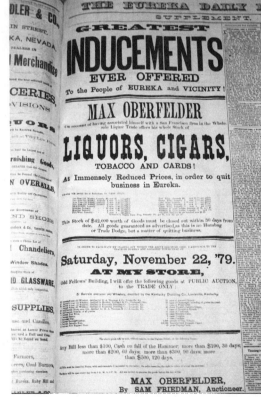

Max Oberfelder, one of Eureka's first proprietors, sold out after the 1879 fire. He advertised five-year-old whiskey for $3.75 per gallon—cash only. *Eureka Daily Leader,* 1879. (Courtesy of Tina Hubbard)

Eureka, site of Nevada's first permanent Jewish congregation, as it looked in the 1870s. (Courtesy of Nevada Historical Society)

Hamilton, Nevada, 1869, became home to hundreds of Jews before the disastrous fire of 1873. Alexander Cohn was tried and convicted of arson, although he and a host of others maintained he was innocent. (Courtesy of Nevada Historical Society)

Carson City Brewery, cofounded by Jacob Klein and erected in 1864. Jews regularly held their religious services on the second floor, which was also home to the Masonic Lodge. (Photograph by author)

Left: Leah Sutro; and *right:* Adolph Sutro. Adolph Sutro engineered a tunnel from the Comstock to Dayton, Nevada, completed in 1878. He later ran unsuccessfully for the U.S. Senate from Nevada. Leah nearly killed his alleged paramour in Virginia City, and Leah and Adolph permanently separated. (Courtesy of Nevada Historical Society)

Mark Strouse, Virginia City chief of police, treasurer, and purveyor of kosher meat, as depicted in Myron Angel, *History of Nevada* (1881).

Elizabeth Rosenstock, her daughter Essie Rosenstock Reinhart, and Milton Reinhart, Elko, 1894. (Courtesy of Northeastern Nevada Museum)

Joseph Rosenstock and his grandson Milton Reinhart, Elko, ca. 1900. Rosenstock opened his first store in Carson City in 1860 before moving his family to Elko. (Courtesy of Northeastern Nevada Museum)

Albert A. Michelson received an appointment from Nevada to the U.S. Naval Academy in 1869. He is seen here in 1873, the year he returned to Virginia City. He later won the Nobel Prize in Physics for measuring the speed of light. (Courtesy of Special Collections and Archives Division, Nimitz Library, U.S. Naval Academy)

Third and fourth from left: Selig and Isaac Olcovich in front of their *Carson Weekly* print shop with George T. Davis and Charles Piper (*on the left*) and Isadore A. Jacobs (*far right*), 1892. (Courtesy of Nevada State Museum, Carson City)

Seated: Ida Platt; *left to right* her maternal uncle Hyman Basch, friend Edna ("Evelyn") Armor, and brother Sam Platt, in miners' costumes, ca. 1890. (Courtesy of Sylvia Olcott)

Extended Hyman Olcovich family, Carson City, ca. 1899. *Left to right:* Isadore Friedenthal, Henrietta Olcovich Friedenthal, Pearl Friedenthal, Jacob Olcovich, Pauline
Saft Olcovich, Nevada Olcovich, Leo Friedenthal, Hyman Olcovich, Selig Olcovich,
Alden Olcovich, Annie Olcovich, and Louis Olcovich. Isaac Olcovich had recently
died. (Courtesy of Irwin Olcott)

Top step: Dr. Henry Bergstein and son with the staff of the Nevada State Mental Hospital, ca. 1897. (Courtesy of Nevada Historical Society)

Thomas Barnett store, Reno, ca. 1882. The families of Isaac and Thomas Barnett were active in Reno's Sabbath school. (Courtesy of Nevada Historical Society)

Settlers at the Wellington, Nevada, Jewish agricultural venture, 1899. *At left, on horses:* Maurice and Hyman Nudelman. *Standing near tree:* Moishe Nudelman. *On porch:* Joseph and Fanny Nudelman and families. *Standing around rock wall:* Shapiro and Bloom families. (Courtesy of Eugene Nudelman)

Sol Hilp, Ely merchant and White
Pine County assemblyman, 1893.
(Courtesy of Nevada Historical
Society)

Nick Abelman, copropri-
etor of Goldfield's Bon
Ton Club, 1907. (Courtesy
of William Pettite)

Tonopah and the Big Casino, managed and co-owned by Nick Abelman, ca. 1915. The town's red-light district is in the foreground. (Courtesy of Nevada Historical Society)

(*Opposite, top*) Politically active and controversial Benjamin Rosenthal with his wife, Vesta, Goldfield, ca. 1907. (Courtesy of Nevada Historical Society)

(*Opposite, bottom*) Benjamin Rosenthal, up for reelection as Esmeralda County commissioner, is caricatured in the Republican press for borrowing money from the school fund to maintain a deputy sheriff force. *Goldfield Chronicle*, October 17, 1908. (Courtesy of J. Dee Kille)

"HANDS OFF!"

Abe Cohn holding a basket made by Dat-So-La-Lee, Carson City, 1924. (Courtesy of Nevada Historical Society)

Temple Emanu-El, Reno, erected in 1921. (Courtesy of Nevada Historical Society)

Top center: Pearl and Rabbi Harry Tarlow at their second kosher board-inghouse near the county courthouse, 1936. (Courtesy of Mervin Tarlow)

Temple Emanu-El Sisterhood, with Felice Cohn barely visible (*right rear*), ca. 1943. Cohn authored the woman's suffrage amendment to the Nevada Constitution, adopted in 1914. (Courtesy of Mervin Tarlow)

Seder for northern Nevada servicemen at Reno's Temple Emanu-El, ca. 1944. (Courtesy of Mervin Tarlow)

Partying

Life in early Nevada could be particularly dreary in the winter, wrote one Jewish observer, "when our hills are enveloped in a cloak of dazzling snow, our thoroughfares and roads covered with the very finest knee-deep alkali mud." At times like these, the Jews would "band together, start societies, give soirees, arrange tea parties, etc., scorning the hoary frost by artificial heat, and whiling the long winter evenings pleasantly away." The Comstock was alive with ethnic balls and parties, and the B'nai B'rith lodges and the Comstock's Purim Club were the chief organizers of Jewish galas.[54]

From the early celebrations of birth, bris, or marriage to the modern fundraising events in Las Vegas, Jews in Nevada have demonstrated that they loved a good party. The ritual welcome of a newborn son was as much a religious service as an occasion of gift-giving to the child and having a festive meal. Even the formation of the new King Solomon B'nai B'rith lodge at Virginia City in 1865 was not simply a business meeting. The city's correspondent to the *Hebrew* described what happened and hinted at what might have been:

> Of course there was a supper after the institution of the new Lodge; such a repast as only sage brush [*sic*] Washoe can get up. My mouth waters even now, when I call to mind the many delicacies that covered the table. Turkeys and chickens, and ducks and geese, without end—roasted, fried, boiled and stewed; a person had only to express a wish, a preference, and it was immediately gratified. Social as the gathering was, however, the new made B.B. took particular pains to confine the mirth that pervaded the assemblage, in its proper bounds, by conducting the supper on an entirely *temperate* principle, so much so, indeed, that no hired temperance lecturer could find fault with them.

After the dinner came speeches and many toasts to B'nai B'rith members past and present. Some of the newly elected officers went home early, but their confreres were not about to let them rest. They went first to the house of Joseph Barnett, "who had the [miss] fortune to get married lately, and arriving there, we made the air resound with many a joyous song." After making sure they had roused the sleepers, they moved on to several other homes, singing all the way. At the last stop, the choristers found that the owner had anticipated their arrival and prepared "a splendid lunch, consisting of all kinds of drinkables, of which we good humoredly and condescendingly partook."[55]

Several months later, Jacob Kaplan was leaving town and received a send-off from his B'nai B'rith lodge brothers. The formalities were followed by a late dinner at a private home, with numerous toasts and speeches. But they only signaled the beginning of Act II. Kaplan went home to sleep and awakened to a band playing "When the Swallows Homeward Fly" outside his window. More farewells, momentary silence, and the band moved down the street in the wee hours to the home of John A. Moch, local restaurateur and lodge vice president. The musicians were dismissed, but the party went on at Moch's place until five in the morning, when Kaplan's stagecoach left the city.[56] Such were the early precedents for parties on the Comstock.

B'nai B'rith balls became so popular that in 1870 the organizers announced that no tickets would be sold. The event was by invitation only, but the festivities were not limited to Jews. Comstock newsman Alf Doten attended the annual event in 1873 and congratulated himself that he managed to be in bed by one in the morning.[57]

One of the liveliest, most entertaining of all feasts that Jews observed was Purim, which celebrated Esther's storied intervention to save her people from persecution. Traditionally, participants came to their synagogue dressed as characters in the Purim story. The villain of the biblical piece was Haman, and whenever his name was mentioned in the ceremonial reading from the book of Esther, it was customary to boo or stomp one's feet.

Virginia City's Purim celebration, a masquerade ball open to the public, was even more boisterous and extravagant. Famed San Francisco costumer Madame S. F. Paullin fashioned costumes of characters drawn from literature, the Bible, history, or a stereotypical ethnic figure. Although tickets were once limited to one hundred participants, the number of revelers reached several hundred by 1878 and had to be held at the large National Guard Hall. It was later moved to Piper's Opera House, which was jammed with people from floor to gallery. Tickets cost five dollars and included free carriage transportation. Handsome prizes were awarded in a variety of categories, with Purim Club members excluded from competition.

The annual balls received elaborate notice in the local press, which took pains to identify the masked participants and comment on their ability to act out the character. The Purim balls were, according to the *Territorial Enterprise* reporter, the finest parties ever given in the city and perhaps among the best masquerade balls on the West Coast. By 1880, it had become an "established institution . . . an occasion not to be missed, unless by anchorites and people whose cynicism and pervert dispositions are so thoroughly engrafted upon their lives as to render their hearts insensible to innocent mirth and jollity." Streamers, colored lights, wall decorations, and illuminated transparencies added to the festive atmosphere. A brass band and full orchestra provided a variety of musical selections for the dancing, which was interrupted at midnight by the "unmasking" and then continued "until broad daylight."[58] The Purim balls attracted as many Gentiles as Jews, and were open to young men and women of marital age. They also included virtually every ethnicity on the Comstock. The Chinese were a noticeable exception.

Women, Their Children, and Their Occupations

Jews migrating to Nevada in its first twenty years were usually young bachelors who tended to get married late in life and to considerably younger women. Jewish men already married or engaged usually traveled alone to Nevada and later brought their families to the state, if the prospects proved promising. A few Jewish men and women never wed, and others married outside the faith.

Finding a Marriage Partner

Nevada's isolation and small population exacerbated the problem of finding a Jewish mate. Unmarried adult Jewish women were virtually invisible until 1880, and they were largely the late teenage daughters of early settlers. Nevertheless, some young Jewish men and women found each other through kinship and friendship networks—usually "arranged" liaisons that in the case of Nevadans often involved a partner from a faraway city. Jewish newspapers chronicled only eleven Nevada Jewish marriages in the 1860s and 1870s, and these customarily involved a partner from San Francisco. One Pioche resident, A. M. Cohn, took no chances on finding the right woman in Nevada. He returned to his native Exin in Polish Prussia, where he married Valeria Cohn.[1]

The paucity of eligible Jewish women was not limited to Nevada. "Hebrew bachelors in the far West make frequent complaint that the lack of Hebrew maidens in their vicinity compels them to forego the joys of married life," reported New York's *Reformer and Jewish Times.* The newspaper deplored the growing number of intermarriages in the East and applauded Jewish men in the West who were "still violent in their opposition to any intermarriage with Christians." The writer recommended that if a Jewish man could find no woman to marry within his religion, he should stay single, but he added that "a large number of Hebrew maidens in New York . . . of marriageable age . . . would welcome offers of marriage from desirable young Jews."[2]

The problem was how to reconcile the eastern plethora of women with the western demand. The *Reformer and Jewish Times* reluctantly admitted to allowing a western merchant to advertise in its pages for a wife. The merchant received a multitude of responses, but the *New York Sun* judged that the best women would hesitate to accept such a proposal. It recommended instead that western bachelors put aside any false economy in such an important matter and buy a train ticket to New York.

Births and Infant Mortality

Where there were marriages, there were proud parents doting on children. San Francisco's and Cincinnati's Jewish newspapers joyfully reported dozens of Nevada-born children whose parents never made the census rolls or city directories. They were among the many Jews on the move. The babies received the kind of attention given to all newborns, and they responded with the squawks and screams that soon became words of need or satisfaction. Then they started to die. Infant mortality across the country was devastatingly high, and the recently settled West was no exception.[3] The Jewish press reported a handful of such deaths in Nevada, but tombstones etched with the phrase "Tief Betrauert" (Deeply Mourned) revealed even more. Infants' and children's graves constituted one-third of Virginia City's Jewish burials and three of the four remaining headstones in the Eureka Jewish cemetery.

Westerners may have become hardened to the deaths of small children. Jacob Kaplan described the grief of those attending the funeral of a child in the morning, and by afternoon "there was hardly a trace of sorrow left on the countenances of those [attending a B'nai B'rith celebration]. . . . 'Out of sight, out of mind,' however is the great maxim of society; and well it is so, that man can so easily forget his sorrows, for if not, he would be wretchedly depressed in his spirits for the greater part of his existence."[4]

Once Jewish couples were committed to settling down, they often had large families. In Carson City, Pauline and Hyman Olcovich raised seven children. In Virginia City were the Harris Block family of five, twenty-three members of two extended Cohen and Cohn families, Jake Goodfriend's brothers and young family, a dozen ubiquitous Harris family members with ties to the Carson City Harrises, the Kirschbrauns, Jacob and Frances Levy's small family surrounded by a bevy of unmarried Levy men, Rosaline and Samuel Michelson's brood of seven, the Louis and Pauline Lowensteins, three Mayer families with children in school, pioneer Jacob and Rose Pinschower with their four daughters and son, town barber Louis Peyser and his four children, and the Rosenbrocks, Rosenthals, Samuels, and Wertheimers in abundance. By 1880, more than half of Nevada's urban Jewish population were children. Marriages and the ensuing children had turned even rugged Virginia City into what its historian described as a "family town."[5]

A Nevada "Mortara Case"?

An international furor erupted when the world learned in 1859 that a young Catholic servant had secretly baptized six-year-old Edgardo Mortara and spirited him away from his Jewish parents to a monastery under the pope's orders. At a mass meeting in San Francisco, future Nevadan Morris B. Ashim, as president of the B'nai B'rith lodge, and others raised their voices in protest against this invasion of religious rights and called upon the United States to restore Mortara to his parents. The protests were of no avail, and the young man went on to be ordained a priest.[6]

A similar incident unfolded at Virginia City in 1871. The daughter of a separated Jewish couple had been placed by her mother in the Nevada Orphan Asylum, operated by the Daughters of Charity. When the mother died three years later, the father applied at the orphanage for her release. The sisters declined to release her, until several prominent Jewish citizens attested to his identity. The child expressed a wish to remain with the Daughters of Charity, who then refused to give her up unless compelled by law. The local B'nai B'rith lodge appropriated funds for legal action, and a court date was set for late January 1871. No record of the adjudication has been found. The sisters had a close working relationship with Jewish families on the Comstock, and the matter was probably settled amicably out of court.[7]

Education: Public and Private

Although most nineteenth-century Jewish immigrants to Nevada brought little formal schooling with them, learning English was a necessity for anyone hoping to succeed in the United States. A number of German Catholic immigrant groups clung desperately to their mother tongue to maintain their culture and religion. This was not true of the Jews, with a few exceptions.[8] Sabbath schools (as in Eureka) taught Hebrew, but English was the common language of instruction and preaching. The only place where such training could be received systematically was in a public or private school. The public school system in the United States routinely used New Testament readings from the Protestant King James Version of the Bible. This practice incited textbook wars in New York and Philadelphia in the mid-1840s, with Catholics and Jews on the same side of this explosive issue. Catholics countered the Protestant influence by developing their own parochial school system. Isaac Leeser, the *Occidental's* Orthodox editor, urged Jews to develop their own Hebrew school system, whereas other Jewish leaders, such as Isaac Wise, strongly supported public education as long as it was religiously neutral.[9]

In Nevada, that neutrality was in jeopardy. The 1863 Constitutional Convention delegates opposed "sectarian education" in the schools, but expected general "religious instruction." One legislator pointed out that because all religious instruction was Christian, Jews would regard it as "sectarian."[10] Nevertheless, no evidence has been uncovered of Jewish public dissatisfaction with the religious neutrality of the Nevada public schools or with the theology that imbued Catholic private schools. The Daughters of Charity staffed Virginia City's St. Mary's School and orphanage and prided themselves on their cordial relationship with Comstock Jews. Not only did Jewish girls attend the school; some were boarders. Their families donated cash, merchandise, and treats to the sisters during holiday seasons. The sisters considered their relationship with Jews a unique characteristic of their work.[11]

Jewish children in Nevada were on the record as avid readers. Carson City residents inherited a unique opportunity when, shortly after statehood, authorities established a library for state and county officials. Although originally intended for their exclusive use, the rules relaxed to allow individuals with a reliable record to borrow books with written approval from a judge, legislator, and (several years later) the head librarian. Library records revealed greater usage by the children of Jewish families than one might expect from their relatively small numbers. For example, in 1889, virtually every page of thirty-five listed users included the name of an Olcovich, Tobriner, Cohn, Bergman, Jacobs, or Platt child. They were reading everything from the latest novels and classics such as *The House of the Seven Gables* to Bible commentaries and a the *History of the People of Israel*. Selig Olcovich, turning eighteen in 1896, returned a *History of the United States* and borrowed *How to Be Happy though Married*.[12]

Private music lessons were available to those who could afford them. The

Tobriner, Platt, Bergman, and two Olcovich families in Carson City had pianos, and music was a part of their children's education. A grandson recalled more than a century later that "music lessons were routine: piano for the girls, violin for the boys." "Sammy" Platt was a precocious exception as a pianist. These children were active in musical and thespian productions as well as in the juvenile versions of masquerade balls.[13]

Eureka's Jewish community had its own academically and artistically promising children. The local press in 1877 singled out the exceptional progress of public school attendees: Arnold and Isidore Goodfriend; Gussie, Ada, and Alma Manheim; Tillie, Fannie, and Mamie Steler; Percy and Louis Goldstone; Jacob Schiller; Lillie Berg; Esther and Sammy Leventhal; and Gussie Moch. Young Michael Banner had so developed his skills as a violinist that he was invited to give performances in Chicago and at Steinway Hall in New York. His family took leave of Eureka and settled in Cincinnati, where Michael could pursue music studies.[14]

Albert Michelson: One Who Got Away

One of Virginia City's prodigies, Albert Michelson, was not a product of Nevada schools. Born December 19, 1852, in Strzelno, Poland, to Samuel and Rosaline, who migrated with their growing family to Murphy's Camp, California, and in 1866 to Virginia City, Albert lived in the family residence above the Michelson store when he was not attending San Francisco Boys High School. His reputation as an excellent student was not lost on his father, who used his influence to further his son's education.[15]

Republican Thomas Fitch, Nevada's congressman, nominated a Nevadan from a poor family to the U.S. Naval Academy, which quickly dropped him. On June 17, 1869, he petitioned President Grant to consider Albert Michelson for the opening. "His father is a prominent and influential merchant of Virginia City," wrote Fitch, "and a member of the Israelite persuasion, who by his example and influence has largely contributed to the success of our cause, and induced many of his co-religionists to do the same. These people are a powerful element in our politics, the boy who is uncommonly bright and studious is a pet among them."[16]

However, Grant had exceeded his allotment of appointments and initially refused one to Michelson. He reversed himself at the behest of the academy's superintendent, who had been impressed by the young man's examination results. Michelson was admitted in the fall of 1869 and returned to Virginia City for a visit in 1873. The new Virginia and Truckee train could practically deliver him to his parents' doorstep. We know little of his stay except that his uniform was ruined in a tiff with a gang of boys who "resented this apparition of cleanliness and military bearing invading their territory." He fought off the gang with a can of ice cream, much of which ended up on the uniform. The Michelson family moved to San Francisco in the eighties, where their fortunes rose and fell according to the luck of Samuel's risky investments.[17]

Albert Michelson married churchgoing Gentile women, but he never adopted their religious faith or professed Judaism. He received an appointment to the University of Chicago in 1892, where he successfully measured the velocity of light. In 1907, Michelson was awarded the Nobel Prize in Physics, the first person of Jewish ancestry to be so honored.[18]

Children in the Working World

No census data provides children's occupations. In fact, they had chores, helped with the family business, held down odd jobs, and in rare cases became private entrepreneurs. In 1880, Bernhard Olcovich's wife, Carrie, shocked the family by leaving him and the five children to fend for themselves while she moved to San Francisco. Meanwhile, the eldest child, twelve-year-old Pauline, had a major responsibility for rearing her siblings.[19]

Two of Pauline's cousins turned out to be literate products of the capital's public schools. At ages ten and twelve, respectively, Selig and Isaac Olcovich (sons of Hyman and Pauline) debuted as editors of a chatty newspaper, the *Sun*, in 1886. This four-page semiweekly was filled with advertisements and never missed an opportunity to note when a Jewish person visited or left the area. It became larger and more successful as the *Weekly* in 1891. The teenagers wore their religion on their sleeve when they noted that the October 5, 1891, issue was smaller because the previous two days were "the Jewish New Year, and as we belong to that faith, we do not work."[20] Isaac's interests turned to the family business in 1898, and Selig took over the paper. When he attempted to raise the annual subscription rate to $1.50, he lost all but his most faithful customers. He suspended publication in January 1899, and the *Carson Appeal* absorbed the newspaper.[21]

Women's Other Occupations

German Jewish journalist Israel J. Benjamin devoted a chapter in his observations to the "upbringing of Jewish women." He noted with disapproval that American women were aggressive and dominating. To the contrary, he added, "it is only in Jewish circles the privileges of women and the power they experience have limits."[22] Benjamin visited the Comstock in 1861 and failed to notice (or chose to ignore) the Jewish women in business for themselves. Although the majority of those from the old country generally were self-described housewives, a significant number of them and their Americanized daughters were cut from different cloth than Benjamin would have admired. He might have choked had he stayed long enough to read Minerva Morris's denunciation of the local Comstock press, whose view of women matched Benjamin's. Chiding the *Gold Hill News* for its coverage of "questionable stock reports" and incidents of crime, she challenged the newspaper to acknowledge the "wives, maidens, and children" whose influence was notably responsible for the increased "moral excellence of our famous Territory." Warming to the point, she urged the newspaper to transcend the traditional view that women's place was at home and not in the public sphere.[23]

Although census records identified most Jewish married women as "keeping house," wives routinely stocked shelves and worked the counter in their husbands' stores. Unlike agricultural communities elsewhere, mining towns provided ample opportunity for women to crack their traditional mold as wives and mothers. The accepted notion of gender-based work in the home expanded in Nevada, where Jewish women were boardinghouse keepers, restaurateurs, saleswomen, teachers, grocers, and saloon keepers—doing business in their own names.[24]

More than Milliners

Many nineteenth-century Nevada Jewish merchants were in the dry-goods and clothing businesses, and a number of Jewish women engaged in ancillary occupations. Of the forty-one female milliners listed in the 1880 census records for Nevada, six were Jewish. On the Comstock, four of the twenty-one milliners were Jewish. The relative overrepresentation of Jewish women in this profession is underscored by the prominence of two of them in Nevada's early history. They did more, however, than design women's hats.

Polish-born Sarah Loryea, who first opened a millinery shop at Carson

City in 1861, was also the first to advertise fine women's wear on the Comstock. She and her Russian-born husband, Joseph, came to Carson City with their son, Milton, and while in Nevada they had a second child, Harry. In the summer of 1861, Sarah moved her business to Virginia City, on the second floor of her husband's Almack Saloon. The Loryea store carried a stock of imported merino woolens, perfumes, fine glassware, kid gloves, mantillas, and bonnets. Loryea advertised that all of her goods would cheerfully be shipped to "ladies in the interior" who supplied her with "their age, complexion and the color desired." At this time, the only such settlement of women was the Reese River Mining District around Austin.[25]

In 1863, Sarah (not Joseph) opened the Loryea House Hotel in Virginia City as a lodging establishment, and a day later, she delivered champagne to the local newspaper staff.[26] The Loryeas moved to Oregon and then California and added two more children to their family. They were members of Congregation Bickur Cholim in San José in 1867. During a period of eight years of raising children and moving four times, Sarah—not Joseph—was the major breadwinner. U.S. Census records for 1870 show Sarah's personal property estimated at two thousand dollars, whereas her husband's net worth was set at five hundred dollars. The Loryeas severed their affiliation with the San José synagogue in 1876 and returned to Virginia City and later settled in Eureka. Sarah Loryea is one remarkable example of a talented fashion designer who moved at least seven times in three western states, gave birth to at least four children, and ran a prosperous business wherever she landed.[27] Clearly one of Nevada Territory's earliest private entrepreneurs, she was never acknowledged as a "pioneer." That honorific title was reserved for men only.

Virginia City's most enduring millinery establishment was that of Russian-born Louise E. Jackson. She arrived with a family of four children in 1861. Her husband—a native of Prussia—clerked at the J. Barnert (later Barnett) and Company clothing store, while she opened her own dressmaking shop about a block away. He soon teamed up with her, and they moved across from the International Hotel. Louise bore the fifth of her six children at the time she was becoming an outspoken women's suffragist. Scholars of the Comstock needleworkers have singled out the Jacksons as the only husband-and-wife working team on the Comstock. The Jacksons were an integral part of the Comstock Jewish community for more than a quarter century.[28]

Another milliner-clothier doing business in her own name was Prussian-born Fanny Mayer, who operated a shop on the Comstock above her husband's saloon and was advertising as early as 1863. She still worked as a milliner in 1880, when her fifty-five-year-old husband showed no occupation. Fanny may well have been supporting the family along with her eighteen-year-old daughter, also a milliner.[29]

When Rabbi Jacob Sheyer of Carson City died suddenly in April 1875, Amelia Sheyer was left to carry on with her three daughters. The partnership of Sheyer and Morris had ended, but the old store was still available. Amelia Sheyer became the sole proprietor of Sheyer and Company clothing store. Keeping house with large families could be a daunting task, and of the fifteen Jewish families in Carson City, ten had one or more live-in servants or cooks. Amelia Sheyer had none. Her daughters doubtless helped in the business, but they soon left the nest. Pauline married Morris Cohn in 1875, and the two lived for a time with Amelia, Lizzie, and Rose. In 1879, Lizzie married Prussian-born Henry Morris, a Virginia City barber, and Rose wed Sol Levy of Reno, one of the mainstays of the city's Jewish religious organization and a prosperous merchant. With her daughters successfully married, Amelia retired to Reno, where she died on June 30, 1895.[30]

Educators: The Early Days of the "First Female Rabbi," Ray Frank

Perhaps to offset any undue Christian influences in the public school system and because teaching was one of the few professions open to them, Jewish women across the country began to fill positions as instructors.[31] The first Jewish teachers in Nevada came from California. Rachel ("Ray") Frank journeyed each school term from San Francisco to Eureka to teach school from 1879 to 1886. Frank was born in San Francisco in 1861 to Bernard and Leah Frank. The Polish-born Bernard reportedly attended Orthodox services regularly and earned a modest living as a peddler and fruit vendor. Ray had two older sisters, Esther (unmarried) and Rosa, who married Aaron Berg, had three children, and lived in Eureka, Nevada, where Aaron was a major stockholder in the Philip Sheridan Mine. Ray and her sister Esther moved to Eureka in 1879 to teach and to care for Rosa, who was sick at the time. Rachel and Esther were two of the thirteen teachers listed as working in Eureka County in 1881, and Esther taught at Elko and Wells in succeeding years. In no other part of Nevada were Jewish women represented in the educational profession beyond their minuscule percentage of the population.[32]

Frank taught children at Ruby Hill and evening classes for adults. She also read a paper on educational theory at the Teachers' Institute in Elko.

Former student Joseph Arthur remembered her as the teacher of his first four years of schooling at Ruby Hill near Eureka. He described her as having "black, shiny hair and eyes, a very bright woman of Polish descent, who later in life became the first woman rabbi in the United States." Actually, she was never ordained. Little more is known about Ray Frank's early teaching, except that she later identified her seven years in Nevada as the determining period of her life. Eureka was alive with social and cultural events and a predominantly Prussian-Polish Jewish population, which was more religiously observant than anyplace else in Nevada. Eureka's Judaism was also Reform, providing this modern woman with an alternative to Orthodoxy.[33] A decade later, Frank achieved a command of Hebrew, philosophy, Jewish history, and its traditions, and became a widely sought speaker. Under Isaac Mayer Wise in Cincinnati, she gained additional education and pedagogical skills necessary for ordination, but they both opposed women in the ordained rabbinate. Frank became superintendent of a Sabbath school in Oakland and gained a reputation for her ability to convey the teachings of Judaism to mixed audiences. This began a speaking career, which brought her back to Reno in 1895, where she was headlined as "the Girl Rabbi." Governor John E. Jones feted her in Carson City, where Frank spoke about the importance of her experience at Eureka.[34]

Selig and Isaac Olcovich's sister Annie matriculated from Carson City High School to the University of Nevada for her teaching credential. At eighteen, she began four years of teaching at the county's Clear Creek School, before moving to a lifetime career of teaching in Denver in 1894. Her sister Nevada Olcovich also became a teacher, as did Pauline and Julia Michelson of Virginia City.[35]

Felice Cohn, daughter of Morris and Pauline Sheyer Cohn, graduated from Carson City High School in 1894. She took courses at Nevada Normal School and Stanford University and earned elementary-school teaching credentials.[36] Sam Platt, son of Joseph and Malvina, taught at Carson City High and in Gardnerville. Platt and Cohn had lifelong productive careers as lawyers in Nevada—on opposite sides of the political fence.

Restaurateurs and Grocery Mavens

Regina Moch, Sarah Levanthal, and Matilda A. Ashim all operated their own dining establishments in Eureka in 1879. Moch was the first to own and manage a business in her own name. She and her husband, John, had run the

Merchant's Exchange restaurant in Virginia City as early as 1864 and opened a second restaurant, the Lunch and Oyster Saloon, in Reno in 1868. Regina was the gourmet cook of the two. They moved their family first to Hamilton and then to Eureka in the mid-1870s. There Regina Moch ran the Epicurean Restaurant under her own name.[37]

Sarah Levanthal was a "restaurateur" with her husband, Edward. They had lived in Eureka since 1871, when they lost one infant to death. Within a decade, they had four children between the ages of four and nineteen, two live-in Chinese cooks, and a young teamster boarder. Although Sarah was in the restaurant business, she also sold fine groceries.

Matilda A. Ashim was born in New York and married wholesale grocer and Prussian-born Simon Ashim. She was the mother of four, including Mark Twain's former stenographer Baruch. The family had moved from South Carolina to Georgia and then in 1863 to Carson City. They were in booming Hamilton by 1870, where Simon reported a net estate worth of twenty-eight thousand dollars. After the Hamilton fire of 1874, they—like many others—relocated to more promising Eureka.[38]

Prostitutes

Contrary to the mythology that includes fantasies about prostitutes in new mining camps, most adult women were married, accompanying a husband and sometimes with children in tow—like Sarah Loryea and Louise Jackson.[39] The 1860 Territorial Census indicated that most Nevada women over fifteen were married and in traditional housekeeping or other professional roles; no prostitutes were so designated. Ten years later, the U.S. Census recorded 242 prostitutes or harlots for all of Nevada, of whom 157 were on the Comstock—about 10 percent of the total female population and equal to the total of all other female-listed professions. But the census enumerator's assumption that Chinese second wives and concubines were harlots may have inflated the number of prostitutes.[40]

Miriam Michelson, who grew up several blocks from the cribs, remembered "Julie [sic] Bulette, Cad Thompson, Stagecoach Nell, and others like them with a professional understanding of the place such women occupy in a rich, new mining town." She speculated that they were listed "in early directories discreetly, but not too definitely disguised, as seamstresses or teachers of foreign languages or what not." Others lived "on the borderland between admission and denial of the manner in which they made their living." With the exception of those provided residences by wealthy lovers, Virginia City prostitutes lived in what Michelson described as uncurtained "little white boxes of houses" in the D Street red-light district.[41]

Rose Benjamin operated one of Virginia City's "fancy" brothels in the 1870s. In individual dwellings and one large house adjacent to her own resided twenty-three prostitutes with an average age of twenty-five, all American-born, save four—some showing personal assets as great as five thousand dollars. Prostitution went unmentioned in the published letters from Nevada correspondents to Jewish newspapers. Nor did local newspapers raise the subject unless some scandal was associated with a particular person or house—as with Benjamin, whose brothel housed teenagers on laudanum and engaged in commercial sex. But whether this forty-year-old madam who provided opium for her customers was Jewish is not clear. The record reveals no ethnicity or any relationship with the five other male Benjamins in northern Nevada. She was born in England in 1830; beyond that, her ethnic heritage remains unknown.[42]

Elsewhere, the Mammoth Lager Beer Saloon in Austin advertised openly to satisfy the needs of all "votaries of Bacchus, Gambrinus, Venus or Cupid." Samuel Bowles, editor of a Massachusetts newspaper, journeyed through Nevada in 1865 and stopped to test the Mammoth's claims. He asserted that all he found was "a fat, coarse Jew girl [who] proved the sole embodiment and representative of all these proclaimed gods and goddesses." Whether this account was factual or simply a play to eastern readers' perceptions of Jews is not known. The saloon was not listed in the 1865 city directory.[43]

In Hamilton, the eastern bonanza in White Pine County, Bertha Cohen was noted in the U.S. Census of 1870 as "keeping house." That would have been a normal occupation for a wife, but because Cohen's dwelling was near those of eight other relatively prosperous unattached women from various parts of the world who were also "keeping house," the occupational designation was certainly dubious. A study of women and divorce on the Comstock noted that "keeping house" was sometimes a euphemism for "prostitute."[44] Cohen reported her birthplace as Hesse-Darmstadt in 1838 and lived next door to eighteen-year-old Rosa Steel from Hesse-Cassel who was also alone and "keeping house." Cohen claimed to be unmarried at the age of thirty-two with an estate valued at five hundred dollars. Also living in Hamilton in 1870 were ten men named "Cohen," all unmarried, between the ages of twenty-two and forty, mostly from Prussia or Poland. No evidence suggests that any of these men were related to Bertha. The Hamilton fire of 1874 displaced many citizens, one of whom was Bertha Cohen, who dropped off Nevada's record of documented citizens.

Family-operated Jewish prostitution became an endemic social problem in New York at the turn of the century and was the object of civic and religious attention. This was not the case in Nevada. Goldfield had its share of prostitutes during its twentieth-century boom days, and Russian-born Fannie Stein took her place among the cribs on Reno's Front Street in 1910. She was the only prostitute with a documented relationship to a resident Jewish male, Ely pawnbroker David Stein. Based on the records, Nevada Jewish women were underrepresented in this ancient profession.[45]

Women as Custodians of Judaism

Women often played a role in Jewish Sabbath schools in eastern cities by 1869, after which "most American Jews who received any formal Jewish education likely learned most of what they knew from female teachers."[46] Nevada was no exception. After his 1877 visit to the West, Rabbi Wise applauded the economic successes of the men but criticized them for observing only the High Holidays. At Sacramento, Wise was shocked that the congregation of fifty-five could barely gather the required ten men for a formal Sabbath service. He found little evidence of Sabbath worship among men even in the large San Francisco synagogues. He observed that women constituted "three-fourths of the congregations in the temples every Sabbath" and shepherded their children to the Sabbath schools. Wise emphasized on several occasions that because of male Jewish religious tepidity, women maintained Judaism. This critique, he wrote, applied equally to Nevada.[47]

Preparing and initiating the Sabbath ritual was, in fact, the mother's responsibility. At dusk she lit the Shabbat candles and invoked the first prayer. The father of the household then blessed bread, wine, and the children and then prayed:

> Y'varech'cha Adonai v'ish-m'recha,
> Ya-eir Adonai panav eilecha vichuneka
> Yisa Adonai panav eilecha
> v'yaseim l'cha shalom.[48]

> (May the Lord Bless you and keep you,
> May the Lord cause his spirit to shine upon you and be gracious unto you.

May the Lord turn His spirit unto you
And grant you peace.)

Whether Jewish women went so far as to substitute for a missing father and bless the children themselves is unknown, but Jewish women in Eureka had enough education in Hebrew and rituals to teach in the Sabbath school. In those instances where Jewish men married unconverted Gentile women, the Sabbath ritual was probably not observed.[49]

Religious Education in Eureka, Reno, and Carson City

A highlight for Eureka Jews was the 1878 arrival of San Francisco rabbi Aron Messing, who was soliciting funds for a new synagogue. He stayed on to establish a religious school, and Eureka was ready. Dr. Morris Rockman became the school's superintendent and Ben C. Levy the president.[50] Samuel Goldstone reported the Hebrew Sunday school as thriving six months later: "It may seem incredible that in twelve consecutive Sundays . . . children who had never before as much as seen a Hebrew alphabet, should be able to read Hebrew fluently."[51]

Despite such successes, Goldstone publicly chided the majority of Eureka Jews for religious lukewarmness. Having commented on their high net worth, he cited only a handful as contributing to Judaism. "The rest," he wrote, "are apathetic, indifferent and selfish, except in pursuit of gain or pleasure." He then challenged card-playing bachelors and married men to visit the Sunday school with a few words of encouragement and candies for the children. With such poor role modeling from the men, the responsibility for maintaining religious observance fell to the women. When Dr. Rockman returned to San Francisco, Matilda Ashim, Esther Steler, and Lena Levy continued the teaching at the Hebrew school.[52]

Although men served on Reno's Sabbath School Board, the instructors were Hulda Barnett and Sophia Prescott, with teenage assistants Leah Frederick, Henrietta Russack, and Fanny Barnett.[53] At the time Rabbi Messing was assisting in the formation of Hebrew Sabbath Schools in Nevada, almost all of Carson City's Jewish children were still of preschool age. Four years later, some of their parents publicly bemoaned the lack of a religious school. In California and Nevada, one of the Harrises reported "in every town of any size a number of Hebrew children growing up to manhood and womanhood, without having the least idea of what Judaism means. They are called Jews," he continued, but consider it a "disgrace" and (in a poor analogy) added that "some of them know no more about the religion of their ancestors than a Piute [sic] Indian." When Carson City Jewish leaders solicited pledges to hire a Hebrew teacher for their children, the response in support of a salary reached only seventy-five dollars per month. "We can get no man for that amount," complained one of the organizers, "to educate our children in the religion of our forefathers."[54] This was a sharp indictment of the city's reasonably prosperous Jewish merchants. And instead of looking for a "man," they might have searched for a Hebrew-literate Jewish woman, several of whom taught in Eureka and Reno.

An alternative kind of religious education went on besides formal schooling. Nevada Jewish children read periodicals. The newspapers covered national and international matters of Jewish interest, and their editorial styles were models of well-written English. The correspondence to the newspapers from Virginia City, Eureka, and Carson City was similarly unblemished—even when laced with outrage or cynicism. The newspapers were tolerant to a fault of these letters. They published damaging criticism as well as exaggerated praise and chronicled births, brises, bar mitzvoth, marriages, deaths, and "coming-out" parties for eligible young women.

The *Hebrew Sabbath School Visitor,* edited by the Reverend Dr. Max Lilienthal at Cincinnati, was specifically directed toward children. "Uncle Sam," as he called himself, mixed morals with hard news, as when he used the occasion of visiting the Chinese in San Francisco to preach on the evils of opium use. Jacob Olcovich, eldest son of Pauline and Hyman in Carson City, had read about the plight of eastern European Jewish orphans in this publication, and the editors duly acknowledged his supportive contribution of forty-five cents. More important, Jacob identified with Jews half a world away, and his parents encouraged the relationship by subscribing to the periodical. Annie Olcovich, three years younger than Jacob, wrote her own letter to the editor: "My brother Jacob takes your paper, and I think it is very interesting. I am thirteen and in the highest grade of the Carson Public School. I study higher arithmetic, physiology, philosophy, grammar and algebra. I do not think you receive many letters from Carson, as we have only six Jewish families residing here, and we have no synagogue. Carson is only a small city."[55]

Conclusion

In the 1930s, Marcus Lee Hansen studied ethnic enclaves in New York and other eastern cities and concluded that the children of immigrants often rejected their parents language, culture, and religion, but the children of the third generation wanted it all back. Second-generation religious tepidity was common in Nevada from 1860 to 1900. Many of the children mentioned in this chapter separated themselves from Judaism, and "marrying out" was often its first step. Morris and Lina Badt of Wells (and later Elko) had decided early on that when their children reached school age, Lina would rear them in San Francisco to enjoy educational advantages and Jewish religious participation unavailable in northeastern Nevada. The parents chose a "commuter marriage" to preserve their children's Judaism. Lina, in addition, wrested a promise from each of their children that they would never marry any but a Jewish person.[56] The Badts' commitment and attendant sacrifice met with mixed success.

The women teachers in Sabbath schools and mothers who encouraged Judaism in their homes epitomized what scholar Ann Braude concluded in a recent study: that "women's history *is* American religious history."[57] A corollary applies to Nevada: where Judaism flourished, it was fostered by committed Jewish women.

Coping with Depression

When Frederick Jackson Turner announced in 1893 that the frontier had ended three years earlier, Nevadans were not cooperating. Turner and the director of the census, Harold Simonson, theorized that settled civilization began and the frontier ended when the average population reached 2 persons per square mile. Though an average 2.4 Nevadans per square mile had settled on private land, the federal government controlled 86 percent of the state's acreage. Population figures aside, the Turnerian characteristic of the frontier as a place in the process of conquest did not end in Nevada in 1890. Despite a declining population, new mining discoveries after the turn of the century gave Nevada a "frontier" appearance it was not quick to shed.[1]

From its beginnings, Nevada's economy had depended almost completely on mineral production. The high tide of a gold or silver bonanza lifted miners, brokers, speculators, and support agencies. Despite the cyclical character of mining, with bust following boom, depression was an experience to which no one was accustomed. Calls for the free coinage of silver resonated from the Nevada platforms of both the Republican and Democratic Parties. Nevada's population, which had been growing geometrically since the Comstock discovery, plummeted more than 30 percent between 1880 and 1900. The slide in mineral production, which began in 1878, halted only with the early-twentieth-century discoveries at Tonopah and Goldfield. An entire generation remembered nothing but depression.

Virginia City: Down and Out

In 1881, the San Francisco *Jewish Progress* correspondent from Virginia City hoped to connect with those "whose liveliest, if not happiest days may be traced back to a former residence in this once thriving and prosperous camp." The writer noted that "the day of resurrection has not yet arrived to instill into the dispirited and almost lifeless population new life and activity." Some Jews succumbed and moved to California, "while the rest remain, endeavoring to sooth their troubled minds by the delusive creations of an over-heated imagination, wearing a magnificent but unsteady fabric of glitter and tinsel, that may fall to pieces at any moment." The only silver-lined cloud in the Comstock's bleak spring was the "invitation-only" Purim celebration by "the elite of Virginia City."[2]

Three months later, the Jewish community's mood was funereal. The correspondent to the *Jewish Progress* wrote dispiritedly: "Pesach [Passover] has come and gone, and passed over our city perhaps at such a height that its presence was imperceptible to the majority of our co-religionists. I have heard, however, from trustworthy sources, that a real old-fashioned Seder held high carnival at the homes of some of the more orthodox." Those who distracted themselves with the occasional theatrical amusements were disappointed by the visiting troupes' lack of ability. The writer, who signed himself optimistically as "B. O. Nanza," closed with the hope that "we may yet see our thriving camp reassert its claims to the proud distinction of being the liveliest and richest camp in existence." It was not to be.[3]

Isidor N. Choynski, San Francisco's correspondent to the *American Israelite*, had worked Aurora's mines with his father-in-law, Morris B. Ashim, and knew the exhilaration and despair of boom and bust. He often visited northern Nevada as an officer of San Francisco's B'nai B'rith Grand Lodge. In 1882, he called Virginia City the once-proud "depository of the mineral wealth of this coast and the gambling table of the world" and now "the most wretched town that ever tolerated a Piute [*sic*] or harbored a mining sharp." The city that once numbered up to five hundred Jews, Choynski wrote, was reduced to about thirty—"all anxious to get away as the mines are played out and ergo, the business has gone to the dogs." The B'nai B'rith lodge, once the "most solid and flourishing in the United States," with $20,000 in its treasury "and a thousand ready to give to a new-comer—is today a mere wreck of its former self, ready to transfer itself to this city, where most of its members now reside." Choynski speculated that Jews who spent thousands of dollars erecting stores and fashionable homes in Virginia City "would gladly give a quitclaim deed to their premises if they could get the price of freight for their iron doors and shutters."[4]

Although Virginia City's Jewish population declined severely, most of the B'nai B'rith lodge's fifty-seven members nostalgically continued to pay their dues in absentia. Miriam Michelson's family had retreated with many other Jews to San Francisco. When refugees from the Comstock gathered, she wrote, "They'll be old, poor, disillusioned; bitter, of course . . . but presently they will begin to speak of the one subject that's worth talking about—the old camp."[5]

Although Carson City avoided the sudden "bust" of played-out mining towns, property values steadily fell from 1880 to the turn of the century. The well-to-do Olcovich brothers' investments declined in value, but they continued to buy properties at seemingly bargain prices—only to sell them near the end of the century at a loss.[6] The dominance of Jewish clothiers and other merchants in Carson City for thirty years was changing. By 1883, Gentiles owned as many cigar and tobacco shops as Jews. Farrells and O'Connors competed with Aronsons and Tobriners. Although Jews still owned seven times as many dry-goods and clothing stores, demographic and religious attrition was in process, and the tide was turning.

A Lonely Observer of Jewish Tradition in Central Nevada

In 1864, Austin was Nevada's third-largest town and had a Jewish population of 150 with a benevolent society and a Jewish burial ground. By 1882, the Jewish numbers had dwindled to 11, six of them single men. The only family was that of New Yorker Abraham Sower, his convert wife, Louise, and their three children, ranging in age from three to eleven years—all Nevada-born. Sower's German-born father, Morris, lived next door and was likely the anonymous correspondent to the *American Hebrew* in that year. He described Louise "as sincere a Jewess—though a liberal-minded one—as though she had been born of Jewish parents." He applauded his son Abraham, who, some years before, had hired a mohel from San Francisco at a cost of $250 for his newborn son's ritual circumcision. This was all the more remarkable, wrote Sower, because Abraham "pays no attention whatever to religious observances." The correspondent continued to describe a religious situation that was fast becoming the norm elsewhere in Nevada: "Though [Abraham] does not fast upon Kippur Day, yet he closes his store, which is more than I can say for [the three] others of the same faith in this town. At the last Passover he was the only one here who had matzos, although others who had lately come from the Old Country were not ashamed to eat leaven." Now there were too few Jews in the entire county to hold a formal service. As though to underscore the depressing state of affairs, Sower noted that the only two Jews buried in the cemetery met violent deaths: one killed in a mining accident and the other murdered.[7] Abraham Sowers left Nevada within a decade, but their son remained unmarried and worked in Austin as a miner and laborer for more than thirty years.

Jews and the Chinese

Nevada's depression years included an increasing hostility toward the Chinese, who were perceived to be in competition for fewer jobs. Nevadans were not above making fun of any immigrant who had a colorful quirk, and newspaper reporters were known to suspend journalistic standards to embellish a good story. One such appeared in the *Gold Hill Daily News* involving an alleged encounter on Virginia City's C Street in 1868 between a Chinaman and a "Hebrew second hand clothing renovator." "Take dat, you tam China rice-eatin' son a b-h," was reportedly countered with, "Ah! yes Goddam Jew, you tinkee me Jeezyclyste, hey? you takee dat." Whether the Chinese man made the less-than-subtle allusion to the Jews killing Christ or it was simply a piece of creative writing is unknown, but the reference would not have been lost on the *News*'s heavily Christian readership.[8]

A leading scholar of Nevada immigrants generalized too broadly: "The lengthy and frequent articles which reported the hand-to-hand and verbal combat between Jews and Chinese were thought hilarious," he wrote. "Grotesque insults were exchanged, and 'the heathen' regularly enlarged on the Jew's responsibility for the death of Jesus Christ."[9] There is no such volume of newspaper or other printed materials pitting Chinese against Jews. The reported incident had less relevance to factual relationships between Jews and Chinese than to the fanciful writing of a Comstock reporter who attributed to both scuffling parties a common view found among the general populace.

"If American people were ever cursed by anything, it is by this miserable, thieving, murderous, licentious, filthy, pestilential race of heathens." So wrote Mary McNair Mathews of Virginia City.[10] One factor contributing to the common prejudicial view of Chinese was the stereotypical portrayal of a Chinaman by the popular poet Bret Harte. Though only a handful of people knew it, Harte's grandfather was a prominent New York Jewish merchant and longtime secretary of the stock exchange.[11] Harte's poetic description of Ah Sin, "the heathen Chinee," appeared in the *Overland Monthly* in 1870 and characterized him as a "peculiar heathen" who could trick card-playing Irishman Bill Nye with a sleeve full of jacks.[12] Harte portrayed Ah Sin using pidgin English. The literary device found its way into a growing ridicule of the Chinese, who could not pronounce the English letter *r.* Harte never intended his depictions of Ah Sin as anything more than an ironic disparagement of Irish prejudice, but the satirical purpose was lost on his less-than-sophisticated readership. The poem was quoted in Congress in 1871 and "worked to shape the debate over immigration policy in ways that Harte could neither have foreseen nor approved."[13] One of the few who knew of Harte's Jewish lineage, Mark Twain, described Harte as a "liar, a thief, a swindler, a snob, a sot, a sponge, a coward, a Jeremy Diddler, he is brim full of treachery, and he conceals his Jewish birth as if he considered it a disgrace." Harte was secretive about his Jewish heritage, but he showed no animus toward Jews or the Chinese.[14]

In the end, the fundamental issue concerning the Chinese was not morality or even religion; it was economics. The threat of Chinese expansionism in the western imagination reached paranoid levels in Nevada whenever mineral production dipped and jobs became more scarce. Whereas many unionized miners singled out the Chinese for wholesale discrimination, owners needing cheap labor prized them for their willingness to work for half the white man's wage. On the emerging issues of whether to trust, hire, boycott, or totally exclude the Chinese, Jews divided among themselves.[15]

Rabbi Isaac Wise characterized the Chinese as "nimble, quick, frugal and servile." He also admired their work ethic and maintenance of Chinese traditions. He considered Chinese laborers essential to the West's growth, and therefore in need of protection.[16] Eureka's Samuel Goldstone, a Wise admirer, had little sympathy for the Chinese and was a leader of Eureka's anti-Chinese immigration effort.[17] The difference in outlook between Wise and Goldstone was typical of the divided Jewish response to the Chinese question.

Chinese occupations ranged from physicians and druggists to barbers, gamblers, tailors, woodchoppers, and cooks or servants residing in households, such as those of Carson City Jewish merchants Frank Boskowitz, Jacob Levy, Morris Cohn, and tailor Adolph Jacobs. These latter Jews were among those initially opposed to the anti-Chinese movement. The 1879 legislature passed acts to prohibit Chinese immigration, employment of Chinese on state properties, and the right of Chinese to own real estate. In 1880, the national and state political platforms of both major parties included anti-Chinese provisions, and the Nevada ballot allowed voters to express their opinion on the subject. Of 17,442 votes cast, only 183 favored allowing Chinese to enter the United States. A significant number of Jews voted in this minority, but lawmakers were attentive to the overwhelming majority.[18]

The 1881 Nevada legislature passed resolutions encouraging Congress to restrict Asian immigration, which it cheerfully accomplished with the Chinese Exclusion Act of 1882. This action stiffened the backbone of northern Nevada patriots, who wanted to send the Chinese home. By 1886, Nevada's anti-Chinese committees had multiplied and become more heavy-handed. Boycotts of Chinese employers were next, and Carson City was a major battleground. The *Morning Appeal* headlined on February 21, "The Boycott Begins: The Chinese Lovers Throw Down the Gauntlet." Businesses employing Chinese were listed and admonished. The dress shops of Morris Cohn and Amelia Sheyer became the first to feel the pinch.[19] Boycotters urged Sheyer and other Chinese employers to sign an anti-Chinese agreement, which they could do at the stores of Max Aronson, Joseph Platt, and Jacob Tobriner.

Within two weeks, Morris Cohn had succumbed and was one of the 360 Carsonites of all ethnic backgrounds to sign a public agreement not to "sell, lease or sub-let or rent in any manner whatever (except actual present leases) any part of a farm, town lot or real estate, to any Chinamen or Chinese for any purpose whatever; neither will he employ any Chinamen or Chinese in any capacity . . . and use all peaceable means to discourage the patronage and employment of Chinese." The Olcovich brothers were among the few Jews who signed the document but openly flouted the anti-Chinese crusade. These merchants owned a Chinese washhouse that continued to do business a few hundred yards from the state capitol building.[20]

Thirteen Jews ultimately signed. Of these, nine belonged to the B'nai B'rith lodge. Significantly, fourteen B'nai B'rith members refused to sign the anti-Chinese document. The "Sons of the Covenant" clearly were divided, but the lines were blurred. Tobriner, a leader in the anti-Chinese campaign, had served in the state assembly; Frank Boskowitz had just completed a term in the assembly and refused to sign. Former Douglas County treasurer Al Livingston signed, but Koppel Rice, former superintendent of public instruction and Douglas County administrator, declined. Mill owner and proprietor of the popular Emporium, Abe Cohn, signed, but not Louis Morris, a small dry-goods dealer with much to lose. The four Harris brothers, who owned the largest clothing store in town along with some ancillary establishments, were not signers. The Olcovich and Harris families were among the city's most observant Jews and were on opposite sides of this issue. On the Chinese question, Carson City Jews were at odds, and no common denominator explained the differences.

The Chinese presence in a state filled with ethnic and religious minorities raises a question: did anti-Chinese sentiment protect other minority groups from the prejudices of an increasingly xenophobic society? The case has been argued and put to rest that prejudice against blacks in the South was a "lightning rod" preventing discrimination against other groups, such as Jews.[21] A similar question could be raised as to whether widespread anti-Chinese bigotry sheltered Indians, Jews, blacks, Italians, or any other minority group from discrimination.

Little evidence supports such a theory in Nevada's case. A bias against the Chinese did not neutralize popular sentiment toward the Paiute or Washoe Indians. Nor did it protect Italians in Eureka from exploitation by mine owners and even the Italian padrones. As for the Jews, they needed no protection. They were a part of Nevada's establishment before any major Chinese presence. They were so much a part of the local power grid in northern Nevada that individual self-assured Jews felt free to take opposite positions on the treatment of the Chinese.[22]

Lights Going Out in Carson City

A decline in subscriptions to the *American Israelite* in Nevada caught the eye of its caustic San Francisco agent, Isidor Choynski. In one of his meaner moods, he wrote, "Carson City, in our neighboring State of Nevada, has but two four-bit subscribers—the Olcoviches and the Harrises—and the other rich men in that town have no ear for the orphans." One of the Carson City Harris brothers responded to Choynski's "cheeky" observations, emphasizing the Hebrew Orphan Asylum's assets of $164,000 and only forty orphans to care for. He criticized San Francisco synagogues for requiring visiting Nevadans to produce a "ticket just the same as if we were about to enter a theater." Harris recounted that when in 1880 a visiting rabbi solicited funds for San Francisco orphans in Eureka, Reno, Carson, and Virginia City, "he carried away more money with him than a Nevada man would have received in San Francisco had he gone there on the same mission." Noting the difficult position most Nevada merchant Jews experienced in the continuing economic slide, Harris recalled when Nevadans could be counted on for generous donations to any worthy cause and complained that when "misfortune befalls us . . . and [we] are without money, we are looked upon as thieves and bad men." Charity begins at home, he retorted. "We take care of our poor," he stated, and observed that locals had failed to raise enough money to hire a Hebrew teacher during these difficult times.[23]

The lack of formal Jewish education in Carson City was a symptom of religious apathy among adults and a signal that they lacked personnel within their own community to teach and manage a Sabbath school. Meanwhile, children followed the lead of less observant adults or rejected the Old World traditions of their parents as they interacted at school with American-born Gentiles. Such was the case of Isaac Olcovich, who was about to get married. His future seemed bright, as he took responsibility for his father's business. The local newspaper noted that his "honest dealing had gained [the] confidence of everyone."[24] The Olcovich name, in evidence since 1863, appeared destined for permanence in the city. The marriage, however, was not celebrated in traditional Jewish fashion. Elizabeth was Episcopalian, and the Reverend J. B. Eddy performed the service. Two weeks later, young Isaac Olcovich died of tuberculosis. Reverend Eddy presided over the funeral in the deceased's new home, which was filled with mourners. His parents attended neither his marriage nor his funeral. For the traditional Olcoviches, a marriage outside the faith was already a funeral. He was buried in the center of Lone Mountain Cemetery, far from the plots set aside for practicing Jews.

Economic decline, kinship, and the threat of a loss of commitment to Judaism among their children had led Hyman and Pauline Olcovich to move to Denver in 1898, several months before Isaac's marriage. There they joined daughter Annie, Henrietta Olcovich Friedenthal, and Saft relatives of Pauline. Their son Louis married a Gentile woman and settled in the Pacific Northwest. Selig stayed in Nevada and later continued his printing profession with the *Goldfield News*. Annie and Vada never married. Jacob Olcovich remained an observant Jew and married Florence Saft, a cousin. Their son, Irwin (Olcott), later married Joseph Platt's granddaughter, Sylvia Platt Gutstadt. The Carson City Platts and the Olcoviches had lived two doors apart for more than twenty years, and according to family lore, the mistresses of the households were not on speaking terms. The families reunited two generations later in a marriage that celebrated their religious tradition.[25]

The death of Jacob Tobriner in 1890 and the departure of the Boskowitzs and the Olcoviches were part of a pattern in the Carson City Jewish community. The following notice appeared on October 3, 1898: "Today the Jewish residents will observe Yom Kippur and the merchants will close their stores

until 6 P.M." In addition to being unusually brief and unreinforced by advertisements, the date was off by a week! It was as if no one cared anymore. In
1900, Cohn, Platt, and Bergman ran upbeat ads, but when it came time for
High Holidays, there was no mention of closings. As if to betoken the state of
things to come, Al Bergman's ad announced a "Closing Out Sale . . . on Account of the Dull Time."[26]

Within a decade, gambling had been declared illegal, and on September
29, 1910, Carson City casinos were closing down before the legal ban went
into effect. Joseph Platt died in 1907, and a Gentile, Joe Smyth, had bought
out William Lilienfeld's place. The Bergmans had left. The Harris brothers
had sold out to Gray, Reid, and Wright. Adolph Jacobs was still tailoring but
not advertising. Henry Rosenbrock took over the Magnolia Saloon on Carson
Street, and Abe Cohn at the Emporium ran lavish ads for everything from
fresh fruit and Paiute baskets to the latest fads in fashion. Children were finding employment outside the old family businesses, and women were working
in professions unthought of a decade earlier.[27] The dominance of the Jewish
merchants in dry goods and clothing had evaporated, leaving only two such
Jewish establishments in 1907, compared with five Gentile-owned stores.

Two of Carson City's native-born Jewish children brightened the lives of
their parents at the depressing turn of the century. Samuel Platt (1874–1964)
had all the advantages afforded by his family's prosperity. He was a talented
musician, awarded for proficiency in oratory, and taught in local schools before attending Stanford and Columbian Law School. He was admitted to the
Nevada bar in 1897 at the age of twenty-two, elected to the state assembly
in 1900, and served as its Speaker in 1905. President Theodore Roosevelt appointed him U.S. attorney for Nevada in 1906.[28] His marriages and his political career as Republican torchbearer for almost a half century were still
ahead.

One of Platt's neighbors in Carson City was Felice Cohn (1878–1961), eldest of Morris and Pauline Sheyer Cohn's six children, and granddaughter
of Rabbi Jacob Sheyer. After taking courses at Stanford and Washington
LawSchool, she passed the Nevada bar in 1902. Cohn was the first native
Nevada woman practicing law in the state, and she shared offices in Carson
City with her senior and mentor, Platt, with whom she later crossed swords
over woman suffrage.[29]

Abe Cohn and Dat-So-La-Lee's Basketry

The common lament that Carson Street was dark because the Jews were celebrating was now a bitter memory. Abe Cohn had married a Gentile and evinced less interested in Jewish traditions, but his Emporium became one of Nevada's larger general merchandise stores. In 1895, Cohn became reacquainted with a former family servant, Louisa Keyser, whose Washoe Indian nickname was Dat-So-La-Lee or "Big Hips." She was in her sixties, severely obese, suffering from edema, and producing some of the most unique native Washoe baskets to be found anywhere in the West. Her weaving style, *degikup,* had the distinctive circular shape of an expanded middle with base and opening of the same size. Her promotion began in earnest with the 1900 publication of a pamphlet by Abe's wife, Clarisse Amy. It attempted to make the Washoe weaver a unique artist with ties to John C. Frémont in her youth and to Abe Cohn as a child. The romanticized legend of Dat-So-La-Lee was now in print.[30]

According to scholar Marvin Cohodas, the hype was pure fabrication. What was genuine was Dat-So-La-Lee's artistic ability. Cohodas explains the dilemma facing the Cohns and even contemporary basket weavers: "The general public considers basketry too humble a product to be worth adequate compensation for the skill and labor required. Only by emphasizing its curio value as the product of a known individual, can the price of a basket be brought up to anywhere near its true worth."[31] The Cohns consequently invented a function for the baskets. Documentation certificates now carried not only Keyser's initials and a number but also the assurance that this was, for example, a ceremonial mortuary basket.

In 1919, Cohn took Dat-So-La-Lee and her baskets to the Industrial Exposition at St. Louis. The exposure eventually placed her baskets in great demand, fetching prices of up to five thousand dollars each. Clarisse died shortly after their return from St. Louis, and Abe married Episcopalian Margaret Jones a year later. Dat-So-La-Lee weighed more than three hundred pounds and moved around with difficulty. Cohn reportedly provided her with the most modern household appliances and the best doctor's money could buy. However, at the end of her life, she spurned them in favor of Native customs and tribal medicine. She died at her Carson City home in 1925 at the approximate age of seventy-five.

Abe Cohn died on January 27, 1934, and was cremated and interred at Cypress Lawn Cemetery, a nonsectarian facility in Colma, California. None of his pallbearers was Jewish, and his obituary made no reference to Jewish lineage. What was emphasized was his important relationship to Dat-So-La-Lee. Although neither Cohn nor either of his wives appears to have exploited Dat-So-La-Lee, their promotion of the basketry and its creator was flawed. Cohn's newspaper advertising for the Emporium had always been flamboyant and given to exaggeration, which knowledgeable customers rewarded with record sales. Nevertheless, Abe and Clarisse Amy Cohn's reimaging of Dat-So-La-Lee pushed the envelope of legitimate salesmanship by fabricating the artist and not simply hyping the goods, which were exquisite in themselves. In the end, greed was not an issue. Abe's second wife made no profit on the baskets. She sold twenty to the State of Nevada for seventy-five dollars each in 1945. They are valued today at six thousand times that amount.[32] Although his marriages and lack of religious practice were part of a growing trend of assimilation, Cohn never repudiated his Jewish heritage and preserved for posterity some of the greatest basketry produced in the West.

Reno: Up and Slowly Coming

In 1879, a devastating fire consumed 350 structures in Reno's downtown area—including most of the Jewish-owned stores—but rebuilding was immediate.[33] Reno Jews numbered ninety in 1880—more than 7 percent of the town's thirteen hundred citizens—but Reno was still very much in the shadow of the Comstock. Its location on the railroad line and serving as a distribution center to the struggling camps and towns to the east and south were the keys to its relative stability. Over the next thirty years, the numbers increased, but the proportion of the Jewish population decreased. Most of the men were dry-goods, clothing, and tobacco merchants. The only certainly Jewish woman in business for herself was prostitute Fannie Stein. The late-nineteenth-century mainstays of the Reno worshiping community included the Jacobs, Pechners, Levys, Cohns, Fredericks, Marymounts, and Lachmans. The local newspapers regularly noted meetings of the benevolent society, the harvest festival of Sukkoth, and the playful Feast of Purim. On at least one occasion, as many as forty adults and children masqueraded as Queen Esther, the hated Haman, the faithful Mordechai, and King Ashuerus, visiting Jewish homes—much as some Gentiles celebrated Halloween.[34]

The Hebrew Benevolent Society had a steady membership of about twenty-one in the 1880s and 1890s. Meetings were routinely argumentative. The minutes revealed an inordinate amount of business devoted to who was a member in good standing, suspensions, reinstatements, and resignations, along with interminable discussions about the validity of excuses given for missing a meeting. The records hinted at underlying personal enmities, which gave rise to resignations. At this time, members were suing each other over such civil matters as easement rights on a common alley.[35] The organization met monthly except for special meetings, and mercifully, some kind of social or card playing followed the business meeting.

Besides providing a social outlet, the benevolent society maintained the Reno Hebrew Cemetery, preserved the *sefer* Torah, arranged for High Holidays, made modest charitable contributions, presided over the burial of members, and aided in the internment of nonmembers who were "without means." Benevolent-society members were also affiliated with Carson City's B'nai B'rith, which struggled to stay healthy in light of the capital's decline.

In 1895, the Reno society voted to disband and cede the Reno Hebrew Cemetery and *sefer* Torah to the newly formed B'nai B'rith Washoe Lodge no. 450. The Carson City lodge merged into the Washoe lodge. It included "nearly all" Reno Jewish males, a few from eastern California, and Carsonites such as Harry Leter and Seymour and Philip Jacobs, who had become part of Reno's merchant class. Its first elected president was Sol Levy of the Palace Dry Goods Store.[36] The first anniversary of Reno's B'nai B'rith lodge was the occasion of a reception and banquet for fifty members and their families. Reno's Jews were always up for a party, and music was featured at this elaborate event. In an editorial accompanying a description of the B'nai B'rith lodge's banquet, the writer contrasted the feast to the area's depressed economy.[37]

The next dozen years of northern Nevada's Jewish religious organizations are murky, at best. The new B'nai B'rith lodge included most Jews in northern Nevada and eastern California, but for unknown reasons it faltered and dissolved. The Reno cemetery temporarily fell into legal limbo. In 1907, members of the former Reno Hebrew Benevolent Society attempted to resurrect the society to save the cemetery. When this failed, the few diehards ceded ownership of the cemetery to themselves: merchants Harry Leter, Phil Jacobs, Sol Jacobs, and Sol Levy.[38] It was the beginning of Reno Hebrew Cemetery's torturous twentieth-century history.

In 1908, more than sixty-five Jewish men formed the Young Men's Hebrew Association (YMHA)—the national Jewish response to the Young Men's

Christian Association. The organization held its first major social reception in December, with seventy-five couples in attendance. Its officers and the social-event planners had been active in one or another of the defunct B'nai B'rith lodges and the Reno Hebrew Benevolent Society.[39] The YMHA had no staying power, and in 1911 the new Reno B'nai B'rith Lodge no. 759 formed, but struggled with multiple suspensions and an expulsion. It disbanded and re-created itself in 1920 as Lodge no. 760. Its membership over the next eight years included eighty-eight men, of whom only nineteen were suspended. The women's B'nai B'rith auxiliary and a group of old-timers calling themselves the Pioneer Jewish Ladies sponsored socials and educational gatherings separated from the men. Both organizations would provide the base for a permanent religious congregation.[40]

Reno's Nonreligious Jews

Missing from the rosters of the Reno Jewish organizations at this time were some of the city's most prominent Jews. One was Moritz Scheeline, born in San Francisco in 1859 and schooled in the banking business by his uncle, Daniel Meyer. Sent to Eureka, Nevada, in the 1880s to supervise his uncle's interests, he married Agnes Hall, a member of the Protestant Episcopal Church. In 1890, the Scheelines moved to Reno, where Moritz established the Bank of Nevada, the state's largest institution of its kind for more than a decade. In 1907, he formed the Scheeline Banking and Trust Company, which weathered that year's financial crisis. The Scheelines were generous benefactors of the American Red Cross, to which they donated fifty thousand dollars before Moritz's accidental death in 1917. The Episcopal rector and Elks Club directed his funeral. The Scheelines' son, Harry, inherited the banking business and the Episcopalian religious affiliation.[41]

One who treated disease but fell victim to his own demons was Dr. Henry Bergstein. Bergstein merits more attention because he was the longest-tenured nonnative Jew in Nevada—from his arrival as a young physician at Pioche in 1871 to a few years before his death in 1930. During that time, he was professionally and politically active beyond the average, he married "in" and then "out," and his relationship to Judaism eventually was beyond reach. His religion was medicine, to which he was devoted until the end of his life.

Bergstein and wife Pauline Michelson moved to Reno from Virginia City in 1883. He had alerted Nevadans earlier about how their indigent-insane were being ill-treated in a rented asylum at Woodbridge, California. It was the impetus Christopher Columbus "C. C." Powning needed as Republican state senator and editor of the *Nevada State Journal* to bring about a commitment from the legislature to construct a facility on Reno's outskirts in 1882. Bergstein's well-known scientific approach to medicine, and the coincidence that Republican Powning and physician Bergstein became public advocates together for the Silver Party, led Silverite governor John E. Jones to appoint Bergstein superintendent of the State Hospital for the Indigent Insane in 1895.[42]

He inherited a mess. According to a Reno historian, "Patients were bathed in herds, one scrubbing the other down with brooms and soapy water," and they were used to work on the previous superintendent's ranch. The customary regimen for handling therapy or punishment was electric shock treatment. Hospital personnel admitted to experimenting and punishing patients in inhuman ways. Determining the extent of unexplained deaths was impossible. The state's declining revenues during the depression forced patients to grow their own gardens, feed themselves, and perform other chores to offset hospital expenses. To make matters worse, whenever Nevada's leadership changed from one party to another, a new director was appointed. He, in turn, fired and replaced the asylum staff. A lack of continuity and professionalism was an understandable consequence.[43]

Upon becoming superintendent, Bergstein halted some of the asylum's flagrant abuses, such as allowing weekend visitors to gawk at the inmates. He also recommended sterilizing the insane in those cases "where mental disease appeared in the second generation." Based on the conventional wisdom of the time, he argued that because 75 percent of all insanity was genetically inherited, sterilization should be considered. No action was taken.[44]

Bergstein came under investigation for misallocation of monies used in finishing a portion of an addition to the asylum. Politics commonly determined contracts and concessions for state institutions. Whether Bergstein resisted or accommodated this practice is unclear, but his name was in the news for months before the complaints subsided. Bergstein ended up firing his business manager, who turned around and charged him with "performing unauthorized autopsies on patients, then throwing parts of their bodies in the nearby Truckee River." When confronted by the state board, Bergstein acknowledged that he had "made a casual comment to the attendant about disposing of the deceased man's brain in the Truckee River, . . . [but] he was unaware that the attendant had taken him seriously." In his defense, he argued that "when patients were deceased and without families, what he did with their bodies made no difference." Although such a statement ran contrary to traditional Jewish treatment of body parts, common decency, and public health considerations, the board of commissioners voted two to one to clear Bergstein of the charges. In a less controversial matter, he informed the legislature of his opposition to visits of large numbers of legislators to the asylum. Crowds, he said, created too much excitement for patients. He recommended that to maintain an atmosphere of serenity at the facility, he would personally conduct tours for small groups of legislators anywhere in the institution they chose to visit. Bergstein also changed the facility's name to the Nevada Hospital for Mental Diseases.[45]

Over the next few years, Powning and Bergstein became friends as they engaged in joint speaking engagements advocating Silverite issues. During this period, Henry and Pauline's marriage was under such stress that they lived apart. He resided at a home on the hospital grounds, and Pauline and their three sons lived at their other home at the corner of Second and Chestnut (later Arlington) Streets.[46]

Powning died suddenly in October 1898. So deep was the city's respect for him that the university, public schools, and businesses across the city closed to pay tribute to his civic-mindedness. Coincidentally, the anti-Silverite *Reno Evening Gazette* took the opportunity to resurrect the previous year's charges of Bergstein throwing a cadaver's brain into the Truckee. The editor sarcastically suggested that such a person was "too 'enlightened' an individual to discuss anything with."[47]

Given all of these factors, most expected the new gubernatorial administration that came into power in 1899 to follow precedent and change the leadership of the state hospital. Meanwhile, Bergstein prepared his annual report to the legislature opposing legislation making it too easy to commit people to the asylum—particularly the practice of unloading paupers on the hospital on the assumption that they were mentally ill. Bergstein also identified the manpower shortage at the hospital: only 8 attendants for 190 patients; whereas the national ratio of patients to attendants was 14.5, Nevada's was 24.5. Implicit in his report was the need for a state board of medical examiners to replace the Board of Commissioners for the Indigent Insane and become what his beloved State Medical Society had never been: a regulator of the practice of medicine and surgery. The legislature created just such a board in its ensuing session. But after four years of what was by contemporary standards a professional administration of the state hospital, Bergstein was predictably replaced.[48]

Meanwhile, six months after Powning's death, Pauline Michelson divorced Bergstein, alleging desertion and abandonment.[49] A year later, Bergstein married Powning's widow, Clare Poor Powning. The friendly *Nevada State Journal* tersely recorded that the two married in Reno at the bride's home, with University of Nevada president Dr. Joseph Stubbs performing the ceremony. Only a "few intimate friends and relatives were in attendance."[50] The marriage notice said that they were to reside in San Francisco, but Bergstein was practicing medicine and residing in downtown Reno in a few years.[51] Little is known about Bergstein's family life. The first years after his divorce were tumultuous, as Pauline Michelson badgered him in the courts for unpaid child support and at one point alleged he had a gambling problem. His inability to pay his Reno hotel rent in 1906 indicated some fiscal irresponsibility or embarrassment. In a 1907 court hearing, Bergstein claimed to be "broken in health, spirit and mind" and asked to be relieved of a reduced alimony payment of fifty dollars per month. His wife Clare had to reside in San José due to his alleged poverty. His appeal was denied, but by 1908 he was making regular alimony payments.

Clare died sometime before 1910, and thereafter Bergstein began a new life. Over the next decade, he was active in civic medical affairs. In 1911, he publicly commented on pending state legislation that would open the field for "quackery." He wrote the history of medical practice in Nevada for Sam P. Davis's two-volume *History of Nevada,* published in 1913. Washoe County's district attorney named Bergstein to help determine the sanity of a woman who had murdered her husband. In 1915, he became the city health officer and put Reno bars and restaurants on notice that they were liable for practices that could be a menace to public health. He resigned that post after fifteen months but remained a member of the Reno Board of Health. At the age of seventy-two, Bergstein still worked as a physician and surgeon in downtown Reno, through 1921. He died in San Francisco in 1930.[52] Bergstein was neither a model of virtue nor a cad without redeeming qualities. His final years of life were as much a paradigm of the state's economic woes as they were, in the end, a sign of recovery.[53]

While the state slid further into a decline of material resources and people, Reno grew steadily. With the exception of the brief demographic blip at Goldfield in 1906, Reno remained the "biggest little city" in Nevada for a half

Table 7.1

Nevada Statewide Jewish Population

Nevada general population figures are from the U.S. Decennial Census reports at the Nevada State Library and Archives, Carson City. The estimates of Jewish population for the nineteenth century are based on published articles and correspondence and the author's data files based on city directories, census reports, and Jewish organization rosters. After 1860, the figures are estimates. Twentieth-century data figures for the Jewish population depend, to some extent, on reports of the *American Jewish Year Book* (*AJYB*), published since 1900, which in the early years are not dependable. In the case of 1900, I have adjusted the *AJYB* figures down from 2000. In later years up to 1980, only Reno and Las Vegas population figures were reported. I have therefore adjusted these figures up slightly to reflect the rural and small-town populations.

Year	General	Jewish	Percentage of total
1860	6,857	27	<1
1870	42,491	420	<1
1880	62,266	900	<1.5
1890	45,761	450	<1
1900	42,335	350	<1
1910	81,875	400	<1
1920	77,407	480	<1
1930	91,058	375	<1
1940	110,247	408	<1
1950	160,083	1,100	<1
1960	285,278	2,720	<1
1970	488,738	3,780	<1
1980	800,493	15,300	<1
1990	1,201,833	54,400	4.5
2000	1,998,257	113,500[a]	5.7

[a] Metropolitan Las Vegas Jewry numbered about 100,000 in 2000, greater Reno/Incline/Carson City Jewry numbered about 13,000, and the Nevada's rural areas accounted for another 500.

century. Although depression was the moody hallmark of late-nineteenth- and early-twentieth-century Nevada, desperation was tempered by the diggings of hopeful prospectors, the initiatives to attract tourists to championship prizefighting and legal gambling, and the promise to triple the state's population with relocated eastern European Jewish farmers. All of these adventures were to be short-lived, except one.

Dashed Hopes, New Discoveries, and the Goldfield Bubble

1890-1920

When the state's economic prospects seemed so bleak, Ephraim Deinard of the Hebrew Agricultural Society of the United States unveiled a plan to triple Nevada's population with thousands of East European Jews.[1] In August 1897, Governor Reinhold Sadler delegated Republican Theodore R. Hofer and entrepreneur Morris Cohn (father of Felice) to take out an option on fifty-five hundred acres offered for about twelve thousand dollars by Sam Wymore in Wellington, forty-five miles south of Carson City. The Occidental Land Company, with Daniel Schwartz as recruiting agent and Harry Bell as president, became the corporate entity under whose umbrella the settlers were to purchase the land.

A Jewish Colony at Wellington, Nevada, 1897–1902

The collectivist arrangement was that everyone was to own a house and share ownership and production of the land. Prospective settlers were initially skeptical about the fertility of Nevada soil, but Cohn and Hofer assured them that the land had plenty of water and nine hundred acres were already under cultivation. Jacob Voorsanger, rabbi of Temple Emanu-El in San Francisco, knew Cohn and was skeptical of the deal from the start. Cohn's intent, Voorsanger believed, was "to do business, not practice philanthropy." The colonization plan was, he wrote, "a brainless movement," a "nefarious scheme," and "an attempt to boom Nevada lands at the expense of poor deluded Jewish artisans."[2] The *Jewish Progress* was critical for a different reason. Editor Abe Seeligsohn regarded such ventures as elitist and un-American and hoped to have "heard the last of this 'Jewish' colonist business."[3]

Undeterred by the warnings, sixty-two Jews in eighteen families set out as the first detachment to Nevada in November. Twelve other families were to follow shortly.[4] Their leader, Joseph Nudelman from Odessa, Russia, in 1881 had organized several immigrant families who homesteaded for a decade in Dakota Territory and later farmed with other colonists in central California.[5] The group included Joseph's single and married brothers with their families and married children's families—for example, Joseph's son Samuel and daughter Sophie who also had children. Surnames of others outside the extended Nudelman family were: Bloom, (Isaac) Cohn, Friedman, Katz, Kriner, Levitt, Lehrer, Lloyd (Loged), and Shapiro. Among them were a carpenter, cobbler, tailor, blacksmith, wagon maker, kosher butcher, ritual circumciser, and a cantor with a *sefer* Torah on loan from a San Francisco congregation.[6]

The Nevada press reacted like boosters cheering a team recruitment. The *Elko Independent*, three hundred miles away, predicted that if the Wellington project succeeded, it would "be the dawning of a new era for the state." The *Yerington Rustler* warmly greeted the "energetic and industrious looking Hebrews" and commended to them "the good will of the entire valley." The *Carson News* quoted Cohn as calling the colonists "tickled to death" and receiving numerous inquiries from outside the state for more settlement opportunities.[7]

The reality, however, was grim. Within three weeks, they learned that the property sale had soured. Rabbi Voorsanger had been correct. Cohn and Hofer planned to make a quick profit from a hefty brokerage fee to be borne by the colonists. Wymore intervened, bought out Cohn and Hofer, and negotiated directly with the colonists and their agents, Bell and Schwartz. On January 5, 1898, Wymore deeded to the Occidental Land Company fifty-three hundred acres for fourteen thousand dollars. Wymore was the company's treasurer. The colonists had become, in effect, renters with options to buy.[8] The several Nudelman families rented a small adobe building, and the other colonists packed into a twelve-room two-story house nearby.[9] Patriarch Joseph Nudelman arranged a lumber purchase, new houses arose, and additional colonists arrived to fill them. Wellington suddenly had more Jewish residents than any Nevada town except Reno.

Early on, a disagreement arose among the men about who was in charge. Although he had agreed to be part of a "cooperative arrangement" involving group decisions, Joseph Nudelman wanted to run the colony on more individualistic principles. "Knowing there would be no harmony," wrote the family historian, "he decided to leave." At the end of January 1898—just ten weeks after reaching Wellington—Nudelman rented the Haines ranch near Genoa. Joining him were his sons Sam and Maurice and two of his brothers, Israel and Samuel, with their families. His two brothers soon departed for San Francisco, but the Kriner, Bloom, and Friedman families took their places.[10] There were now two Jewish farming communities with Nudelmans working on both. One in Genoa grew potatoes, wheat, and hay on already cultivated land, and the other at Wellington scrambled to prepare fertile (but partly uncultivated) land and improve the water supply for spring planting.

There were enormous hardships. Under Wymore's direction, the able-bodied rearranged the flow of dammed water from the West Walker River, digging what the press described as a four hundred–foot tunnel through a hillside whose soil had been unable to support the ditch water. In the course of their digging, they burrowed through fifty feet of solid rock—all that remains today of the tunnel. "The colonists are poorly housed and some of them poorly clad," reported a local newspaper, "but we are told that they make no complaint and are looking forward hopefully to better homes . . . , productive fields and independence," and to more families joining the colony soon. Within a week, the *Genoa Weekly Courier* reported that the number of colony students at the Wellington School had jumped from twenty to thirty-six, and seventy people were living in one dwelling.[11]

Treachery Aborts the Dream

The colonists planted their first spring crop of alfalfa, which proved salable thanks to an abundant water supply. However, the summer of 1898 turned so dry that it was necessary to carry water by horse-drawn wagon from the river. Harry Bell and Daniel Schwarz mortgaged the forthcoming fall crop for fifteen hundred dollars, ostensibly to cover land-rental and operating costs. The two then absconded with the funds, a pair of the best horses, and colonist Lehrer's wagon. Repeated attempts to apprehend the scoundrels were unsuccessful, and the bank foreclosed on the Wellington colony's Occidental Land Company.[12]

In August, the colony's crop, cattle, and equipment went up for sale. Joseph Nudelmen intervened to have family cows considered personal property and exempted from the auction. On December 8, 1898—in temperatures recorded at below zero in the region—forty men, women, and children abandoned the Wellington colony. The San Francisco Hebrew Benevolent Society paid for their journey. Five families remained in the area, including the Joseph Nudelmans, Friedmans, Blooms, Shapiros, and Cohns. There is no evidence of any financial assistance to the settlers from the declining Carson City Jewish community.[13]

The press analyzed the reasons for failure. San Francisco's Isidor Choynski blamed it on the colony's officers. "This scoundrel Schwartz and . . . Harry Bell, whose real name is Ganef Stinkowicz [thieving son of a stinker], will be apprehended someday, and may the Lord have mercy on their black Russian hearts." The *American Israelite* in Cincinnati attributed the colony's demise to its having been organized "on so-called socialistic lines."[14]

In January 1899, Joseph Nudelman and Ephraim Friedman purchased from the Occidental Colony Company 5,300 acres subject to a mortgage in favor of Samuel Wymore for fourteen thousand dollars. The plan was to divide the property into 80-acre parcels and recruit settlers from as far away as Kansas. To help make it work, he farmed the spring crop from the Haines ranch in Genoa and sold his homestead in North Dakota.[15] The Wymores moved away, and the Nudelmans moved from the Genoa farm to the Wymore house.

Joseph gave parcels of land to his sons Maurice and Sam, another to his son-in-law, Jack Levitt, and still more to four other settlers, who were likely the Cohns, Blooms, Shapiros, and his brother Moishe, who had remained single and did not leave during the worst of times with his brothers. The Wellington Jewish agricultural venture was no longer a communal experiment. Those choosing to remain were now private entrepreneurs.[16]

By the spring of 1900, Joseph Nudelman owned 360 acres free and clear, with two irrigation ditches, a family house, two stables, a 10-acre apple orchard, alfalfa fields, horses, and cattle carrying a registered brand. The Nudelmans sold milk, apples, and other fresh fruit throughout the summer to miners in nearby Bodie, California, while Joseph's sons Maurice and Hyman were put to work rounding up wild horses into a huge corral from which they were sold to the U.S. Army.[17]

Setbacks and Destruction

The settlers were doing well when more adversity struck. In November 1900, Sam and Sophie Nudelman's five-year-old daughter fell into a vat of hot milk and had to be taken first to Carson City and then to San Francisco for treatment. They never returned to the Wellington ranch. Likewise, the Levitts left for Milwaukee. A large number of cattle in the area were lost to disease, but winter brought an end to the epidemic, and 1901 was a quiet year.[18] Prosperity, Joseph Nudelman hoped, was at hand.

The apple orchard in May 1902 was loaded with fruit, the Bodie mining camp was filled with hungry miners in need of fresh fruit, and the grain was in excellent condition. One midmorning, Joseph, Maurice, and Robert were irrigating the fields when dark clouds appeared over the mountains. The boys were directed to saddle up, ride to the dam, and close the ditch gates. En route, they encountered sheets of rain with heavy hail, and the ditches were filled with mud and rocks. When they reached home, they found the grain flattened though salvageable, but the marble-size hail had stripped the orchard. This event triggered Joseph Nudelman's decision to abandon his dream of being a rancher and farmer. He sold his entire spread and animals to neighboring rancher John O'Banion for about fifteen dollars per acre. In late fall, the family moved to Portland in time for Hanukkah, where most of Nudelman's extended family settled.[19]

Although the experiment in farming had ended for the Nudelmans, the Isaac Cohn family remained on adjacent land for about ten years. Daughter Becky taught at the Wellington elementary school for a year and later married prominent valley rancher Daniel C. "Cap" Simpson. Another daughter, Dora, went away to high school, and son Percy stayed on with his parents on their farm. The Cohns continued to cultivate and irrigate the orchard and to sell fruit to nearby ranchers.[20] The Nudelman property was later sold to the Saroni family, but old-timers referred to the dam and main ditch leading to the property as "Jew Dam" and "Jew Ditch" until recently. The old orchard is still sprouting.

The promised "tripling" of Nevada's population with eastern European Jews had turned out to be a fanciful dream. In 1900, the total state population had slumped further to 42,355, and ore production was at one of its lowest levels in forty years. Despite what appeared obvious to insiders, the *American Jewish Yearbook* increased its estimate of the Nevada Jewish population from 780 in 1878 to a whopping 2,500 in "about 1900." This figure was realistically reduced to 300 over the next decade.[21] In fact, there were more uncounted in the state's tiny hamlets. In Yerington, a few miles from Wellington, Mich Segal managed J. I. Cohn's Cash Store in 1896. He and his wife, Chasha, emigrated from Russia directly to Nevada in 1885 and settled in Mason Valley, where Mich worked as a mechanic and their four children attended school. By 1910, Hungarian-born Harry Samuels and his German-born wife, Hannah, were running Cohn's Cash Store. Small numbers of eastern European Jews continued to find employment in a state desperate for new blood.[22]

Industrial Removal Office

Nevada's experience with the Industrial Removal Office (IRO) exemplified both the state's need to attract immigrants and the lack of interest in resettling there. In one of several efforts to reduce the concentration of eastern European Jews in New York, a group of (German) Jewish Americans in the East created the Industrial Removal Office to relocate immigrants out of the New York region into towns across the nation. The class arrogance of German Jews toward Polish and Russian coreligionists died hard. The very name of the "removal" organization showed a mechanical insensitivity to the hardship of leaving family and neighbors. The references by some IRO officials to in-transit immigrants as "shipments" or "orders" carried an eerie connotation of the Holocaust, but the organizers were largely well intentioned and compassionate. From 1901 through 1913, the IRO transplanted more than seventy-one thousand underemployed Jews. Sixteen of them were sent to Nevada—the smallest contingent to any state.[23]

Morris Clink and Calman Aronson, proprietors of the Reno Tailors, made a request in February 1906 to the IRO for assistance and were told that the organization had no one to send. After waiting more than five months, Aronson struck on a plan to bring his brother-in-law's family to Reno. With elegant penmanship supporting his halting grammar and spelling, he wrote to IRO headquarters: "Gentlemen, I send you a letter a fue Months ago abouth getting me a Tailor till this time I did not got any one so I received a letter from my Brotherlaw his name is Sam Bluestein that he wold lik to get away from New York because he can make no leaving and as I need a Tailor I wold like to ask you to send him allso his Famelie to me I could give him a steady position. I allso right a letter to him and he will come to your Office and show my letter so you will know he is the right Man."[24] David Bressler, the IRO's general manager, responded promptly by postcard that he would give the matter his immediate attention. Aronson undiplomatically badgered him by return mail, stating that he could not understand his vagueness and demanded to know: "Are you going to send this family out to [me] or not? . . . Please telegraph me at my expense if you are going to send Bluestein out here at once or not & also why or what causes the delay. Thanking you for past favors." Bressler's response was a telegram requesting ninety dollars to defray transportation costs. Aronson wired the money, and the Bluesteins were "sent" to Reno in August 1906. Subsequent requests by Clink and Aronson for "tailors, pants makers and vest makers" met with regretful denials from the IRO.[25]

Reno, Carson City, and Ely were the destinations for fifteen other Jewish immigrants between 1905 and 1914. One, Mrs. N. Richmond, took the time to send a note penned exquisitely in Yiddish to thank the IRO for sending her to Ely. J. I. Star, proprietor of the Union Shoe Repairing Shop in Winnemucca, requested in Yiddish that the IRO send him a shoemaker he would pay five dollars per week plus board and lodging and a raise, if he is "worth more." But the IRO could find no one in New York available or willing to relocate in Winnemucca.[26]

The Industrial Removal Office liberated urban Jews from the New York ghetto and served the patrons to whom they were sent, but the overall effect on Nevada Jewry or the state's population decline was negligible. Had the IRO sent clusters of ten families to small towns such as Elko, Ely, or Winnemucca, they might have encouraged the development of worshiping communities, but the IRO's mission did not include a commitment to Jewish religion.

White Pine County's Merchant, Miner, Assemblyman, and Druggist

Henry, Ferdinand ("Fred"), and Solomon Hilp were brothers born in Cincinnati of Orthodox Jewish parents. They went to White Pine County, where they had general stores in mining towns from Hamilton and Treasure City to Ward (where Henry became postmaster in 1881), Mineral City, Taylor, and eventually to Ely. Sol's son, Lester, remembered his father as religiously "active." How he practiced his religion in White Pine County is a mystery, because there were rarely enough Jews in the small towns where he worked to have a minyan. His brothers were devout, however, and may have observed some rites together.[27] Henry left Nevada for San Francisco, where, at age forty, he married Emma Greenberg in 1887. Fred followed soon after. Henry's marriage to a Jewish woman and living in a city with a Jewish infrastructure brought some assurance of an observant progeny. The maintenance of Jewish religious traditions in eastern Nevada, however, would be a challenge.[28]

Sol Hilp bought out his brothers' business interests and, at the age of thirty-five, married his Virginia City–born wife, Emma, in 1887. She had been a student at Bishop Whittaker's Seminary for Girls in Reno and maintained an Episcopalian affiliation. Hilp soon opened a large general store in Ely, where he also served as a notary public and conveyancer of deeds. The economy in Ely and many White Pine towns was struggling at this time, and Hilp provided liberal credit to his customers.[29] He routinely received stock certificates in exchange for goods sold to miners who had more hope than cash. He eventually had interests in forty mines, most of which went belly-up before they showed any profit. In 1890, he had to file for bankruptcy. "Mr. Hilp deserves well of this community," the *White Pine News* editorialized. "He has carried it for more than two years, and if he could only get in one-half of his just dues, his San Francisco creditors should be appeased at short notice." Within a month, Hilp was back in business and even added a registered pharmacist to his Ely store. Nevada had its first Hilp's drugstore. Generosity with customers and a fifteen-year tenure in Ely likely contributed to his next success. He won election in 1892 as assemblyman on the People's Party ticket.[30] Declining prospects in Ely, however, led Sol to move his wife and three children to Reno.

Hilp's Reno years were filled mostly with part-time jobs and public-service contributions. But his devotion to Judaism had flagged. He never affiliated with Reno's Jewish organizations. Hilp's children were not raised in the Jewish faith, but those of his brother Henry and wife Emma Greenberg maintained their religion into modern times. He died of a lingering illness on October 6, 1917. His legacy to northern Nevada was an interest in pharmacy, which he passed to his son, who became a pharmacist and opened Hilp's Drug Store, a Reno landmark for more than a half century.[31]

Jews in Lincoln County

For Nevadans, the prosperity a Republican victory promised in 1900 was nowhere in sight, but news of a gold strike 150 miles south of Ely offered some hope. The area, named Delamar, was the state's most active mining area in that year. It was also the deadliest. The gold was embedded in a silica quartzite. The dust produced by the mining and milling allegedly caused the death by silicosis of "at least three hundred men." The Delamar Mining Company was in decline when prominent Utah Jews Simon and Jacob Bamberger gained control of the enterprise. The operation failed to meet its potential. The Bambergers suspended work in 1909. Simon Bamberger went on to become Utah's first and only Jewish governor, in 1917.[32] Eastern Nevada's mining prospects were at a low ebb; it had to wait for a wealthy Jewish family, the Guggenheims, to resurrect it from obscurity.

Hawthorne and the Rosenthals

Hundreds of miles west of Ely, the tiny hamlet of Hawthorne on the southern shore of Walker Lake was an oasis compared to much of the state. Peddler Jacob Levy of Carson City was one of the "traveling merchants" who serviced the area. Created in 1881, the town was the Carson and Colorado Railroad's southern terminus. Russian-born Davis Rosenthal came to the United States and settled in Hawthorne in 1882 with his Polish wife, Augusta Golden, and their four children. He purchased the Lake View Hotel and ran it until his death in 1901. Youngest son Benjamin was born in California and educated in the public schools of Hawthorne. He married Episcopalian Vesta M. Rice in 1892 and became proprietor of the Lake View Hotel upon his father's death. Rosenthal promoted local baseball and in 1904 was grand vice chancellor of the Pythian Grand Lodge of Nevada. Like many Nevadans, he was a Silverite politically. The Rosenthals were among the first to move from Hawthorne to Goldfield, when that place showed promise, and where he became one of its most colorful political figures.[33]

The "Southern Camps": First There Was Tonopah

Although mineral production had plummeted in the last quarter century, hundreds of prospectors continued to burrow into Nevada's mountains. One of them was hay farmer Jim Butler, generally credited with the 1900 discovery of a silver-gold deposit in an area he named "Tonopah." In local Paiute language, the name means "a place of little water." Actually, it was an area unburdened with any visual assets aboveground. It resembled a lunar landscape. Within a year, however, the population was nine hundred and rising.[34] The Tonopah discovery led to thousands of mining claims, which citizens of Reno and Carson City dubbed the "southern camps."

One unlikely resident was Josephine Sarah Marcus Earp. "Josie" was born to traditional German Jewish parents in New York in 1861. She had a streak of independence that eventually led her to Tombstone, Arizona. She fell in love with Wyatt Earp, whose first wife had died. A second marriage failed while he and Josie were having an affair. They never married, but they cohabited for nearly a half century. The two traveled widely in the West and ended up at Tonopah in 1902, and Wyatt's brother Virgil became a Goldfield lawman. Wyatt became part-owner of the Northern Saloon and served as an occasional deputy U.S. marshal. The Earps did not remain in the area for the boom years but moved to various other western towns in 1904. Although Wyatt apparently never adopted his wife's religion, he was buried next to her in the Jewish section at Hills of Eternity Cemetery near San Francisco.[35]

Also among the first arrivals at Tonopah in 1901 was Louis L. Blumenthal, whom President Grover Cleveland earlier had named U.S. inspector of customs and chairman of the Civil Service Commission in Alaska. Ten years later, he and his wife, Sadie Loeb of Portland, settled in Tonopah in the mercantile business. That first winter occasioned a severe pneumonia epidemic, killing fifty. The well-to-do family provided personal and material care that was never forgotten.[36] Blumenthal became cofounder and supreme chancellor of the Tonopah Knights of Pythias; a member of the Elks, Eagles, and Masons; and a three-term Nye County public administrator. In 1909, Blumenthal sold his store to focus on his expanding real estate and mining interests, including the vice presidency of the North Star Mining Company.[37]

Tonopah had a slow-growing but stable mineral production that helped it survive into modern times. For a short time, however, the town lived in the shade of a new gold strike, which many expected to secure Nevada's economic future.[38]

Goldfield

The Goldfield Mining District, thirty miles south of Tonopah, based its instant fame on a mineral find made by Harry Stimler and William Marsh in 1902. The town grew from about 50 residents in that year to 13,500 by 1907, had a ratio of men to women as high as 20 to 1, and was suddenly the state's largest and wildest town. Soon Tonopah and Goldfield were connected by a railroad that ran north to Carson City and Reno and later south to Bullfrog, Beatty, and the railhead of Las Vegas.[39] Nevada was again the new El Dorado. The rush to Goldfield included Jewish prospectors, merchants, lawyers, saloon keepers, gamblers, teamsters, newsmen, and speculators.

The Jewish Citizenry

Goldfield's Jewish population was modest even during the boom years. In 1907, an estimated 160 men, women, and children were of Jewish heritage. Samuel Cohn's Columbia Toggery and Frank Friedman and George Elkus's Gold Bug Store were two small specialty clothing shops. Max Meyer's giant dry-goods and clothing emporium was one of Goldfield's "three good stone buildings" amid a "sadly hideous aggregation of tents, huts, shacks, adobes

[and] frame homes." Woolf Bair's Furniture and Hardware business was among the city's largest, but it exerted no monopoly on the trade.⁴⁰

Occupations were even more diverse. Mine broker Harry Epstein and engineer Henry Eisenberg could have purchased real estate through Sarah Morris and cigars from Max Hecht, dined at Mrs. Leishman's deli or Sarah Bair's upscale restaurant, and bought their meat from John Lobenstein and their tea from the Nathan and Simon Nevada Tea Company. Selig Olcovich—recently from Carson City—worked for the *Goldfield News.* Jews with expendable income invested in mines. Additionally, there were Jewish and Gentile peddlers in such a booming environment.⁴¹

Woolf and Sarah Bair: Dogged Itinerants

Woolf Bair started as a peddler and ended up in a stable furniture business. He was born in Poland in 1850 and married to Sarah, born in England of German parentage, in 1882. They moved from the East Coast to Minnesota, Illinois, Wisconsin, Oregon, and Montana, where Woolf left his wife and four children to try his hand in the restaurant business in Sodaville, a railroad depot between Reno and Tonopah. It failed, as did his lodging house in Tonopah and a mining excursion to Bullfrog, on the edge of Death Valley. Sarah was left with the children in Montana, and, if one can read between the lines, she was unhappy with her husband, who could find no predictable income to keep them all together. He received a usurious loan at 50 percent per annum to start a used-goods store in Goldfield and was able to send ten dollars to Sarah in Butte. She wrote to say that with such stability, she was coming to join him. He wrote back: "Not yet, for God's sake. I am not ready for you." She is said to have replied that she was coming not for Yahweh's sake but for her own.⁴²

Upon arrival, Sarah reportedly wept at the poverty of her surroundings. She asked where Woolf's money had gone, and he painfully admitted to losing it prospecting. Sarah then opened a delicatessen, which she turned into an elegant, high-priced restaurant. She called her daughter in Portland to assist her and left the restaurant business after one year with ten thousand dollars, mining stock profits, and a residence thrown in for good measure. Meanwhile, Woolf built an addition to his store, which was now selling furniture and hardware. Two sons, Isaac "Isal" and Maurice, were his chief salesmen. A third son, Samuel, owned a paint shop. As a family, they succeeded while others failed in the mines or the stock market. *Goldfield Gossip* editor

Sydney Flower celebrated their success by praising the entire "race" of Jews for their "alert sense of enjoyment," "business insight," and commitment to home building and the honor they bestowed on their parents.[43]

Benjamin Rosenthal: Controversial Politician

Benjamin Rosenthal, recently from Hawthorne, was Goldfield's leading pharmacist and jeweler and, by 1905, a director of Goldfield's Chamber of Commerce. He had an easy smile, and for a while was the toast of the town. On February 19, 1907, Silver-Democrat governor John Sparks appointed him Esmeralda County commissioner. Rosenthal reluctantly accepted the post, but warmed to the job and became a leader in Democratic politics. Ten months after his appointment as commissioner, Governor Sparks asked Rosenthal to resign for flagrancy in the discharge of his duties. Rosenthal responded that he could not comply, claiming he had done his duty and a county grand jury had approved his actions.[44] Within ten weeks of being characterized as inspiring, public-spirited, and generous, Benjamin Rosenthal was being vilified in the partisan *Goldfield Chronicle.*

Esmeralda County was still reeling from two bank failures and residual effects of the 1907 national economic depression. The treasury was bankrupt. Rosenthal and Sheriff William Ingalls wanted to maintain a twenty-four-man deputy sheriff force, while reformers called for the numbers to be cut to one officer. Rosenthal borrowed money from the school fund to pay for the deputies and other county bills. The outcry was deafening from Republican partisans. As the 1908 general election drew near, the formerly "smiling Benny" and local first baseman was now being caricatured as domineering "Big Mitt" Rosenthal, with his hand in the school-fund cash drawer.[45]

Nor did their support for union labor during recent strike activities endear them to mine owners. The *Goldfield News* (the *Chronicle*'s Democratic counterpart) denounced the Mine Operators Association for their campaign against Rosenthal and other Democratic candidates supporting unions. Even Rosenthal's partisan critics never accused him of dishonesty or appropriating money for his own use.[46] Despite the *News*'s strong intervention, Ingalls and Rosenthal lost. Local magnate George Wingfield had been active in bringing radical unionism to its knees months before and may have been instrumental in the candidates' defeat.[47]

Rosenthal was still around two years later as proprietor of his drug and jewelry store and clerk of the Esmeralda County Court. He and former sheriff Ingalls were politically influential well into Goldfield's declining years. Rosenthal was also not above being clownish on the baseball field. "He was as funny as a crutch!" gushed Lena Hammond. "You'd forget about the ball game, and you'd watch him. . . . Everybody loved him."[48]

Speculation, Entertainment, and Other Distractions

The Goldfield Stock and Exchange Board allowed women to participate in the feverish pace of buying and selling—though they were restricted to the "ladies' corner." The exchange was ever in the shadow of the San Francisco Stock Exchange, but it reflected the same energy and occasional chaos. The press noted the Goldfield exchange's ethnic diversity of "bright and quick thinking Jews, the sturdy and slow going Germans, the restless and lucky Irish, who have acquired for themselves at least a temporary prosperity."[49]

In a town largely populated by single men, one of the leading distractions for lonely miners and merchants was the red-light district. A local constable estimated that at Goldfield's peak period, more than five hundred women plied their trade in the tenderloin. Max Meyer and Company dry-goods and clothing store was also in that neighborhood, and its first-class goods attracted the ladies.[50]

Meyer fell for one of the working girls from a brothel on Main Street. Known to his store employees as "Miss Raymond," she was a "most refined, good-looking girl," one of them said. "Rae," as she called herself, also loved Max and wanted him to marry her. Meyer said that he could not marry her. He may have had reservations about marrying a Gentile, he may have been committed to another woman elsewhere, or the relationship with Rae Raymond was more one-sided than she thought. Whatever the reason, she unexpectedly committed suicide—with a shot to her head. Her funeral procession included a local band accompanied by a large contingent of mourners. According to one version of the story, Meyer abruptly left Goldfield on the excuse of taking a vacation and promptly disappeared. Neither his brother nor his partner, Jacob Cohen, knew of his whereabouts. They sold out the Max Meyer and Company inventory and moved to San Francisco. The year was 1908, and Goldfield was building substantial structures and elegant homes as if the mineral resources would continue to break records.[51]

By 1907, Goldfield prided itself on its twenty restaurants and forty saloons. Earlier, the Nevada state legislature had passed statutes requiring "hurdy-gurdy" house proprietors to pay a license fee of five thousand dollars every three months.[52] The amount was usurious, and politics prevailed. In 1905, the legislature cut the fee to a modest five hundred dollars per quarter. The state made money, and so did owners like Jacob "Jake" Goodfriend, who led the entertainment business in both Tonopah and Goldfield. Goodfriend's commitment to his Jewish heritage is uncertain. In 1896, he wed Miss E. Sparks of Boise, and in 1906 he married for the second time to "Maggie."[53] Goodfriend had residences in both Goldfield and Tonopah, where he owned nickelodeon-style theaters—one of the few sources of legitimate amusement for children. He also had a hardware and general-provisions store, "Goodfriend and Liebes."

He was best known for catering to adult cravings for gambling, dancing, and hurdy-gurdy shows as well as serious eating and drinking. Jake's Dance Hall was one of Goldfield's most popular watering holes. Mannie Sylvia, Harry Flack, and Jake's relatives Louis and Eugene Goodfriend were responsible for music, entertainment, purchasing, personnel coordination, advertising, and promotion. Jake Goodfriend also owned a string of properties adjacent to the club that housed his managers, waiters, cooks, musicians, and showgirls.[54]

One unadvertised feature of the dance hall was the private "club" in the rear, which provided faro boxes and poker games. In response to Progressive and Prohibitionist pressures, the state legislature had made gambling illegal statewide, effective October 1, 1910. Goldfield historian Sally Zanjani observes that the illegal amusement remained widespread in private homes and clubs, and the "law gradually dissolved in a welter of exceptions, legalistic obfuscations, and indifferent enforcement."[55] This assessment of gambling activity remained accurate for the entire state until the law was reversed in 1931. Meanwhile, Jake's Dance Hall, as well as George Lowen and Nate Opperman's Palace Saloon and almost forty other entertainment establishments, provided apprenticeships for the future proprietors of legalized gaming.

Religion

From Goldfield's earliest days, Christian missionaries held services in private homes or hastily constructed tent churches. Late in 1904, the Ladies Aid Society raised money for a substantial hall, which became the temporary setting for religious services of all faiths. Goldfield's Jewish population was so small that it never organized the customary Hebrew Benevolent Society or purchased a dedicated cemetery. Nevertheless, Jews were invited to celebrate Yom Kippur and Rosh Hashanah at the multipurpose hall.[56] Some people may have been privately observant, but most appear to have been ethnic or secular Jews seeking a profitable investment away from someplace else called home. That may have been Nick Abelman's original intention, but he became a Nevada fixture over the next half century.

"Jew Nick" Abelman: Miner, Saloon Keeper, and Casino Operator

Nathan Abelman was born of Yiddish-speaking parents in 1876. They moved to Bessemer, Michigan, where he ran a saloon in 1897. Abelman came to Goldfield in 1906 and became co-owner of the Bon Ton Club, an unpretentious "sawdust" gambling parlor serving up beverages, entertainment, and legal gambling. He opened a garage, which leased traditional stagecoaches and cars to adventurous and wealthy speculators, such as Wingfield and George Nixon, who influenced Goldfield as bankers and owners of the major Goldfield Consolidated Mines Company.[57]

Abelman developed a friendship with Harry Stimler, who introduced him to the technicalities of spotting potential mining sites. Although he may have viewed such sites personally, he provided equipment or funds to skilled prospectors, who received partial ownership of the claim. To maintain title to a claim (usually about 20 acres), a claimant had to complete at least $100 worth of "location work" each year and file a "proof of labor" with the county. Eventually, a worked claim could be "patented"; then the claimant owned the land itself and not simply the mineral rights. In 1907 alone, Abelman, personally or with a partner, registered nineteen ore claims with Esmeralda County authorities—the last of which was a fully patented claim.[58]

As Goldfield declined, Abelman moved in 1913 to the more stable Tonopah, where he was called "Jew Nick"—a nickname from which he never shrank. The two largest entertainment centers in the area were the Big Casino and the nearby Tonopah Club—owned by George Wingfield, who asked Abelman to manage them. Over time, Abelman agreed, on the condition of having controlling interest, which occurred in 1916. James McKay and William Graham held minority positions in the properties. The arrangement linked all four men in mining and future gambling ventures in Reno.[59]

Tonopah became Abelman's center of operations for his mining activities. Over the next two decades, he appeared on hundreds of claims in Nye and Esmeralda Counties. Some of them were multiple and adjacent claims as large as 180 acres and so remote that neither the claimant nor the county recorder could determine the mining district where they were located. His mines included the much overused names of Ajax, Mohawk, and Opulence, as well the more impish Never Sweat no. 1 and two adjacent sites named Jew and Nick. Abelman's business association with Harry Stimler gave instant credibility to those claims that carried his name. The Gibralter North Extension, for example, which Abelman owned with Stimler and Jack Jordan, sold for $20,000, even in its declining years.[60]

Abelman was known to set up a saloon and gambling room with faro and poker anywhere his mining interests led him. His clubs in the southern camps never got him into trouble, indicating a working relationship with the sheriffs, who received the legal licensing fees. He also was affable. Desert prospector Herman Albert heard about the Landmarks claims owned by Abelman and McKay. The sale price was $150,000. Negotiating the purchase was a harrowing experience, wrote Albert, "especially as regarded the grasping, cold-blooded McKay." His impression of Abelman was "just the opposite—fine to do business with."[61]

At the age of forty-six, he was older than most Jews to take a wife. On October 14, 1921, he married Montana-born Audrey Marie Porter in Goldfield in the presence of Justice of the Peace J. R. Bradley. "May" Porter may have had Jewish lineage, but a rabbi never solemnized their wedding.[62] The two had no children. They lived in Tonopah for the next six years. Abelman had exploited the region's mining frenzy and the locals' need for entertainment for twenty-one years before becoming one of the pioneers of organized gambling in Reno. All of his businesses contained a high element of risk to both life and fortune. Some of his employees and partners had less-than-sterling reputations: McKay and Graham were later convicted of illegal activities in Reno and landed in federal prison. The powerful George Wingfield, who was known to display shadowy ethics, liked and trusted Abelman, who was learning to dance with wolves.

Goldfield Visitors: Felice Cohn, Bernard Baruch, and Jacob Herzig

Because of Goldfield's relatively short period of mineral production, almost everyone turned out to be a visitor. In 1905, a young woman came to Goldfield who did not match the profile of the husband seeker, stock speculator, or hurdy-gurdy girl. She immediately captured press attention not only because she was a woman but also because she had the credentials of a male-dominated profession. Felice Cohn had arrived to litigate competing land claims. Professional women were rare in mining towns, and Cohn turned heads for the six months she quartered in Goldfield.[63] Although by 1907 the town had several woman physicians and a dentist, a reporter felt compelled to ask Cohn why a woman would choose the legal profession. She confidently replied, "I have a great liking for the law and I find it entirely within a woman's powers." The reporter pressed the issue—apparently to assure his readers of attorney Cohn's femininity—and concluded: "There is nothing about her appearance or manner to suggest that she is at all masculine nor . . . that would suggest that she was other than a well reared woman of refined tastes."[64] Cohn had become an expert in mining and corporate law and soon was in great demand both within and outside Nevada.

Another Jew who made a well-publicized appearance in Goldfield was Bernard Baruch. His family was from Kempen in Poznán, and he was related by marriage to Carson City's pioneer Olcovich brothers.[65] Baruch loaned $1 million to U.S. Senator George Nixon and George Wingfield with an option to purchase a million shares of their Goldfield Consolidated Mines Company. The city was in the throes of labor disputes in 1907, and with the stock down, Baruch chose to cut his losses by accepting $160,000 in cash and $154,000 worth of Consolidated Mines. Baruch lost money in the deal, but his continuing presence in the local press spurred interest in Goldfield stocks. As he invested or sold, the market followed. Baruch and Wingfield had reputations as "market-makers," but not as stock manipulators.[66]

In this respect, they were in contrast to a Goldfield visitor whose stock frauds became legendary. Jacob Herzig was born in New York in 1870, the son of prominent Syracuse Jewish furrier Simon Herzig. At an early age, Jacob forged drafts against his father's company, for which he spent two years in the Elmira reformatory. Herzig continued to steal from the company and served four years for larceny at Sing Sing Prison. At this time, he decided to distance himself from his shady past by changing his name to George Graham Rice.[67]

Herzig/Rice was a seasoned con artist when he turned up in Goldfield in 1904. He set up an advertising bureau to drum up the sale of mining stock through his L. M. Sullivan Trust Company and cosponsorship of a championship fight between Joe Gans and Oscar "Battling" Nelson. He and his associates were parties to throwing the fight in favor of Gans, to the crowd's delight and to Herzig/Rice's financial gain in the betting. The September 1906 event brought him instant recognition and thousands to add to his list of sixty-five thousand "suckers." His success was short-lived: the Sullivan company failed in 1907; he fled his creditors and moved to Reno and then decided to promote an entire mining town.[68]

Rawhide

The Rawhide camp, located about sixty miles east of Carson City, boomed in 1907 and began its bust in 1908 before attracting almost ten thousand to its ninety saloons, Barbary Coast–type row of easy houses, and mines. To cover himself, Herzig/Rice advertised the Rawhide prospects under the name of his associate Nat C. Goodwin, a well-known actor and comedian, also of Jewish heritage.[69] Credulous out-of-state visitors picked up on the Goodwin publicity, but when Herzig/Rice's connection to Goodwin was exposed, the scam collapsed.[70]

Herzig/Rice never called Rawhide his home, and few other Jews did. Of the ten clothing stores, two may have been Jewish-owned: A. Frieman's Clothing Store and A. M. Rosenberg's High Grade Clothing Store. Sol Lasky and Jake Abrams stayed long enough only to manage a notice in the once-published city directory. Abram I. Rosenberg, thirty-four, a single man born in New York of Yiddish-speaking parents and serving as bookkeeper for a mining company, was the only identifiable Jewish remnant in Rawhide in 1910.[71]

The Guggenheims Revive Ely

The Ely economy—in a slump for years—was about to change. In 1900, two young miners burrowed into a mountain and produced a tunnel surrounded by copper ore, which attracted buyers, including Solomon Guggenheim and his brothers, who owned copper mines all over the world. The phenomenally wealthy family managed to buy out competitors, secure water sites, and build reduction facilities. In one year alone, their Nevada Consolidated Copper Company increased production tenfold to more than six million dollars in 1909. It was the state's most productive mining venture, and the nearby tiny city of Ely was back on the map.[72] Whereas the Guggenheims may have paid a token visit to their highly productive mining region, other Jews came to call it home.

Ely's New Jewish Population

During the first two decades of the century, Yiddish could be heard in the Ely area. Sam Bernstein owned the Leader Clothing Company in Ely and later moved to nearby McGill with his wife, Esther, and two children. He was elected to a statewide office in the Knights of Pythias. Ben and Sadie Bergman and two young children were among the several merchant families in the area. Max Fisher and Abe Wolfe were single clothing merchants, and Michael Levy toiled as a laborer in Consolidated's company town near McGill. Shoemaker J. I. Star, soon to move to Winnemucca, was a married man without his wife, as was pawnbroker David Stein. Sam Bloom appeared in the 1910 census as a "gambler." Morris and Esther Glick—from Cleveland and, later, Crested Butte, Colorado—were proprietors of a restaurant in McGill, where they lived for several years with their first three children. Their grandson Milton Glick became president of the University of Nevada at Reno in 2006.[73]

By the 1920s, all but a few families and a single man had left the area. Jacob A. Rosenberg was selling "gents' clothing" in Ely. Michael Cohen and his wife, Philipena, had moved from the Delamar camp, operated the Fair Store, and was elected White Pine County commissioner in 1914.[74] Ben and Sadie Bergman added a third daughter to their family in 1920. Four years later, three armed men entered the Bergman Clothing Company store and emptied the cash register. When Ben attempted to grab a gun from behind the counter, the robbers killed him. Ely merchants posted a five hundred–dollar reward for information leading to the arrest of the murderers, who were captured and sentenced to life in prison in 1926 but paroled nine years later.[75] Descendants of the Bergmans remember that Ben and Sadie did not celebrate Christmas—an indication of their ties to Jewish tradition in a place without a worshiping Jewish community. One of Sadie and Ben Bergman's daughters, Bernice, married an observant Jew in Los Angeles, and Sadie became president of the Hollywood branch of Hadassah.[76]

The Scoundrel Returns

Ely's copper mines were flourishing under Guggenheim control when George Graham Herzig/Rice came up with yet another plan as manager of publicity and promotions for the New York–based B. H. Scheftels and Company in 1909. Ely Central Copper Company stock had been sliding after 1906, but it suddenly surged—thanks to a price manipulation by Herzig/Rice. The gullible public bought up shares of the mine—further inflating the price. It was a "New Scheme to Hook Suckers," wrote the *Engineering and Mining Journal.*[77] The stocks took a nosedive, and the *White Pine News* reported that "Scheftels & Co Are Closed Up." Local police had raided the company on orders from the U.S. Department of Justice and arrested Herzig/Rice on charges of mail fraud. He eventually pleaded guilty. Herzig/Rice went to federal prison, where he wrote an unapologetic account, "My Adventures with Your Money."

In 1920, he returned to Reno to promote the Broken Hills Silver Corporation, and in less than a year his Reno office equipment was attached to pay creditors. Over the next few years he was active in Weepah, Nevada, but in 1928 he was convicted of stock fraud and sentenced to four years in the Atlanta penitentiary. As one mining newspaper wrote: "You can't keep a good swindler down when there is a public that needs trimming."[78] Herzig/Rice was arguably the most colorful, imaginative, and unscrupulous exploiter of Nevada's resources. Newspapers that once had supported him now characterized the man as "the most malign influence of the world of Get-Rich-Quick Finance" and a "master necromancer in the art of inducing small investors to take long chances."[79] None of the negative reports ever mentioned Herzig/Rice's Jewish lineage.

Building a Tourist Economy and a Permanent Synagogue

Before and after the Goldfield excitement, a central issue facing Nevada was diversifying its economy. Exploiting Nevada's vast unsettled land agriculturally required better management of water resources. Until then, other expedients were necessary. Jewish state senator Herman Freudenthal introduced the first substantive bill of the 1903 legislative session, calling for an appropriation to send a display of Nevada products to an exposition in St. Louis. The bill received widespread support in the legislature but had little economic impact. Others looked to attract outsiders to enjoy pastimes and benefits illegal elsewhere. One of these was prizefighting at a time when boxing at the national level was becoming a Jewish sport.[1]

Promotions of Prizefighting

Al Livingston, one of Genoa's first settlers, was an architect of a tourism approach to financial exigency. Livingston twice ran afoul of the law in his capacities as a public official and barkeeper, but neither incident affected his popularity.[2] A founding member and officer of several fraternal organizations and past president of the city's B'nai B'rith lodge, he married May Novitzky after the death of his first wife and raised three daughters. He may have had the latter in mind when he installed a soda fountain at his Ozark Saloon to treat children accompanying parents who were there for adult beverages.[3] As state revenues declined, Livingston became active in promoting events to attract visitors and their capital.

Boxing had long been a favorite male spectator sport in Nevada's saloons and even in the Virginia City Opera House. Livingston organized "The Fight of the Century" in 1897 between heavyweight champion "Gentleman Jim" Corbett and Bob Fitzsimmons. Prizefights were illegal in the United States, but the Nevada legislature—desperate for revenue—pragmatically approved a statute licensing previously forbidden "glove contests." Accordingly, the sheriff of a county could issue such a license for the sum of one thousand dollars, of which 10 percent went to the county and the rest to the state. The prizefighting statute was the top priority and emerged as the first bill to be signed into law. The legislation included conditions that eased its swift passage. Whereas early local contests in Virginia City and Carson City were often fought with skintight two-ounce gloves or bare fists, the legislature required four-ounce gloves, a physical examination of the fighters, and a ban of alcohol. Livingston provided complimentary ringside tickets to media representatives, whose coverage appeared in newspapers all over the nation. The event under-filled an eighteen thousand–seat arena specially constructed at the Carson Race Track. It was Nevada's first venture into economic diversification through tourism, and it showed promise.[4]

Former lawbreaker Livingston vaulted into the role of state lawmaker. In 1899, he began the first of two terms in the state senate as a Silverite. He sponsored ten bills and introduced two concurrent resolutions. One of his successful bills provided for reclamation of water used for irrigation purposes. State resources, however, were meager. A wholesale solution to the state's water shortage had to await federal subsidization. Livingston's resolution to support the direct election of U.S. senators was unbeatable, coming as it did during a session in which incumbent Senator William Stewart defeated Representative Francis Newlands in a hard-fought, corrupt campaign. Newlands had retained his congressional seat of ten years and was addressing the water concerns of Nevadans, like Livingston, at the national level. Newlands's leadership in establishing a national water-reclamation service led to his cosponsorship of what came to be called the Newlands Reclamation Act of 1902.[5]

In 1903, the legislature's actions reflected the state's desperate need for revenue and the desire to monopolize boxing events in Nevada by discouraging their promotion elsewhere. A new law required those promoting boxing *outside* the state to pay for a license amounting to one thousand dollars per month plus seventy-five dollars per month for engaging in out-of-state activity. Such were the first stumbling efforts of state leaders to create new revenue sources by attracting visitors for entertainment banned elsewhere. One way in which Nevada and a few other states sought to control boxing was to require a licensed athletic club. In 1905, Livingston, considered "Nevada's premier prize fight promoter," was elected first president of the Reno Athletic Club, hastily organized to sponsor a contest between Marvin Hart and Jack Root, who were top contenders for the heavyweight title when Jim Jeffries retired after defeating Fitzsimmons. The match drew four thousand spectators and was, by all accounts, a tourist-producing success.[6] Livingston died in 1908, but his promotional legacy lived.

Another opportunity for Nevada to sponsor a major boxing event came in 1910, when the governor of California canceled a contest between two of the world's best-known boxers: black heavyweight champion Jack Johnson and Jim Jeffries. The "Great White Hope," as Jeffries was dubbed, had come out of retirement with his Jewish manager, Sam Berger, the former Olympic heavyweight champion in 1904. Although some local religious reformers railed against the forthcoming match as a disgrace that would bring the dregs of society to Reno, the mayor and governor assured the fight promoters that they would not be pressured into canceling the contest. Johnson won the fifteen-round event, and Jeffries's vaunted comeback failed.[7]

Nick Abelman used prizefighting to draw patrons to the Tonopah Club in 1915. The match pitted Swede Sundberg and Jack Dempsey, locally known as "Kid Blackie." Abelman recalled that Dempsey knocked Sundberg down nine times but punched himself out. Sundberg then proceeded to kick Dempsey all over the ring and earned a draw. Each man received $130 for his trouble. Dempsey was "broke and hungry," Abelman reported, but the boxer sent the entire purse to his mother in Salt Lake. A dozen years later, Dempsey was drawing million-dollar gates. Abelman and Dempsey remained friendly, especially after Abelman moved to Reno.[8] Prizefighting as a tourist attraction never became a significant revenue source until sponsored by Las Vegas casinos late in the twentieth century.

Horse Racing

Most Jews and Gentiles were simply spectators in the rich man's sport of horse racing. However, merchants invariably profited from an event that brought new people and money into town. Horse racing proved to be a tourist attraction and a modest fifty thousand–dollar source of state revenue in 1920.[9] Another twenty years passed before Jews were involved in the promotional wagering on horse races, using wire services to bring results to the bettors. Meyer Lansky was running illegal sports-book operations in various parts of the United States in the 1930s, and it was an obvious option to consider doing business in Nevada, where all-out gambling became legal.

Table Gambling: Illegal in Nevada but Widespread

Flying in the face of the most popular form of entertainment in Nevada mining camps, the territorial and state legislatures had long earlier declared gambling illegal. Despite the bans Nevadans neither observed nor enforced the law, and gambling flourished throughout the state. Governor Henry G. Blasdel condemned it as an "intolerable and inexcusable vice" that sapped the foundation of morality, but in 1869 the legislature overwhelmingly overrode his predictable veto. What the Methodist governor described as the "root of all evils" and a crime throughout the Union was now legal in Nevada. Counties here and there attempted to restrict the hours or the area in which gambling could be conducted and exacted a licensing fee. But gambling was then a pastime and not an industry. The thought of taxing it was as unthinkable as imposing a levy on picnics or baseball games.

Early in the twentieth century, Reno women's groups, Prohibitionists, and Progressives rallied the state's latent reform sentiments, which had produced such changes as direct election of U.S. senators. The legislature responded with a bill to outlaw gambling effective October 1, 1910, leaving plenty of time for people attending the summer's big fights to gamble with abandon. The next biennial legislature succumbed to pressure from gamblers to legalize poker and certain other card games, but this law was reversed in 1913.

In the next biennial session, the forces of economic diversification introduced bills to reduce the waiting period for divorces, reinstate legal gambling along with the newfangled nickel slot machines, and revise a restrictive racetrack betting law. Former senator Herman Freudenthal wrote urgently that changes in the law were a "return to formal disgraceful conditions in this State [and] would be a blot upon the good name of the State and inconsistent with the higher purposes of morality and decency."[10] His action did not deter the opportunistic and revenue-hungry legislature from legalizing card games with alternating deals and allowing pari-mutuel betting where the race was being held. Meanwhile, other forms of illegal gambling continued to thrive in most Nevada towns. It remained widespread in private homes and in private backroom "clubs" whose membership was open to anyone paying the token "dues" at the door. Unlike Freudenthal, most Nevada Jews came to terms with gambling as a moral issue and profited from it. The only known Jew owning gambling clubs in these upside-down days was Nick Abelman in the southern camps.

Legalized Gambling and a Lower Residency
Requirement for Divorce, 1931

Nevadans were aware of widespread illegal gambling and the collateral lack of law enforcement. Many favored a legal taxation of the widespread amusement, while others—Christian spokespersons and women's groups—predictably opposed gambling as immoral.[11] Legislators in 1931 were loath to be the first to introduce an enabling bill, but once on the floor it passed easily.

Reno and Las Vegas clubs were ready for the new legislation. They expanded their hitherto illegal operations, which drew thousands of Californians by rail and motorcar. The state placed gambling controls squarely on local authorities and in return received one-quarter of the revenues. The opportunities for out-of-state syndicates to move in and control gambling was acknowledged but not prevented. Informed that Al Capone might be interested in relocating to Nevada, Reno's chief of police allegedly responded with Old West arrogance: "Al Capone is welcome in Reno as long as he behaves himself."[12] Such bravado proved ominous.

Jewish law permitted divorce, and most local Jews had no quarrel with changes in Nevada's six-month residency requirement. Other states had tightened residency restrictions, but Nevada's law had remained unchanged and attracted future divorcées. Divorce became a Reno "industry."[13] When several adjacent states lowered their residency requirements to six months, the Nevada legislature countered in 1927 with a law reducing the period to three months. Divorce was big business—despite the unsavory publicity it generated. It took little ingenuity to adjust the requirement even lower to six weeks in 1931, and the seeming "flood" of divorcées in the mid-1920s became a torrent in the thirties. Between 1931 and 1936, Nevada courts granted more than twenty-three thousand divorces—most in Reno—for an estimated five million dollars per year.[14]

Attorney Felice Cohn criticized the reduction in residency for reasons related to economics and morality. She opposed it because it cheapened the process. The three-month requirement, she said, would bring a better class of divorce seeker to the state, who would "pay better attorney fees, and spend more money with the merchants of Reno, and the inn-keepers." Cohn had handled more than fifteen hundred divorce cases by 1933 and attributed the large number of divorces nationwide to quarrels over money. A longer waiting period presumably allowed more time for reconciliation.

Cohn also viewed the lack of uniform divorce laws among the states as immoral. New York in 1933 had a single ground for divorce (infidelity), South Carolina none at all, and in Nevada grounds included desertion, cruelty, non-support, impotence, adultery, drunkenness, and imprisonment. This, said Cohn, led to the "absurdity of a person being single in one State, married in another, and a bigamist in still another, all at one and the same time." Such conditions, she said, "make for immorality and often directly promote, rather than retard, the number of divorces."[15]

Out-of-state barristers filed their credentials in Nevada, but local attorneys had an early edge on business. They could more easily make arrangements for a prospective client—from being met at the train station and squired to the law office to sociable escorts for a night on the town. Occasionally, a lawyer offered his house to a celebrity seeking greater privacy. Sam Platt owned a residence at Elk Point on Lake Tahoe, which he made available to Elliott Roosevelt and other clients. The law firm of Platt and John S. Sinai allegedly had a "lock" on the well-heeled East Coast divorce seekers.[16]

Friendships commonly developed between soon-to-be-single couples, and a marriage often followed the divorce proceedings. In some instances, the lawyer-client relationship moved from business to pleasure. In mid-1917, Helen Marks Faith, a Roman Catholic, traveled to Reno for a divorce. Platt was her lawyer. On January 30, 1918, they married in Carson City. Helen was athletic, gregarious, and deeply protective of her new husband. On at least one occasion, old-line Republican Platt's political differences with Progressive George Springmeyer ended in a fistfight at a downtown Reno café. Platt was bruised and bloodied in the mismatch. A trophy-winning golfer in Scarsdale, New York, Helen was accused on several occasions of driving her golf ball into Springmeyer's foursome at the local country club. Her attempt to run over Springmeyer with her golf cart resulted in a warning to Platt, ending further trouble. The two divorced in 1933, Helen died in 1934, and Sam remarried in 1936, to another Catholic woman, Antoinette L'Ecuyer, daughter of a Reno lumberman. Platt's marriages did not prevent him from formal affiliation with the B'nai B'rith lodge or being the Reno contact person for donations to the Jewish Anti-Defamation League.[17]

Nevada's First Permanent Synagogue

Reno's B'nai B'rith leadership's most enduring legacy was the 1914 formation of Congregation Temple Emanu-El. In lieu of a permanent synagogue, services were held variously at Beebe Hall, Labor Hall, Masonic Hall, and the Century Club. These temporary locations also served as meeting rooms for Jewish organizations and a Sabbath school reorganized in 1918. The congregation also had a steady cantor in Max Gottlieb from 1917 to 1924. The Jewish community in the 1920s was relatively prosperous, and a few of them donated a thirty-by-seventy-foot lot at 426 West Street for the building site. Attorney Sinai contributed architectural plans, while others divided up the city among themselves, seeking support for the project from both Jews and Gentiles.[18]

The fund drive officially began on February 27, 1921, with a dinner at the Century Club. More than 175 guests attended. Music, dancing, encouraging speeches from California rabbis, and local Fred Phillips congratulated Reno Jews on the end of their "wandering." Platt's speech addressed Judaism's ideals in light of other religions. Pledges as high as one thousand dollars from merchant Benjamin Lipschutz took no luster from the five-dollar promises from children.

Sol Jacobs, chairman of the building committee, turned the first spade of dirt on May 3, 1921. Its cornerstone was set two weeks later, and the first services were High Holidays in October. Platt had handled many of the temple's zoning and paralegal issues and was called to speak on Yom Kippur. The edifice was completed in December at a total cost of thirty-five thousand dollars, of which twenty-five thousand was in hand, with the remainder guaranteed by notes from local Jewish merchants. The building never had a mortgage. It was dedicated in time for 200 people to celebrate the 1922 High Holidays.[19]

The finished Temple Emanu-El was of tapestry baked-brick construction and comprised two stories. Over the main entrance arch, a large circular window depicted the Star of David and the Ten Commandments inscribed in Hebrew. The facility's ground floor was divided into small meeting rooms, a kitchen, and a larger area that could serve for banquets or religious seders. The upstairs portion included a small room for Sabbath school, with the remainder for services. The synagogue was the pride of its congregation and became the focus of Jewish social and religious life. Until a resident rabbi could be hired, however, Hebrew-literate members of the congregation and Cantor Gottlieb conducted Sabbath services. Rabbis from San Francisco, Oakland, and Sacramento routinely visited to lead High Holiday events until 1931, when the temple welcomed its first permanent rabbi.[20]

Reno's First Rabbi and Kosher Boardinghouses

Orthodox rabbi Hirsh Abraham Opoczynski accepted a call from Temple Emanu-El to serve as rabbi for the salary of one hundred dollars per month. Born in 1897 and educated in his native Poland, he joined a Zionist youth group there and settled in Palestine. After ordination in 1923 and certification as a *shochet* and *sofer* (scribe), he served as rabbi at a Tel-Aviv synagogue for more than three years. Opoczynski encountered persistent difficulty obtaining a visa to the United States, but written assurances to the consul general at Tel Aviv that he had a job broke the bureaucratic logjam. Soon after arriving in San Francisco in 1931, he altered the spelling of his surname to Oppochinsky and changed "Hirsh" to "Harry."[21] His selection as rabbi resulted in part from his marriage to Pearl Schmerlowski, who was related to temple president Sol Jacobs.

Together with their young son, Haskell, the Oppochinskys resided in a home one block south of the temple at 330 West Street. Harry's pittance of a salary demanded that the couple create additional sources of income. Reno's divorce trade provided the opportunity. They took into their home Jewish boarders for their six-week residency. The demand for Jewish ambiance was great enough to warrant purchase of another residence at 316 South Center Street, a short distance from the courthouse.

The Orthodox leanings of some Temple Emanu-El members as well as visitors desiring "ethnic" food presented another business opportunity. Louis Vinitz announced the grand opening of Reno's first kosher restaurant at 358 North Virginia Street on July 3, 1931. Although the restaurant had a short life of one year, the demand for kosher food continued. Pearl Oppochinsky already maintained a kosher household, and it was an easy step to provide kosher meals to her boarders and the public. Their second son, Mervin, clearly recalled one of the owners of Parker Brothers Western Store stopping by from time to time for a one-dollar kosher meal.[22]

The Oppochinskys became naturalized citizens and changed their name to Tarlow—Harry's mother's maiden name. Tarlow was an Orthodox Jew called to serve a people with no uniform or formal Jewish affiliation. His was a polyglot congregation, bound loosely by a synagogue and a common Jewish heritage. Its members included those who liked to think of themselves as Orthodox, anti-Zionists who sided with the old Reform movement, Zionists like Tarlow, those embracing Solomon Schechter's new Conservative movement, and pro forma members of the congregation who simply paid annual dues. From the start, regular temple Sabbath worship generated little interest, and the Sabbath school begun in 1918 had long since closed. Tarlow led Sabbath services whenever a minyan gathered and prepared young men for their bar mitzvah. Stern and deeply committed, Tarlow had difficulty inspiring an observant following. His son Mervin stated that even he resisted his father's attempts to prepare him for bar mitzvah. Tarlow succeeded in imbuing his son with the ideals of Judaism, but the boy's Hebrew barely passed muster.[23]

Pearl Tarlow was active in the temple Sisterhood, the women's arm of B'nai B'rith, and the local chapter of Hadassah—a support organization for Palestinian Jews. These groups used the temple for regular meetings and open social events. The men's B'nai B'rith organization also met regularly on the first and third Thursdays at the temple. Minutes kept by Abe Melner beginning in 1933 reflected a fairly mundane set of meetings, often family affairs with amateur-night events and door prizes to encourage attendance. In the late thirties, the men of B'nai B'rith began discussing political affairs. In October 1939, for example, they were on record questioning the Neutrality Act, which prevented U.S. involvement against Germany. As the war in Europe raged, the organization sponsored essay contests on the conflict.[24]

All of these otherwise healthy activities appeared to be a substitute for regular Sabbath services. However, Reno Jews rallied for marriages and funerals. And Tarlow was regularly in the news representing the Jewish community at interfaith events as well as being involved in civic benefits and national Jewish affairs.[25] The congregation's disinclination to gather for regular Sabbath services was just one symptom of the group's religious diversity. The desire for a more liberal approach to Judaism motivated sixteen members to break away and form a new congregation. It was 1940, the country was on the brink of war, and Temple Emanu-El had to cope with its first schism.

A Reform Rebellion: Temple Beth Or

Joseph Gumbiner came to Reno about 1938 from Selma, Alabama, to obtain a divorce. While in Reno, he met and married a Jewish divorcée from Los Angeles. The couple opened the Gumbiner Book Store and Rental Library at 3 North Virginia Street.[26] Gumbiner affiliated himself with Temple Emanu-El, although no references to him as a rabbi appeared until October 9, 1941, when, while giving a book review, he made public his ordination. A small group of self-styled "younger Jews" from Temple Emanu-El insisted on meeting with him "in the back of his book store." This splinter group called itself the Nevada Association for Reform Judaism and wrote a constitution.[27] Its letterhead in February 1940 read: Joseph H. Gumbiner, rabbi; Abe Melner, president; Bert Goldwater, secretary; and Maurice Berman, treasurer. Attorney Goldwater formally notified the county authorities that the group existed with a Sunday school and adult study group. It soon formally joined Reform's near century-old Union of American Hebrew Congregations, the only such affiliation since Eureka's in 1876.[28] Gumbiner kept meeting with the B'nai B'rith lodge members in Temple Emanu-El while serving as rabbi for the new Beth Or congregation. The situation could not have been more awkward for Rabbi Tarlow.

Like the early members of Temple Emanu-El, Temple Beth Or's Reform group met in rented space. The founding families leased their first worship site at a dance school on Reno's south side. Members of the breakaway group maintained their affiliation with the B'nai B'rith and its women's auxiliary, occasioning conversations across congregational lines. Families at Temple Emanu-El debated whether to join the dissidents or remain in a congregation headed by an Orthodox rabbi. Some regarded those who chose to depart as traitors. In a few months, the new congregation had swelled and moved to temporary quarters in the Knights of Pythias Hall.[29] But those still affiliated with Temple Emanu-El were not all committed to Orthodoxy. The Conservative movement was then the fastest-growing branch of American Judaism, and some congregants were whispering about abandoning Orthodoxy for Conservativism.

The small salary provided to Beth Or's Rabbi Gumbiner was insufficient to keep him from being lured in 1942 to a Tucson congregation. Beth Or's trustees hired German refugee Rabbi Hans J. Zucker, who served the group from 1942 to 1945. His background placed him in high demand as a speaker on war issues and at patriotic rallies. In the meantime, he enlarged on Gumbiner's successes with a trained choir and Sabbath school. One of the rare high points of cooperation between the two congregations was a Passover seder service that Rabbis Zucker and Tarlow conducted in 1943 at Temple Emanu-El for members of the armed services. Temple Emanu-El, on its own, hosted university students and troops from nearby military bases for High Holiday services.[30]

Zucker resigned late in 1945 to lead a larger congregation in California.[31] Beth Or's secretary, attorney Norman H. Samuelson, penned an urgent request to Hebrew Union College in Cincinnati, whose president, Julian Morgenstern, requested more information. By return mail, Samuelson reported thirty-nine members, twenty-four of them dues-paying, and anticipated that proper spiritual leadership would increase this number by 50 percent. The congregation, he advised, wanted a young man in his late twenties or early thirties, preferably unmarried, because the proposed salary of eighteen to twenty-four hundred dollars would likely not attract a married man. Samuelson was considerably out of touch with the postwar job market. Morgenstern responded that newly ordained rabbis commanded annual compensation between thirty-six and forty-two hundred dollars. Beth Or's proposed salary, he wrote, "would hardly suffice, even for an unmarried rabbi," and he urged the Reno congregation to provide a more realistic and attractive salary or accept a retired rabbi.

An exchange of offers of older personnel and haggling over salary followed. Samuelson insisted that the congregation was set only on having a dynamic young rabbi who could attract half of the unaffiliated Jewish population and secure eight or ten families from Temple Emanu-El. He added that a new Reform rabbi who was "progressive and has a pleasing personality could supplement his income" from among the Jewish portion of 18,500 marriages performed each year in Reno.[32]

Morgenstern responded with understanding, graciousness, and a dose of reality for Beth Or's exaggerated expectations. He offered yet another candidate who, like Zucker, was a German refugee and ominously concluded that Beth Or would be making a grave mistake not to accept him. Beth Or's board of trustees mulled over the recommendation and concluded that it was incapable of securing "the type of rabbi desired at a salary within its means." Samuelson informed Morgenstern that Reno's Beth Or board had dissolved the congregation as of March 29, 1946. Stunned and regretful, the seminary president urged the trustees to consider temporary part-time student rabbis. Samuelson responded gratefully but noted that the congregation had thoroughly discussed the matter. Congregation Beth Or was defunct, and the future affiliation of its members was in doubt.[33]

Reno Businessmen and Gamblers and Their Religious Affiliations—or Not

The occupations of Reno Jews up to 1940 were related mostly to clothing and dry goods, general merchandise, and junk dealing. However, the number of lawyers such as Platt, Goldwater, Sinai, Cohn, and Samuelson and physicians such as Emmanual Berger and Samuel Blatt was on the rise with other white-collar businessmen, and their relationships to Judaism differed.

Sam Frank, Nevada's First Jewish Mayor

California-born Sam Frank came to Reno in 1903 at age thirty. He was in the wholesale liquor business for seventeen years prior to Prohibition. In 1912, Frank won his first election to the Reno City Council—a position he held almost continuously for twenty-three years. Reno's B'nai B'rith initiated Frank in 1914 but suspended him two years later for reasons unknown—possibly his marriage to Gentile Jeannette Ott—while his brother Benjamin remained a member. In 1919, the two brothers co-owned a soft-drink manufacturing company that Ben managed, while Sam supervised several livestock ranches in Lander and Churchill Counties east of Reno. Sam was uninvolved in the dedication and building of Temple Emanu-El and appeared—unlike Benjamin—to have terminated any formal religious affiliation.[34] In 1925, Sam partnered with Ben Barbash to build Reno's largest automotive establishment, the Grand Central Garage, and later the contiguous service station. The Franks circulated in Reno society, which included Jews and Gentiles. Before Jeanette died from pneumonia in November 1931, the couple were guests at the Abelmans' South Lake Tahoe property.

When Mayor Edwin E. Roberts died on December 11, 1933, the city council named Frank acting mayor—a position he had held several times before. Frank probably could not have been accorded again the mayoralty had he not concurred with the gambling status quo and received George Wingfield's blessing. He served in that capacity for two years, while also directing and managing Reno's municipal airport. Although he was reported to have been a popular leader, Frank lost the election for mayor in 1935 to John A. Cooper. Frank died of a heart attack on June 26, 1937. His cremated remains were interred at Cypress Lawn Cemetery in San Francisco.[35] His brother Ben died in 1950; he and his family were buried traditionally in Reno Hebrew Cemetery.

Abe Zetooney: Clothier and Builder of the El Cortez

A native of Damascus, Syria, Abe Zetooney came to Reno in 1920 at age twenty-seven. He opened the Silk and Linen Shop (later the Vogue). Business was brisk, and he managed a down payment to build the art-deco Hotel El Cortez—at seven stories, Reno's largest building—across from the Catholic

Cathedral. The El Cortez also was upscale, charging rates three times those of nearby hotels. Just in time for the influx of divorce seekers and the legalization of wide-open gambling in 1931, the El Cortez also was the only major hotel with its own casino. Zetooney leased the entire property to the local Bulasky brothers, Joseph, Solomon, and Louis, which Zetooney parlayed into a fortune as a real estate broker. He and his wife, Rae, were active in civic affairs and an integral part of the Temple Emanu-El congregation. When he died in 1949, he left an estate well in excess of one million dollars, which was distributed to his wife and several dozen relatives around the world. He and his family were buried in Reno Hebrew Cemetery.[36]

Nathan Bula(w)sky: From Peddler to Investor

The Bulasky brothers had been in Reno for several years before wide-open gambling. Their father, Nathan (spelling his name Bulawsky), came penniless to Reno from Russia in 1914. He started in the junk and waste business as a peddler, then opened a scrap-metal yard and shipped tons of metal to San Francisco. Bulawsky also invested in real estate, including the future site of Harolds Club. He and his wife were charter members of Reno's Temple Emanu-El in 1921. They had four children, and all three boys became lawyers before becoming involved in Reno casinos and changing their name to Bulasky.

Upon taking over the El Cortez, the Bulasky brothers added more rooms and a small showroom called the Trocadero. Among the entertainers who played there were Sophie Tucker, Victor Borge, and Chico Marx. They also assumed control of the Waldorf Club in 1938. Although their father was an active and observant Jew, the Bulasky sons limited their involvement to temple and cemetery financial support, although Joseph was an officer in Reno's last B'nai B'rith lodge. Even after they left Reno, Temple Emanu-El activist Harriet Abelman Wolfe was able to squeeze an annual donation from them and from her uncle Nick.[37]

"Jew Nick" Abelman: The Quiet Gambler

George Wingfield supposedly invited Nick Abelman to Reno to run some of his properties. What they might have been is unclear, for Wingfield had his fingers in many pots.[38] One of Wingfield's problems was the tarnished reputations of his friends and associates William Graham and James McKay, both locally regarded as shady characters or petty gangsters and openly involved in running illegal speakeasies and the notorious cribs near the center of town. Wingfield's biographer implies that her subject may have owned the land on which some of the nefarious activities occurred, but he was not directly involved in illegal gaming operations. He was, however, an architect of legislation to legalize table gambling in 1931, and, says his biographer, "in the public mind, George Wingfield was culpable simply by association with Jimmy McKay."[39] Wingfield needed someone he could trust who was experienced in handling money and property, respected for honesty, in good odor with law enforcement authorities, and not a political lightning rod. When Abelman arrived in Reno, Wingfield was preoccupied with a scandal that could ruin his banking interests and allegations that he was tied to embezzlers. Wingfield was even more in need of someone to oversee some of his Reno properties.

Abelman became owner and proprietor of the Ship and Bottle Club, on Wingfield land, which officially opened in 1932. The club had a history as a "private" gambling house and dance hall, because it was mentioned as one of the stopping-off places for future divorcées in residence before gambling was legal. Local newspapers regarded it as one of Reno's first elegant casinos.[40] Within a year of the club's opening, Abelman suffered the loss of his young wife, Marie, after a three-week bout with pneumonia. Her pallbearers included the chief of police and county sheriff, and Baptist minister Brewster Adams conducted the service. Although Abelman never repudiated his Jewish heritage, neither he nor Marie had any formal Jewish affiliation. Several years later, he married divorcée June Pettite, an Episcopalian whose sons Nick adopted.[41]

In the meantime, Wingfield's financial problems worsened considerably. To offset his losses and indebtedness in 1933, Wingfield leased most of the Riverside Hotel businesses to Nick Abelman and his associates Steve Pavlovich and Bert Riddick. Wingfield was known to stop in with a bodyguard to collect his "rent" in cash. Forced by bank receivers to liquidate all his assets, Wingfield arranged to auction his 640-acre Spanish Springs ranch in 1935. Mysteriously, the only bidder was Nick Abelman, who secured title for a mere three thousand dollars. Abelman used the ranch as his own until Wingfield was well out of trouble. Then, perhaps on a handshake and quitclaim deed, he transferred the ranch back to Wingfield's estate.[42]

At this time, it was not unusual for casino owners to do business on a cash basis, relying on a nod and a promise that could be broken only at one's peril. Abelman had no known checking account. He kept hundreds of thousands of dollars in the safe of his fashionable home among Reno's nabobs. He routinely carried wads of hundred-dollar bills and had a reputation for generosity. On one occasion when he was a pallbearer for former employee Sam Erlich, he slipped a few c-notes to Rabbi Tarlow for a cleanup of the cemetery.

At the Riverside, Abelman entertained the rich and famous, as well as his old prospecting friends from central Nevada. Reportedly, when two of Abelman's scruffy pals on their annual pilgrimage to the big city appeared at the posh Riverside, they asked the bartender for "Jew Nick." The bartender consulted his manager, who went to Abelman's office to ask if the men should be thrown out. Abelman reportedly replied, "Tell them Jew Nick will visit them shortly and all drinks are on the house." At his South Lake Tahoe property, Abelman sheltered the children of Jack Sullivan, Jim McKay, and other associates who preferred to be out of Reno from time to time. He is said to have carried a gun only when Bill Graham or Doc Stacher was in the house.[43] Nick Abelman died in 1951 and was buried in Mountain View Cemetery.

Jack Sullivan and "Doc" Stacher

Jack Sullivan was born Jack B. Scarlett of Jewish parents in Canada. He came to Tonopah in 1906—the same year as Abelman—as a hopeful miner and prizefighter. The ring announcer jokingly introduced him as "John L. Sullivan," and Scarlett chose to keep the name. He struck up a relationship with McKay and Graham, and the three later developed a partnership at Reno's Willows nightclub and the Golden Hotel's Bank Club, where Sullivan was the bouncer. Although Sullivan never worked for Nick Abelman, they were friends. Nick seemed to get along with everyone—including Gentile felons like Graham and McKay, who served six years in Leavenworth, while Sullivan managed the Bank Club for Wingfield from 1939 to 1945. In 1950, Sullivan tried to sell his third of the Bank Club to Joseph "Doc" Stacher, a well-known former associate of Meyer Lansky in the bootlegging business. Stacher had been arrested in the 1920s for a slew of felonies, all of them dismissed. Nevertheless, the Nevada Tax Commission blocked the sale to Stacher, who went to Las Vegas to seek a piece of casino action. Neither Sullivan nor Stacher had any known ties to Reno Jewish organizations.[44]

Joseph and Sadie Zemansky, Sanford Adler, and Charlie Resnick

Joseph and Sadie Zemansky came to Reno in 1937 after Joseph's stint managing heavyweight champion Jack Johnson. He also ran a chain of jewelry stores and a successful resort in Mexico. Upon arrival, the couple became owners of the Club Fortune, whose location had its own Jewish history. Its two-story property on East Second Street between Virginia and Center was originally the Palace Dry Goods store owned by William Levy. In 1936, Levy sold the property to McKay and Sullivan, who, in turn, sold it to the Zemanskys. The Club Fortune was among Reno's finest nightclubs from 1937 to 1947, when the property lease expired. The Zemanskys were active in the club's day-to-day operations, generous contributors to Jewish causes, and strongly affiliated with Reno's Temple Emanu-El.[45]

Sanford Adler and Charlie Resnick, Las Vegas–based Jewish gamblers with alleged organized-crime backgrounds, purchased the Club Fortune's building and reopened the casino in 1948 as the Club Cal-Neva. At the time, Adler and Resnick also owned the Cal-Neva Lodge at Lake Tahoe and the El Rancho Vegas. Although Adler seemed in relatively good standing with state gaming authorities, they barred him from the industry in 1955 for failing to respond to a state subpoena concerning relicensing of the Cal-Neva Club.[46] Neither Adler nor Resnick had any formal relationship with Reno civic or Jewish organizations.

The Wertheimers, Hornsteins, Weitzes, and Masons:
More Reno Jewish Gamblers

Two other Jewish casino owners who came to Reno with impeccable syndicate-related credentials were Mert and Louis Wertheimer. Both had been active in illegal gambling ventures in Michigan and Florida, but served no time. Unlike Doc Stacher, they were able to secure Nevada gambling licenses. Mert Wertheimer was actually actively involved in strengthening state controls on gambling. Comparing some of his past adventures to his Reno casino ownership, he was quoted as saying, "The thing I like about it here is that you don't have to pay anyone off." In 1949, Mert took over the gambling franchise at the Riverside Hotel from Nick Abelman. Joining him at the Riverside was his brother Lou, who had co-owned the Bonanza Club from 1944 to 1947 and leased the gambling operation at the fashionable Mapes Hotel with Bernie Einstoss and Leo Kind. The Wertheimer brothers, with Ruby Mathis (Reuben

Mathews) and Baldy West, purchased the Riverside outright from Wingfield in 1955. The Wertheimers were, according to one longtime Jewish resident, "loosely connected" to the Reno worshiping community. Ruby Mathis was Jewish but not religiously affiliated.[47]

Other Jewish casino operators who came to Reno in the 1930s included brothers Joseph, George, and Henry Hornstein. All three were involved in various casinos and race and sports books. Joseph had the Nevada Turf Club from 1946 to 1955, and Henry and George owned the Colony Club (later the Colony Turf Club) from 1956 to 1974. Joseph was also a major partner in the Palace Club and co-owner for a few years of the El Morocco Club in Las Vegas with his brother-in-law Jack Austin, who was also Jewish. In 1974, all three Hornstein brothers sold their Reno Turf Club interests to Austin. None of these men was religiously active—in fact, some held them in contempt for their failure to contribute to Jewish causes.

Other Jewish partners in Reno's flourishing Palace Club in 1953 were United Jewish Appeal (UJA) organizer Frank Cohen, Russian-born Harry Weitz, and his American-born brother William, who was killed in an auto accident several years later. Cohen, too, died early in 1957. Members of the Jewish community considered Harry Weitz a "nice guy," who likely donated to the local temple from afar. Popular with his employees at the Palace Club and the Tahoe Palace because he gave them cash "under the table" if the house was particularly prosperous that day, he explained the largesse this way: "It wasn't that I was such a nice guy. I just wanted to keep them honest." Harry lived more than forty years in Reno and died there in 1991.[48]

Maury Mason built casino and hotel properties in Miami and Las Vegas. In 1955, he received a share in the recently constructed Riviera Hotel in Las Vegas instead of a cash payment. He soon divested himself of that property and moved to Reno, where, in 1967, his sons Stuart and Walter became partnered in the Horseshoe Club. They had succeeding interests in the Sparks Shy Clown Casino and Reno's Silver Spur through 1988. Although the Mason family was not fully affiliated with the local synagogue, Walter Mason and his wife, Cheryl, reportedly contributed all the chairs to the temple. One of the Masons' erstwhile managers at the Horseshoe Club, Sam Silverberg, won $112,000 in a wrongful-termination suit against the club in 1975. Silverberg was active in Jewish religious affairs and retired as cantor emeritus from Temple Emanu-El. Although Jewish influence dominated Las Vegas hotel casinos, it was waning in Reno with the deaths of Nick Abelman, the

Wertheimer brothers, and Joe Zemansky in the 1950s and the departure of the Hornstein brothers in 1974.[49]

...

With the exceptions noted, leadership of northern Nevada Judaism in the mid-twentieth century was not to be found among the Jewish hotel and casino owners. The mainstays of Reno's religious community were the clothing merchants, pawnbrokers, jewelers, junk dealers, lawyers, real estate brokers, card dealers, and a few physicians. What had happened in the first half of the twentieth century was the state's extrication from dependence on mineral production and transition to a tourist economy, which included boxing, horse race betting, slots, and table games. Jewish owners and managers were prominent in Reno's gambling business from the start, but the ascendancy of their fellow Jews in Las Vegas soon overshadowed them.

The Early Years of Las Vegas

Las Vegas started as a watering stop on a trail—and later a railroad line—that came and went to more important places. Neither born of a mineral bonanza like so many Nevada towns nor the product of Benjamin Siegel's alleged desert vision, it had one of the state's oldest recorded place-names. Its abundant springs led to its being named "the Meadows" (Las Vegas) by travelers on the Old Spanish Trail early in the nineteenth century—well before the United States acquired the area.[1]

Solomon Carvalho in the Meadows

The first known Jew to traverse Las Vegas was Solomon Nunes Carvalho, born in Charleston, South Carolina, in 1815 to Sephardic and Portuguese parents. He attached himself to the expedition party of John C. Frémont in 1853 and served as photographer, artist, and chronicler. On May 29, 1854, he wrote in his log that he and his party had "camped on a narrow stream of deliciously cool water, which distributes itself about half a mile further down, in a verdant meadow bottom, covered with good grass. This camp ground is called by the Mexicans, Las Vegas."[2]

During his travels to Las Vegas, Carvalho refused to eat porcupine, because "it looked very much like pork. My stomach revolted at it, and I sat hungry around our mess, looking at my comrades enjoying it." He attempted to maintain the regimen of avoiding horse meat, but to avoid starvation, "I then partook of the strange and forbidden food with much hesitation." When dying animals were slaughtered and their blood drained into the camp kettle, he resolutely never touched the food.[3] Remarkably, the first identifiable Jew to pass through Las Vegas tried to be observant. More than a century would pass before a strictly kosher option was available to Jews in the area.

Las Vegas was on a mail-run trail that Congress established in 1854 from Salt Lake City to San Diego. In 1855, the first white settlers, Mormons, built a fort-mission to protect themselves and to proselytize local Paiutes, but they abandoned the area by 1858. In 1865, Octavius Decatur Gass and some friends obtained rights to the old Mormon fort, and the area became a sprawling ranch supplying fruit, vegetables, and livestock to passing travelers.[4] Likely, Jewish peddlers were among them, but there is no documentation to name even one.

Adolph Levy at the Las Vegas Town Site

The Gass ranch fell into the hands of Archibald Stewart, who was killed in a shootout, and his widow, Helen, sold the property to Senator William Clark of Montana in 1902. Pioche senator Herman Freudenthal helped to pass legislation in 1901 allowing Clark to build a railroad across Lincoln County. Clark valued the nearly two thousand–acre Stewart ranch as the ideal watering stop for his trains, and the area soon teemed with surveyors and railroad workers. The San Pedro, Los Angeles, and Salt Lake Railroad line was completed in January 1905, and Clark and his partner, the Union Pacific, auctioned a town site to the highest bidder. Alcohol was to be restricted to Block 16 on Fremont Street.[5]

Even before the railroad's completion, a competing town site west of Clark's lots came to be called Ragtown and later the Westside or West Las Vegas. Las Vegas was a launching pad for supplies going north to the mining districts of Bullfrog, Rhyolite, and, by 1907, Goldfield. Two of those from Rhyolite who depended on this supply line were A. Cohen, a furniture merchant, and Sylvan Cohn, sole proprietor of the Richelieu Saloon. It was also a place for local peddlers and other merchants serving the fast-growing area. One of these was Las Vegas's earliest Jewish settler, Adolph Levy, who remembered Ragtown "with its tent stores and large freight outfits" charging "extortionate prices." Those were the old days, Levy wrote a year later; the "new Las Vegas" demanded a different class of merchant, and he contended that he was the master of "twentieth century merchandising" who could provide the best goods and services at the lowest possible price.[6]

Levy had emigrated from Germany in 1883 and married Rose in 1895. They peddled their way across the country, with Rose giving birth to their first child, Pauline, in Illinois in 1902. They passed through Arkansas en route to Missouri and on to Nevada. Levy saw himself as more than a grocer. He personalized his advertisements with an enticing lead-in story for six consecutive weeks in the local newspaper, concluding with special offers on products from soap to fresh mackerel, but his promotions did not end with his merchandise.

It was time, he wrote in 1906, "to incorporate our city." He criticized the "drones and mossbacks" who had come to Las Vegas merely to speculate, and urged his readers to "get their shoulder to the wheel and build GREATER Las Vegas." The city, he observed, needed a "High School, a City Hall, a Park, Library, Church and well equipped Fire Department." It could be accomplished, he urged, if people put aside petty strife and joined hands to "have a city that no one will feel ashamed to call their home." Levy was promoting Las Vegas as much as he was touting the excellence of his goods and services. He predicted "a nice thriving city of 6000 or 8000 people in a few years," and he planned to meet "every many, woman and child in the city" to encourage their civic-mindedness and attract their business.[7] The census enumerator identified Rose as the Levy store's saleslady—clearly involved in the family business.

Levy invested in mines west of Las Vegas and opened a lumberyard in partnership with Las Vegas's first mayor, Peter Buol. He sold his store, which had expanded to clothing and general merchandise. He erected a two-story building on Fremont Street that succumbed to fire. Although he moved his family to Los Angeles in 1913, he remained heavily invested in Las Vegas and continued to visit it often. The *Las Vegas Age* quoted Levy assessing the business climate in Las Vegas as "more healthful and prosperous" than any "little city in the west." Reno and Goldfield might have quarreled with such chutz-pah, but by the time he was buried in the Home of Peace Jewish cemetery in Los Angeles in 1936, Las Vegas's population had reached his predicted figure of more than six thousand people.[8]

Religious Observance with Barely a Minyan

A common indicator of a Jewish presence in Nevada communities was typically the local newspaper's notification of High Holiday observance. The first such clue appeared in the *Las Vegas Age* in April 1913, which reported that "most of our Jewish population" was observing Passover. Nevada's Jewish merchants advertised lavishly, but the local newspaper noted only the presence of Levy's Economy Store. Who, then—besides the Levy family—were the other Jewish worshipers? One was Julius F. Fox, born in Russia of Polish-speaking parents, who operated a small farm on First Street but had no taxable real estate in 1910. Two other members of the minyan may have been

New Jersey–born Abraham Hofman, nineteen, working in a furniture store, and the young, single electrician Abraham Blaustein of Germany. The 1910 census also noted families of Bermans, Bergmans, Richters, and Vogels—all without any certain Jewish lineage. The *Las Vegas Age* briefly noted the passing of High Holidays in 1914, with no reference to the local Jewish community. The next token four-line notice did not appear until nine years later and then disappeared again.[9] By then, the town lacked any significant observable Jewish presence. Las Vegas simply was not attracting new entrepreneurs.

The town had begun to suffer reversals early, which deterred any significant in-migration. For example, on New Year's Day of 1910, a warm rain prematurely melted the mountain snows, reducing 110 miles of the railroad to a "mass of wreckage." A train that had departed Las Vegas for Salt Lake was caught in the flooding. Although passengers received alternative transportation, the Los Angeles Limited remained trapped for five and a half months. With no trains operating, and no railroad men in the city to spend their payroll, local businesses suffered accordingly. Several fires destroyed the local school and some stores during the same year. In 1921, Clark sold his share of the railroad to the Union Pacific. The decline of mining activity in Goldfield and Tonopah occasioned the dismantling of the railroad connecting them to Las Vegas. In 1922, a strike against the Union Pacific split the populace; the railroad soon moved its repair shops up the line to Caliente in retaliation against the strikers.[10] Las Vegas appeared to be driving in reverse gear. It was not an attractive prospect for an energetic Jewish merchant.

The Jewish population of Las Vegas was in decline or at best static during the city's teenage years. Traveling Jewish merchants, such as Edward A. "Ike" Blum, passed through town en route to Los Angeles or mining sites during Las Vegas's early decades. Blum was in Las Vegas for the land auction in 1905, then departed for Rhyolite, where he worked in a cigar store, and at the age of thirty-five was still single. In 1920, he was on record as a widower in Tonopah clerking with a mining company. A 1928 arrival in Las Vegas remembered Blum as being certainly Jewish, having a type-A personality, and working for a local newspaper.[11]

Although a bare handful of Jews called Las Vegas home, one reportedly visited the city annually in search of a minyan with whom to worship on the High Holidays. Joe M. Cohen was born in Utah in 1902 to Benjamin and Sophia (Siegel) Cohen. He moved to Pioche in 1926, opened the successful Leader Store, and in 1936 married Sarah Berlin of Hollywood. Caliente native Ralph Denton remembered Cohen as the lone Jewish merchant at Pioche in the 1930s and no Jews whatsoever in Caliente, leading Denton to ask his father why he heard occasional antisemitic remarks. The elder Denton sagely summarized the phenomenon as the result of hating "every son of a bitch in the country that's smarter than I am." Cohen openly described himself as both a Democrat and a Jew. He went on to become chairman of the Selective Service and Office of Price Administration Ration Boards during World War II, president of Pioche's Chamber of Commerce and Lion's Club, and grand master of the local Odd Fellows. He was likely the legendary figure who joined Las Vegas's tiny Jewish worshiping community in the late 1920s and 1930s.[12]

Las Vegas: "Gateway to Boulder Dam," 1928

Announcement of Boulder Dam's construction sparked a migration of workers and speculators to southern Nevada. The federal government allocated more than seventy million dollars for development, which included the erection of a "company town," Boulder City, to provide housing and services for the workers. The project employed up to five thousand people with an annual monthly payroll of a half-million dollars. The dam "rescued Las Vegas from a whistle-stop fate," wrote historian Eugene Moehring, but Las Vegas itself had no identity other than being its "gateway."[13]

One of those hearing of the dam construction in 1928, Alexander Salton, had run away from home in Belorussia. He managed to buy a steerage ticket to the United States and joined the American expedition to track down Pancho Villa in 1917. Salton met and married Belorussian-born Rebecca Leboff, who had migrated to New York, where she dabbled in socialist politics. They had two children, Charles (b. 1922) and Adele (b. 1926). According to Charles, his father consulted a fortune teller who told him he would make money on raw land. Charles remembered Las Vegas in 1928 as little more than five short paved roads around Fremont Street—with not a Jewish store in sight.[14]

The few Jews young Salton recalled as already in Las Vegas when the family arrived were attorney Louis Cohen; brothers David and Sam Stearns; and Mike and Sally Gordon, whose daughter was reported to be the first Jewish child born in the city. Polish-born Kitty and Louis Wiener Sr. arrived a couple of years after the Saltons and opened a tailoring shop on Fremont Street. According to granddaughter Valerie Wiener, he designed suits "for men who ran the red-light district, and my grandmother made the dresses for the women who worked there. That's what put food on the table." Lawyer Abraham J. Schur and his family also settled in Las Vegas. The Wieners, Gordons, Schurs, and Goldrings were all related. When Louis Wiener Jr. announced he wanted to become a lawyer, Uncle Abe Schur (Kitty's brother) reportedly discouraged the move. "This is a handshake town," he told young Wiener. "People don't sign contracts; you'll go broke." Wiener completed law school, passed the bar, and later represented—among many others—the city's major casino owners.[15]

Nate Mack and a Flurry of New Arrivals in the 1930s

Nate Mack, born in eastern Europe in 1891, had owned a supermarket in Los Angeles before relocating to Las Vegas. His brothers, Harry and Louis, followed him and earned good livings in real estate. Nate's occupational history was decidedly more varied. He tried his hand at a haberdashery early on and then decided to look into opportunities in Reno in 1936. Reno's winter drove him back south to Boulder City, where he sold tires and batteries. Mack was running a restaurant when he noticed that the poor highway between Boulder City and Las Vegas was the site of many accidents. He opened a towing service and a wrecking yard, with stations at both ends of the highway. Not long after these new starts, he bought out Sam Friedman's popular clothing store on Fremont Street.

Amid his many businesses, which now included the sale of produce, a liquor store, and a bar on Fremont Street, Mack invested in Roccola jukeboxes and new Jennings slot machines, which he placed in bars at Tonopah, Beatty, Round Mountain, Manhattan, and Pioche. He earned 50 percent of the revenue on all machines. How and why he was not cheated by the local managers is a testament to how he conducted business. Mack often said that he looked to make a small profit and leave something for the next guy. And "should there ever come a day when the next man does not make a profit, we are all in trouble."[16]

Near one of his Las Vegas wrecking yards, Mack purchased a block of lots for eight thousand dollars. He had a "hunch" that the investment would pay a modest profit. There was yet more to gamble. Mack was among the first to invest in casino properties with other Jewish Americans. His early partners included Moe Sedway, Sanford Adler, Gus Greenbaum, Charlie Resnick, and Art Rosen—all of whom had alleged criminal pasts. These associations went uncriticized in both the Jewish and Gentile communities. His heavy eastern

European accent, which he carried to the grave, was no barrier to his ability to communicate. Nate Mack became one of the most influential citizens of Las Vegas—as well as a founding father of its organized Jewry.[17]

Herb Waldman was another newcomer in the 1930s. He sold wholesale beverages. Waldman married Kitty and Louis Wiener's daughter Katheryn, further linking the Las Vegas Jews through marriage. Others coming to Las Vegas in the 1930s included Ethyl Rappaport, operating a liquor business in her name; tailor Louis Abrahams; grocer Harry Levy; Flora Chochinsky, known later as social activist Flora Dungan; clothing merchant Louis Friedman; Art Brick, who owned the Palace Theater and later a piece of the Golden Nugget; Mark Shulman, selling wholesale meat; Dr. Mandel Coblentz, the town's only Jewish physician; and Morris Rose, who sold groceries and bootleg supplies. Charles Salton vividly remembered the hooch, because his father, Alexander, occasionally made deliveries for Rose.[18]

The Silvers were yet another extended family of three brothers, Ben, Morris "Bill," and Mike, who were born in Germany and settled in Los Angeles. Morris partnered with Harry Samett (who once boarded at the Saltons) to run Silver's Building and Restaurant Supply Company. Morris Silver had been working in Las Vegas as early as 1931, but did not relocate his wife and family of six children to Las Vegas until 1933. A few weeks after they took possession of their new house, Morris was called upon to preside with A. J. Arthur at the funeral of the infant daughter of Mr. and Mrs. Charles Bain. Las Vegas Jews had no burial society or their own cemetery; knowledgeable laymen provided the religious internment ceremony. Following the trade of his father, Mike Silver set himself up in plumbing and sheet metal, and soon had two stores. In an interview, he joked about early mistakes and credited his success to his customers. An outspoken supporter of President Franklin Roosevelt, Silver was active in organizing local plumbers, whose union he was voted to head in 1933.[19]

Coming Together for Worship

In 1931, the Gordons, Schurs, Macks, and about twenty other families began gathering in the back of a store to pray and teach the Torah to their children. They called themselves the "Sons and Daughters of Israel." Whatever the accuracy of the date, something was stirring within the growing Jewish community by 1932. The *Las Vegas Age* published a front-page, twelve-column-inch, center-copy description of the beginning of the Jewish New Year.

The article, written by E. A. (presumably "Ike") Blum, had all the earmarks of an author versed in Jewish tradition. This piece was in stark contrast to the four-liners buried in prior editions of the *Age* fifteen years earlier. Its prominence betokened a significant number of well-known Jewish residents to whom the readers could relate. The Jewish community was large enough that March to have a Purim Ball at the Meadows Club. The seeds of a formal congregation were germinating. The faithful remnant celebrated the major Jewish Holidays, with Sally Gordon developing a model seder for families to follow using supplies from San Bernardino. Mike Gordon's cousin Reba Gordon Saiger recalled that their grandfather Abraham occasionally presided at High Holiday services. Louis and Kitty Wiener and Sally Gordon's father, Herman Adler, joined the Christian Science church during the Depression and later rerooted themselves in Judaism. Such was the pattern of observance before formal organization.[20]

World War II Establishments

As German aircraft bombed London in 1940, America's lend-lease program clearly needed to include the vital element of weapons-grade magnesium. In July 1941, the federal government bankrolled the erection of Basic Magnesium, Inc., fifteen miles southeast of Las Vegas. It was to produce ten times that of Germany's output and employ ten thousand workers with their families. Boulder City and Las Vegas together lacked the infrastructures to accommodate such an influx. The shacks around the plant were transformed into a town, which was renamed in honor of Charles Henderson, a longtime Nevada politician who headed the Reconstruction Finance Corporation that helped set up Basic Magnesium.[21]

Las Vegas leased its inadequate airport eight miles northeast of town to the U.S. Army Air Corps for a dollar a year in October 1940. The site became the Las Vegas Army Air Corps Gunnery School. With the onset of formal hostilities, the base expanded, and by 1942 it was graduating four thousand combat-ready bomber pilots and gunners every six weeks. Las Vegas's population rose accordingly and included about one hundred Jews. Although the temptations of Las Vegas's red-light district and the area's legal gambling bothered air corps brass, the average airman considered the environs "good duty." Jewish base chaplains provided weekly services, and Las Vegans invited the men into their homes for Passover seders as well as other social events away from the city's nightlife. The war and its exposure of the Holocaust

helped some Jewish servicemen and women redefine themselves unasham-
edly as Jews.[22] Several people who trained at the gunnery school brought that
dedication back to Las Vegas and a congregation about to be born.

The Jewish Community Center

The 1940 schism of Reform elements from Reno's Conservative temple gave
Las Vegas Jews reason to ponder their new congregation's religious affili-
ation within the spectrum of Judaism. Most of the earliest Jewish settlers
had childhood ties to the Union of Orthodox Jewish Congregations, and the
Salton family claimed no fewer than four Orthodox rabbis.[23] Some younger
newcomers were more inclined to affiliate with the Reform UAHC. The Las
Vegas compromise was to affiliate in 1946 with the United Synagogue of
America (now the United Synagogue of Conservative Judaism). For many,
Orthodoxy was no option, being considered too outdated and "Old World"
for such a modern city as Las Vegas. The germs of future dissent were already
in place.

The first synagogue, or shul, was the Jewish Community Center located at
Thirteenth and Carson Streets. Not simply a place of worship, in the tradition of American Conservative Judaism, it was an outreach and community-
building enterprise, with its board of directors theoretically distinct from
the congregation. The first president of the new Beth Sholom Congregation,
Abraham "A. J." Schur, served from 1943 to 1945—succeeded by Nate Mack
(1945–1949) and Mike Gordon (1949–1951). Mack was unfamiliar with the
niceties of Robert's Rules of Order, and Schur occasionally helped control a
meeting that had run amok.[24]

The driving force behind the building project, Nate Mack, humbly refused
to take full credit for the center's construction. He singled out Dave and Sam
Stearns, Mike Gordon, Bill Mendelsohn, Murray Wollman, Al Goot, and Ira
Goldring. Unmentioned by Mack were A. J. Schur, Art Brick, Al Salton, and
Harry Levy, who also provided essential organizational and construction
skills. Mack's financial contribution, however, was a sine qua non. The Jewish Community Center members elected him their president for the next
nine years, during several of which he served as state chairman of the United
Jewish Appeal.[25]

The Jewish Community Center was a humble establishment whose external Jewish distinction was the Star of David in a circular window above

the main entrance. Besides serving as a place of worship on High Holidays, it housed Las Vegas's first Jewish gift shop and display. Women in the Sisterhood, such as Edythe Katz, traveled to Los Angeles to purchase religious goods at discount prices for resale. Nowhere else in Las Vegas could one buy a mezuzah (doorpost Torah scroll) or even Hanukkah *gelt* (the traditional foil-wrapped chocolate treats for children).

The Las Vegas population tripled between 1940 and 1950. These were the so-called golden years in which much money was made in land sales. Most Jews migrated to Las Vegas for no other reason than that Las Vegas was a growing city. Others associated with organized crime came to enjoy Nevada's legal gambling environment, in which they were joined by Italians with whom they had been in partnership elsewhere.

Jewish and Italian Cultural Values

Southern Italians and eastern European Jews reached American shores en masse after 1880. The merger of Jewish and Italian business interests was noticeable in the first quarter of the twentieth century in the East Coast needle trade. There Italians joined Jewish garment unions to strengthen their common cause. Italians saw the Jewish unionist as "the standard bearer of Italian labor interests." Jews and Italians brought no prejudice against each other from Europe, and they were uninfected by the hostilities between other ethnic groups that developed in the United States. Italians admired Jews as upwardly mobile, educated professionals who also maintained their ethnic identity.[26]

According to Jewish historian Rudolph Glanz, "Currents of tension are apparent only in two relationships: Jew-Irish and Irish-Italian, whereas the Jew-Italian association remained free of tension." The Italian-Jewish cooperation was "without exaggeration, the most successful achievement of the new immigrant groups in American labor."[27] The Triangle Waist Company fire on March 25, 1911, at the Asch Building in New York City was a tipping point. Some of the 146 women and men who died jumped to their deaths because the ninth-floor doors were locked. Most victims were recent Jewish and Italian immigrants eking out a living in this sweatshop owned by Isaac Harris and Max Blanck. The two were acquitted in their manslaughter trial because they allegedly did not know that exits from the factory had been locked. The fire and its aftermath strengthened the International Ladies Garment Workers Union and the union movement in general.[28] Italians and Jews shared a common preventable tragedy, and they worked together through the relief effort, overlooking their wide theological differences.

There was little social group interaction between Jews and Italians, but common characteristics contributed to future alliances. One of the cultural similarities shared by Jews and Italians was their attitude toward alcohol consumption and gambling. Unlike the Protestant view of both activities as sinful, neither Jews nor Italians considered them morally wrong as long as they were characterized by self-control. The term *temperance* for mainline Protestants meant "total abstinence," whereas Catholic moral theology viewed the same term as synonymous with "moderation." Both groups had a zest for gambling. One early commentator called these two ethnic groups "habitual gamesters." The only difference was that Italians gambled openly in their saloons, whereas Jews cultivated the practice in their homes, "far from the eyes of reporters, who nevertheless did not miss this fact." Catholic moral theologians, at the time, recognized the potential social evils that could arise from alcohol abuse and high-stakes gambling. They did not, however, condemn as sinful moderate social drinking and "pastime" gambling.[29]

For the record, one exception to Jewish temperance was the mitzvah based on the Talmud's Megillah 7b to get so drunk on Purim that Haman (the villain in the Esther story) and Mordechai (the hero) were indistinguishable. Jewish scholars disagree on how to dispatch this duty. Hard-core traditionalists explain that whereas reason and temperance are the order for 364 days, Purim is the one day to dismiss reason in exchange for a jubilant experience of oneness with the divine power that liberated the ancient Jews. Other Jews—less hidebound by tradition—find the practice quaint but unrefined.[30]

Southern Italians in particular suffered from the taint of criminality cast upon the entire ethnic group by the machinations of the "Black Hand," or Mafia, which operated with impunity in major cities as early as the 1860s. By the turn of the century, a few unscrupulous Jews used the symbol of the Black Hand to intimidate even coreligionists. When deals between Jewish and Italian gangs were violated, Jews perpetuated execution-style murders against offending Jews.[31]

Young Jewish boys taunted on the street formed gangs for self-preservation. Poverty, disaffiliation of young people from their parents' Old World values and traditions, divorce, desertion, and family destabilization pushed second-generation Jews into prostitution, gambling, extortion, embezzlement, and white-collar crimes. "These crimes probably were the perverse result of the American desire to rise, as much as they were the result of deprivation," wrote one observer.[32] Although Jews and Italians came together in union causes, they had no formal affiliation with organized crime until the Eighteenth Amendment to the U.S. Constitution.

The onset of national Prohibition in 1919 complicated the moral issue of alcohol production, transportation, sale, and consumption. Over the next fourteen years, Jews and Italians were engaged in all of these proscribed activities as well as illegal gambling. Some of the cooperative ventures led to personal friendships and legal—though suspect—relationships.

Jews in the Las Vegas Gambling World

The first known Las Vegas Jewish gambler with ties to organized crime was Moe Sedway. He had a police record dating back to the 1920s in New York. On orders from Meyer Lansky, Sedway visited Las Vegas in the early 1940s to compete with—or take over—the local wire service, which provided horse-race results to betting booths. The syndicate's version was the Trans-America Wire Service. Sedway used a methodology that was straightforward and in the spirit of supply and demand. He simply offered his wire to the Las Vegas bookies at a lower rate than his competition. Once Trans-America was the only service in town in 1942, Sedway increased the rates and demanded a share of the profits in a permutation of the old "bait and switch" operation. Sedway took the profits to invest (for himself and silent partners) in other casinos.[33]

Lansky had given Benjamin Siegel responsibility for expanding Mob involvement in Las Vegas, but Siegel hated the desert, turned over operations to Sedway, and headed back to California, where he hoped to make his mark in movies and was involved in underworld activities. In 1945, Siegel purchased the El Cortez Hotel with other investors, including Sedway, Greenbaum, Lansky, Israel "Icepick Willie" Alderman, Chickie Berman, and the man once considered "the toughest Jew in America," Chickie's brother Davie. Earlier, Siegel reportedly drove with Meyer Lansky to Las Vegas via the Los Angeles Highway. The details get murkier in the many accounts and cinematic portrayals of what happened next. The prevailing myth has been that Siegel stopped outside of the city, looked around, and bragged that he would build on this spot the biggest and fanciest casino resort—called the Flamingo. Hollywood purveyors of Las Vegas mythology credit this Jewish mobster with a "vision" of the modern Las Vegas "Strip."[34] The Flamingo was to be a luxurious cut above its competition, but this one casino did not alone create the Strip. There were other venues and some intervening Gentile players, and in several versions, Lansky was the actual visionary.

There were others with dreams and ambitions. Former Los Angeles cop Guy McAfee owned the old Pair-O-Dice in 1939 and first described the area as the Strip. Hotel developer Thomas Hull purchased a parcel of land at the corner of Highway 91 and what is now Sahara Avenue and built the El Rancho hotel and casino, which opened in April 1941 several feet outside the Las Vegas city limits. With its pool and gardens, it was Las Vegas's first resort hotel. Rupert E. Griffith opened his more lavish Last Frontier in October 1942. And inveterate Los Angeles gambler, publicist, and nightclub owner W. R. "Billy" Wilkerson bought a thirty-three-acre site between the El Rancho Vegas and the airport, as distant from future competition as the El Rancho was from Fremont Street, where he could indulge his gambling addiction. If he lost at the tables, he won as the owner and vice versa. He named it the Flamingo.[35]

On February 26, 1946, Wilkerson signed a contract with Lansky's agent, Harry Rothberg, for a syndicate of investors to buy 60 percent of Wilkersons' property for one million dollars. The financially besieged Wilkerson resumed construction. A month later, Sedway and Greenbaum visited him on the site. "They brought with them a loudly-dressed character," Wilkerson's son later wrote, who turned out to be Siegel.[36]

Eventually, the Mob completely bought out Wilkerson. Under Siegel's watch, the Flamingo construction costs soared, it failed to open on time, and it was a financial disaster. Siegel was murdered in his Mob-related paramour's Beverly Hills home on a June 1947 evening. Within minutes of the event, Sedway and Greenbaum by prearrangement took control. The Jewish "mafia" was in command of the Flamingo, forming a lavish bookend with the El Rancho Hotel, which they also soon controlled. Thus began what one observer called "kosher nostra." Some scholars, history buffs, and Strip casino decorators credit Siegel's Flamingo opening as "the crucial event which transformed Las Vegas from a recreational to a full-fledged resort city."[37] But others should share responsibility and credit, including the hapless Wilkerson. As for Siegel, the man who would not tolerate his nickname to be used, he has been commonly known, after his death, as "Bugsy."

Siegel is not to be idolized here as the Strip's patriarch, because a host of Jewish developers, owners, and managers actually created the reality. Professor Alan Balboni's summary of Jewish involvement in Las Vegas's hotel-casino industry between 1947 and 1967 succinctly communicates the overwhelming Jewish dominance:

> Most of the hotel builders were Jewish Americans. Jay Sarno [often misidentified as Italian] and Nate Jacobson were associated with Caesars Palace; Moe Dalitz, Morris Kleinman, and Sam Tucker with the Desert Inn (and, along with Jake Factor, with the Stardust after [Tony] Cornero's death); Sidney Wyman, Al Gottesman, and Jake Gottleib with the early years of the Dunes; Gus Greenbaum, Moe Sedway, and Charlie Resnick with managing the Flamingo after Bugsy Siegel's death; Ben Goffstein, Willie Alderman, and Davie Berman with the building and running of the Riviera; Milton Prell with the establishment of the Sahara and then with the transformation of the Tally-ho into the Aladdin; Hyman Abrams, Carl Cohen, and Jack Entratter with the ownership and operation of the Sands; and Ben Jaffe, Phil Kastel, and J. Kell Houssels (the latter of Anglo-Saxon background) with the construction and operation of the Tropicana.[38]

In addition to casino operators, those unaffiliated with organized crime, such as Murray Wollman, Nathan Adelson, Nate Mack, and Irwin Molasky, were among the Jewish developers of Las Vegas's infrastructure of housing, malls, and hospitals.

Isolating the Strip from the City of Las Vegas

A less likable character with known underworld connections, Gus Greenbaum, played an essential role in the Strip's creation and control. His plan was to separate the area legally from the City of Las Vegas. Greenbaum lobbied the Clark County Commission to create the unincorporated township of Paradise on December 8, 1950. To be lobbied by Greenbaum was to be intimidated. Dick Odessky, a longtime Las Vegas publicist and journalist, called him the "most frightening man" he ever met, a heavyset man whose "personality was as dark as his physical being." "His mouth turned downward," wrote Odessky, "and his jaw jutted at you almost like the end of a gun barrel." His notorious background and alleged bad habits—"heroin, gambling, and showgirls"—did not prevent him from becoming the unofficial first "mayor" of Paradise. The effect of Greenbaum's intervention was that a city hungering for tax dollars could not annex Strip hotels, and the arrangement would continue as long as the county commission reaped the tax benefits. It was also one of the first times that Strip casino owners' interests meshed with those of elected politicians, beginning a symbiotic relationship of money and influence.[39]

Kefauver Investigations and Sassy Las Vegas Witnesses

After Siegel's death in 1947, the Nevada Tax Commission began requiring licenses for wire services, temporarily suspended Sedway's license, and in 1950 outlawed wire services altogether. This was the desert, however, and the camel's nose was already under the tent. Tennessean Estes Kefauver's Senate Committee on Organized Crime in Interstate Commerce held hearings that millions watched on the relatively new medium of television. Politicians from Maryland to Missouri with alleged ties to the underworld's financial support opposed the committee's work from the start, but it was popular with the rank and file. Kefauver's patronage of racetracks apparently did nothing to diminish his credibility. At a meeting with Meyer Lansky, the gangster challenged Kefauver's campaign against gambling in view of his habits. The senator did not deny his own gambling proclivities but added: "But I don't want *you* people to control it."[40]

In mid-November 1950, the committee arrived at Las Vegas in the wake of Kefauver's threat to hold Lansky in contempt of Congress. Wilbur Clark openly admitted selling 74 percent of the Desert Inn to Moe Dalitz and his associates. Although Dalitz managed to elude the Las Vegas hearing (he was questioned later), the committee grilled Clark about Dalitz, whom they linked to illegal gambling in Ohio and Kentucky and to known criminals Lucky Luciano, Siegel, and Lansky.

Beginning in the legitimate laundry business of his father in Detroit, Boston-born Moe Dalitz moved to transporting bootleg alcohol from Canada to casinos and speakeasies in Ohio and Kentucky during Prohibition, which associated him with Detroit's infamous Purple Gang. Dalitz owned illegal casinos and bars outside Cincinnati and Youngstown and across the Ohio River as well as a short-lived illegal dog track. He had as many legitimate holdings in real estate, ice cream, and the Chicago and Rock Island Railroad. He served as a second lieutenant in World War II before considering purchase of Reno's posh Riverside Hotel and Casino in 1949. Instead, he turned his attention to Las Vegas and the Desert Inn, which Clark was struggling to build, and Dalitz and some Cleveland cronies bailed him out for 74 percent of the action. Dalitz was also involved with Lansky in some Havana investments from which he beat an early retreat. He had an uncanny sense of timing.[41]

Columnist John Smith considers Dalitz "arguably the most important, and least understood, gambler-developer in the history of Las Vegas." He credits Dalitz's shrewdness with his ability to have survived scrutiny by law enforcement authorities from his twenties to his dying day. Although he was indicted for bootlegging and tax evasion, the charges were dropped, and, notes Smith, he was "never convicted of so much as jaywalking." Clark's reaction to the questioning made him appear, to some observers, to be "a confused little fish who had been bodily swallowed by the sharks" from Cleveland.[42]

The committee also asked Bill Moore, a Gentile owner of the Last Frontier and state tax commissioner, why the tax commission had licensed alleged Reno vice lords William Graham and James McKay (who had been around long before), along with Sedway and others who had traceable connections to the Syndicate. Moore's response pussyfooted around a grandfather clause that protected established casino operators. He asked the senators why a man's prior associations elsewhere should matter in Nevada, where gambling was as legal a profession as practicing law. The committee asked Moore how much money had escaped federal taxation. Moore claimed to have no knowledge of such matters, though virtually everyone working the Strip was aware of the skim. Las Vegans cared more that those with prior criminal associations "conduct themselves properly," keep the streets clear of violent crime, and boost the city's economy.[43]

Reno police Chief L. R. Greeson naively mentioned the hearsay that Joseph "Doc" Stacher, while at the Bank Club, had boasted he would spend $250,000 to buy off Nevada politicians. Stacher—once connected to Kansas City's Tom Pendergast machine—was now in Las Vegas, and committee members were prepared to accept hearsay as fact. Under oath, Sedway appealed unsuccessfully to the committee's sympathy for his many serious physical infirmities. Although he admitted having met, in passing, people such as Lucky Luciano and Frank Costello, he was now an aging businessman "making a living for my family, and not making a lot of money." When asked how he might have lived his life differently, Sedway was sassy and defiant: "We don't get as rich as you think we do. This is hard work. I would not do it over again. I would not want my children to do it again. No Senator, the first thing I would do would be to get a good education like I am trying to give my children, and when I got real learned I would become a United States Senator like you."[44]

Dalitz evaded the committee's subpoenas until—under threat of arrest—it caught up with him in California. Kefauver exposed Dalitz's past illegal activities from smuggling to money laundering, and referred to the rum-running area around Lake Erie as the "Jewish lake," with Dalitz and his henchmen as "the Big Jewish Navy." Dalitz sheltered himself under the Fifth Amendment privilege, as he wove his way through the barrage of questions and accusations. In one widely quoted interchange, Dalitz accused Kefauver and his political supporters of hypocrisy on the issue of illegal booze. "If you people wouldn't have drunk it," he said, "I wouldn't have bootlegged it."[45] Whereas the senate committee painted Dalitz as a crook, Robbins Cahill, a longtime Nevada Tax Commission official, "greatly admired" him. Looking back almost forty years later, Cahill characterized Dalitz and other former bootleggers and gamblers not as gangsters but as men who wanted to do legally in Nevada what had been illegal elsewhere.[46]

The Kefauver committee spent less than two days in Las Vegas and allotted only four pages of its lengthy report to the hearings there. Nevertheless, it criticized Nevada's licensing policy for providing an ineffective "cloak of respectability" to known gangsters. Most casino figures identified in the report as allegedly associated with organized crime were Jews: Morris Rosen, described as an old associate of the New York Mob, and Mert Wertheimer of Reno's Riverside, characterized as formerly in partnership in Florida with "such notorious gangsters as Joe Adonis, the Lanskys, and Frank Erickson." It charged that Nevada was inextricably and publicly connected to the underworld and needed major changes.[47]

The Crusading Hank Greenspun

Herman Milton "Hank" Greenspun almost single-handedly chose to take on the role of city reformer. The maverick who later challenged the power structure of Senator Pat McCarran, confronted corruption in the county sheriff's office, and helped broker civil rights for Las Vegas blacks also targeted some of his fellow Jews. Born in Brooklyn in 1909, he was steeped with a sense of his Jewish heritage and identity. His father was an ascetic Talmudic scholar in the Orthodox tradition who depended on his wife, Anna Bella, to keep bread on the table and raise four children. Early in life, Greenspun received a lesson from his mother in dealing with antisemitism. One of his paper-route customers refused to pay him and laced his intransigence with antisemitic remarks. Anna Bella sought out the miscreant and physically attacked him; he never bothered the boy again.[48]

Greenspun earned a degree at St. John's University and read the law under Vito Marcantonio, a liberal Republican New York lawyer, to pass the bar exam. Although the training was useful, Greenspun disliked the profession. Drafted into the army during World War II, he worked in ordnance. One of the decisive moments in his life came while attending Yom Kippur services in a French synagogue. There, he said, "I became aware of Jewish responsibility for the fate of all Jews." He married Jewess Barbara Joan Ritchie in Ireland in 1944. Having received France's Croix de Guerre, Greenspun briefly returned to practicing law, which occasioned a career-changing meeting. One of his clients, Joe Smoot, offered him a partnership in building a racetrack at Las Vegas. He visited the city in 1946 and was so charmed by the surrounding beauty that he telephoned his wife to pack up everything, including the baby, and relocate to Nevada.[49]

The racetrack scheme fell through, and Greenspun turned to journalism. With two other reporters, he published *Las Vegas Life*, an entertainment magazine, which led to Siegel hiring him as the Flamingo's publicist in 1947. After Siegel's murder, Wilbur Clark offered Greenspun the same position at the Desert Inn, for which he would receive 15 percent of the operation. He had no scruples about gambling and took the job. Almost immediately, some relatives asked him to provide arms for the new nation of Israel. He initially hesitated, but eventually threw himself into the dangerous and illegal smuggling, lying to friends and family about his secretive trips abroad.[50] To what extent this activity was the product of religious idealism, adventurism, or self-interest is speculative. He was so successful in running guns to Israel and wooing Latin American capitalists to support Israel that he was indicted and convicted for violating the Neutrality Act. Greenspun pleaded guilty, received a suspended sentence, paid a fine of ten thousand dollars (likely covered by "friends of Israel"), and lost his right to vote. While Greenspun was away, Clark sold control of the Desert Inn to Moe Dalitz and members of the so-called Mayfield Road Gang. The deal left Greenspun with just 1 percent of the property.[51]

In 1950, he landed on his feet with a one thousand–dollar loan from Nate Mack to run the *Las Vegas Free Press*, which he renamed the *Las Vegas Sun*. He soon took on his competition, the *Evening Review-Journal*, claiming, "The paper had long specialized in labor-baiting as well as 'Jim Crow' and antisemitic items." The *Sun* became Greenspun's bully pulpit to crusade against what he considered political or gambling corruption and to support the rights of the underprivileged. His supporters considered him brilliant, heroic, charming, and irrepressible in the face of perceived injustice. His critics found him self-serving, grandiose, acerbic, and brazen—but always colorful. Republican Greenspun joined Democratic governor Grant Sawyer and other politicians and casino owners in desegregating casinos and won a pardon from President Kennedy and a restoration of his right to vote. In 1962, Greenspun ran for governor against Sawyer and was roundly defeated in the primary, thanks, in part, to opposition and money generated by Dalitz. Over the next three decades, Greenspun used the *Sun* to become one of the most influential players in Las Vegas's future. He also became wealthy. CBS's *60 Minutes* news program later characterized him as the "second largest landowner in Las Vegas."[52]

The United Jewish Appeal

Support for Israel was the cement that held together the devotees of disparate Judaisms as well as secular Jews. Three funds to aid Palestine and provide assistance to European refugees merged in 1939 to form the United Jewish Appeal. Lacking any religious trapping, the UJA was a way for a nonpracticing Jew to make a commitment to Jewish survival. The phrase "I am because I give" identified their level of observance.[53] It became the nation's largest postwar philanthropy. Solicitors for this and other Jewish causes were often overbearing. Reno merchants recall Orthodox volunteers from the East detraining and heading immediately to Jewish downtown shops. Even the beleaguered owner's claim that he had "given at the Temple" did not deter the black-coated fund-raisers, who often refused to leave the store until they received a donation.[54]

In Las Vegas, the dons of the Jewish community chose Moe Sedway to head the United Jewish Appeal for four years. Congregation president Jake Kozloff chaired it in 1951, and Gus Greenbaum had the honor in 1952.[55] Another casino executive and former bootlegger, Sam Tucker, chaired the UJA from 1953 to 1956, followed by his partner Dalitz. In 1956, Ed Levinson, a Sands and Fremont co-owner later caught on an FBI tape discussing Meyer Lansky's share of the skim, rounded out the leadership of UJA chairs.[56] The group reflected the variety of casino personnel involved in Las Vegas Jewry's contribution to Israel. More significantly, however, the high visibility and responsibility of those with questionable pasts betokened their desire for respectability. Many of the same personnel who had proved their fund-raising ability for the United Jewish Appeal also would help build the new synagogue.

Nick Abelman in front of his upscale Ship and Bottle Club, Reno,
1932. (Courtesy of William Pettite)

Riverside Hotel lessee Nick Abelman with wife June at their Reno
home, 1946. (Courtesy of William
Pettite)

Judge Bert Goldwater, cofounder of Reno's short-lived Temple Beth Or, and, later, president of both Temple Emanu-El and Temple Sinai, seated next to statue of Mark Twain, ca. 2000. (Courtesy of Bert Goldwater)

Marvin Abrams holding a photo of his grandfather at his bar mitzvah celebration, Temple Emanu-El, with Dr. Nathan Joseph and Rabbi Tarlow (*left*), 1944. Tarlow was Nevada's first rabbi affiliated with a permanent congregation. (Courtesy of Mervin Tarlow and Marvin Abrams)

Sam Platt, appointed U.S. attorney for Nevada by President Theodore Roosevelt. He ran unsuccessfully for the U.S. Senate four times. (Courtesy of Sylvia Olcott)

Las Vegas's Jewish Community Center erected in 1943 by Congregation Beth Sholom, now a Christian academy. (Photograph by author)

The Temple Beth Sholom Gift Shop moved from the Jewish Community Center to the new synagogue in 1955. Its proprietors were (*left to right*): Pauline Shlisky, Edythe Katz, Rabbi Bernard Cohen's wife (first name unknown), Anne Nussbaum, and Sophie Katzman. (Courtesy of Edythe Katz Yarchever)

Las Vegas's first Temple Beth Sholom on Oakey Boulevard, erected 1955. (Photograph by author)

Louis Wiener Jr., early Las Vegas resident and attorney, ca. 1985. (Courtesy of Valerie Wiener)

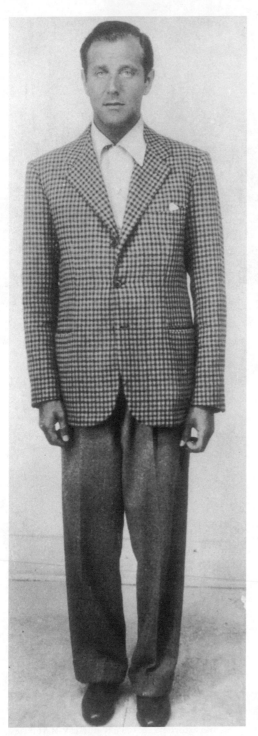

Benjamin "Bugsy" Siegel was sensationally depicted in the media as a visionary of the Las Vegas Strip. He was murdered in 1947. (Original Work the Property of the University of Nevada–Las Vegas, Las Vegas, Nevada)

Moe Sedway (*left*) and Gus Greenbaum took over control of the Flamingo hotel and casino after the murder of Bugsy Siegel. They were among those with organized-crime affiliations who owned and managed early Las Vegas gaming properties, ca. 1948. (Original Work the Property of the University of Nevada–Las Vegas, Las Vegas, Nevada)

Fiery editor of the *Las Vegas Sun* Hank Greenspun and his wife, Barbara Ritchie, in a footlight moment. (Original Work the Property of the University of Nevada–Las Vegas, Las Vegas, Nevada)

Past presidents of Temple Beth Sholom, ca. 1964. *Left to right, standing:* Melvin Moss, Jack Entratter, Harry Wallerstein, Al Goot, David Zenoff, and Jerry Mack; *seated:* Nate Mack, Mike Gordon, and Lloyd Katz. (Courtesy of Edythe Katz Yarchever)

Mel Hecht, rabbi of Las Vegas's Temple Ner Tamid, with its prominent donor Moe Dalitz, ca. 1981. (Courtesy of Rabbi Mel Hecht)

Reno's new Conservative Temple Emanu-El dedicated in 1973. (Photograph by author)

Reno's Temple Sinai erected in 1970 and scheduled to be replaced. (Photograph by author)

Lloyd Katz, leader in desegregation of Las Vegas movie theaters, 1955. (Courtesy of Edythe Katz Yarchever)

Eileen Brookman, eight-term Nevada assemblywoman and civil rights activist, ca. 1987. (Courtesy of Deborah Brookman)

Martha B. Gould, 1988 ACLU Civil Libertarian of the Year and member and chair of the U. S. National Commission on Libraries and Information Science, 1993. (Courtesy of Martha Gould)

Ruth Dickens, civil rights proponent and president of Reno's Temple Sinai, ca. 1975. (Courtesy of Robert Dickens)

Sheila Goodman, Las Vegas cocktail waitress who actively promoted local desegregation, 1972. (Courtesy of Katherine Goodman Selinsky)

Abraham Feinberg, peace activist, rabbi-in-residence at Reno's Center for Religion and Life and Temple Sinai, and outspoken advocate for senior citizens, ca. 1980. (Courtesy of Patricia Blanchard Feinberg)

Sanford Akselrad, student rabbi at Reno's Temple Sinai and Las Vegas's Temple Ner Tamid pulpit rabbi since 1988. (Courtesy of Temple Ner Tamid)

Milton Badt, Elko lawyer, fluent in Hebrew, and justice of the Nevada Supreme Court, ca. 1965. (Courtesy of Nancy Badt Drake)

Reno Lubavitch Rabbi Mendel Cunin in front of the facility to house the Lubavitch Chabad's sanctuary, kosher restaurant, and David and Parvin Farahi Jewish Day School, 2006. (Photograph by author and courtesy of Rabbi Mendel Cunin)

Mikveh near Reno's Lubavitch Chabad Center, 2006. *Mikvehs* are used for Orthodox women's purification rites and also for conversions by some Conservative and Reform Jews. (Photograph by author and courtesy of Rabbi Mendel Cunin)

Las Vegas Lubavitch Rabbi Shea Harlig and family; *top to bottom and left to right:* Motti, Rabbi Shea, Levi, Binie, wife Dina, Mendy, Chayala, Charie, and Yossi, 2005. (Courtesy of Rabbi Shea Harlig)

New Temple Beth Sholom in the Summerlin area of Las Vegas, 2000. (Courtesy of Temple Beth Sholom)

Felipe Goodman, pulpit rabbi at Las Vegas's Temple Beth Sholom since 1998. (Courtesy of Temple Beth Sholom)

Edythe Katz Yarchever, civil rights activist, foundress and chair of the Governor's Advisory Council on Education Relating to the Holocaust, and a living encyclopedia of early Las Vegas Jewry, 1989. (Courtesy of Edythe Katz Yarchever)

Reno Hebrew Cemetery, established no later than 1877 and vandalized in 1985. The cemetery is shared by Reno's Conservative and Reform congregations. (Photograph of unknown origin)

Dr. Judith Eaton, president, Community College of Southern Nevada, 1979–1983. (Courtesy of Judith Eaton)

Milton I. Schwartz, Las Vegas businessman and founder of the Hebrew Academy named after him, 2007. (Courtesy of Milton I. Schwartz)

Oscar B. Goodman, criminal defense lawyer, former president of Congregation Beth Sholom, and elected mayor of Las Vegas, 1999. On this latter occasion, he gave thanks at the local Lubavitch Chabad Center. (Courtesy of Oscar B. Goodman and photographer Les Stone)

Howard Rosenberg, television movie critic, art professor, and University of Nevada regent, 1996. (Courtesy of Howard Rosenberg)

Valerie Wiener, Nevada State Senate minority whip from
Las Vegas, 2005. She is one in a long list of Nevada Jews
who have served in the legislature since 1864. (Courtesy
of Valerie Wiener)

(*Opposite, top*) Three generations of the Reno Farahi family at Sasha's bat mitzvah;
left to right: Ben, David, Sasha, Bob, and John. The Farahi families have subsidized
intertemple youth trips to Israel and other Jewish causes. (Courtesy of John Farahi)

(*Opposite, bottom*) Shelley Berkley, five-term U.S. congresswoman from Las Vegas.
(Courtesy of Shelley Berkley)

Milton Glick, grandson of early-twentieth-century McGill merchant Morris Glick, became president of the University of Nevada, Reno, 2006. (Photograph by Jeff Ross)

Art Marshall—banker, businessman, board member of United Jewish Community/Jewish Federation of Las Vegas, member of the Nevada Gaming Commission since 1997, and University of Nevada Distinguished Nevadan, 2005. (Courtesy of Art Marshall and Audrey Dempsey/Infinity Photo)

Building a Temple, Keeping a Rabbi, and Schisms North and South

1950–1980

At midcentury, Congregation Beth Sholom had a full-time rabbi, David Cohen, cantor Herman Kinnory, and a Jewish Community Center it had outgrown. Jake Kozloff, a former Pennsylvania brewer who had just purchased the Last Frontier, was president of Beth Sholom when its members decided to build a temple at Sixteenth Street and Oakey Boulevard. Kozloff's restaurant at the Last Frontier was the late-evening meeting place to discuss such business.[1]

A building project of this magnitude required leadership and diplomacy to reconcile divergent opinions on architecture and tradition. Everyone had a slightly different understanding of what it meant to be a Jew. For some, it meant not denying their Jewish lineage and distancing themselves from all religious trappings. For others, it was to preserve the faith by educating children in Judaism, observing the Sabbath, and being part of a studying and worshiping community. For most others, "being a Jew" was interpreted broadly or strictly between these two poles. Success marked the careers of many families who were the core of Beth Sholom, but the most visible source of Las Vegas wealth was with the Jewish casino owners and operators—some with storied connections to organized crime. To spring the capital for a new synagogue from such a diverse population required a delicate touch.

Builders of Temple Beth Sholom

Attorney David Zenoff chaired the building committee, and construction chairpersons were local developer Irwin Molasky, Jean Messing, and contractor Melvin Moss. Ira Marschak, a former postman who got his start in architecture through correspondence courses, donated the plans for the synagogue. The initial fund-raiser for Temple Beth Sholom, produced and directed by Edythe Katz in the spring of 1955, was a simple "box supper" event held at Kozloff's New Frontier. Despite initial limp ticket sales, it turned out to be a well-attended function involving the entire Las Vegas community and cleared a neat six thousand dollars.[2] The construction and furnishing of Temple Beth Sholom continued for eight years through the presidencies of Harry Levy, Lloyd Katz, Al Goot, Zenoff, Moss, and Jack Entratter.

The congregation delegated community fund-raising to Merv Adelson, a builder of elegant homes outside the city limits. Cochairing with Adelson was his business partner, Moe Dalitz of the Desert Inn, who was a natural choice to help lead the fund-raising effort for Temple Beth Sholom. His targets were other recently arrived Jews who had made an investment in Las Vegas gambling.

One of the less well-known was Ruby Kolod, who helped Dalitz finance the Showboat, had a "reputation as a killer and blackmailer," and was allegedly involved in "a shady oil deal."[3] In later years, Kolod was unfavorably remembered by some members of the Jewish community and with genuine affection by others as a generous man who wanted to atone for and expunge his past misdeeds. "Now all of a sudden Ruby Kolod, married to Esther, can own a house and not look over his shoulder," recalled Mel Moss. Kolod gave money to the building effort, which included a youth center dedicated to his son, who had died in a Lake Mead boating accident. Although Kolod became a lightning rod for future governor Grant Sawyer, Lloyd Katz in 1954 respected him enough to ask him to serve on the temple's board of directors. "You don't want somebody like me," Kolod replied, and he remained a temple supporter from the sidelines. A decade later, the state tried to add him to Nevada's "Black Book."[4]

Melvin Moss and the Gin Rummy Tournament

Funds to complete the temple construction and add necessary furnishings had flagged, when Melvin Moss took over as president in 1957. Moss came from Detroit to the Las Vegas Army Air Corps Gunnery School in 1943. He met his future wife, Corinne "Corky" Wollman, at that time. They married in 1946, returned to Detroit, and then came back to Las Vegas with two children. "The financial support which we got from the Strip for the synagogue was very important," Moss later recalled. "But for the most part, the people on the Strip who identified themselves as being Jews were more superstitious than they were religious. They would come to the synagogue one day a year to do the Kaddish for their dead and then ask where they could send the check." The "check" was, perhaps, the remedy for a pricked conscience. Support for the temple also came from more religiously motivated individuals, such as Joe Bock, the Desert Inn's food and beverage purchasing agent. He was devoted to the temple's construction and "hustled money from every purveyor he did business with—from the Stardust to the Desert Inn."[5]

Harry Wallerstein and Max Goot were partners in a furniture store on South Main Street. When the synagogue seemed to be in serious jeopardy, the two came up with the idea of getting the casinos to sponsor a national gin rummy tournament to benefit the temple. It would take $250,000 to publicize the event nationally, host the tournament, and guarantee something for the temple. The plan was to approach ten Jewish owners or operators of casinos for a participant fee of $25,000.

Nine of the casinos contributed, but the Riviera held back. The Strip's first high-rise hotel, opened in 1955, belonged to a Miami group supposedly tied to Lansky, with the casino portion held by the Chicago Mob. It was slow to show a profit. Within months, Gus Greenbaum reluctantly came out of his Phoenix retirement to take over the Riviera, "only after being threatened by Tony Accardo and Jake 'Greasy Thumb' Guzik," to whom Greenbaum allegedly owed a million dollars from his Flamingo days.[6] Greenbaum pulled around him a group of Jewish investors and managers including Israel "Icepick Willie" Alderman, who had been so named because of the tool with which he enforced gang demands. Also in this group were Davie Berman and Ben Goffstein, from whom Temple Beth Sholom was attempting to solicit $25,000 for the gin rummy tournament. They were under severe pressure from Chicago and Miami to make the Riviera profitable.

Moss and his father-in-law, Murray Wollman, repeatedly tried and failed to enlist Goffstein's participation. However, one day Goffstein telephoned Moss for lunch and said he needed a favor. He wanted to build Las Vegas's first convention center and have John Creedman of Los Angeles as the builder. Creedman was not licensed in Nevada, but Moss was. The arrangement was that Moss would secure the permits to build the facility and hire his out-of-state partner, Creedman, to do the actual construction. Moss and Goffstein shook hands, and Goffstein proffered a check for $25,000 toward the gin rummy tournament.[7]

Eddie Gambarana and Jack Entratter

Another contributor to the building project was Italian Catholic Eddie Gambarana who accompanied Jack Entratter to the Sands from New York's Copacabana Club, where Gambarana was one of his key people. What Bock did with his purveyors and suppliers for the temple project, Gambarana matched. "He shook them down for every fund raising affair the Temple had—including money to build the building," Moss remembered. The gesture was one more example of Jewish-Italian cooperation in business and religious matters.[8]

As director of Sands entertainment, where he adamantly opposed any form of nudity, Entratter succeeded in bringing the most famous Hollywood celebrities to the Strip. He and the Sands were also mainstays of Temple Beth Sholom. Entratter succeeded Moss as congregation president from 1959 to 1963 and was elected again in 1966. The synagogue's exterior was subsequently completed with his personal gift of cash and the fourteen-foot Philippine mahogany doors at a cost of $25,000.[9]

Finding and Keeping a Rabbi

The transition from Jewish Community Center to Temple Beth Sholom occasioned disputes over rabbinical leadership and revealed how involved the Jewish gamblers were in synagogue affairs. Conservative David Cohen was the first rabbi to serve Beth Sholom while it met at the Jewish Community Center. His successors were Herman Kurtz and Arthur Liebowitz, whose tempestuous tenure included lawyer David Goldwater trying but failing to organize a new Reform congregation. (David's brother, Bert, was an officer of Reno Congregation Beth Or's earlier break from Temple Emanu-El.) Beth Sholom's board disagreed over whether to renew Liebowitz's contract. Some were concerned about the rabbi's ability to handle stress, and others thought he showed "signs of Reform." Although Hank Greenspun did not like him because he had been critical of Jews killing Palestinians in a bus incident, Katz was one of the rabbi's lifelines. Another supporter, Davie Berman, claimed to have been responsible for bringing Liebowitz to the Jewish Community Center.

The ensuing pressure of trying to maintain his position took its toll on Liebowitz, whose contract was up for a vote in May 1957. Many of the rabbi's strongest supporters on the board also owned or managed the town's casinos. On the fateful day when Liebowitz's contract was to be voted up or down, casino owners received notice that Frank Costello had been shot in the foyer of a New York apartment building. As surgeons removed the bullet, police authorities lifted notes from his clothing containing the exact dollar amounts of the skim from a Las Vegas casino for him and others. Because casino executives supporting the rabbi were caucusing about the Costello incident, they missed the selection meeting. Liebowitz failed to garner enough supporting votes, and his contract was not renewed. The search was on for another rabbi.[10] The incident was one more example of how religious and business interests could be intertwined in midcentury Las Vegas.

Being Beth Sholom's spiritual leader was a form of hazardous duty. Agreement on hiring and keeping a rabbi caused major strife. The agency recommending candidates was not enthralled with Las Vegas due to its sordid reputation and lack of culture. Consequently, the pool of rabbis available for an assignment there was not large. Moreover, once assigned, the rabbi was expected to be all things to all adherents of all branches of Judaism. Liebowitz's successor, Bernard Cohen, served during the transition from the Jewish Community Center to the newly completed synagogue on Oakey Boulevard. Rabbi Harry Sherer also had a brief term after Cohen's departure.

Aaron Gold, who became Beth Sholom's rabbi in 1964, had a longer-than-average tenure. His first sermon so captivated editor Jack Tell of the *Las Vegas Israelite* that he headlined it "All That Glitters Is Gold." As a child, the Polish-born Gold moved to Brooklyn, where his father served a Hasidic congregation as rabbi, cantor, and *shochet.* Originally ordained as an Orthodox rabbi, Gold later joined the Rabbinical Assembly of the Conservative movement. Immersed in interfaith and human rights activities, he served as president of the Clark County Ministerial Association and made news by talking down a potential suicide from a perch on the Fremont Hotel in 1968. Oscar Goodman later characterized Gold as handsome, charismatic, and dynamic. "His congregants adored him," Goodman recalled.[11]

Gold was in his ninth year at Beth Sholom when adversity struck. Israeli Avram "Abe" Schwartz had been hired as a Hebrew teacher shortly after Gold came to Beth Sholom. Schwartz dabbled in real estate, and Rabbi Gold was among his partners. At one point, they co-owned five downtown motels, but the investments went sour. Irwin Fish bought the Baghdad hotel from Schwartz but refused to pay him. Needing the money to cover other debts, Schwartz dunned Fish for payment. On May 15, 1972, Schwartz disappeared.

Liable for his partner's unpaid bills, Gold was forced to declare bankruptcy. The ensuing investigation led to allegations that at least one of the motels had catered to a dubious clientele. Gold could neither stand the publicity nor face his congregation. The Temple Beth Sholom board terminated him a month later.

In September, Schwartz's body was found in a shallow grave outside the city limits with a bullet in his head. One of the guilty parties turned state's evidence, revealed the grave to the authorities, and identified the killers as Irwin Fish and Douglas Webb. Gold was in no way implicated in any illegality, and, according to some, unscrupulous partners had duped him. Although a few congregants considered the rabbi a little too "slick," others characterized him as mellifluous. Mel Hecht, a Reform rabbi well distanced from Beth Sholom, mourned his departure as a major loss to Las Vegas Judaism.[12]

Temple Beth Sholom was the pride of Las Vegas Jewry, but the seeds of disenchantment over rabbinical leadership continued to be sown. Several former congregation presidents recalled that it seemed as if "we used to play 'Get a new Rabbi' every year."[13] Additionally, a growing interest in Reform Judaism within Beth Sholom eventually led to a schism similar to the exodus about to take place from Reno's Conservative Temple Emanu-El.

Reconciliation and a Vibrant Community at Temple Emanu-El in Reno—for a While

The strain of the Beth Or schism from 1940 to 1946 took its toll on Rabbi Harry Tarlow. Perhaps no Orthodox rabbi could have kept this disparate congregation together. Forces of reconciliation, however, emerged to consider a reorganization and reunion. Board members agreed to abandon their identification as an Orthodox Jewish congregation and affiliate with the Conservative United Synagogue of America. Former dissidents accordingly agreed to rejoin Temple Emanu-El. The reunification capped Tarlow's fourteen years of service, but his tenure with the officially Conservative congregation was now in jeopardy.

In 1947, the rejuvenated synagogue called Conservative rabbi Baruch I. Treiger to lead it. Tarlow privately admitted to his family that he felt betrayed. He had been, however, invited to remain as rabbi emeritus and received a five hundred–dollar annual stipend for five years to perform incidental duties as requested by the temple's board of directors. Heated discussions arose over whether Rabbi Tarlow or Rabbi Treiger ought to administer the B'nai B'rith welfare fund. Tarlow broke the impasse by moving that the fund be placed entirely in Treiger's hands. This gesture of goodwill won unanimous consent. The controversy was a signal for Tarlow to lower his rabbinical profile. While the Tarlows' sons attended local schools, Harry and Pearl continued to operate their kosher boardinghouses.[14]

Under Treiger's leadership, Temple Emanu-El became the focal point of Jewish religious, cultural, and educational life in northern Nevada. Treiger was the model, as chairman of the Washoe County Ministerial Association, on the Governor's Committee for the White House Conference on Children and Youth, as well as chaplain-on-call for the Jewish men at Stead Army Airbase and the Reno Veterans' Hospital. His wife, Leah, served on the Reno Council of Church Women and became vice president of the Reno League of Women Voters. She was also the temple's public relations expert, making sure that every significant synagogue event made the newspaper. Well-publicized and -attended lectures open to the entire community on topics of local and national interest turned Temple Emanu-El into a moral presence in Reno.[15]

B'nai B'rith meetings at the temple continued regularly but with a noticeable decline in attendance. "There was," wrote temple secretary Abe Melner, "just too much going on." The men decided to turn the regular evening B'nai B'rith meeting into a luncheon gathering.[16] Meanwhile, some controversies concerning race and religion showed how divided the lodge and the congregation could be—even though they shared much of the same male membership.

For several years, some lodge members encouraged support of an interfaith and interracial Boy Scout troop, which they deemed consistent with the congregation's outreach to the wider community. But some members openly disagreed, arguing that it diluted the lodge's focus on specifically Jewish matters, and they similarly opposed giving the lodge's Americanization Award to a Christian. In the latter case, debate was so fierce that the lodge dropped the idea altogether. The scout troop's future was also in jeopardy. Nevertheless, a majority agreed to establish a troop whose nucleus was "3 colored boys, 4 whites and 1 Japanese-American." The troop was to have a "colored scoutmaster, with former Bro. Bert Tannenbaum as Asst. Scoutmaster." Thought to be the first "Brotherhood Troop" in the state, the scouts met at the First Christian Church, but the lodge members, led by Louis Dickens, wanted it to meet at Temple Emanu-El. The congregation's board refused to allow it. Consequently, this groundbreaking interfaith and interracial group, which had grown to fourteen, met at the home of Sol Abrams, the new assistant scoutmaster and lodge member in good standing.[17] It was the Reno B'nai B'rith lodge's last stand. Its final recorded meeting was September 27, 1951.

The temple's success was another matter. Its accomplishments resulted in the United Synagogues of America singling it out to receive the Solomon Schechter Award for Distinguished Congregational Achievement during the years 1948–1950. Treiger was quick to remind his people that this award was not a "number drawn from a huge fish bowl of names of congregations through the United States and Canada," but the result of "concentrated, intensive labor . . . [to] serve as a new impetus to all of us."[18]

The reunited congregation flourished with its religious school, headed by Dr. Samuel Blatt, the Sisterhood presided over by Rae Zetooney, and a temple choir led by Madge Tillim. Within a few years, former Beth Or congregants had completely reintegrated themselves. The presidents of the congregation were a diverse group of community leaders: Dr. Sidney Tillim, superintendent of the State Mental Hospital; George Parker, co-owner of Reno's Parker Brothers Western Wear; attorney Bert Goldwater; Dr. Nathan Joseph, a Reno optometrist; and banker Herbert Brown. The presidencies of Goldwater and Brown, former officers of Temple Beth Or, symbolized the successful melding of the two congregations.

Just when Temple Emanu-El seemed to have consolidated, the Treigers announced their departure to accept an assignment at an eastern pulpit. Thus began a search for a new rabbi—a process that would dog Temple Emanu-El for the next fifty years. The temple turned to its retired rabbi, Harry Tarlow, to lead services before the family left for Los Angeles in 1953. Temple Emanu-El continued to carry Tarlow's name on its stationery for more than two decades thereafter as "Rabbi Emeritus."[19] The congregation hired Rabbi Meyer Schwartz, who departed five years later. Optometrist Nathan Joseph conducted serves during a three-year search for a rabbi.

The congregation called Rabbi Phillip H. Weinberg in 1961. During his four-year tenure, Weinberg was as active in civic affairs as any of his predecessors and was honored with the Outstanding Volunteer Award for his notable work for the United Fund. Temple Emanu-El was in the public eye and gave every appearance of having a congregation and rabbi in a marriage made in Zion. But clouds on the horizon eventually became the eye of a hurricane and threatened to tear the temple asunder.

Dissatisfied Jews Disconnect from Reno's Temple Emanu-El

Although Temple Emanu-El was officially "Conservative," its members' inclinations ran the spectrum of Judaism. The Orthodox members were, in the view of some congregants, intransigent on certain traditional practices. The small group of Beth Or Reform Jews who had remerged with Temple Emanu-El resented the consistent use of Conservative Sabbath and High Holiday prayer books. Personal disputes contributed to a roiling of one or another group in the congregation, thus blurring the differences along strictly religious lines.

Disagreement within the board of directors was common, but as one observer noted, "it had been going on for over forty years."[20] The discord went beyond matters of worship and concerned mainly procedures and personalities. Some staunchly Conservative and Reform members were particularly galled at the majority's support of Rabbi Weinberg, whose ethics they considered suspect. Several of them had received complaints from local bakery and dairy providers that Weinberg assured congregants that the products of a competing bakery and milk producer were "kosher." Weinberg's availability for quickie marriages also offended some people. By April 1962, the situation had, in one critic's words, become "intolerable, and the alliance fell apart."[21]

In a final dispute over extending Weinberg's contract for three years, more than two dozen couples walked out of the board meeting and resigned from the congregation. Casino employee and former boxer Jake Garfinkle was president at the time and resigned after the meeting to join the dissidents. Some, like the Garfinkles, wanted to form a second Conservative synagogue. Clearly, the break with Emanu-El was as personal as it was religious. After consulting with the regional rabbinical leadership, they determined that Reno could not support two Conservative congregations. Members of the dissenting group also predicted that Reform Judaism would be more attractive to Reno's unaffiliated Jews.[22]

The defectors finally agreed to affiliate with the Reform UAHC. Regional director Rabbi Joseph Glaser responded, and within weeks the new Congregation Temple Sinai was formed. The five founding couples were Eugene and Bea Brown, Sam and Judy Cantor, Louis and Ruth Dickens, Stanley and Frances Fielding, and Jake and Mary Garfinkle. Eugene Brown suggested the name "Sinai." It has been claimed by some and denied by most that the name acknowledged the generous donation from attorney John Sinai's estate, possibly to attract additional support from his son, David. All agreed that the name was appropriately common for a Reform temple.[23]

In addition to the founders, charter members included the Gumbert, Garell, Zentner, Melner, Jaffe, and Chernus families, with more quickly to follow. The Reno Reform group worshiped at the Masonic temple beginning in September 1962. In preparation for this historic event, the congregation's president-elect, Louis Dickens, built an ark and hand-carved Decalogue tablets in his basement. Dickens was a plumber by trade and not a carpenter, and the movement of the oversized ark took out the staircase wall of his new home. Gene Brown made a hurried trip to San Francisco to borrow a Torah, because Temple Emanu-El refused to release the Beth Or Torah it inherited in the 1946 merger. Obviously, feelings and tempers were raw across the Reno Jewish community.[24]

With a donated organ and a hired accompanist and soloist, Milton Gumbert led a mixed choir of ten nonprofessionals. Ethel Jaffe assumed preparation of young men for their bar mitzvoth. At the UAHC regional leadership's urging, the congregation formed a religious school that met first in a rented YMCA room and then at the Garfinkle and Zentner homes. A Sisterhood formed around Frances Fielding, and the congregation received the twice-monthly services of visiting rabbi Julius Liebert, who gave the congregation his personal Torah. The scroll was formally dedicated on May 26, 1963—apparently the first such ceremony held in Nevada. Nevada justice Milton Badt was the service's main speaker.[25]

Temple Emanu-El authorities tried to reunite the two congregations and met privately with Louis Dickens on a merger. However, the groups were beyond reconciliation. Reunification failed, and the tiny Congregation Temple Sinai was on its own.

Northern Nevada's Temple Emanu-El Fell and Rose

Rabbi Weinberg's tenure ended under a cloud in 1965. An allegation had arisen that the community-activist rabbi had received kickbacks from funeral parlors to which he directed business. For some congregants, the allegation—true or false—sealed his termination. Temple Emanu-El was fortunate to enlist Rabbi Jack Frankel as his successor for a three-year term. He had served during World War II with an army intelligence unit in France, where he met his future wife. Frankel's zest and charm contributed to the sense of unity and purpose that Temple Emanu-El needed.[26] He left for a post at Santa Rosa, California, in 1969.

Frankel's departure occasioned the decision to abandon the Emanu-El synagogue, whose support timbers had rotted away. Many in the congregation wanted to save the venerable structure for historic reasons. The City of Reno intervened, however, and condemned the building, which was formally vacated on December 31, 1970. After its demolition, it became the site of a high-rise parking garage for the Silver Legacy Resort Casino.[27] The new synagogue site was in fashionable southwest Reno.

Jacques Morvay served as temple president during the three-year construction transition, while Dr. Nathan Joseph was called again to lead religious services, assisted by cantor Sam Silverberg. Rabbi Maurice Lazowick of Capitola, California, led High Holiday services in the new Reno Centennial Coliseum. The board persuaded him to revisit Reno on alternate weekends to lead services and conduct bas and bar mitzvah classes—a heroic task he performed for six years.

Groundbreaking took place in fall 1972, and the building was dedicated the following April. The temple exterior, designed by local architect Graham Erskine, was considerably more modern than the West Street synagogue, but many of the interior furnishings on the bimah and around the ark had been in the original Temple Emanu-El a half century earlier.

One last-minute addition turned out to be an amusing error. During demolition of some structures in the oldest part of downtown Reno, workers uncovered a hundred square feet of ceramic tiles arranged in the form of a six-pointed star. Rabbi Lazowick was the only authority called upon to identify the artifact. He judged the design to be a Magen David (Star of David and symbol of the State of Israel) and possibly from the floor of a *mikveh* (ritual bath). The archaeological discovery was given to the temple and promptly cemented outside the synagogue's main entrance. Several years later, specialists from the University of Nevada studied both the design and the original location of the ceramic. They correctly concluded there was no evidence of a Jewish worship center on the Center Street site and noted that the Masons commonly used the design.[28]

Temple Emanu-El experienced a problem that plagued many American Jewish congregations: it could not or would not retain a rabbi for any length of time. The new synagogue's first rabbi, Bernard S. Herzig, lasted only a few months. Maurice Lazowick was hired part-time in 1971 but retired due to poor health six years later. Irnie Nadler had a stormy six years with the temple board and left to join the staff of Hebrew University in Jerusalem. Kalman Dubov lasted one year before returning to a navy chaplaincy. C. Joseph Teichman was a troubled man who died of a massive heart attack in 1988 at age forty-six. The temple had no rabbi for another year, hired Erwin Cuttler in 1989, and terminated him the following year. After another two-year hiatus, Arnold Stiebel served one four-year term, but his contract was not renewed. Avraham Keller, hired in 1997 and greeted like the Messiah, left Reno in three years to give his children a better Jewish education in Israel. Dany Melman stayed two years and left for a larger congregation in the South. Menashe Bovit, ordained in the Orthodox tradition, made accommodations to lead this Conservative-Orthodox congregation, which terminated his contract in March 2005 for what was described as "poor performance," which Bovit strongly disputed.[29]

Why could the temple not keep a rabbi? In many cases, the congregation did not *want* to keep the rabbi under the conditions he requested or because one of his actions—or inactions—offended the board. Rabbis reported leaving due to salary, the need for a Jewish school, and the lack of a Jewish infrastructure within the community.[30]

Building Temple Sinai and Hiring a Rabbi

Whereas Temple Emanu-El hired, fired, or let go eleven rabbis between 1965 and 2003, Congregation Temple Sinai was just trying to make ends meet. A fire at the Masonic temple in 1965 forced the Sinai group to move its services to the Reno Musicians Hall through 1970, as the group searched for a permanent home. Louis Dickens sold the congregation a three-acre parcel of land on the northwest outskirts of the city for eight thousand dollars. After several false starts, the synagogue began to rise in February 1970, at an initial cost of forty-five thousand dollars. Dickens provided plumbing fixtures, Sam Cantor donated electrical fixtures, and George Jaffe provided installation labor. Jake Garfinkle was responsible for landscaping and planting trees and shrubbery. The new structure was dedicated in August 1970, with Rabbi Julius Liebert in attendance as well as Rabbi Joseph Gumbiner, around whom the Beth Or group had rallied thirty years earlier. With some financial help from Jews living at Lake Tahoe, the congregation paid off the remaining twenty-eight thousand–dollar mortgage. County librarian Martha Gould and Eric Hobson supervised the children's religious school, while Abe Melner led a monthly study group for adults.[31]

Temple Sinai could not afford a full-time rabbi. It contracted with Hebrew Union College in Los Angeles for a student rabbi to officiate at services and meetings from Friday through Sunday evenings. Over the next decade, the congregation received well-remembered leadership from its first student rabbis, Michael Berk and Erin Petuchowski, to their last, Sanford Akselrad, who later played an essential role in the Reform movement's growth in Las Vegas. While in Reno, Akselrad married a member of Temple Emanu-El. Temple Sinai congregants boycotted the wedding despite their affection for Akselrad. Sinai members still considered Emanu-El hostile territory.[32]

The search for a permanent rabbi began in 1980. During the lengthy process, Sinai benefited from the temporary services of a remarkably talented rabbi retired from Blossom Temple in Toronto, Abraham Feinberg, who presided over the congregation's marriages and funerals. Although Feinberg's politics were to the left of most, his religious liberalism and social activism won great respect. Rabbi Paul Tuchman arrived in the summer of 1982 and presided over a growing congregation before accepting another position in Alabama in 1984. With the help of regional UAHC officials, Sinai's president, Robert Dickens (son of Louis and Ruth), hired Nevada's first female full-time rabbi, Myra Soifer.[33] The larger community initially considered her controversial and provocative, but she soon won appreciation as a principled, civic minded leader. She proved to have staying power into the twenty-first century.

Las Vegas's Congregation Beth Sholom

Every Jew is familiar with one or another version of the story about the man who was shipwrecked on a desert island and built two synagogues: he attended one and would "not be caught dead" in the other. In 1865, Virginia City formed two temporary synagogues for High Holidays, due to disputes over ritual and language. Temple Emanu-El in Reno survived twenty years before the Beth Or break. Beth Sholom in Las Vegas resisted a similar fate for almost three decades.

This single Las Vegas congregation formed in 1945 was officially Conservative, but its membership was religiously diverse. One way Beth Sholom served its constituencies was through a variety of organizational activities. The men had their own B'nai B'rith chapter and a temple Men's Club. Women's groups included the temple Sisterhood, B'nai B'rith Women, as well as local chapters of Hadassah and the society for Occupational Rehabilitation and Training (ORT). These organizations had teas, card parties, fund-raising events, and charitable ventures such as hospital visitations and seders for shut-ins. The fashion shows were gala events held at major casinos and often included celebrity performers. Additionally, a Senior Club worked with the aging population, and a Yiddish Club served those wishing to brush up on the lingua franca and ironic humor of their youth.[34] Beth Sholom served a polyglot Judaism from 1945 until 1974, and those early members who are still alive remember a strong sense of camaraderie, especially in their common support of Israel. Stress factors, however, were evident from the start. Internal bickering over the choice of rabbis reflected the disparity of Judaisms within the congregation.[35] A split was in the making.

Congregation Ner Tamid

The origins of Congregation Ner Tamid (Eternal Light) are clouded in a fog of anecdotes and conspiratorial accounts, and the truth has many faces. Modern Las Vegas Jews recall "old-timers" recounting the secret nature of Temple Beth Sholom dissidents' early meetings in private homes, the counting room of a local casino, and even a casino safe. For the most part, the early partisans were more recently arrived Reform Jews who simply wanted their own place of worship. Longtime members of Beth Sholom—even those with Reform leanings—were loath to leave friends and family for another congregation. As the number of dissidents grew, their leaders consulted with West Coast authorities of the UAHC for guidance. Once enough families could be counted on to make the break, the leaders—veterinarian Eugene Kirschbaum, and dentist David Wasserman—announced the formation of a new Las Vegas Reform congregation.

The as-yet-unnamed group of thirty-five families held its first services on Friday, June 7, 1974, in an auditorium of the West Charleston Baptist Church. Two hundred people attended the event, led by Rabbi Erwin Herman, a regional UAHC director. The guitar strumming of cantor William Sharlin set the tradition-breaking tone of Reform. Kirschbaum, who was to become the congregation's first president, announced that dues for the year were $300, plus another $100 toward a building fund. Thirty-five people signed on as charter members of Ner Tamid. Rabbi Stephen Weisberg arrived in 1975, and added to the one hundred–family congregation he had inherited.[36] Cantor

Regina Yarchever co-officiated at Ner Tamid's 1978 High Holiday celebration at the Las Vegas Convention Center. It was further evidence of the Reform movement's openness to women's full participation.

Weisberg left in 1978, and over the next decade the congregation went through a revolving door of rabbinical and lay leadership. One such casualty, Rabbi Mel Hecht, came with master of Hebrew letters and doctor of divinity degrees from Hebrew Union College of the Jewish Institute of Religion, Los Angeles. He disagreed with the lay board on financial matters, but before relations disintegrated, Hecht presided over a legacy that was pure Las Vegas.

Hecht told the story this way. Moe Dalitz was a larger-than-life figure whose religious interests reached well beyond his affiliation with Temple Beth Sholom. Dalitz had attended High Holidays led by Rabbi Hecht at a temporary synagogue and afterward invited the rabbi to see him. Hecht and Kirschbaum visited Dalitz at his Sundance office (now Fitzgeralds, downtown). Dalitz's attorney, future Ner Tamid president David Goldwater, was also present. Dalitz asked, "What do you need?" Hecht was unsure, so Dalitz started to put the numbers together. First of all, offices and a meeting place of about sixteen thousand to eighteen thousand square feet would cost about $750,000, plus another $250,000 for furnishings. The sanctuary could be built later. Dalitz then commented that Las Vegans expect to be "comped" for everything. So he pledged a half-million dollars that the congregation needed to match. Substantial donations followed, such as a five-figure sum from businessman Herb Tobman for a playground. The rest of the pledge was matched in ten weeks. A generation later, those who knew Dalitz only by his reputation with the Mob wondered why their social hall, library, and offices were named after a gangster.

Rabbi Hecht admitted to being a controversial figure within the congregation. He was too liberal for some and said, "They could not control me." The lay board had demanded that he give back to the congregation a portion of the stipends he earned from weddings and private services. Hecht refused, and the matter eventually went to the regional UAHC authorities, who sided with the board. The result was what Hecht later called a "divorce" of rabbi and congregation that, he acknowledged, "was good for both of us." Hecht's successor, Ed Moline, died soon after his installation. The membership plummeted from 350 families to a low of 80 families before the congregation succeeded in finding a rabbi who could provide Ner Tamid with long-term leadership.[37]

The new Reform congregations resulting from schisms at Conservative temples Emanu-El and Beth Sholom were products of internal politics, personality conflicts, and religious ideology. Later, geography and demography became additional causes for the proliferation of new congregations, particularly in the rapidly growing cities of southern Nevada.

Joe Yablonsky's Meteor and Some Intertribal Warfare

Joe Yablonsky's short passage across Nevada produced a tiny blip on the radar screen but a 5.0 reading on the Richter scale. Howard Hughes's takeover of Las Vegas casinos beginning in 1966 created the assumption that Mob rule had ended in Las Vegas. Yablonsky's appointment as an FBI special agent in charge in 1979 demonstrated the agency's belief that the city still needed work. Edythe and Lloyd Katz, Milton Schwartz, and a host of other well-wishers welcomed Yablonsky into Temple Beth Sholom. He shortly became a member of the temple's governing board.

Soon Yablonsky was publicly claiming that untold millions of casino profits were still going untaxed. One of his favorite targets was temple stalwart Dalitz, along with public officials who had taken bribes. Hank Greenspun, who had used the pages of the *Las Vegas Sun* for his own reforming crusades, took umbrage at Yablonsky's roiling of the waters. When Yablonsky targeted some of Greenspun's friends, the editor drowned him in the *Sun*'s ink.

Within a year, Yablonsky was being portrayed to the community as a pariah. Although widely quoted as saying, "The Jews treated me worse than anyone else," he retained supporters such as Katz, Schwartz, and others. After claims that Dalitz's matching gift of $500,000 to the new Ner Tamid was a protest against Yablonsky's position at Temple Beth Sholom, those willing to speak on the record in recent years have denied that Dalitz would have been so petty. Upon retiring in 1983, Yablonsky found himself virtually blackballed from the usual former FBI jobs in casinos. He shook the dust from his feet, left Las Vegas, and settled in Florida. Mention of his name still arouses strong feelings of affection and contempt.[38]

Antisemitism in the Twentieth Century

Nineteenth-century Nevada Jews were largely untouched by overt acts of discrimination or prejudice. This benign environment was due to Jewish civic leadership, their economic contributions, the smallness of the Jewish population itself, and the fact that Jews were just one ethnic minority in a state with the highest percentage of foreign-born citizens. At the turn of the century, antisemitism was rife in East Coast cities, where overcrowding and crime fueled a bias against immigrants, and Nevada began to reflect the growing malaise.[1]

Antisemitism in Nevada must be read through the prism of the Jews' millennial battle for acceptance in a dominant Christian society. Those who emigrated from central and eastern Europe in the mid-nineteenth century left behind discriminatory laws depriving them of property ownership and citizenship and an environment that regarded their religion as inferior. They were among the earliest survivors of a culture endemically hostile to Jews. The Holocaust could not have been carried out without massive denial and a lingering religious belief that Jews deserved to pay for the death of Jesus.[2] The examples of antisemitism in Nevada were a vestige of this mind-set nourished by ignorance and the need to scapegoat society's ills.

The Specter of Antisemitism Nationwide and in Nevada, 1900–1950

A kind of malevolently capricious anti-Jewish sentiment existed in the private conversations, personal correspondence, and diaries of Nevadans from the beginning of the century to its end. One of these appeared in a 1905 letter from Governor John Sparks, who had made his fortune as a cattleman in Elko County. There he would have known, firsthand, members of the large Badt family, who were also ranchers and merchants in both Elko and Wells. When Mel Badt sought his younger brother Herbert's appointment as U.S. postmaster of Wells, Sparks complained to his friend Senator Francis Newlands. Herbert Badt, wrote Sparks, was a "wild Jewboy," and Mel was "a rich

Jew" and "the worst enemy we have in this state." He expressed his intention to write directly to President Theodore Roosevelt to support the incumbent Wells as postmaster and consequently "knock out a rich Jew."[3]

Twenty-one when Sparks tried to prevent his brother's appointment, Milton Badt was unaware of the governor's bias. "There was no prejudice against Jews, as far as I could see," he later said of his early years in Nevada. Badt recalled being treated with the greatest consideration and, he noted, elected "Master of my Masonic Lodge, the Exalted Ruler of my Elks Lodge, [and] the President of the Chamber of Commerce."[4] The attitude toward Jews represented by Sparks doubtless was shared by some, but not expressed in public or polite society.

The mood nationwide, however, was growing otherwise. At about this time, Mark Twain became caught up in a dialogue with a *Harper's* reader who asked, "Will a Jew be permitted to live honestly, decently, and peaceably like the rest of mankind?" Twain responded that Jews were "quiet, peaceable, industrious, unaddicted to high crimes and brutal dispositions," no burden on local charities, and benevolent toward others. But he acknowledged that the common view of Jews was quite the opposite. It was the reputation "for small forms of cheating, and for practicing oppressive usury . . . arranging cunning contracts . . . [and] smart evasions." Consequently, Twain predicted, the Jews would always be regarded as "strangers-foreigners" wherever they were.[5] Harvard professor Harry Austryn Wolfson later confirmed this view. "Because of our Judaism we must be prepared to give up some of the world's goods," he wrote in a pamphlet titled *Escaping Judaism.* He then countered the American adage that all men are born equal: "Some are born blind, some deaf, some lame, and some are born Jews."[6]

Jewish historian Henry Feingold has claimed that antisemitism in the 1920s and 1930 was discontinuous and episodic.[7] Although immigration restrictions and Klan activities in the twenties fell into such categories, a form of antisemitism was pervasive within many Christian churches. Catholics and Protestants singled out Jews as part of their ongoing missionary conversion strategies. Such efforts were based on the deeply held belief that Christianity superseded Judaism and salvation was possible only through baptism. Marriage between a Catholic and Jew was null and void in the church's eyes, and participation in Jewish religious services was forbidden. On Good Friday, Catholics chanted "Amen" to two consecutive prayers for the conversion of the Jews, who were characterized as "perfidious," "treacherous," and "blind." The notion that Jews had a responsibility for killing Christ was widespread and provided a religious excuse for discrimination. Modification of these views and practices did not significantly change for another fifty years. American citizens were officially tolerant of all religions, but some Christian churches officially maintained a deep sense of religious superiority, which provided a sacred basis for institutional discrimination across the nation at universities and in social and country clubs.

Jews interviewed for this study, who grew up in Nevada in the 1930s, initially responded that they experienced no antisemitism in their youth. Invariably, however, they added something like, "Of course there were the occasional name-callings in the school yard or the cat callings of a bully."[8] The Gentile hecklers likely had no ideological basis for their feeling about Jewish classmates but had picked up the baiting habit at home or on the street, where groups had their nicknames—mick, spic, dago, kraut, fish-eater, or kike.

Masonic and Fraternal Orders: A Change in National Policy

The editor of one of San Francisco's Jewish newspapers announced to the world in 1896 that "there is more freedom from bigotry and fanaticism on this Coast than anywhere in the world."[9] This optimistic assessment contrasted with ominous signs in the East, where the heretofore welcoming arms of Masonic and other fraternal orders were restricting membership to Gentiles.

Why had Jews in the West been so actively involved with Freemasonry, the International Order of Odd Fellows, and the Knights of Pythias? The answer in its simplest form was that Jewish men were gregarious, successful, and desirous of being accepted as Americans. The "universalism" that characterized the constitutions of most fraternal organizations reached across ethnic and religious affiliations, though racial bars remained high. Historian of Freemasonry Lynn Dumenil includes both the nineteenth and twentieth centuries when she writes, "Jews (when they were admitted to the order), assuming they could ignore the occasional slip in prayer reference, could also find in Masonry a religious spirit congenial with their traditions and could have the satisfaction of knowing that much of Masonry was drawn from the Old Testament."[10]

Some Gentiles avoided an affiliation with Freemasonry due to the common belief that Masons and Jews were together bent on controlling the world. The French Rothschilds—international symbols of wealth and power—struck many as the example par excellence of Jews with world-dominating aspirations. The Dreyfus Affair (1894–1899), in which a French Jewish military officer and affiliated Mason, Alfred Dreyfus, was accused of a treasonable breach of French security, helped connect Jews and Masons in the public mind. The bogus *Protocols of the Elders of Zion,* disseminated in the 1920s through Henry Ford's newspaper, the *Dearborn Independent,* nurtured this view.[11]

Fraternal organizations across the country in the twentieth century consequently experienced a decline in Jewish membership. The attrition was due not only to membership restriction. Jews avoided groups that promoted a xenophobic Anglo-Saxon Christianity. As religious spokesmen like Josiah Strong argued for identifying "America" with Protestant mores, Masonic and other fraternal lodges became more self-consciously Christian. The rising spirit of antisemitism along with the more explicit identification of lodges with Christianity moved Jews in large cities to form their own separate Masonic lodges. No such trend was evident in Nevada, where Jews were charter members and state officers of these organizations.[12]

On the first Yom Kippur observance at Reno's new Temple Emanu-El in 1921, Samuel Platt took the occasion to criticize Henry Ford's slander of Jews as "money-getters" rather than "money-makers." He reminded his audience that Siegfried Marcus, a Jew, was credited with inventing the first gas-powered machine—the basis of Ford's own "money-getting."[13] Still a faithful adherent of Freemasonry, Platt was a prominent Jew who as a young man was chosen master of the Carson City Masonic Lodge no. 1. When invited to address the Carson lodge for its centennial in 1962, Platt, then eighty-eight, fondly recalled "the mysterious, magnetic pull of Masonry, perhaps nurtured in part by a revered and devoted father, with a spiritual philosophy of life and living I could never hope to emulate." A Jewish heritage was no barrier to Masonic membership, and Platt's father went so far as to affirm that Freemasonry was the only religion a man really needed.[14]

Northern Nevada Jews maintained their memberships in Masonic and fraternal groups well into the twentieth century. Relationships between Jews and these organizations were consistently cordial. When Reno congregations were without a permanent synagogue, they routinely used the Knights of Pythias, Odd Fellows, or Masonic halls for services. By contrast, Las Vegas Jews had no tradition of charter membership in fraternal or civic organizations. They had to break down the barriers of membership discrimination.

The Ku Klux Klan in Nevada

The resurgence of Waspish feelings toward eastern Europeans in the United States contributed to the passage of federal immigration-restriction laws in 1921 and 1924. The largest allocations of immigrants were accorded to those from Great Britain, Ireland, and Germany, reflecting the "old immigrants" of the nineteenth century. Such emphasis on "Nordic" populations was consistent with Ku Klux Klan's description of "American." The Klan underwent a revival during the xenophobic twenties. Between 1924 and 1926, ten Klaverns organized in the Nevada towns of Reno, Carson City, Elko, Las Vegas, and Caliente.

Their first major appearance was the burning of a fiery cross announcing a meeting at the Reno Odd Fellows Hall in April 1924. A June 28 cross burning on Peavine Mountain was visible to the entire city and heralded the first initiation of a local citizen into the Klan. The organizational headquarters and recruiting station in Reno were Jake Wainwright's Standard Oil Station and the Sierra Street Garage.[15] The organization produced 130 marchers for a parade celebrating "100 percent Americanism" on October 17. The event attracted thousands of spectators—some of whom hurled tomatoes at the participants. Although Jews and Catholics were among the traditional scapegoats for the Klan, the weakness of anti-Catholicism and antisemitism in Nevada provided poor soil for the Klan's sowing of hatred.[16]

Political Case Studies: Platt, Georgetta, and McCarran

Sam Platt and George Wingfield were rivals for the position of Republican National Committeeman from Nevada in 1920. Wingfield has been described as one "whose crude prejudices were never far below the surface." When he learned that some Reno City Council members supported Platt against him, he lumped them together and complained that "the Jews at city hall are counting us out." Such sentiments were uncommon in Reno, which had just broadly encouraged the erection of the first synagogue.[17]

Northern Nevada had no wholesale restrictions on Jews. Platt was a member of the Reno Country Club, a member of Carson City's Masonic Lodge, a Reno Rotarian, co-owner of the *Reno Gazette Journal,* president of the Nevada Historical Society, a founder of the Reno Community Concert Association, and member in good standing of Reno's B'nai B'rith lodge. He had run unsuccessfully for congressional office three times. He lost his first by forty votes in his 1914 bid for U.S. Senate against Francis G. Newlands. In 1916 (when he endorsed a national suffrage amendment) and again in 1928, he lost to Key Pittman and was poised to try again in 1940.

Pittman was a hard drinker whose binges were well known to insiders. Reno postmaster Pete Petersen wrote his friend Senator Pat McCarran that Pittman was drunk most of the time, and "Sam Platt is hammering away, turning out great crowds wherever he has appeared, and if it were not for the fact that he is a Jew, no one knows what could happen in November."[18] Days before the November election, Pittman was drunk, and his managers decided to keep him out of public view. They were quoted as saying they were keeping the senator "on ice." He made no public appearance during the days before the election. Platt carried his home county but lost the election two-to-one statewide.

The rumor spread that Pittman had died before the election and was literally "kept on ice" at the Mizpah Hotel in Tonopah, where he had been scheduled for a preelection speech. Platt could not believe that he had lost the election to a dead man, and he was correct. Recent research has unequivocally determined that Pittman was in a suite at the Riverside Hotel where he took sick after a drinking bout. He was taken to the hospital and died several days after the election.[19] Isolating a single reason for Platt's loss to Pittman is impossible. The incumbent simply may have ridden the coattails of Franklin Roosevelt's landslide victory. Whatever latent antisemitism may have existed within the populace-at-large proved less important in Platt's several congressional defeats than his consistent refusal to cooperate with Wingfield's bipartisan coalition. Platt ran as a loner, paying his own way, depending on the correctness of his views and the power of his oratory but lacking a sufficiently broad two-party base.

Platt was a Jew who never denied his ancestry and donated to Jewish causes because he knew he should. At the age of sixty-five, his political career over, he kept speaking and writing about Nazi atrocities before and during the war. His rhetoric was strongest against the murders of innocent people in concentration camps, and he called for the harshest punishments of the perpetrators. He was also a proponent of outlawing war altogether. His outspoken views received wide circulation in the press.[20]

One of those taking a great interest in the 1940 Platt-Pittman race was Clel Georgetta, a native-born Nevada attorney who considered himself senatorial timber and hoped one day to defeat the alcoholic incumbent. Born "Cleleo," in 1901, on a White Pine County ranch, he carried the baggage of a lifelong bigot. His well-kept diary told of an early encounter at Gold Hill, Nevada, with a young woman he identified (almost with a leer) as attractive, clever, and well read. "If she were not Jewish," wrote Georgetta, "I would go back to see her sometime."[21]

A dozen years later, his opinion of Jews was still quite plain. He was defending a client whose adversary was represented by the New York firm of Javits, Javits, and Max Steuer. When, in his words, "the bluffing Jews" refused his offer to settle out of court, he commented that he could not "conceive of a Jew turning down a virtual gift of $4,500." Days later, he recounted his reprimand to a firm member for not negotiating the settlement: "No doubt I expected too much, considering your breed," he claims to have said to the Jewish lawyer, "which I am now thoroughly convinced is the lowest, the smallest, the cheapest, skunkiest type of Kike Jew, a breed that contaminates the world wherever it is found." Georgetta lost the case, and his partner blamed him for a "lack of sound judgment . . . based on my dislike of the Jews." Georgetta's inflated ego erupted, as he characterized his partner as small and petty. At about the same time, Georgetta had been invited to represent a family in a small-claims case against a Reno Jewish hotel owner who cut a branch from the family's front-yard tree, which obscured the hotel sign. Georgetta chose not to take what he considered a penny-ante damage suit. His diary comment was that he had no such time, "much as I would enjoy it, as I love to sue a Jew."[22]

As the 1940 November election neared, Republican Georgetta peppered his diary with anti-Roosevelt statements and comments on the race between fellow Republican Platt and Pittman. Georgetta attended a preelection rally at which Platt spoke for an hour. Georgetta criticized the silver-tongued Platt's speech as repetitive of Fourth of July rhetoric. "To me," wrote Georgetta, "he was a flop."[23] Whether Georgetta was able to bring himself to vote for Platt is unknown. Although a staunch Republican himself, Georgetta likely preferred that Pittman win so that he might become an easy mark for Georgetta six years later. Pittman's death foreclosed that option, but despite his antisemitism and demeaning attitude toward Mormons and women found in his diary, Georgetta served as White Pine County assemblyman in 1931 and was appointed to a vacant district court judgeship, which he retained for a single term.[24]

Pittman's death removed one of the last obstacles to political domination for his longtime opponent, the junior Democratic senator from Nevada, Pat McCarran. McCarran's attitude toward "the Jews" was hostile and paranoid. He blamed "the Jews" for opposition to his anticommunist initiatives. When Rabbi Harry Tarlow approached McCarran after World War II to expedite his brother-in-law's immigration to the United States, McCarran instinctively asked, "He isn't a Communist, is he?"[25] In McCarran's mind, "Jews" and "communists" were coterminous—not unlike the conflation of the two terms by Nazis, though the comparison likely would have embarrassed McCarran.

A few years later, Reno postmaster Pete Petersen suggested a political strategy for McCarran that would give the appearance of being opposed by "the Jews." Petersen's rationale was, "I don't think that particular race is too well thought of in this state."[26] This was doubtless a good-faith assessment of his own personal feelings or those he attributed to his friend. The Mc-Carran-Walter Immigration Act of 1952, vetoed by President Harry Truman but overridden by Congress, favored immigrants from northern and western Europe, which negatively affected Jews attempting to leave eastern European countries. Its substance was under discussion during the 1952 presidential campaign between Adlai Stevenson and Dwight D. Eisenhower. "It seems both Stevenson and Isenhower [sic] are dumb as to law," McCarran wrote to his wife. "They both show gross ignorance as to my bill. . . . The Jews are misleading both of them." The Democratic nominee for U.S. Senate from Nevada, Thomas Mechling, had also criticized McCarran. "He too," McCarran countered, "is being led by eastern Jews, and 'Commies.'" When the Jewish U.S. senator from New York, Herbert Lehman, opposed the restrictive legislation, McCarran referred to him and other opponents as part of the "cloak-and-suit" crowd from New York's garment district.[27]

One of those who resented McCarran's thinly veiled jibe was Hank Greenspun, who took on McCarran as well as the *Las Vegas Review Journal*, which the senator controlled and Greenspun also considered racist and anti-semitic. Suddenly, in 1952, forty casinos dropped their advertising in the *Las Vegas Sun*. Greenspun was able to verify that a call from Washington, D.C. (presumably initiated by McCarran), had triggered the boycott. Greenspun sued McCarran and the involved casinos, whose lawyers urged them to settle out of court. Although McCarran was never formally implicated, the hasty settlement of more than eighty thousand dollars to Greenspun spoke volumes to anyone paying attention.

McCarran died making a speech in Hawthorne, Nevada, in September 1954, and Greenspun—through his newspaper—elevated his role as an influence broker in southern Nevada politics. One Jew who considered McCarran a friend was Eddie Ginsberg of Reno's Home Furniture. He was an honorary pallbearer at McCarran's funeral for which the Anti-Defamation League and the local B'nai B'rith lodge officially reproached him. Morton Saiger, McCarran's Las Vegas occasional chauffeur, experienced no anti-Jewish bias during their many encounters. McCarran's antisemitism may, indeed, have been directed to faceless Jewish communists rather than to friends and acquaintances.[28]

No Jewish Faculty at Reno's University of Nevada—for a Time

Between 1938 and 1955, a University of Nevada dean let it be known privately to his department chairs that he had no interest in employing Jewish faculty. He openly admitted to one chairman that he simply had a prejudice against Jews. Though no documentary evidence supports such a ban, a number of faculty and administrators have attested to having heard that this person made it clear: "As long as I am in this office, there will be no Jewish faculty." One departmental chairman reportedly followed his dean's order by requiring pictures of faculty candidates in order to peruse them for "Negro" or Jewish features.[29]

Robert M. Gorrell, chairman of the English Department (1946–1952), was fully aware of the administrator's bias but recommended Milton Miller for a short-term lecturer position. Miller had indicated on his application that his religion was "Jewish." Gorrell elected to suppress this datum in the paperwork forwarded up the line, and Miller was hired. Ironically, Miller ended up teaching English to the dean's son, who "thought he was the best teacher he'd ever had."[30] Although Miller remained with the university for only three years, he may have been the only Jewish faculty member hired during the period of the unofficial ban. Shortly before his departure to complete doctoral work, Miller was married in a Jewish ceremony held at the Gorrell home. Faculty children present at the fireside ceremony were stunned when Milton crushed a wineglass on the hearth. It was a brief teachable moment on Jewish tradition.

After 1955, the door opened to hiring faculty without reference to Jewish heritage or religion. The English Department hired George Herman in 1957, though the department chair later claimed to have been ignorant of his Jewish heritage. He was also active in the Reno Little Theater, taking the role of figures such as Otto Frank and "a traditional Jewish papa." Although he received rave reviews for his acting and kudos for his teaching, Herman was not widely known to be Jewish. Herman has affirmed that he experienced no antisemitism as a faculty member.[31]

The decisive moment in Nevada's attraction of Jewish scholars was the hiring of two professors in the Department of Psychology who had international reputations. Gerald Ginsburg was previously affiliated with the prestigious World Health Organization, and Alan Gardner astonished the scientific world with his successful experiments in teaching sign language to chimpanzees. After 1963, Jewish hires spiked significantly, thanks also to the growth of the University of Nevada, Las Vegas (UNLV), which began as a branch of the Reno university in 1951 and was spared the residual antisemitism of the 1950s.

Postwar Decline of Antisemitism, Jewish Idols, and Catholic Accommodations

Historians commonly agree that antisemitism declined after World War II, but there is no consensus on the cause. People were only marginally aware of the Holocaust or of Jews serving in the armed forces. Although Jews were thrilled with Bess Meyerson's crown as Miss America and Hank Greenberg's crack-of-the-bat World Series win for Detroit in 1945, Gentiles did not seem to notice their ethnicity. Popular movies such as *Gentlemen's Agreement* in 1947 and Herman Wouk's *Caine Mutiny* in 1954 highlighted the worst side of antisemitism and may have contributed to Jews being understood by some as simply Americans with a different religion. Although their names had been anglicized, Jewish comedians such as Jack Benny (Benny Kubelsky) and George Burns (Nathan Birnbaum) were making all of America laugh. Eddie Cantor and Al Jolson had been among the country's popular singers. Fred Astaire danced to the syncopations of George Gershwin, whereas Rodgers and Hart and Hammerstein provided music and lyrics for Broadway. Jews were everywhere in the entertainment world, though many had succumbed to the assimilation strategy of changing their names, including Paulette Goddard (Marion Levy), Lauren Bacall (Betty Perske), and John Garfield (Julius Garfinkle). Americans sought advice from Ann Landers (Esther Pauline Friedman Lederer) and her sister, Abigail Van Buren or "Dear Abby" (Pauline

Esther Friedman Phillips), but few knew the Jewish ancestry of these prominent entertainers and self-help personalities.[32] Their ethnicity did not figure
noticeably as a cause of the postwar philo-Semitic atmosphere.

Coinciding with the postwar thaw of antisemitism was a revolutionary
and more substantive development in Catholic theology, which led to a re-
freshingly new understanding of the Jews' role in the death of Jesus. While
liberal Protestant and Jewish theologians labored over the theories of the
origins of the Hebrew and Christian scriptures, Catholic biblical scholarship
was mired in literalism until in 1943 it moved beyond hidebound interpretations. The ensuing new era provided a basis for collaboration among Catholic, Protestant, and Jewish exegetes.[33]

Two decades later, Pope John XXIII breathed new life into the Catholic
Church with his proclamation of an ecumenical council. The documents resulting from the 1963–1965 deliberations of Vatican II were iconoclastic and
controversial. Among the council decrees were that Catholicism was not co-
extensive with the "true church"—thus reversing the long-standing edict that
"outside the Church there is no salvation." Thanks to the efforts of American
theologians, the council agreed that everyone should be allowed to exercise
freedom of religion. Moreover, Jews were to be regarded as redeemed by reason of the promises to their fathers and therefore not to be proselytized. John
XXIII's successor, Paul VI, opposed the latter initiative and attempted to di-
lute its language. After much debate and with strong support from German
bishops, the council agreed that the death of Jesus "cannot be blamed upon
all the Jews then living, without distinction, nor upon the Jews of today. . . .
The Jews should not be presented as repudiated or cursed by God, as if such
views followed from the holy Scriptures." Paul VI capitulated and promul-
gated the council's action.[34]

Overstating the impact these decrees had on interfaith relationships is almost impossible. Although ultraconservative Catholics were upset that their
"unchangeable church" made such momentous adjustments, the widespread
euphoria over the new openness characterizing the official church temporarily
muffled their voices. Dialogues between Catholics and Protestants and among
Jews and Christians became part of the wave of increased tolerance. The Holy
Week liturgy no longer referenced the "blind and perfidious Jews." Instead,
Catholics were being taught to regard Jews as kindred spiritual Semites.

Interfaith Cooperation

University-campus chaplains in Nevada responded to the Vatican II initiatives by establishing Centers for Religion and Life in Reno (1968) and Las Vegas (1973). Their long-range purpose was to rise above the parochial goals and activities of Newman Clubs, Luther Leagues, and Wesley Foundations by living out in the present a future ideal of cooperative ministries. Hillel Foundations did not exist in these early days at either university campus. Rabbi Jack Frankel joined the Catholic and Methodist cofounders to make the Reno Center an interfaith effort. His successor, Abraham Feinberg, became rabbi-in-residence at the center, from which he vigorously encouraged social activism beyond sectarian lines.[35]

Protestant and Catholic efforts to study and ameliorate the historic causes of antisemitism and racial divisions reenergized the stately National Conference of Christians and Jews. Its Reno and Las Vegas chapter members included the area's religious, civic, and political leaders. In the 1960s, future governor Mike O'Callaghan, Lubertha Johnson, Flora Dungan, and Eileen Brookman all figured prominently in the Las Vegas citizenry's bridge-building efforts across religious and racial lines.[36]

In Reno and Las Vegas, mainline Protestant ministers and liberal Catholic priests occasionally exchanged pulpits—a practice unthinkable for Roman Catholics before the 1965 Vatican II decrees. Although the same practice did not obtain between synagogues and churches, the respect and level of cooperation among Christians and Jews grew as they invited each other to their lecture halls and study groups.

In Las Vegas, Italian Catholic Eddie Gambarana, a contributor to Jewish causes, called upon his Jewish friend Melvin Moss to lead a building drive for Las Vegas's Catholic Home of the Good Shepherd for unmarried pregnant women. Moss had just completed a major fund-raising drive for Temple Beth Sholom, and he declined. The wily Gambarana asked Moss to reserve his judgment until he met with the home's mother superior. Moss recalled that the woman looked like she had been cast for the role in *The Bells of St. Mary's*. He explained that the temple fund-raiser had depleted his resources and contacts. The same people gave to all the good causes, and he had already become a pest. Consequently, he argued, he doubted much money could be raised. Moss remembered she looked him square in the eye and said, "Just help me with this project, dear. Don't worry, we'll make it. . . . The Lord will provide." Moss melted, succeeded, and enjoyed the challenge.[37]

A Roman Catholic leader of interfaith efforts in Las Vegas was the Reverend Patrick Toomey, C. S. V. Toomey's experience as a military chaplain extinguished any anti-Jewish bias to which he may have been exposed on Chicago's South Side, where he was raised. He inherited a plan to build a church in the heart of the Las Vegas Strip. It started as a storefront operation with a debt of $29,662 until he put together a fund-raising group, which included his friend Moe Dalitz. The Desert Inn had earlier contributed land then valued at $50,000 at 302 Desert Inn Road. The Tropicana, Flamingo, Sands, Riviera, Thunderbird, Sahara, and Fremont hotels contributed an average of $20,000 each to start construction of what came to be the Guardian Angel Shrine in 1963. The Jewish-controlled hotel-casinos accounted for an estimated $175,000 toward its construction.[38]

Toomey was not simply a convivial Irishman who had kissed the Blarney Stone. When the Six Days' War broke out in 1967, he was at the forefront of a massive inter-religious rally with Rabbi Aaron Gold in support of Israel. At a time when Catholics were getting accustomed to the idea of Jews no longer being "perfidious," Toomey publicly declared his love for them as part of the people of God. Most important for this rally, he stood for Jews' "right to exist, and exist as a nation." He denounced the erection of a statue of Jesus in front of the Las Vegas Convention Center as "a source of embarrassment for the Jewish citizens who live and work in Las Vegas and participate in events at the Convention Center."[39] Upon Toomey's departure in 1970 to head a graduate program at the Washington Theological Coalition, the Jewish community feted and honored him. Temple Beth Shalom recognized him with its Israel Award. *Las Vegas Israelite* editor Jack Tell congratulated him as "responsible, more than anyone else, for the development of the finest relationship anywhere among Protestants, Catholic and Jews."[40]

Also notable was Donal "Mike" O'Callaghan. Before being elected governor in 1971, O'Callaghan had established a relationship with George Brookman based on a special affection for Israel. In addition to his many supportive postgubernatorial editorials in the *Las Vegas Sun*, O'Callaghan joined the Sar-El, the Israel Defense Force volunteer work program. George Brookman accompanied him on one of his visits, where the two helped repair tanks. Between 1985 and 2004, O'Callaghan served the Israeli cause though the Sar-

El program twelve times. The only conditions he required from the Sar-El organization were, first, to call him "Mike" and, second, a vehicle and directions to a place where he could attend daily mass.[41] The Las Vegas Jewish Federation and the David L. Simon Foundation honored O'Callaghan with the David L. Simon Bridge Builder for Peace Award on February 8, 2004, at its annual Champions of Freedom Dinner Gala. O'Callaghan died of a heart attack on March 5, 2004, while attending mass in Las Vegas. His acts of devotion to Israel and his leadership in racial equality endeared him to the Jewish community and prompted Danny Greenspun (Hank's son) to say of him, "As a devout Catholic, Mike was the best Jew I ever met."[42]

Breaking Down Barriers in Social, Civic, Fraternity, and Sorority Groups

Before World War II, virtually all business and social clubs nationwide barred Jewish membership, and almost two-thirds continued to do so into the early 1960s. Northern Nevada was an exception. The Reno Country Club membership included anyone—Jew or Gentile—with the money and disposition to join. The Reno Prospectors' Club was a prestigious organization, and as one old-timer observed, "The Jews always had a table [there]." Exceptions to the open membership of fraternal groups after World War II were the Greek societies at colleges and universities, which often maintained a white-Christian-only policy.[43] The University of Nevada's fraternities actively recruited high-profile Jewish students such as Buddy Garfinkle and Sinclair Melner. However, in 1947, football players Leonard Marmor and Kenneth Sinofsky pledged and lived at the Phi Sigma Kappa fraternity. At the end of the pledge period, the fraternity accepted Sinofsky, but Marmor was shocked to learn he had been blackballed because of his alleged "Jewish traits." In protest, a half dozen of Marmor's Jewish and Gentile friends left the fraternity for good. There was no known repetition of fraternity discrimination against Jews thereafter.[44]

Several of the university's sororities had a reputation for denying membership to Jewish women. When Judi Havas (later Kosinski) matriculated from her Las Vegas home to the University of Nevada at Reno, a friend advised her not to rush for a sorority. The challenge immediately engaged this young woman, who hoped one day to work in a kibbutz. She applied to four sororities. Two turned her down, bluntly stating, "We do not take Jews." Two others, Gamma Phi and the Tri Deltas, allowed her to rush, and she chose the latter. During the pledge period, she experienced no antisemitic prejudice, but she voluntarily chose to drop out.[45]

Las Vegas did not have northern Nevada's track record of Jewish pioneers when it was founded after the turn of the century. Social organizations were closed to Jews even after World War II. One exception was the Desert Inn Country Club, owned and operated by Moe Dalitz and some of his Cleveland associates. Jake Gottlieb, Major Riddle, and Irving Kahn's Dunes golf course a decade later matched the Desert Inn club's elegance.[46] Unlike Jews elsewhere in the United States who founded their own country clubs due to exclusionary policies, Las Vegas's newest golf venues were owned by Jews and open to Gentiles. Some older local organizations, however, excluded Jews by policy.

In 1946, twenty-four civic-minded women established the elite Service League of Las Vegas. The city's premier women's social group, it provided leadership in ameliorating some of Las Vegas's social blights and barred Jewish women from membership. Corinne "Corky" Wollman came to Las Vegas in 1934 with her parents, Murray and Agnes. Murray Wollman was actively involved with civic leaders in the city's early development as a tourist destination. Corky thought that if her father could work hand in glove with the husbands of Service League matrons, she ought to be able to lend her talents to the group's civic initiatives. After marrying developer Melvin Moss, she established ties with the league's officers and became the first Jewish woman inducted into the organization—now known as the Junior League of Las Vegas.

David Zenoff and Mel Moss had been doing business with many members of the local Elks Club and were offended that the organization was closed to Jews. When first proposed for membership in the 1950s, the power structure blackballed them. Then Oscar Bryan (father of future governor and Senator Dick Bryan), Madison Graves and Archie Grant successfully proposed Zenoff for membership. Harley Harmon, county commissioner and gubernatorial hopeful, recommended Moss. "It was a real break-through," Zenoff and Moss later recalled.[47] As part of good-natured hazing, the two new Jewish members were required to serve everyone corned beef and cabbage at the annual St. Patrick's Day banquet.

When asked whether he had experienced any prejudice, Moss responded, "Never," other than the initial rebuff from the Elks and "some isolated cases in the Army, but nothing serious." He purchased a homesite in a gated community developed by Robert Kaltenborn, who had the reputation of being a "known Jew hater." The Mosses lived there without incident. Zenoff's experience in Las Vegas was similar, but his travels exposed him to the less sophisticated feelings of a few in Nevada's interior. A Las Vegas district judge from 1958 to 1965, Zenoff was appointed to fill an unexpired term in the Nevada Supreme Court in 1965. His background as an observant Jew did not affect his subsequent election to two more terms. Zenoff recalled some incidents when he detected an anti-Jewish bias or stereotype. "One was a gas station attendant at Eureka who said to me, when I introduced myself, 'You're that Jew judge, aren't ya.' And one of my associates, who was dead drunk, one day called attention to the fact that I was a Jew. There, of course, were hidden conversations I may never have heard. But the fact is I did not experience any antisemitism."[48]

Others did—as late as 1971. David Wasserman of Las Vegas encountered a climate of serious discrimination against Jews and other minorities, when he sought a state license to practice dentistry. An Anti-Defamation League study found that between 1963 and 1971, sixty-eight Jewish dentists had taken the state board examination, and none had passed. When governor-elect O'Callaghan learned of the blatant inequity, he told the Nevada State Board of Examiners that if its practices continued, he—not the board—would be granting state dental licenses.[49] The discrimination stopped.

Jewry in Nevada, like everywhere else, was not monolithic, consistent, or predictable. Although Gentiles may have felt they were flirting with antisemitism if they were to characterize the behavior of some Jews as "pushy" or "fractious," Jews had no such scruples. Zenoff flatly stated that "antisemitism or anti-Jewish behavior was often brought on by Jews themselves." The examples he gave were of Hasidic Jews making demands on Reform or Conservative Jews. Additionally, he said, "there are some Jews that Jews don't like—not because they are Jews, but because they exhibit behavior which they find offensive." Sydell Miller, president of Congregation Bet Knesset in Las Vegas, observed strong feeling among Jews against fellow Jews who acted "pushy, boisterous, manipulating, and as always having a scheme."[50] Modern Nevada Jews generally managed to avoid the stereotypes begotten of their own peers. As one Nevada legislator said of Chief Justice Milton Badt, "I never noticed that he was Jewish." Whatever characterized someone as "Jewish" was not always obvious or important.[51]

Rise of Antisemitism Worldwide and in Nevada

Eileen Brookman was elected to the first of eight terms as assemblywoman from Clark County in 1967. She believed that American children knew very little about Nazism and treated its symbols as a joke at a time when neo-Nazism was on the rise in Germany. She introduced a bill that barred "advocating genocide of any racial, ethnic, or religious group; [and] the wearing of Nazi or Ku Klux Klan uniforms or regalia." Greenspun's *Las Vegas Sun* gave the bill only the slightest mention.[52] The legislation went nowhere. Had it passed, Las Vegas might have avoided a disruptive incident twenty years later.

The Great Embarrassment

Ralph Engelstad's prominence as owner of the Imperial Palace on the Strip was equaled by his reputation for easily slipping into anti-Jewish slurs and jokes. It came as little surprise when reports surfaced that he had amassed a collection of Nazi paraphernalia including vehicles, weapons, banners, posters, and other Hitler memorabilia on the fifth floor of his casino's parking garage in what came to be called the "war room." In 1986 and 1988, he held several large parties to show off his toys. He reputedly pressured Jewish employees to cut the cake decorated with swastikas. One of Engelstad's terminated employees fueled the appearance of antisemitism by quoting him as saying he should have built ovens in the war room rather than painting murals.[53]

The Engelstad parties and the war room's existence drew cries of outrage from the thirty thousand–member Jewish community. When the Jewish Defense League (JDL) announced that it was coming to protest, the Las Vegas Jewish Federation urged Irv Rubin and his shock troops to stay away—to no avail. Twenty-five JDL supporters staged a protest outside the Imperial Palace while a sound truck denounced Engelstad to passing tourists. Self-styled "skinheads" provided a counterdemonstration, marching in goose step and taunting the JDL demonstrators with the Nazi salute.

The events drew national attention from *People, Newsweek,* and cable television. Letters to the *Las Vegas Sun* reflected the spectrum of support for Engelstad and the outrage of those offended by his Hitler exhibit and parties. His supporters pointed to his contributions to Catholic and Jewish causes, whereas others called for his banishment. The pressure was on to discipline Engelstad and neutralize the negative national publicity. In December 1988, the Nevada Gaming Control Board filed with the Nevada Gaming Commission its two-part complaint against Engelstad for security breaches in his hotel and indiscretions reflecting negatively on the state. The outcome was a prearranged settlement whereby Engelstad agreed to pay a $200,000 fine and another $1.3 million in three installments over two years.[54] The debacle was the last major public demonstration involving antisemitism in Las Vegas in the twentieth century. Las Vegas Jewry's conflicts over the next two decades were internal.

Attack on Reno's Temple Emanu-El

The most aggressive antisemitic actions occurred in northern Nevada, where Jews were relatively invisible. On November 30, 1999, a group of self-proclaimed white supremacists hurled a cement-filled bottle through a window of Temple Emanu-El, followed by a Molotov cocktail that fell harmlessly to the ground, burning only the sidewalk. The incident was a wake-up call to the entire community. In January 2000, eight hundred people of all faiths and political persuasions gathered at a local casino in a statement of solidarity against antisemitism and bigotry of any kind. The temple's rabbi, Avraham Keller, recalled his grandfather's Berlin synagogue being "vandalized and shattered" in 1938. U.S. congresswoman Shelley Berkley warned that such incidents were symptomatic of a state of mind that developed "when the intolerable somehow became tolerable."[55]

The five perpetrators from Reno and California were apprehended quickly and brought to trial seven months later. They all pleaded guilty to a variety of federal charges and were convicted and sentenced to up to fifteen years in prison. Rubin and the JDL organized a rally on the steps of Reno's federal court building at the time of the trial in July. The half-dozen protesters burned Confederate and Nazi flags and called for Jews around the country to arm themselves in the face of growing violence. Reno Jews did not support the militants or their tactics, which, the Anti-Defamation League regional director said, were "counterproductive and could just end up exacerbating tensions in the community."[56]

In his address to the eight hundred gathered at the January interfaith rally, Rabbi Keller had noted that Internet hate sites listed Temple Emanu-El as "an unfinished job." Almost a year later, on January 1, 2001, an unknown person sprayed the temple's front door with a combustible substance and set it on fire. The door was charred, but there was no further damage. A broad spectrum of the larger community filled Temple Emanu-El in a demonstration of support against the violence. Local newspapers and religious and civil rights organizations condemned this crime, which, to date, has gone unsolved. Neo-Nazis vandalized the small Temple Bat Yam synagogue at South Lake Tahoe in December 2004, but the congregation remained steadfast—encouraged by generous support from the surrounding Gentile community. This crime, too, has remained unsolved.[57]

Victims of Antisemitism in Nevada

Holocaust survivors moved to Nevada not for its low level of antisemitism but more often to be near relatives and friends. One of these was Joseph Kempler, born in 1928 at Kraków, Poland. His personal account began with the German army's arrival in 1939. When ordered to report to the nearest ghetto, his mother bribed the enforcing Polish police officer by granting him a sexual favor. The family fled to the woods, where Kempler decided to abandon his family in the interest of his own safety. His parents accepted his decision quietly. In what he described as an "emotional shutdown," he chose to survive at any price. He tried to pass as a Christian but was eventually caught and sent to what he called "a bad part" of Oskar Schindler's factory camp. Cannibalism of the dead was only one of the unspeakable horrors he experienced in his single-minded desire to live. He acknowledged that many, like him in his early days, "put God on trial, because He failed them," and became atheists or agnostics. Kempler's spiritual hegira led him to rediscover the Jehovah's Witnesses with whom he had been interred in a concentration camp.[58] Kempler's conversion was an exception to the continued identification of most Holocaust survivors with their historic tradition.

Las Vegas survivor Henry Schuster and his wife, Anita, organized a Holocaust survivor group in 1995. The original group numbered thirty-five, but in only five years the organization's list exceeded three hundred. Like their counterparts all over the world, many of these Jews suffered "survivor's guilt"—including the inclination to be silent about the unforgettable. As antisemitism showed itself worldwide, survivors overcame their earlier reluctance. The Holocaust Survivors Group of Southern Nevada became outspoken about the events of their childhood under the motivational slogan "Never Again." Its speakers' bureau sent volunteers to area schools requesting a firsthand description of the Holocaust, which is now being studied in a Holocaust curriculum spearheaded by Edythe Katz Yarchever.[59]

Conclusion

Despite examples of institutional prejudice displayed by national and local organizations, Nevada Jews experienced relatively little overt discrimination in the twentieth century. Although individuals expressed a bias against Jews, no wholesale expression of antisemitism existed within the electorate at large. Jews regularly won local and statewide political and judicial offices. Anti-Jewish vandalism was, however, a troublesome problem for several synagogues in the North.

Civil Rights and Uncommon Causes

"Both Jews and Blacks are a pariah people—a people who had to make and remake themselves as outsiders on the margins of American society and culture." Black professor Cornel West thus introduced his 1995 dialogue with Rabbi Michael Lerner on how to begin the healing of hostile relations between the two—particularly in large East Coast cities.[1] Jews moving to Nevada from these areas carried memories of friction and camaraderie. The difference was that from the earliest days, Jews were not on the margins of Nevada society and culture. From its position of relative prosperity and security, Nevada Jewry provided an uncommon leadership on issues of civil rights and social justice. Rank-and-file Jews did not, however, uniformly share the same passion.

The Supreme Court decision to desegregate public schools in 1954 and Rosa Parks's courageous refusal to move from the white section of a bus catalyzed a civil rights movement. For many Jews, it was a moral issue, and they were indisputably overrepresented in early civil rights activities. They were advisers and fund-raisers for Martin Luther King Jr. and James Farmer, about half of the white civil rights attorneys were Jewish, and more than half of the white freedom fighters were Jews. Jews linked the black experience to the biblical Exodus.[2] Nevada had its Jewish prophets who anticipated and then fought to end discrimination, in a state that had a reputation as the "Mississippi of the West," where black entertainers were not allowed to lodge or publicly eat where they worked in casino hotels owned by Jew or Gentile.[3]

One of Judaism's controlling principles is *tzedakah*, which literally means "righteousness" but more broadly "acts of loving kindness to meet the needs of others." When it was under siege, the Jewish community deflected the charity and social justice inwardly to support Jewish life. To have applied the duties of righteousness to Gentiles required Jews to feel physically and psychologically secure. In short, when Jews climbed the ladder of social acceptance and economic freedom, they remembered those who did not.[4] This last condition was generally characteristic of Jewish life across the nation after World War II and in Nevada's two major urban areas, particularly within the rapidly expanding Las Vegas Jewish community. Nevertheless, many Nevada Jewish civil rights militants faced criticism not only from Gentiles but also from Jews who considered such activities "kooky" and a potential liability for Jewish tranquility.

Color Bars in Reno and Las Vegas

Only 134 African Americans lived in Nevada in 1900 and were hardly a threat to anyone. Nevertheless, Reno expelled unemployed blacks in 1904.[5] In 1940, Las Vegas had a population of about 8,400, which included relatively few blacks. They had been barred, however, from the brothels on Block 16, the El Portal Theatre, and Hoover Dam construction jobs. Recruitment and hiring of hundreds of blacks at the Basic Magnesium plant during the war years led to their segregation in Las Vegas's poor and unpaved Westside. Restrictive covenants on new housing to the east effectively isolated the emerging black community. The National Association for the Advancement of Colored People (NAACP) statewide tried to secure a comprehensive Nevada civil rights law in 1939 and 1949, but both died in legislative committee.[6] As yet, there was no visible Jewish presence in the effort.

Since gambling had been legalized in 1931, Reno blacks had not been permitted to patronize "white" casinos or even enter the front door to work as porters or maids. Black servicemen stationed at the Army Airport (later Stead Army Airbase) were regularly denied entrance to the clubs. Sammy Davis Jr. of the Will Mastin Trio was among dozens of African American entertainers who worked Reno clubs, such as Joe Zemansky's Club Fortune, which barred black patrons. The attitude of other Reno Jewish hotel and casino owners to publicly accommodating blacks was uneven, at best.

At the Bank Club, Jewish bouncer Jack Sullivan had a reputation for heavy-handedness toward cheaters. However, his treatment of blacks was slightly more humane. As they approached a table game, he "discouraged" them by simply declaring the table "closed." This was repeated until the black patrons got the message and left.[7] Before 1947, a few performers such as Lena Horne and Eartha Kitt could eat, sleep, and gamble where they entertained. But when Paul Robeson, the black actor, singer, and civil rights activist, came to Reno for a community concert in 1949, Reno hotels barred him—as much over race, perhaps, as his leftist political views. He temporarily stayed at the home of Jewish attorney Charlotte Hunter Arley until Mert Wertheimer, the new lessee of the Riverside Hotel, agreed to put him up.[8]

The following year, NAACP cofounder Alice Smith made reservations for regional officials at the El Cortez Hotel and Casino, owned by the Syrian Jew Abe Zetooney and leased by the Bulasky brothers. When the officers arrived, they were refused service. Smith turned to her unofficial secretary, Ruth Dickens, who contacted Wertheimer, who also had a loose affiliation with Temple Emanu-El and assured Dickens that the black officers were welcome. He personally met them upon their arrival at the Riverside and made clear to his employees that these guests were to be treated cordially and comped them for dinner. The breakthrough had Reno's restaurant owners buzzing.[9]

As Las Vegas began to draw more southerners, the "Jim Crow" atmosphere deepened. The Ames Brothers, Eddie "Rochester" Anderson, Sammy Davis Jr., and other black headliners had to rent rooms on the Westside, and Last Frontier casino worker Mort Saiger chauffeured many of them. He compared the discrimination to "the way I was treated in Poland, as a Jew." Saiger's employer did not permit black employees in the kitchen. Saiger recalled having to bring them sandwiches at a picnic table set up outside behind the kitchen. "That was criminal," he said, but the Jewish and Gentile casino owners considered "integration" bad business. Dr. James McMillan complained that the Jewish hotel owners could have ended segregation years before it finally came about. In fact, some members of the Las Vegas Jewish community were already laying the foundation for an end to discrimination.[10]

Strip casinos declined to serve restaurant food to their black workers, but Foxy's delicatessen across the street from Milton Prell's Sahara Hotel was an exception. Whereas "White Only" signs adorned Las Vegas restaurants, Foxy's had booths reserved for blacks. It was an oasis of tolerance surrounded by neon discrimination. Lubertha Johnson, president of the NAACP, remembered Julius Fox's restaurant as a kosher-style place and that "the NAACP gave him an award for being willing to serve Negro people."[11]

Lloyd Katz came to Las Vegas with his wife, Edythe, in 1951. Katz took over the Fremont, Huntridge, and Palace movie theaters, which allowed admittance to blacks a decade before the integration of casinos. There was segregated seating before 1955, but Katz changed the policy and directed his employees to "let people sit where they want." He refused to capitulate to those in the power structure who opposed his open seating policy. "The opposition eventually blew itself out," said his wife, Edythe. He was a model of humanitarianism who motivated others. Dorothy Eisenberg, active in the League of Women Voters, gratefully remembered him as "my mentor."[12]

Charlotte Arley, Early Reno Civil Rights Proponent

Charlotte Hunter Arley faced discrimination on several occasions as a child and adult due to her ethnicity and gender. She was born in New York, the daughter of Russian-born Lottie and Morris Gancharov, who changed their name to "Hunter" before settling in Springfield, Massachusetts. Lottie kept a kosher household, and Arley claims she never tasted pork until she was eighteen—away from home. A Polish adult escorted her to school through the Polish Catholic neighborhood, where children otherwise would hurl stones and call her "Jidov" (Jew). She passed the Massachusetts bar at age twenty-three in 1935; came to Reno in 1940; met her future husband, Jacques Arley, at Temple Emanu-El; did some paralegal work; and passed the Nevada Bar in 1947. Veteran Felice Cohn, Emilie Wanderer, and Charlotte Arley were three Jewish women of the four female lawyers practicing in Nevada at the time.[13]

Between her friendship with Paul Robeson and her appearance with him at a rally for Henry Wallace, subsequent newspaper coverage implied that Arley was a communist. Amid the "Red" hunting during the McCarthy era, the Soroptimists dismissed Arley. It was a dark time of her life, because the rumor followed her everywhere. While walking down Reno's main thoroughfare, lawyer Kenneth P. Dillon accosted her and said threateningly, "If we go to war, I'll get you first." She postponed application to the American Bar Association, fearing that she could be blackballed, based on a single lawyer's charge of her alleged affiliation. Arley's lifetime membership in the American Civil Liberties Union (ACLU) lent credence to those who linked the organization to Jews and communists. She followed her husband to Portland, Oregon, where they remained until his death in 1970. She returned to Reno to practice law, when the collective memory of the communist threat had faded and Arley was beyond the shadow of suspicion.

In retrospect, Arley denied any association with the Communist Party and blamed her youthful naïveté and the political climate for the suspicions. Arley's commitment to civil rights never wavered. She was a longtime member of the NAACP, freely took the cases of black clients, and was active in child-advocacy matters. Even in her late eighties, Arley was assisting someone being deported due to a lack of understanding of American law.[14]

George Rudiak and the 1953 Civil Rights Bill

George Rudiak emigrated with his parents from the Soviet Union at the age of five and served more than three years in the U.S. Army Air Corps before coming to Las Vegas in 1943. Having passed the Nevada and California bars, he focused on defending victims of unlawful evictions, championing Nellis Air Force Base soldiers' right to vote, and spearheading a petition for repeal of the "Right to Work Law." Rudiak opposed capital punishment and urged legislation to appeal every capital case, stating that it was "better to let ten guilty persons escape than to execute one innocent man."[15] Rudiak's intensity was both an asset and a liability.

As an assemblyman from Clark County in 1953, he defied the odds by introducing a civil rights bill, "an Act concerning the rights of citizens in places of public accommodation or amusement; providing for the admittance to places of amusement and entertainment on presentation of tickets or prices of tickets." It eventually lost by a single vote. As a Reno newspaper announced: "Race and Color Still Can Keep People Out of Public Places."[16]

Rudiak ran for the Nevada Senate in 1954. His paid advertisements highlighted his support of education, disability insurance, and pro–labor union issues. He had served as attorney for the Teamsters—an affiliation that helped to defeat him in view of negative publicity about the union—an irony, given that Teamster loans later underwrote many Las Vegas projects such as Greenspun's country club and Dalitz's hospital. His opposition's ads asked, "What foreign country did he come from?"[17] At that time, American newspapers were filled with anticommunist, Red-scare rhetoric, and the Russian-born Rudiak lost badly.

James McMillan believed that Rudiak's defeat in his bid for state senate in 1954 directly resulted from his sponsorship of the civil rights bill. "Not only did [opponents of equal accommodation] defeat him, he lost a lot of his clients after that."[18] In the long run, however, he gained more than he lost. Rudiak contributed generously to Temple Beth Sholom's building fund but was not particularly active in religious affairs. His focus was elsewhere. He chaired the Nevada Equal Rights Commission (ERC) in 1965 and later was Nevada's delegate to the National Board of the American Civil Liberties Union. His closest allies often found him abrasive and intractable. In the end, he was single-minded and courageous according to those who respected him, and a dangerous cryptocommunist to those who did not.[19]

Integrating Nevada Casinos

In 1955, a group of white investors, including Jews Louis Ruben and Will Max Schwartz, had opened the Moulin Rouge Hotel and Casino on Las Vegas's Westside.[20] The first integrated facility in Las Vegas, it was a residential alternative for black entertainers, who were previously limited to rooming houses far from the all-white casinos. Although the Moulin Rouge failed within less than a year, it became a symbol of what liberated blacks and whites wanted for the entire city. The Sands' heavily Jewish ownership and manager Jack Entratter agreed that year to let its black entertainers reside at the hotel.[21] Nevertheless, the Jim Crow atmosphere persisted.

The resort industry's service-level positions attracted blacks, whose numbers swelled to more than eleven thousand, when early in 1960 the Las Vegas NAACP chapter threatened to march on the casinos if segregation did not end by six o'clock on the evening of March 26. With memories of similar events shutting down businesses in Selma and Montgomery and activists descending on the South to encourage integration, local casino owners who had opposed integration in the past agreed it was now good business. Moe Dalitz communicated to the NAACP's James McMillan that he and all blacks were welcome at the Desert Inn. Greenspun and McMillan jointly called for a meeting of the mayor, sheriff, and other local leaders to discuss an agreement on casino integration. The complex negotiation came to be called "the Moulin Rouge Agreement." About 90 percent of the casinos complied.[22]

One of those slow to integrate was the Dunes, whose owner, Major Riddle, weakly defended his racial policies based on "customer opposition to negroes." One of his employees at the time, Sheila Goodman, a Jewish cocktail waitress, worked the Viva Les Girls Revue. During her shift, a black couple and two racially mixed couples entered the showroom. Guards stood by, prepared to evict the couples, and awaited a signal from Goodman. The couples "were all only 21," she recalled. "I seated them all on the aisle. . . . They were scared to death; they all ordered cokes, none of which they drank. They were waiting to get kicked out. HAH!! I waved the guards away. They looked at me in amazement, but complied." Later in the year, Riddle acknowledged that "things are changing" for the better in the casino's treatment of blacks.[23] The civil rights agitation in Las Vegas and the Reno-Sparks NAACP's unsuccessful efforts to leverage the forthcoming Olympics at Squaw Valley to end discrimination in public accommodations focused attention on the issue in the 1961 legislative session.

While the legislature debated a bill to establish an Equal Rights Commission, blacks conducted a sit-in at Reno's "whites only" Overland Hotel. The senate was prepared to kill the ERC bill, but new demonstrations picketing major Reno gambling establishments, the Nevada Bank of Commerce, and the legislature itself on March 27, plus pressure from Governor Grant Sawyer, led to its passage by a slim majority. To obtain enough votes, the bill's sponsors capitulated to swing voters who demanded the commission have only a token annual budget of twenty-five hundred dollars and no staff.[24]

Sawyer appointed Reno Jewish lawyer Bert Goldwater to chair the commission. Goldwater also sat on the Nevada Gaming Commission but was, by his own admission, "too dogmatic and focused on human rights" to be a popular choice among casino owners. He had also made his civil rights statement by resigning from the Hidden Valley Country Club, the Elks, and the prestigious Prospectors' Club in protest over their barring blacks—and, in the case of the Prospectors' Club, women—from membership. The 1961 legislature determined that only one person from the same profession could serve on its commissions. Because another lawyer already sat on the gaming commission, Sawyer asked Goldwater to lead the Equal Rights Commission. The ERC held its first meeting at Las Vegas in January 1962. On the agenda were complaints of civil rights violations. The commission, however, lacked not only staff but also subpoena power.[25] The group was so besieged by numerous lawsuits and applications for injunctions that Goldwater resigned in frustration. Thomas West succeeded him in 1963, followed by George Rudiak in 1965.

Open Housing, Equal Opportunity, Reapportionment, and, Finally, Fair Housing

Until 1948, it was common to find in a housing contract for sale the agreement not to sell, lease, or transfer the property to anyone of the "colored," "Ethiopian," or "Semitic" race. In *Shelley v. Kraemer*, 245 U.S. 60 (1948), the U.S. Supreme Court held that such restrictive covenants violated equal protection under the law. The Civil Rights Act of 1964 outlawed discrimination in all public accommodations, but Nevada towns and many other American cities remained essentially segregated. Eileen Brookman recalled that she and other delegates to a Reno convention stayed at the Mapes Hotel, which did not want to accommodate black attendees. "I told 'em to put a roll-away in my room for Lubertha [Johnson]," said Brookman. "And they did! But they didn't like it!"[26]

The state legislature remedied the situation in 1965, but some agencies were slow to remove the prejudicial language.[27] When Sheila Goodman was buying a home two years later, the title company said it would "cross out" the racially restrictive wording rather than reprint thousands of new forms. Goodman said she told the title officer, "Dump them all, I am not signing until there is a new printed form." The title company capitulated.[28]

One of the barriers to passing civil rights legislation was the underrepresentation of Nevada's urban counties, where blacks were most concentrated. In the early 1960s, the U.S. Supreme Court directed states to reapportion their legislatures to reflect the guideline of "one man, one vote." Nevada legislators were loath to make the change, but Las Vegan Flora Dungan forced the issue by suing. The U.S. District Court accepted the case of *Dungan v. Sawyer* in 1965. Before making a decision, the court delivered an ultimatum: Governor Sawyer needed to call a special legislative session to resolve the matter, or the court would reapportion the legislature. The court upheld the legislature's 1965 adjustments, which lasted until 1972. According to political scientist Eleanore Bushnell, Dungan had—through sheer determination—"brought about the end of a legislative era."[29]

The same legislature had also enacted a law banning discrimination in employment and public accommodations. Sheila Goodman had been recently employed as a cocktail waitress at the Frontier and was among those the casino fired in order to hire three black cocktail waitresses. When asked if she was upset, she replied, "Heck No!! It was something I had fought for all my life."[30] Although never in public office or a board member of the NAACP or ACLU, Goodman proved to be a feisty, one-woman, rank-and-file Jewish supporter of the civil rights movement in Las Vegas.

Civil rights advocates in the legislature pushed for an open housing law in 1969, but its proponents were divided, and it failed. In 1971, under threat of federal intervention and with the strong backing of Governor O'Callaghan, who had a reputation for actively supporting racial equality and the ability to reconcile warring factions, the passage of an open housing law seemed possible. He was no flaming liberal, but his head and heart were with the oppressed, as he saw them. Even McMillan acknowledged that as governor, O'Callaghan "was decent with us. He appointed Blacks to positions and he was responsive to the NAACP." The 1971 Fair Housing Bill overwhelmingly passed the assembly and the senate. O'Callaghan signed the bill. Fair housing was now the law in Nevada, but the battle for women's equal rights was still ahead.[31]

The Equal Rights Amendment and Pro-Choice Movement

The historic role of the woman in Judaism was to assist her husband and children in maintaining all Torah prescriptions. Orthodox Jewish men traditionally awoke each day to pray, "I thank Thee, Lord, I was not created a woman" (Menahot 43b). Women were officially barred from the rabbinate, because the male leadership considered them incapable of making judgments concerning Jewish law. Reform Jewish women were the first to organize and promote ordination. Their first candidate was ordained in 1972. Conservative Judaism allowed women to be counted in a minyan but did not ordain its first female rabbi until 1985.[32] Even Jewish Orthodoxy was the target of Blu Greenberg's withering discovery, critique, and ultimate rejection of her religion's thorough male dominance. Despite accommodations for Orthodox women to study the Torah, female ordination to the rabbinate remained out of the question.[33]

The reconsideration of women's religious roles was an outcome of the earlier feminist movement of the 1960s, which included a disproportionately large number of Jewish women. Betty Friedan delivered the first manifesto in 1963 with *The Feminist Mystique.* Bella Abzug, a three-term congresswoman from New York, and Gloria Steinem, founder of *Ms.,* were two high-profile Jewish women who inspired the revisitation of women's rights in all religions and American society.

The struggle for women's equal rights in Nevada began unsuccessfully in 1869. The only Jewish woman identified at the time with the female suffrage amendment was milliner Louise Jackson. Felice Cohn's authorship of the Nevada's woman's suffrage amendment, which became law in 1914, was a major step toward equal political opportunity.[34] The modern battle was joined when the federal Equal Rights Amendment (ERA) came before the state legislature in 1973. It lost decisively in the senate, sixteen to four. Among those opposing the measure were the only woman in that legislative body, Helen

Herr, and Republican Jewish senator Chic Hecht. For the ERA to pass in the next biennial legislature, Nevadans had to overcome religious objections as well as surprisingly heavy opposition from women.

Several grassroots organizations formed to support the amendment. Countering them was a "Stop ERA" movement that had heavy support from Mormons and conservative Christians. One pro-ERA Jewish activist recalled that "our main opponents were the 'Hansenoids,' as we called Janine Hansen and her followers from up North and the Church of Jesus Christ of Latter-day Saints in Utah and Nevada and the general population who got cold chills when faced with the thought of 'equality for all' in Nevada." The same attitude also held true for the state's small number of Orthodox Jews.[35]

A Las Vegas effort to reconcile religion and the ERA was People of Faith for ERA, in which a Roman Catholic sister and a Protestant campus minister joined Stephen E. Weisberg, rabbi of Temple Ner Tamid, to "present a statement of their faith in support of equality."[36] The Northern Nevada Women's Political Caucus with Isabel Kimble and Jewish housewife Marion Sieber, supported the effort. Other politically involved women in the Reno area—Martha Gould, Barbara Weinberg, and Mylan Roloff Hawkins—headed northern Nevada's ERA effort. In southern Nevada, assemblywomen Renee Diamond, Myrna Williams, Dungan, and Brookman were among the elected leaders promoting women's rights. When the ERA came to a vote in the 1975 legislature, the assembly approved it twenty-seven to thirteen, but again the senate roundly defeated it.

By the 1977 session, no legislative issue (other than the budget) aroused so much rancor. Brookman was among the most outspoken critics of those who claimed that the amendment's passage would lead to a spate of legislation eroding rights that women already enjoyed, such as the right to be exempt from military combat and to be supported by their husbands. She reminded her auditors that "we" did not live under "a church dominated state." She urged the legislators to join her in her resolve never to be forced to vote her convictions "under the influence of *any religious pressures*." Her added emphasis was a less-than-subtle poke at the Mormon lobby against the amendment.[37]

Renee Diamond from Las Vegas and Mylan Hawkins of Reno—both Jewish—were state cochairs of the ERA ballot issue. They obtained support from the National Jewish Women's organizations in the ERA coalition. Although some Nevada Jewish groups followed suit, Diamond said that "by and large there was not much Nevada Jewish public support or activism connected with ERA."[38] Dorothy Eisenberg, who was involved in the cause with Diamond, Myrna Williams, Edythe Katz, and Helen Meyers, wistfully remembered working with "a great group of women," though the effort had a "bitter outcome." The electorate voted against the ERA by a two-to-one margin.[39] Nevada joined Utah and Arizona as the only states in the Mountain and Pacific West not to pass the measure. The South also uniformly opposed it, giving the notion that Nevada was the "Mississippi of the West" new meaning for some women.

Yet another challenge awaited Nevada women: the abortion issue. Although acknowledging that facing an abortion was "an awful, terrible decision," Hawkins agreed to lead the pro-choice campaign in 1987. The question was whether to bring the matter to the state legislature or use a referendum as a "preemptive strike," which might yield greater success. Hawkins consulted with influential Republican state senator Sue Wagner, who took the matter to the party's legislative leader, William Raggio. "What we got out of Bill Raggio," said Hawkins, "was that [Republicans] would be delighted if it did not have to be a [legislative] issue." With this left-handed blessing, Hawkins and her cohorts—including Martha Gould and Ruth and Dr. Gene Glick—set out to gather signatures for a referendum.

The pro-choice leaders had learned some lessons in the ERA defeat and wrapped themselves in the American flag. This issue, they advertised, was about "freedom," "choice," and the "American way" and was a private matter between a woman, her spiritual adviser, and her physician. The organizers collected more signatures than any other referendum in the state's history, and won 64 percent of the vote. Although the referendum leaders relished the victory, it was bittersweet for some. As Hawkins reflected fifteen years later, "The minute we take care of every human life, it may be unnecessary for a woman to think about an abortion except under the most extreme circumstance."[40]

Gay and Lesbian Rights

Some organized religions, including Hasidic and Orthodox Judaism, took official positions against homosexual behavior. In some instances, the official opposition led gays to "pass," leave the religious group, or—in the case of some Jews—find sympathetic rabbis who ministered to gays and lesbians outside the parameters of Orthodoxy. Reform Judaism had come to terms with the issue, allowing gay and lesbian unions. The Metropolitan Community Church of the Sierras, numbering thirty in 2004, was one of several Reno Christian groups reaching out to Reno gays and lesbians. With the blessing of her congregation and for a very modest rental fee, Rabbi Myra Soifer offered Temple Sinai for the church's Sunday-evening worship.

Deborah Achtenberg was active in the civil rights and anti–Vietnam War movements in the Washington, D.C., office of the National Urban Coalition before accepting a position in the Department of Philosophy at the University of Nevada, Reno, and becoming a member of Temple Sinai. After establishing herself academically, she and her Jewish friend Joyce Nance and Kaye Crawford of Reno Gay Pride and the Metropolitan Community Church cofounded a gay and lesbian support organization called SPECTRUM Northern Nevada. Achtenberg served as its president from 1998 to 2002. During this time, the organization had two hundred paid members and became connected with Jewish lobbyist Bobbie Gang of the Nevada Women's Lobby.[41]

Jewish Leadership in the ACLU of Nevada

The American Civil Liberties Union arguably has had the longest continual focus on the defense of civil liberties of any organization in the nation. In its early years, its causes coincided with those of the American Jewish Committee, the Anti-Defamation League, and Hadassah, one of the nation's largest women's organizations. Additionally, Protestants and Other Americans United for the Separation of Church and State joined the ACLU against public funding for busing parochial-school children. Jews who remembered the violations of their rights by czarist police were sympathetic to dissenters against the established authorities and joined the ACLU in disproportionate numbers. Many became the object of derision, as critics identified Jews with Marxism and referred to the ACLU as the American Communist Liberties Union. Others went so far as to identify the ACLU with "Christ-killers." The organization appeared unmoved by such criticism.[42]

The Nevada ACLU was founded in 1966 amid the continued violations of black and Native American rights. Its official charter of January 31, 1968, included Marvin Sedway, a Las Vegas Jewish optometrist and nephew of Moe Sedway. The southern chapter was little more than a token presence until Jewish-born Sari Aizley revitalized the chapter as its part-time associate director in 1986.[43]

The northern chapter had equally modest beginnings. Between 1966 and 1981, one member called it the "family store" of non-Jews Hazel Erskine and Elmer Rusco with Richard Siegel. Its heavily Jewish executive board over the years included Judi Kosinski, Marty Gutride, Morris Kanowitz, Ellen Steiner, and Alan Greenblatt. For most of its life, Nevada's ACLU chapters had no paid staff, but they were able to elicit the volunteer services of dozens of lawyers, such as Michael Melner in Reno and George Rudiak in Las Vegas. One such volunteer agreed to take a case, pro bono, in the eastern part of the state, on the condition that his involvement with the ACLU not be made public![44] The ACLU's reputation was a liability in conservative Nevada.

Most of the issues the organization addressed were controversial. It opposed capital punishment along with penalties for marijuana users, invasions of free speech, violations of black civil rights, inequality for women, and issues it considered to be in violation of church-and-state separation. Other contentious matters receiving the ACLU's support were prisoner rights, reproductive freedom for women, protests at the Nevada nuclear test site, and the losing gay and lesbian attempts to have their own rodeo.[45]

Richard Siegel has had the longest tenure of any Nevada ACLU official. He was born in 1940 in New York City. His parents were practicing Jews in the progressive tradition, and both helped to found a Reform congregation in Brooklyn. He attended Hebrew school and earned degrees at Brandeis and Columbia universities. He directly connected his social activism to Judaism and particularly the Brandeis experience. The University of Nevada's Department of Political Science hired Siegel in 1965. He joined Temple Sinai in 1969 and became vice president of the congregation a decade later. He had become active in the state Democratic Party but chose to leave politics and to focus on ACLU matters.[46]

Although he was as provocative and controversial as the issues themselves, Siegel never fell under any restraint within the university. He admitted to receiving some antisemitic phone calls and letters and criticism from other Jews. When Carson City authorities planned to have driving-under-the-influence convicts perform public service wearing a distinctive garb indicating their offense, Siegel publicly labeled it "an Auschwitz-type policy." Temple Sinai's Rabbi Paul Tuchman was outraged that Siegel dared to compare convicted criminals to Auschwitz victims. The two met to discuss the matter, but neither convinced the other. Siegel actively opposed religious baccalaureate services in the public schools and succeeded in having the practice stopped. On another occasion, he publicly objected to how the Washoe County School District celebrated Christmas. Some within the Jewish community were embarrassed by this "Jewish" activism and urged him not to roil the waters. Siegel attributed such opposition to an insecure fear of antisemitic backlash.

Siegel's issue-oriented demeanor was often confrontational. "I realize I enjoy defying people," he said. "I rarely say anything publicly without being very forceful. I feel that I speak for others who lack the courage." Whether despite or because of his aggressive style, Siegel served as president of northern Nevada's chapter of the ACLU for the better part of twenty years and was Nevada's delegate to the ACLU National Board from 1975 to 1988. Several years ago, the northern and southern Nevada affiliates consolidated to form a single statewide organization: ACLU Nevada (ACLUN). From the outset, the organization had, according to Siegel, a Jewish membership and financial support greater than the proportion of Jews in the state population. Consequently, a decision was made to locate the state headquarters in Las Vegas, where the Jewish population had skyrocketed. Siegel became board president of the consolidated ACLUN. Fellow Jew Gary Peck of Las Vegas was the executive director, and Allen Lichtenstein, also of Las Vegas, became the organization's general counsel. The three remained the state's most visible and outspoken advocates for the group's many—often unpopular—causes.[47]

Gray Liberation and Abe Feinberg

Born in a small Ohio coal-mining town in 1899, Abraham L. Feinberg was the seventh of ten children of Lithuanian immigrants Nathan and Sarah. Ordained at Hebrew Union College in Cincinnati and called to the second-largest Reform congregation in New York City, he left the rabbinate in 1930 because the "business side" of religion stifled him. Feinberg married Ruth E. Katch before accepting a scholarship to study voice at the Conservatoire Americain in France. He adopted the identity of bon vivant "Anthony Frome" and built a radio career with several appearances in New York's Paramount Theatre at the end of the vaudeville days.

With the onset of Hitler's oppression of European Jews, Feinberg revested himself in rabbinical robes and in 1943 accepted a call to Canada's leading congregation, Holy Blossom Temple in Toronto. During his eighteen-year tenure, he was named one of the country's "seven greatest preachers" and was Canada's best-known Jewish personality. Opposition to the Vietnam War led him to visit Ho Chi Minh in a private effort to negotiate peace. He was associated with Bertrand Russell and John Lennon and Yoko Ono in his protests against the war. Upon his wife's death in 1971, Feinberg moved to San Francisco and affiliated with the racially mixed Glide Memorial United Methodist Church. He returned to radio with a format titled *Gray Lib*—emphasizing senior citizens' rights and encouraging his listeners' involvement in social issues. He relocated to Reno in 1976 to be near his physician son, Jonathan. Friends in San Francisco and Berkeley urged him to stay in the Bay Area, predicting he would be "lynched" in conservative Reno.[48]

In California, Feinberg was active in the Grey Panther organization, whose stated goal was to politicize older Americans and to age rebelliously. After settling in Reno, he announced to the Reno Retired Community Volunteer Program, "I'm ready to get involved with something in this community." He organized a chapter of Grey Panthers and produced a radio program modeled after his northern California venture, which he now called *Gray Lib Plus.* He and gerontology professor and Jewish musician Mark Edinberg opened the show with music, followed by a guest speaker on issues of interest to the aging. He urged seniors to become involved in social issues and engage in romantic trysts. His recommendation was that every senior citizen center should have a dating service.

Jewish matchmakers actively plotted to bring about a possible liaison of the attractive rabbi with one or another of the city's long-widowed Jewish matrons. In one of his gerontology classes, however, he and a young woman on the verge of conversion to Judaism caught each other's eye. Although Feinberg was more than thirty years her senior, they hit it off, dated, and married. She was the love of his life and his caretaker—particularly as his eyes began to fail him.

A buffalo-hide cane given to him by Ho Chi Minh was his walking stick, but Feinberg rarely walked—he ran whenever a civil rights issue was at stake. In 1977, he addressed with customary eloquence a joint legislative session in support of the Equal Rights Amendment. He even convinced some conservative women at the Senior Center that the ERA could benefit them in old age.[49] When he died in 1986, he was remembered not as a partially blind rabbi but as a lively, charismatic, and dogged advocate for social justice and the aging population much younger than himself.[50]

Jewish Activism in Civil Liberties Issues: Setting the Record Straight

That Jewish men and women were so prominently involved nationwide in promoting civil rights for blacks and equal opportunity for women raises the question of whether Nevada Jews were overly represented in the same causes based on their percentage of the population. Jewish women nationally made up about 1 percent of the population but constituted 7 percent of the civil rights leaders.[51] The same women who had spent their volunteer hours tending to family and synagogue activities were, within the Conservative and Reform traditions, enjoying raised expectations of being elected to local boards and even presidencies of congregations, but these otherwise dedicated women were not necessarily interested in public affairs.[52]

Future assemblywoman Renee Diamond came to Las Vegas from the San Fernando Valley in the early 1970s and later wrote that "it was a shock to me that not many Jews were involved in civic and civil rights in Nevada." She observed that the only Jewish activists in the George McGovern campaign were the Rudiaks, the Eisenbergs, Myrna Williams, and Diamond herself.[53] At about the same time, Judi Kosinski of Reno tried organizing a luncheon for Jewish women interested in fostering relations between Israel and the United States. She was unable to attract more than a handful. "I was astounded," she later said, "about how apolitical Jewish women were here in Reno."[54] Several years later, Reno registrations for the National Organization for Women's local newsletter included only five Jewish names out of three hundred.[55]

Several reasons explain why Jewish women in Nevada were less publicly involved on civil liberties issues. One was generational: older Jewish women traditionally saw their place in the home and synagogue, including membership in a Sisterhood or Hadassah. Esther Goldwater, for example, converted her husband, Bert, to a host of liberal causes after their marriage in 1941. Although Bert became an activist in civil rights matters, Esther never involved herself publicly in such causes. This was a common phenomenon nationally, where activist Jewish women received only moral support from their coreligionists—whose status, nevertheless, was elevated like the tide that raises all ships.[56]

The departure of Reform dissidents from Reno's Temple Emanu-El in 1961 and a similar departure from Las Vegas's Conservative Beth Shalom in Las Vegas in 1974 inclined many devoted Jews to focus their voluntarism and philanthropy on shoring up their respective synagogues. One result was that many who might have otherwise become involved in the civil rights agitation and the campaign for women's equality worked on new temple fund-raisers and the multiplicity of committees supporting the religious life of the new and depleted congregations.

Another constraint on broad Jewish public involvement in political affairs was an innate fear of being associated with controversy, which might rain down abuse or criticism on the heads of all. In Las Vegas, a home owner active in the local Jewish Federation objected to placing an "Elect Renee Diamond" lawn sign in the yard because it "might offend someone." A similar timidity could be found among those who preferred not to "overreact" to the antisemitic activities of Ralph Engelstad in the south and the vandalism against Temple Emanu-El in the North. Elsewhere in the country during the civil rights agitation, some Jews counseled "silence in the face of the black struggle" because they assumed that involvement in integration would bring about "social, economic, or physical harm" for all Jews.[57] One interviewee (who asked not to be identified) attributed a lack of Jewish interest in civil rights by some Nevada Jews to a political bias that led them to migrate to a conservative state.

Yet Jews who exercised influential roles in social-action causes were represented well beyond their 2 percent of the population. But with the exception of the Nevada chapter of the American Civil Liberties Union, the prominent leadership exercised by Nevada Jewry failed to generate comparable support from the Jewish rank and file. More important, those in the forefront of civil rights causes in Nevada invariably attributed their goal orientation in some way to Judaism. These volunteers—like the paid public servants—found motivation in the Egyptian slavery and exodus of the early Hebrews, the maltreatment of Jews over the past two millennia, or the deeply religious notion that all Jews are called to works of loving kindness. This was true even of those whose religious piety and full observance was a practice of the past.[58]

The Varieties of Religious Observance

Few better represented the struggle to maintain a Jewish identity in rural Nevada than Morris and Lina Badt. All their children were raised Orthodox in San Francisco schools, spending summers and holidays in Elko County. Milton counted Hebrew among his several languages and abstained from pork but never affiliated with a synagogue. All the Badt children promised their mother to marry Jews. Milton, however, received a dispensation. He and his Christian wife, Gertrude Nizze Badt, raised their children, Nancy and Milton Jr., in a household that observed Jewish and Christian holidays. "On Passover," Nancy recalled, "we lit candles and had matzohs and easter eggs." When Milton Jr.'s son married a Jewish attorney, he publicly rejoiced at another Jewish lawyer in the family.[1] It was a rare example of a return to a tradition, unobserved for a generation, because Milton Badt kept alive the spark of Judaism, which he practiced quietly and in his own way.

Badt was appointed justice of the Nevada Supreme Court in 1947 and then elected for several terms. He and the family moved from Elko to Carson City, where they resided until his death as chief justice in 1966. David Zenoff from Las Vegas served on the state supreme court from 1965 to 1977. Zenoff recalled that Chief Justice Badt asked him in 1966 to be one of the ten men required to have a Jewish service. The necessary tenth member of the minyan was to have been Dr. Stanley Kline. The group gathered, but Kline could not leave a sick patient. The service had to be canceled because they knew no other Jewish man in Carson City to take his place.[2] Such was the sorry state of Jewry in Nevada's capital.

From "No Minyan" to a Reform Congregation at South Lake Tahoe

The next thirty years brought a small in-migration of Jews to the Carson City and South Lake Tahoe areas. Their backgrounds, educations, and professions were indistinguishable from those of the general population. In 1981, Dr. Jeffrey Applebaum was holding together a Jewish group of six to ten families on the south shore of Lake Tahoe. Charna and Allen Silver joined them in 1983 and, with Applebaum, crafted articles of incorporation for Congregation Bat Yam. The unaffiliated group was "hanging by a thread" until it affiliated with the UAHC and qualified for the services of a Reform student rabbi from Los Angeles Hebrew Union College. In 1988, Oren Postrel gave the congregation the lifeblood it needed to grow and stabilize at about sixty-five families—including forty-five children. The congregation later purchased a multipurpose structure on four acres for its growing constituency near the California-Nevada state line.[3]

In the meantime, Jews in Carson City, nearby Genoa, and Minden to the south formed the Chai Sierra Havurah—a fellowship group. It numbered about forty adults who celebrated life-cycle events over a potluck dinner and organized hikes and Passover seders. The *havurah* was not intended to have a religious focus. The people had found, for the time being, diverse ways of being "Jewish," and showed little interest in joining Temple Bat Yam at the lake. Over time, however, the group dwindled, as newcomers were less interested in socialization.[4]

A few joined Temple Bat Yam at South Lake Tahoe, even though the travel time—in good weather—could be an hour each way. In the summer of 2000, ten couples and single persons who resided as far as forty miles apart met at the Carson City home of Judith and Norman Greenspan to share stories about Jewish roots. Some had taken refuge with their parents in Shanghai with the approach of World War II, where Japanese occupiers consigned them to the ghetto. Others told of peddler parents on New York's Hester Street and rabbinical grandparents in Poland. Family histories were peppered with the litany of anglicized name changes—from Olchevski to Olson and Rosenberg to Rowen—the stories themselves garnished with Yiddish.[5] These people were part of Bat Yam's core membership, and their hostess became its president that year.

The congregation hired its first full-time rabbi, Jonathan Freirich, in 2004, and membership immediately swelled to more than one hundred families. Trained in the Reconstructionist tradition, Freirich accommodated himself to a diverse congregation. More than half of the one hundred adults were married to Gentiles, who shared a common concern for their children's Jewish education. A few of the Gentiles had converted, some simply attended temple services with their Jewish spouses and children, and others celebrated both Christian and Jewish holidays. Because the congregation also spanned the political spectrum, its organizers agreed not to discuss politics—a custom continued to the present day.[6]

North Lake Tahoe Hebrew Congregation

Lake Tahoe, at an altitude of 6,255 feet, bridges northern portions of California and Nevada and is home to more than 50,000 permanent residents. Because winter snowfall could isolate the lake from Reno and Carson City, North Lake Tahoe's Jews needed to be self-supporting and independent. The area's congregation began as a *havurah* in 1979 with a handful of couples and single women. Its first community seder was held in April 1982 at a lakeside restaurant, and in a month it affiliated with the UAHC. From 1987 through 1992, student rabbis from Los Angeles served them. Rabbi Irnie Nadler (formerly of Reno's Conservative Temple Emanu-El) joined the staff part-time and became full-time in 1996.

With no permanent home, the congregation held services at a Kings Beach conference center. Fund-raising begun in 1997 yielded a synagogue in five years.[7] In 2004, the congregation membership topped 150 families, with a Sisterhood and a Hebrew School serving about 50 children. Rabbi Nadler died suddenly on February 26, 2004, but a year later the congregation selected Oren Postrel, former student rabbi at Temple Bat Yam across the lake.[8]

Reno's Temple Sinai and Rabbi Myra Soifer

When Temple Sinai hired Rabbi Myra Soifer in 1984, she inherited a file box of records and a congregation of about 45 families and residential clusters. She focused on families' and children's religious education, the routine brises, *brit bat* ceremonies (naming of a daughter), and *B'nai mitzvah* (initiatory reading of Torah by teenage youngsters), whereas Ethyl Jaffe, raised in an Orthodox family, provided Hebrew lessons.[9]

Lacking a mohel, the congregation initially turned to local Jewish physicians for the operation and the rabbi for the ritual. Because Reform discipline requires no ritual preparation of bodies before burial, the temple had no *hevrah kadishah* (burial society); the local funeral home handled everything. As for marriages, Rabbi Soifer received as many as forty requests to officiate and refused to comply with as many as half. Her position was clear: she did not marry people who wanted to marry on a moment's notice. Additionally,

"I will not do mixed marriages," she said, "unless the non-Jewish partner is committed to Jewish education and not affiliated with another religion."[10]

Bright, articulate, outspoken, and fiercely dedicated to Judaism and women's rights, Soifer supported Israel but openly criticized certain of its political positions. Shortly after her arrival in 1984, a Reno newspaper quoted her as saying that the Israeli occupation of the Palestinians was unjust and immoral. Sometime between the High Holidays and Succoth later in the fall, Soifer was attending an event featuring an Israeli choir at the Conservative Temple Emanu-El. President Milton Gann led the service while she participated "loudly" from her place toward the rear.

As Soifer was leaving the event, she heard someone yell at her. It was one of the congregation's stalwart supporters. The only thing Soifer heard from her distant vantage point was the word *traitor*—presumably, in reference to her remarks in the press. She remembered little else except that the commotion was violent and loud. Usually not one to shy away from such a confrontation, she kept her composure, turned to her accuser, and repeated phrases in Hebrew such as "Have a good year!" An apology to Soifer from the congregation arrived several days later, signed by President Gann.[11] The subject of Israel was one that could bring Nevada Jews together, but views on Israeli foreign policy were rarely unanimous.

Although her feminism and outspokenness may have been initially abrasive to some, Soifer began to "wear well" with a growing congregation that still retained members of the old guard who had been part of the original Beth Or break from Temple Emanu-El. By 2004, the congregation had more than tripled to 140 families, including a significant number of university faculty and other professionals. The temple had an active Sisterhood, religious school, Hebrew school for grades 4 through 7, library, and gift shop. Although its annual membership fee was a "flexible" eighty-five dollars per month, Temple Sinai had built a reservoir of donations large enough to plan construction of a new synagogue on the premises.

Soifer was regularly called upon to represent northern Nevada Jewry at civic functions. One of her pet peeves was the lack of sensitivity that some Christian clergy displayed to religiously diverse audiences, such as at the governor's annual prayer breakfast. A typical blessing might end, "We make this prayer through Jesus Christ Our Lord." Over the years, she successfully campaigned for prayer language that was inclusive of non-Christians.

The Jewish community has embraced Soifer, who could be trusted to do the "right thing"—even under duress. In Yiddish terms, she was a "mensch." Soifer served Temple Sinai for more than twenty years, the longest tenure at the same congregation of any rabbi in Nevada history.[12]

Las Vegas's Accommodation to Growth and Dissent

The population of Las Vegas was 8,422 in 1940. It tripled by 1950 and doubled every decade thereafter. It attracted tourists because it was an entertainment center. Service personnel flocked to fill jobs in the expanding resort business. Its warm weather, friendly tax climate, and planned developments in outlying areas like Summerlin and Green Valley drew permanent settlers from all sections of the nation, where, until recently, one might sell an expensive home and replicate it at half the cost in Las Vegas. The Las Vegas metropolitan population numbered 1.7 million by 2004. Of these, Jews numbered about 80,000, though other estimates approached 100,000 to include totally assimilated or alienated Jews. My survey of 321 Las Vegas Jewish residents who died between 2001 and 2004 revealed a predictable average age of 76. The residential tenure in Las Vegas ranged from less than 1 year to 52 years, the average being 16.5 years. Of the deceased, 11.5 percent were foreign-born; 50 percent (mostly New Yorkers) were born in the Northeast; 30 percent in the Midwest; 2 percent in the South; 5 percent in California, the Southwest, and Mountain West; and 1 percent in Nevada. Although this study was representative of only a slim subset of the total population, it indicated the high level of in-migration to the area. In addition, the 1990 U.S. Census reported nearly 1,000 Israelis immigrated to Nevada in the past decade, and many settled in Las Vegas.[13] With so many new and old understandings of "Judaism," more options were needed. Some congregations formed simply because the members lived too far away from their favorite brand of Judaism. Others affiliated or disaffiliated for personal reasons—friendships with other congregants, financial constraints, or disagreements with the rabbi.

Orthodox Congregations and the Kaballah Centre

Temples Beth Sholom and Ner Tamid were, for a short time, Las Vegas's only permanent synagogues. Between 1978 and 1988, two Orthodox congregations emerged. Shaarei Tefilla, founded in 1981, was affiliated with the Union of Orthodox Jewish Congregations of America and located near the Strip.

It invited visitors to reside in its adjacent Hospitality House on the Sabbath so that they could walk to services. Shaarei Tefilla advertised four kosher restaurants under the supervision of its rabbi, Yakov Wasser. It also had a *mikveh* available to the public.[14]

Jewish developers Sam Ventura and Mordechai Yerushalmi built a new neighborhood a few blocks from Ner Tamid. When a significant number of Las Vegas's 10,000 Israelis bought homes in the development, they added a small Israeli-Orthodox synagogue. Although the congregation had a rabbi or two in the past, it was unable to support one full-time. The congregation, Or-Bamidbar, felt uncomfortable with an American Orthodox affiliation and remained independent. Ventura was instrumental in building the synagogue's Israeli Cultural Center. In 2005, he was president of the congregation, and his wife, Rachel, was entertainment director.[15]

In 2000, Israeli Moshe Omer conducted Kabbalah services for as many as 40 people out of his four-bedroom home in a Las Vegas residential community. Complaints about parking and traffic from neighbors prompted city officials to warn Rabbi Omer several times that the services violated zoning regulations. When authorities tried to have the rabbi sign a citation on a Saturday morning in June, he refused because he considered such an act a violation of the Sabbath. He was handcuffed, arrested, and transported to a police station—an act he also considered a Sabbath violation. According to one report, Kabbalist Irwin Molasky complained to Mayor Oscar Goodman, who held a press conference at the residence apologizing for the insensitive treatment of the rabbi. Goodman did not condone the zoning violation, but within a few months the Kabbalah Centre moved to a commercial area a few miles west of the Strip.

Rabbi Moshe Dahan headed this storefront-type synagogue in 2005 and was dedicated to teaching the Kabbalah as interpreted by Michael Berg. His claim was that all can "become like God" with an end to pain, suffering, and even death. Some Las Vegas rabbis did not consider the Kabbalah Centre a legitimate congregation, and others considered it a cult, though it did offer weekly Friday-evening Shabbat services and a minyan service on Saturday morning, followed by an interpretation of the ancient esoteric Jewish texts. It claimed to have approximately 100 students.[16] The center's leadership has changed several times in recent years.

Synagogue Spin-offs

When Ner Tamid did not renew his contract in 1984, Mel Hecht had sufficient support to open an unaffiliated Reform synagogue, Temple Beth Am. It was the first congregation to follow the westward movement toward Summerlin. According to Hecht, Beth Am had a 2005 membership of "200 units, or 400 to 600 people." He has been a pulpit rabbi more than twenty years in a city where rabbinical tenures have been very short.[17]

Gary Golbart had sung with the *Lido de Paris* show on the Strip. Hecht gave him the title of "cantor" at Beth Am and got him licensed to perform weddings—though he had no traditional ordination. The two men had a falling-out, and Golbart left in 1992 to found another group, and some of Beth Am's members followed him. The new congregation was Adat Ari El, and its lay leadership found itself in an irreconcilable dispute with Golbart, who left. The congregation then affiliated with the UAHC—now the Union for Reform Judaism (URJ). It maintained the customary men's club, Sisterhood, pair of cantorial soloists, and youth group. Its meeting place was not a traditional synagogue in 2005, but a temporary arrangement on West Flamingo Road. Hillel Cohn of San Bernardino was its interim rabbi since 2002 and came to the position with a lifetime of ecumenical and civic involvements. Congregations Beth Am and Adat Ari El merged in 2007 to form Temple Sinai, located in Summerlin and affiliated with the URJ.[18]

Golbart, meanwhile, received a diploma through the Rabbinical Seminary International (RSI), which gave academic credit for life experience and other courses. The RSI had no relationship with the traditional Orthodox, Reform, or Conservative seminaries. Golbart formed a new synagogue, Adat Ami ("My People"), which competed for congregants who wanted to be Jewish in a modern way while retaining many traditional practices. It also required no membership dues, which could be burdensome—particularly for young people. In lieu of an affiliation with traditional Jewish movements, Adat Ami designated itself "postdenominational." Its location in 2005 was a few miles west of the university campus.

Temples without Walls

Established in 1991, Temple Bet Knesset Bamidbar was a congregation with a difference. Led by Rabbi Hershel Brooks, this self-styled "traditional Reform" group eschewed brick and mortar for a community of largely retired people who met at Desert Vista Community Center in Sun City Summerlin, in northwestern Las Vegas. The congregation claimed to be the largest in Las Vegas, with thirteen hundred members, though only Sun City residents were eligible. Bet Knesset Bamidbar had an active Men's Club and Sisterhood. Its outreach program included nursing home visitation, regular food collection for the Jewish Family Service Agency (JFSA), and financial support of the Hillel Foundation at UNLV. Its president, Sydell Miller, was an accomplished vocalist and a member of the local *havurah*, Shema Yisroel.

This latter group reflected a mix of thirty Reform and Conservative members who met in homes and at the Mountain Shadows Community Center. Its leader, former Beth Sholom rabbi Louis Lederman, also performed weddings at local hotels. Lederman's grandchildren attended the Lubavitch Chabad Hebrew school in 2005, and he supported Chabad throughout his various ministries. His daughter ran the "kosher aisle" at the local Smith's supermarket. Miller's assumption of Bet Knesset Bamidbar's presidency and Rabbi Lederman's family affiliation with the Lubavitchers were further indications of the diverse expressions of Judaism existing within families and cutting across traditional religious lines.[19]

Also in the fast-growing Sun City area was the small Temple Bet Emet, calling itself Reform—but unaffiliated with the URJ. It had its services twice monthly at the Mountain Shadows Community Center, with Steven Newman, and, later, Craig Rosenstein, as its rabbinical leader.

Temple Ner Tamid

After the departure of Rabbi Mel Hecht and the death of Ed Maline, Ner Tamid struggled. For two years, Eileen Kollins and Leo Wilner provided lay leadership until, in 1988, the temple leadership hired Sanford Akselrad. At the time, he was pulpit rabbi at one the Midwest's largest Reform temples, and he had served Temple Sinai in Reno during his student days at Hebrew Union College. Akselrad inherited a congregation that had dwindled to eighty families. He immediately introduced new programs together with traditional courses in Hebrew, Judaism, and Torah study. He succeeded in creating what one new congregant described as a sense of community and belonging reminiscent of the days when Beth Sholom was the only synagogue in town. Akselrad is the longest-tenured pulpit rabbi in Las Vegas.

Ner Tamid became the largest Reform congregation in Nevada with a membership of more than six hundred families, but it outgrew its physical plant. Over the past few years, the membership's median age rose, and the number of children in religious school fell from three hundred to two hundred. To be nearer its growing membership, the congregation decided in 2005 to relocate south to the donated Greenspun Campus for Jewish Life in Green Valley. The plan was to continue the preschool, start a Jewish day school and adult education center, and phase in a Jewish healing center.[20]

Temple Beth Sholom, Felipe Goodman, and the Clash of Titans

In September 2000, Temple Beth Sholom formally dedicated its majestic new synagogue in fast-growing Summerlin, west of downtown Las Vegas. A $10 million facility on seven acres of prime real estate, the elaborate complex was made possible, in part, by a $4 million gift from an anonymous donor. Acknowledgments of philanthropy, such as that recognizing Dr. Leon and Faye Steinberg, who were instrumental in donating the *mikveh,* filled the corridors. One of the temple's striking exterior features was the immense sculpted doors that Jack Entratter had donated to the original Oakey Boulevard synagogue forty years earlier. Furnishings included a series of weavings depicting the journey from Egypt to Israel, a Murano glass sculpture of Moses, a six hundred–year-old Strauss Torah, and sixteen stained-glass windows illustrating quotations from the book of Isaiah, designed by UNLV art professor emerita Rita Deanin Abbey.[21]

Felipe Goodman was the first Jewish Mexican ordained as a Conservative rabbi. He had received a master's degree from the Jewish Theological Seminary two years before his ordination there in 1996. The young rabbi served in a number of student-leadership roles and had coauthored a Passover service widely used in Latin America. When Goodman arrived with his wife and children to assume spiritual leadership of Beth Sholom in 1998, the congregation's numbers had fallen precipitously—almost 90 percent from its previous high of one thousand families. Reasons for the decline were the subject of speculation and controversy. The most commonly cited cause was the rapid turnover of rabbis. Another was a rabbi's refusal to officiate at a marriage to a Gentile—sometimes leading both parents and children to seek a more liberal congregation. For some, the issue was the annual membership dues. Although a sliding scale made accommodations for hardship cases, the benchmark dues for a family of four was $1,600. For many, the old Oakey Boulevard location in the heart of Las Vegas was simply too far from the growing Jewish population on the outskirts of the city.[22] Finally, Temple Beth

Sholom was in competition with a multiplicity of ways of being Jewish in Las Vegas. Stemming the tide of attrition may have been among Rabbi Goodman's first goals, but even before the new temple was completed, he found himself enmeshed in an ugly dispute involving a prominent congregant and the city's mayor.

Sheldon Adelson, owner of the $1.6 billion Venetian Hotel and Casino, had fended off the Culinary Union attempts to organize his workers when it opened in May 1999. Temple Beth Sholom planned a fund-raising event for the new synagogue-in-progress and approached three resorts about available dates: the Venetian, Four Seasons, and Paris. In deference to Adelson, who had pledged $250,000 toward the building-in-progress, the planners let it be known that the event would be at the Venetian, but no contract was signed. Temple organizers subsequently decided that the occasion would be a roast of newly elected mayor Oscar Goodman and his wife, Carolyn, but when Goodman learned of the location, he was quoted as saying, "I won't go into the Venetian because I don't cross invisible picket lines. Everybody in town knows that I'm a strong union supporter." Organizers pleaded with him to make an exception for the sake of the temple. Goodman refused but offered to withdraw as the roast's honoree and postpone his own involvement to a later date. Adelson met with the event planners and proposed to fly in—at his own expense—a major speaker, such as Ariel Sharon. The organizers would have none of it and scheduled the roast at the Four Seasons. Adelson was insulted and deeply hurt. A dinner meeting between Adelson and Mayor Goodman was arranged at the mayor's home by mutual friends attempting to ameliorate the situation.[23]

A week prior to the event, Las Vegas Jewish Federation president Doug Unger (who had purchased a dinner ticket) announced that he would not attend the roast if it was held at the Four Seasons. According to several sources, Rabbi Goodman responded by declining to participate in a federation-sponsored event with the Jewish Community Center. Shortly before the December 12 event, Adelson visited Rabbi Goodman at the temple, delivered what the local newspaper described as a "tirade," and because he had reneged on the federation appearance declared him "unfit" to lead the congregation. Word spread that Adelson had brought the rabbi to tears, and Mayor Goodman promptly canceled the planned dinner meeting with him. Disparate accounts of the confrontation between Adelson and the rabbi were already afoot and creating their own mischief.

All three of the principal players in the dispute were in vulnerable positions. The Culinary Union had been one of Oscar Goodman's strongest supporters for mayor. Someone reportedly upset by the Venetian's antiunion success scrawled "Dead Jew" on Adelson's cabana mirror, and he expected moral support from his synagogue. Felipe Goodman was relatively new to his rabbinical position and was understandably deferential to the congregation's officers and event planners.

The roast went on as planned at the Four Seasons, and the money raised reached almost $200,000, thanks, in part, to unions that purchased more tables than expected—doubtless to spite Adelson. During the fund-raiser, Goodman's law partner, David Chesnoff, picked up the microphone and pretended to page Adelson from the stage. A roast of Goodman had now become the occasion for embarrassing the man who had wanted to host the event. The Adelsons—already in Israel—were notified of the Chesnoff gaff the following morning and were humiliated. The upshot was that Sheldon and Miriam Adelson resigned their membership at Temple Beth Sholom and redirected their $250,000 pledge to another cause. Contrary to a newspaper report, sources close to the Adelsons firmly stated that the pledge monies were never used as a lever to have the event held at the Venetian and were on the table until after the dinner event.

Adelson, however, was not out of reach of criticism. The newspaper article alleging that he had brought the rabbi to tears was picked up by the *Forward*, a Jewish periodical with international circulation, and Adelson was receiving calls about the matter from all over the world. Prominent Las Vegan Art Marshall, who attempted to bring about a reconciliation, attested that the rabbi did not cry. Any tears were figurative or shed subsequently. National director of the Anti-Defamation League Abraham Foxman defended Adelson in a letter to the *Forward* editor, but the damage was already done.

The incident was more than a trivial load of dirty laundry hung out for public view. It was an unfortunately divisive issue whose effects reverberated years later within the affiliated Jewish community—even as Adelson continued to donate generously to Jewish causes in Las Vegas and elsewhere. The young rabbi had faced a construction shortfall, the loss of at least one family from his congregation, and a spate of ill-feeling toward one or another of the principals. It was not a recipe for success, but Goodman and Beth Sholom survived. Temple president Sandra Mallin expressed confidence that the congregation would step forward to cover the lost pledge. The temple's board, president, and rabbi launched an ambitious educational program (including the traditional religious school) and a variety of activities for young people and adults.[24]

The new temple was particularly proud of its outreach to the elderly. Ruth Goldfarb, who had long urged the construction of a home for the Jewish elderly, formed the L'dor V'dor (Generation to Generation) program at the new temple in Summerlin. Volunteers brought 260 elderly people to the temple every eight weeks to interact with young children in the day school. The bimonthly event included a lunch prepared by celebrity chef Gustav Mauler.[25]

The combination of effort and new construction in Summerlin helped raise the temple's membership from 120 to 680 families—southern Nevada's largest Conservative congregation. Rabbi Goodman articulated his objective over the next few years to make Beth Sholom the "flagship" Conservative congregation in the entire Southwest. The relationship between Adelson and Temple Beth Sholom remained unresolved, but in 2004 Goodman received a second seven-year contract. He was on his way to the longest tenure of any rabbi in Beth Sholom's history, and reconciliations of the various parties were only a few years away.

A Break among Conservative Jews and Other Moves to Henderson, Nevada

Southeast of Las Vegas in Green Valley lies Henderson, among the nation's fastest-growing cities. On October 31, 1994, prominent attorney Mark Goldstein and his wife, Gail Alcalay, gathered nine others at a Green Valley restaurant to discuss building a new Conservative synagogue. All belonged to Beth Sholom. Not only were they dissatisfied with the direction of that congregation, but they also lived at a great driving distance from the Oakey Boulevard temple. After further consultation, the founding eleven and a host of friends held services in a warehouse able to accommodate a Hebrew school and preschool not far from McCarran International Airport. In 1998, High Holiday services held at the Henderson Convention Center drew 600 worshipers. The new congregation took the name Midbar Kodesh and formally affiliated with the United Synagogue of Conservative Judaism. The group broke ground on a permanent synagogue in 1999 on land donated by the Greenspun family. Jeremy Wiederhorn, ordained in 2000, was hired to lead the Las Vegas area's second Conservative synagogue. The rabbi's wife, Riki, had a strong academic background in Jewish education and rabbinics and became an active teaching member of the staff.[26]

Beth El Congregation—also located in Henderson—styled itself as "traditional Reform" but had no ties with the URJ. Its congregation was not then interested in annual dues or expensive building projects. Its head was Simon Bergman, who had been the *hazzan* (cantor) at Temple Beth Sholom until he came into conflict with the rabbi and congregation. Instead of retiring, he followed Golbart's lead, obtaining a rabbinical education and ordination through a nontraditional seminary. The congregation, which had a Men's Club and Sisterhood, had Shabbat services twice a month in 2005 at the Hampton Inn and Suites.

The Reconstructionist movement nurtured by Mordecai M. Kaplan separated from Conservative Judaism in 1968. Its Las Vegas congregation met at the Desert Willow Community Center, with Shabbat services on the first Friday of the month. It called itself the Valley Outreach Synagogue, headed by Rabbi Richard Schachet. Reconstructionism appealed to those Jews who preferred to set aside some of the traditional practices of Judaism in favor of social action directed to the development of a messianic age. When Schachet retired in 2005, his successor was Las Vegas's first female pulpit rabbi, Yocheved Mintz.

Rabbis with Nontraditional Training

Sometimes disparagingly called "mail-order rabbis," Golbart, Bergman, Schachet, Craig Rosenstein, and others were excluded from the Las Vegas Council of Rabbis, composed of traditionally educated and ordained rabbis. Golbart and Schachet, however, were accepted members of the Clark County Ministerial Association, and Golbart wrote a regular column in the *Las Vegas Israelite* along with Rabbis Hillel Cohn, Shea Harlig, and Hecht.[27] The position taken by the Las Vegas newspapers as well as by the Las Vegas Jewish Federation has been that if a congregation of Jews accepts someone as their rabbi, the newspaper and the federation so acknowledge him or her.

Lubavitch Hasidic Chabad and Young Israel Come to Nevada

Lubavitch Hasidism was an international movement whose organizational arm, Chabad, had headquarters in Crown Heights, Brooklyn, New York. Its followers traced their origin to the eighteenth-century rabbi Shneur Zalman, who authored the *Tanya,* a guide to Jewish spiritual awareness. In 1950, Menachem Mendel Schneerson became the Chabad's leader. Known to his followers simply as "the Rebbe," Schneerson intellectually and organizationally stimulated the movement until his death in 1994. He was childless, and no successor was appointed. Chabad leadership decided he would be the last rebbe, and many assumed the movement would not survive. Instead, it grew more than thirty percent, with some followers considering Schneerson the long-awaited Messiah.[28]

The organization's mission was simply to bring every known Jew back to full observance of traditional Judaism as taught by the Rebbe. As such, it was a proselytizing movement within Judaism. In 1999, more than twenty-six hundred Chabad seminaries, day camps, schools, and other outreach institutions were emphasizing self-discipline, Torah study, men and young boys wearing the tefillin (pieces of the Torah worn on the arm) at least once a week, giving to charity, following kosher dietary laws, and observing the Sabbath. According to some, the organization was a strong financial supporter of efforts in Israel to disfranchise non-Orthodox Jews. This alone created discord between Lubavitchers and many other affiliated Jews at the national level. The issue has not yet emerged in the Nevada public forum, though Lubavitchers firmly view their strict Orthodoxy as the only integral Judaism.[29]

For many years, Rebbe Schneerson had opposed any Lubavitch Chabad presence in Las Vegas. A delegation of Las Vegans traveled to Crown Heights to obtain the Rebbe's blessing, and soon afterward he agreed to send Rabbi Shea Harlig to establish the city's first Chabad. Harlig and his followers succeeded beyond the expectation of anyone except the true believers. When Harlig came to Las Vegas early in 1990, he defined his constituency as "every Jew and any Jew." The "Sin City" to which Rebbe Schneerson had not wanted to send emissaries was fertile ground for this ultra-Orthodox Chabad, because Las Vegas had so many nonpracticing Jews. Some of them initially greeted Harlig with scorn, saying something like they "left the East Coast in order to avoid people like you." Harlig initially sported a long black beard and topped his head with the traditional black Hasidic hat. He was likely an unexpected distraction as he walked through a casino en route to a welcoming party.[30]

His presence initially was divisive, but as one established rabbi asserted, "the presence of Chabad has been more positive than negative." Rabbi Harlig received a $1.2 million donation from Venetian owner Adelson, who had separated from Temple Beth Sholom in 1999. Chabad developed three centers in Las Vegas: one downtown, another in Henderson, and a third in Summerlin. All three had Hebrew schools for students up to the seventh grade, and the Desert Torah Academy Day School went up to the eighth grade. Harlig and three other Chabad rabbis offered adult education courses on the Torah, Talmud, Hasidic discourses, and Mishnah. Harlig also assigned another rabbi to provide "more meat and potatoes" to what he considered the heavy docket of social activities at the UNLV Hillel. The *Chabad Times,* mailed five times a year to three thousand Las Vegas homes, covers local and national news of interest to Lubavitchers. Although a few members from Ner Tamid and Temple Beth Sholom joined the Lubavitchers, many of its affiliates were simply financial supporters or occasional worshipers at the daily minyan.[31]

Harlig's success in Las Vegas prompted a small group of Renoites to ask for a Lubavitch Chabad through Rabbi Baruch Schlomo Cunin of Los Angeles. The latter sent his nephew, who had been serving a group in northern California, to spend some time during the summer to assess Reno's potential. He reported back to his uncle that Reno certainly needed a Lubavitch presence, but the appointee, he said, required "nerves of steel."[32] Uncle Rabbi Baruch appointed his nephew, the messenger, to the post.

In 1997, young Mendel Cunin took up permanent residence in Reno, supported by grants from the Los Angeles regional office. Over time, he built up a constituency of small groups from Dayton and Carson City to Incline Village on the shores of Lake Tahoe, with whom he met on a monthly basis or on High Holidays. He purchased a small home on Reno's south side, which also served as his office and a preschool. With generous donations from Lubavitchers in New York and several families affiliated with Temple Emanu-El, he built Reno's first *mikveh.* It was a stunningly beautiful design and, according to the rabbi's wife, Sarah, well used. With thirty donations of one thousand dollars each, Cunin authorized the creation of a handwritten sefer Torah on sixty sheets of cowhide. Chabad scribes in Israel did most of the work. It was completed at the Reno Chabad in 2004 and accompanied under a *huppah* (ritual canopy) to a nearby park, where there was dancing and a kosher feast.[33] In 2006 the Northern Nevada Chabad acquired a two-story office building that now houses a sanctuary, a restaurant, and the David and Parvin Farahi Day Shool.

Another Orthodox presence in Las Vegas was Young Israel/Aish Las Vegas headed by Rabbi Yitzchak Wyne of Edmonton, Canada. Rabbi Harlig initially discouraged Wyne from coming to town because there were too few Orthodox. Wyne assured Harlig that he would not poach on Lubavitch territory. For example, when Wyne learned that Harlig was opening a summer camp for children, he directed Young Israel programs to young adults. Wyne's goal was to stem the tide of assimilation, which meant stopping the practice of marrying outside the faith. His singles programs included "speed dating" and the puckish "Wyne and Cheese." Young Israel's success attracted the attention of a Las Vegas real estate developer who was also from Canada. Eskander Ghermaizian donated to Young Israel a $1.2 million synagogue near Summerlin. Wyne was quoted as explaining, "Everyone needs their billionaire. Harlig has Adelson and I have Ghermaizian."[34]

Yiddishkeit, or Ways of Being Jewish

1931–2005

"Kosher Las Vegas, nu?" This slippage into Yiddish is simply a preparation for what is to come after a taste of traditional Jewish fare. Strictly kosher foods are prepared according to ancient dietary regulations called "kashruth." Meat must come from an animal with split hooves that chews its cud. Fish that lack fins or scales, such as shrimp and lobster, are forbidden, as are birds of prey. Even permissible meat and fish must be killed in a carefully prescribed manner by a certified *shochet.* Foods made with milk may not be eaten or mixed with meat products. Modern Jews disagree about the origins and meaning of kosher laws. Most, however, agree that observance of dietary laws evokes the memory of millennia-old practices, which have reinforced Jewish identity and deterred cultural assimilation.

Reno had kosher restaurants and delis in 1931, but—with the exception of Rabbi Tarlow's rooming-house kosher table—they were short-lived. In modern times, Jews looking for "kosher-style" food patronized a local deli, but the strictly certified version could be found only in specialty markets. In 1997 the Sisterhood of Reno's Temple Sinai started what became an almost annual fund-raiser dubbed "Jewish Fest." It included klezmer music, folk dancing, and kosher foods for sale. The response from the Reno Gentile community was so great that the event was moved to a regional park, where it could accommodate the four hundred to five hundred visitors. The festival became a victim of its own success seven years later when its volunteers realized they could not prepare enough food to meet the demand or cope with the event's increasing complexity.[1]

In recent years, kosher opportunities in Las Vegas dwarfed the Reno offerings. Twenty years ago, choosing to eat exclusively kosher food in Las Vegas would have been nearly as heroic as it was for Solomon Nunes Carvalho in 1854. The city's first kosher meat market and a kosher cafeteria located within Sunrise Hospital did not appear until 1984.[2] Since then, a steady increase in

[248]

the city's vegetarian, gourmand, and Jewish population has generated a new demand for kosher products. Several major supermarkets have provided seasonal offerings of kosher products for years, particularly during Passover and High Holidays. Now these stores have expanding kosher lines twenty-four hours a day, year-round. Several markets have hired a *masgiach* (overseer of kashruth law) to supervise their enlarged kosher departments.

The Smith's supermarket in Summerlin remodeled its store to include what it calls the "Kosher Experience" and had its own bakery providing challah, rye, and other breads and desserts. It had also added tables and chairs for those who want to enjoy a sit-down kosher breakfast, lunch, or dinner. Avi Klein, the *masgiach* at Albertsons, had a three hundred–page list of available kosher food items. During Passover alone, sixty feet of shelf space was stocked exclusively with Passover groceries—a volume that recently doubled within one year. The family-owned Vegas Kosher Mart provided imported foods from Israel and sold kosher food exclusively. By 2005, Las Vegas supported four kosher restaurants. One served meat dishes only, another was a pizzeria providing some dairy dishes, and one of the oldest was the Chinese-style Shalom Hunan. An abundance of delicatessens and specialty houses had catering services, and at least three casinos had kosher kitchens.

The person largely responsible for promoting kosher food in Las Vegas was Rabbi Shea Harlig, head of the Orthodox Lubavitch Chabad of southern Nevada. When he came to Las Vegas in 1990, he found no fresh kosher food. He approached the supermarkets to expand their kosher lines, but at that time, he said, "I couldn't get through the front door." In 2005, he became the kosher supervisor for the Smith's "Kosher Experience," Albertsons' kosher aisle, and three kosher restaurants. Las Vegas Judaism's competitive sense displayed itself when Yakov Wasser, Orthodox rabbi of Shaarei Tefilla, claimed supervision of two of the same places.[3]

Yiddish in Nevada?

The word *Yiddish*, derived from the German *Jhdisch*, or *Jewish*, is an unsophisticated combination of High German, Hebrew, Old French, Old Italian, and Slavic words. *Mishmash* (hodgepodge), *gelt* (money), *kibitz* (to offer unrequested or playful comment), *klutz* (clumsy person), *nosh* (snack), *schmaltz* (flattery), and *schmooze* (chat) are just a few examples of Yiddish words that have made their way into modern usage. Latin and Attic Greek are dead languages, and Yiddish once seemed headed to the same graveyard. The colorful and pungent language that many immigrant Jews considered their *mama loshen* (mother tongue) was on the verge of disuse in this country, but it has been resurrected in recent years, bringing a renewed interest in Yiddish theater and klezmer music.[4]

Jews throughout Nevada commonly interjected a touch of Yiddish into daily conversation, either because the word was untranslatable or had a humorous connotation. To describe carrying or dragging a thing or person as "schlepping" connoted the tiresome nature of the task not found in English. To call someone a "schlemiel" rather than a "loser" somehow seemed more richly descriptive. Conservative Beth Sholom in Las Vegas had a Yiddish Club as early as 1972. Thirty years later, Rabbi Wasser often spoke to his Orthodox people in Yiddish. "Why not?" he said. "It's a beautiful language, and it makes some of our congregants feel good."[5]

The Yiddish revival in Las Vegas was not limited to religious Jews. In 1996, Charles Casper of the Sun City Jewish Friendship Club formed a Yiddish class that grew to thirty participants. In 1999, the Las Vegas Jewish Community Center began sponsoring "Yiddish Vinkle" (Jewish Corner)—devoted to learning or relearning the language. Northern Nevada also had many Yiddish speakers. Among them was Leonard Nimoy (*Star Trek*'s Mr. Spock), who hosted a two-hour weekly National Public Radio program of Yiddish and other Jewish music in 2005. The program's popularity sparked an interest in Jewish culture in an area once described as a Jewish "cultural wasteland."[6] First-generation American Jews who lived through spates of antisemitism and were anxious to assimilate often rejected Yiddish except on funeral occasions. The embrace of kosher fare and Yiddish in everyday conversation by Nevada Jews signaled a new sense of security, maturity, and self-respect.

Three Newspapers and a Magazine Promote Jewish Events and Culture

Henderson's Moritz "Morry" Zenoff started editing and publishing *Boulder City News* and the *Henderson Home News* in the late 1940s. In 1961, he founded the weekly *Nevada Jewish Chronicle,* which carried international and local Jewish news. Zenoff hired Jack Tell as editor and advertising salesman for the *Chronicle.* When Jack and Bea Tell founded, published, and edited the *Las Vegas Israelite* in 1965, Zenoff thought he was victim of a "dirty trick." According to Nevada newspaper historian Jake Highton, Zenoff stopped publication and never spoke to Tell again.[7]

The *Israelite*'s early editions represented the diversity of Jewishness within the population. Editor Tell's devotion to Israel showed in his unapologetic condemnation of United Nations ambassador Arthur Goldberg, who had criticized Israel for denigrating non-Orthodox Jews. It published the *yahrzeits* (celebrated death dates) of those registered at Temple Beth Sholom as well as simplified explanations of Jewish holy days and rituals. The newspaper's readership varied enough in its level of dietary observance for the *Israelite* to carry promotions of kosher food as well as restaurants advertising pork and shellfish. The *Israelite* devoted large quantities of ink to Las Vegas entertainment venues, whose advertising was a source of financial support. "Las Vegas Showcase of the Stars" was a regular feature from the earliest publication and within a decade formed a third of the newspaper, devoted to local entertainment and celebrity gossip.[8]

Judaism and casino life came together onstage and in the pages of the *Israelite*. The popular focus on Israel appeared in a Union Plaza Hotel and Casino stage presentation, and the "Dunes Extravaganza" included a tribute to Israel's first twenty-five years. Perhaps the most humorous conflation of Judaism and pleasure seeking was in reporter Alan Kirschner's coverage of cabaret shows. He began his article with a Talmudic discussion and then proceeded to review a cabaret show with dancing half-naked women.[9]

Since its inception, the *Israelite* has chronicled Las Vegas Jewry, though it has generally steered clear of local controversial issues. In recent years, it opened its pages to regular columns from as diverse a group of rabbis as "postdenominational" Gary Golbart, traditional Reform Mel Hecht, URJ's Hillel Cohn, and Hasidic Lubavitch Shea Harlig. It is published twice monthly and continues to announce itself as "Nevada's English-Jewish Newspaper." In 2006, it added a full-color insert promoting Jewish organizations—in particular, the Southern Nevada Jewish Community Center and Jewish Family Service Agency.

The *Israelite* had no local competitor until the founding of the *Jewish Reporter* in 1976 by Edythe Katz Yarchever and Jerry Countess. The *Reporter* generally carried two-page focus stories and a score of regular features. These latter included news of the federation's beneficiary groups, and—most recently—the latest addition to kosher availability. Unlike the *Israelite*, the *Jewish Reporter* initially had virtually no advertising or special features on casino entertainment. Since 2006 the *Reporter* has vastly expanded its paid advertising. The *Reporter* was free, whereas the *Israelite* listed a modest subscription fee. Both newspapers served as tribunes of Las Vegas's diverse Judaism and Jewishness and had a readership that included northern Nevada Jews.

Caroline Orzes, former editor of the *Jewish Reporter,* launched a new publication in the spring of 2004. *Life & Style: The Las Vegas Jewish Magazine* was a hefty, full-color, slick-paper quarterly with a difference. It provided opinion pieces that were not always politically correct and covered what the editor emphasized as events and issues of interest to the *"entire* Jewish community." It instantly became a bimonthly. In addition to the customary letters, food, book-review, and personality departments, its early issues included stories on the controversial federation reorganization, Jews for Jesus, conversions to Judaism, and the Israeli enclave in Las Vegas.[10] In June 2006, the magazine expanded to include Arizona and altered its name to *Jewish Life and Style: Sun Country.* Editor Orzes resigned in 2007, and the future of the magazine is uncertain.

Jewish Federation in the West

In parts of eastern Europe, Jews formed a *kehillah* to provide for coreligionists so they might not be a burden on society. Although composed exclusively of Jewish elders, a *kehillah* was supervised by local civil authorities and expected to tax Jews for public services. Judah Leon Magnes, rabbi of New York's Temple Emanu-El, established the first *kehillah* in the United States in 1909 to attract Jews straying from the fold and to assist in closing down illegal gambling and prostitution on the Lower East Side. Due to financial problems, as well as the criminals' disregard of its authority, the American *kehillah* lasted only thirteen years.[11]

Its purpose lived on in the form of the Jewish Federation. Northern California's Greater East Bay had a Jewish Federation as early as 1918. Its purpose was, and remained, raising funds for needy Jews locally and around the world. The United Jewish Appeal, established in 1939, focused on the plight of European Jews. Reno came under the California federation's umbrella, but its influence was limited to coordinating donations to the UJA. Reno wanted its own coordinating organization.

Reno's Community Council

The Jewish Community Council of Northern Nevada was a long-awaited dream of Sidney Stern, president of Nevada First Thrift. He gathered around him members of both Reno synagogues, including Mike Brissman, Patricia Blanchard, John Farahi, and Hy Kashenberg. At the outset, in 1982, organizers estimated that at least six hundred Jewish families lived in northern Nevada, most of them unaffiliated with a synagogue. The council was to be a nonreligious Jewish organization, which could provide social services to resident and visiting Jews—similar to the long-defunct Hebrew Benevolent Society. Brissman hoped initially "to develop a sense of solidarity within the local Jewish community—to strengthen it and create a presence."[12] He indirectly acknowledged the twenty-year-old rift created when a half-dozen Jewish families bolted from the Conservative Temple Emanu-El.

Blanchard, a member of the new Temple Sinai, wished the council might inspire the building of a Jewish Community Center, restart a B'nai B'rith chapter, or introduce the general public to Jewish food and traditions. Dr. Leonard Shapiro, president of Temple Emanu-El, was chosen to serve two years as the council's president. Professor Richard Siegel, vice president of Temple Sinai, became vice president of the council and, later, copresident with David Levine. Siegel's view of the Jewish Community Council of Northern Nevada reflected his academic interest in political science. He envisioned merging the goals of the United Jewish Appeal with a local public-policy agenda. According to Shapiro, however, the council was not to be politically oriented. With such differences evident at the start, some lack of focus was inevitable.

The effort was short-lived. With Stern's death, the Jewish Community Council of Northern Nevada also died. It failed to meet the expectations of its founders. The lack of interest from nonaffiliated Jews, coupled with the expenditure of volunteer time devoted to the separate temple functions, sapped whatever life with which the leadership infused the council. With the council's demise, the only issue that could be counted on to bring unaffiliated Jews together in northern Nevada was a public discussion or debate on Israel.[13]

In many places across the country, a federation was the focus of Jewish life. Reno, Incline, Elko, and Stateline Jews remained unfederated and may have contributed to international Jewish causes through the United Jewish Communities. But in these northern areas, those who had a Jewish social life were identified with a *havurah* or synagogue. Only Las Vegas had an active federation.

Jewish Federation of Las Vegas

The United Jewish Appeal was Las Vegas's first major organized fund-raising vehicle. Its chairs included Moe Sedway, Jake Kozloff, Gus Greenbaum, Sam Tucker, and Moe Dalitz, all executives of Las Vegas casinos. The organization morphed into the Las Vegas Combined Jewish Appeal, as did its leadership, which increasingly came from the nongaming community. Jerry Mack, whose interests were in real estate and banking, was the Combined Appeal's first president as well as chairman for years of the Israel Bond Campaigns. David Messing, a Las Vegas certified public accountant, was credited with organizing the Combined Appeal's successor in 1967, the Las Vegas Jewish Federation. Its first president was Mack.[14]

Consistent with tradition, the federation raised millions of dollars in support of local and Israel-related programs. In 2000, it counted among its agencies the Jewish Community Center of Southern Nevada, Jewish Family Service Agency, Hillel Foundation at UNLV, Milton I. Schwartz Hebrew Academy, and Jewish Community Day School (since closed). In addition, it provided partial support for the *Jewish Reporter*, Holocaust Education and Sperling Library, and Israel Independence Day Festival, among others. It was led by an eight-member executive committee and a thirty-five-member board of directors. Past president Doug Unger stated that one of the most important federation goals he helped to achieve was to change its past image of heavy-handed solicitation for funds.[15]

Future challenges included greater emphasis on Jewish young people and building a campus in the fast-growing southwestern part of the city to house the Jewish Community Center and other federation agencies. The federation board hired Meyer L. Bodoff as executive director in 2001, and his task was to develop a new plan of action. The trick was to find a strategy that did not jeopardize the fund-raising autonomy of synagogues and nonfederation Jewish organizations and to maintain a sense of empowerment enjoyed by the federation's own agencies and programs. The politics of the process proved daunting.

Jewish Federation of Las Vegas Joins United Jewish Communities

Bodoff, new president Robert Unger (unrelated to Doug), and members of the board and executive committee created a new model for achieving the vision. It included reducing the board of directors by one-third to eighteen and some internal restructuring to reduce administrative costs. On June 4, 2003, Robert Unger turned over the president's gavel to Michael Novick as chair of the new board. Under the restructuring, Bodoff was Jewish Federation president and chief executive officer. The new organization's stated goal was to build a Jewish community campus. Also under consideration were a Jewish high school, an assisted-living facility, and a home for the aged.[16] So far, so good; but controversy lay ahead.

One national statistic showed Nevada had the highest increase of people sixty-five or older between 1990 and 1998, with the number of elderly possibly doubling by 2005. Since studies showed that 90 percent of the elderly in Las Vegas wanted to remain in their own homes, they tabled the original plan to build a home for the elderly. Instead, with the help of a hefty federal grant, the Jewish Federation created a nondenominational Las Vegas Senior Lifeline to provide in-home services for the elderly, transport them to a senior center for social activities, and investigate high-tech ways of connecting the homebound. The plan appealed to many except those who had dreamed of building a home for the elderly. It also did not address how the services of the Senior Lifeline program related to those that had been the Jewish Family Service Agency's responsibility.[17]

At a special meeting in the fall of 2003, the federation's board unanimously voted to affiliate with United Jewish Communities, a national network of 155 federations and 360 nonfederated Jewish communities (such as the Reno area). The resulting new entity was called the United Jewish Community of Las Vegas. At the heart of the plan was a reorganization of federation agencies and programs into seven Service Pillar Commissions with attendant changes as to how to fund its services. Board member Danny Greenspun called it a "bold new plan to identify and unite" the Jewish community of Las Vegas. Federation past president Hal Ober characterized the move as "more cost effective." The plan was officially to go into effect in January 2004, but the reorganization immediately prompted negative reactions, ranging from the charge that it was a "power play" to a lack of confidence in the United Jewish Community plan.[18]

The federation responded to these objections in the pages of the *Jewish Reporter* and boldly moved ahead. One modest accommodation was to change its name to the Jewish Federation of Las Vegas/United Jewish Community (JFLV/UJC), but the name and initialism were reversed a year later. It was a matter of emphasis needed to accommodate the exigencies of internal Jewish politics. Over the course of 2004, the new agency made other adjustments to criticism and enjoyed some major successes. Israel Independence Day celebrated at a local park in 2001 had drawn fewer than a thousand. In 2004, the event took place at the Bellagio Hotel and attracted an estimated eight thousand. The new organization's fund-raising efforts also broke new records with a two million–dollar annual appeal. But there were casualties in the process.

Jewish Community Center of Southern Nevada (JCCSN)

The concept of the community center originated with Mordecai Kaplan's idea, stated in 1916, that each synagogue needed to have a place where Jews could play as well as worship. The simple notion was to attract otherwise unaffiliated Jews to the center in the hope that they might be motivated to attend religious events. Soon Jewish community centers arose independent of the synagogue, supplanting organizations such as the Young Men's Hebrew Association. The stand-alone community centers began to compete with the synagogue centers after World War II in large urban areas. "But even when the Jewish community center became, in the end, the unifying *ethnic* institution of American Jews while synagogues became the *religious* institutions that divided them," argues historian Jonathan Sarna, "the synagogue-center idea that Kaplan had so powerfully championed remained influential."[19]

So it was at Las Vegas's Temples Beth Sholom and Ner Tamid, until Joyce G. Scheinman founded the Jewish Community Center of Southern Nevada (JCCSN) in 1991. Its stated purpose was "to enhance the quality of life in southern Nevada by providing educational, social, athletic, and cultural programs designed to meet the needs of the Jewish community and the community as a whole, in a way that promotes Jewish values and unites, strengthens, nurtures and enriches all of our lives."[20] For most of its very active life, it was affiliated with the Jewish Federation of Las Vegas.

The JCCSN's myriad activities resisted generalization: weekly card games with "Great Games," the "Lunch Out" or "Dining Out" clubs, "Poetry and Writing Workshop," the "Film Society," "Hiking Out Club," a retirees group called "Enjoying Leisure," and a variety of programs to bring singles together, such as the "Singles Bagel Brunches" program. Some were leadership programs, such as "How to Become a Camp Counselor." Others were ideological, such as Young Judea, a Zionist Youth group. There were summer camps and soccer camps and bowling leagues among the five hundred programs publicized to its four thousand members by mail and online.

In 2004, JCCSN leaders took exception to the funding implications of the federation's affiliation with United Jewish Communities. They severed their ties to the federation, but conversations between federation and JCCSN directors were arranged to heal the breach. One of the issues was whether the land donated to the federation for the purpose of building a Jewish Community Center facility would still be available to the now-independent JCCSN.[21] The organization's future hung in the balance.

Jewish Family Service Agency (JFSA)

Many of the services once provided by local Hebrew Benevolent Societies in Nevada had become the purview of the Jewish Family Service Agency, founded in 1977. Its clientele included Clark County's neediest Jewish people. Its food pantry, long overseen by Shel Kolner, provided more than five thousand meals yearly. The *bikur holim* (visiting the sick) was a cluster of volunteers providing spiritual support for those in hospitals and nursing homes. A team of counselors assisted Holocaust survivors and those with bipolar illness. Workshops and support groups comforted the bereaved and aided families affected by drug or alcohol addiction. The agency also reached out to interfaith families and to gay, lesbian, and transgender Jews.[22]

Director Mitchell Gilbert brought a master's degree in social work and fourteen years of experience to the agency in 2003. At that time, the JFSA was an independent beneficiary of funds raised by the federation, covering one-third of its budget. When the federation decided to affiliate with the United Jewish Communities, Gilbert and his staff feared the loss of their autonomy and left the federation. In prior years, about one hundred people added personal donations to the federation's infusion. After the split, four hundred came forward in support of the Jewish Family Service Agency—more than equaling its former dependence on the federation. The reorganization and affiliation of the federation with United Jewish Communities was, said Gilbert, "a very painful, bloody episode that is splitting the community."[23] Others were of the same mind. In 2006, Eric Goldstein, executive director of the JCCSN, became interim executive director of the JFSA.

Edythe Katz Yarchever and Holocaust Education

Predating the Holocaust Survivors Group were two programs firmly under the Las Vegas Jewish Federation's wing and supported through a governor's council: Education Relating to the Holocaust and the Holocaust Library.

Edythe Katz Yarchever, then a member of Temple Beth Sholom, attended a presentation in the early 1970s by Professor Franklin H. Littell, a United Methodist historian of religion. His subject was "Teaching and Learning about the Holocaust," and it refocused Yarchever's community activism forever. With a persistence that could melt the most tightfisted potential donor or a governor intent on proposing budget cuts, she engineered programs to expedite education about the Holocaust in Nevada's schools. Although such a curriculum was not mandatory until 1989, a large contingent of Clark County teachers earlier attended training seminars and voluntarily incorporated modules on the Holocaust in their classes. With an initial grant of ten thousand dollars, from her mother, Gertrude Sperling, and subsequent gifts from the Mack and Kronberg families, Yarchever established the city's first resource library for Holocaust study in 1980 at the Jewish Federation headquarters. The collection was not simply a stand-alone monument to its donors and the Holocaust itself but also an expanding user-friendly resource for students and teachers whom Yarchever had helped to train over the years.[24]

Governor Bob Miller (1989–1999) strongly supported Holocaust education and urged the legislature to establish the Governor's Advisory Council on Education Relating to the Holocaust. Yarchever has chaired the council since its inception. She was also the spokesperson before the assembly's Ways and Means Committee to lobby for an annual budget, which in 1998–1999 included special instruction for two hundred teachers and university professors. Committee vice chair Jan Evans and Governor Kenny Guinn (1999–2007) acknowledged receiving hate letters based on their support for the Holocaust education program. Evans's correspondent attempted to convince her that the Holocaust was a hoax, and Guinn's critic called him a "Jew lover," which he then publicly acknowledged that he was. He followed up with a proclamation that the first week of May 2000 would be dedicated to remembrance of Holocaust victims, survivors, rescuers, and liberators.[25]

Judy Mack had lost family members in the Holocaust before leaving Germany in 1949. She and her husband, Ronald, helped Yarchever create the Shia Szrut Holocaust Collection, housed in the northwest branch of the Washoe County Library in Reno.[26] The statewide program and its libraries were among a series of Edythe Katz Yarchever's legacies to Nevada Jewry. The Las Vegas Jewish Federation honored her and her husband, Judge Gilbert Yarchever, in 2005 with the David L. Simon Bridge Builder for Peace Award.[27]

A Plethora of Organizations Unaffiliated with Synagogues

Hadassah was an international organization of women primarily devoted to support for Israel. Reno had a very active chapter in the 1940s, but thanks to a dispute among members about whether a portion of the funds raised by Hadassah ought to remain with the temple and a subsequent exodus of members from Temple Emanu-El in 1961, Hadassah fell on hard times. In recent years, the antagonism engendered by the schism abated, and a Reno chapter of Hadassah revived. Its membership included women from both Reno congregations and beyond. The larger Las Vegas Jewish population in 2007 supported nine chapters of the philanthropic group.

Na'Amat was Israel's largest women's social-action program on women's rights and Israeli domestic issues. It had active chapters in Green Valley and another in Summerlin, as did the Women's American Occupational Rehabilitation and Training (ORT). A few women in northern Nevada maintained a supportive relationship with ORT chapters in Nevada or other parts of the country from which they had moved.[28]

The American Israel Public Affairs Committee (AIPAC) is a fifty-year-old pro-Israel organization, considered by many to be the most powerful foreign-policy lobby in Washington. It has sixty thousand members, with chapters in Reno and Las Vegas. Its donors cross political lines. Congresswoman Shelley Berkley served on its board before her election to Congress. She was a beneficiary of AIPAC funds for its various domestic and foreign missions. John Farahi of Reno's Atlantis Casino was AIPAC's northern Nevada coordinator.[29]

The nearly forty organizations independent of Las Vegas synagogues included four chapters of Jewish War Veterans; the Brandeis University National Women's Committee, which promised its coed membership an educational experience; a Jewish fraternity, Alpha Epsilon Pi, and Hillel Foundation; and B'nai B'rith of Greater Las Vegas, with an allied youth group, supplemented the nurturing programs to be found in most area temples. The Jewish Genealogy Society of Southern Nevada was organized for more than a decade and published a monthly newsletter, *Family Legacies.* Under the leadership of Sam Showel, the society initiated a survey of all Jewish graves in 2003, which is now complete and soon will be available online.[30]

The Ultimate Mitzvah: Burying the Dead

Burial in a sacred ground was the last wish for observant Jews and many who had long since distanced themselves from religious observance. As soon as they had a minyan, nineteenth-century Nevada Jews established a cemetery. Preparing a body for burial was considered the most important mitzvah a Jew could perform, because this act of kindness could not be repaid.

The rites themselves are ancient. A lighted memorial candle and the tearing of a garment symbolize bereavement. A *shomer* (guardian) stands vigil with the deceased until the funeral can take place. The *hevrah kadishah*, a society of lay volunteers, carefully washes the body *(taharah)*, covers it with a simple white linen shroud, and prepares it for a plain wooden casket, constructed without nails or metal attachments. Embalming and cremation are forbidden. Traditionally, the body is to be buried within a day of death. After recitation of the kaddish at the grave site comes the shivah, or the initial seven days of mourning. During this time, men often refrain from shaving or even bathing. Even the least-observant Jews reverence their dead by commemorating them annually on their *yahrzeits* by lighting a candle, making a charitable donation, and reciting the kaddish once more. Over the centuries, the Orthodox maintained these practices, whereas Conservatives and Reform Jews modified some.[31]

Liberal religious Jews have recently revived the traditional burial rituals. Ten years ago at Temple Beth Sholom, one funeral a year might have included a *taharah*. In 2004, all but one of the temple's funerals included the ancient practice. The Las Vegas area's two Conservative temples, Beth Sholom and Midbar Kodesh, have cooperated to form a *hevrah kadishah* composed of about twenty-five volunteers trained in the ritual. Although the congregants know who the members are, those performing a particular *taharah* remain anonymous. In Reno, Mel Gordon led the area's only *hevrah kadishah* in recent years, and when a visiting Jewish businessman died at one of the local hotels, the Lubavitch rabbi Mendel Cunin arranged for a *shomer* at the family's request.[32]

All of the nineteenth-century Jewish cemeteries have experienced vandalism. There is no trace of the burial site at Austin. In the 1990s, the county's Honor Camp surrounded the Eureka Jewish cemetery with a heavy chain-link fence. Director Wally Cucine of the restored Eureka Opera House served as the cemetery's unofficial custodian. Virginia City's cemetery—covered by sagebrush and with barely recognizable headstones—recently received a face-lift. Reno's temple men's clubs joined with the Comstock Cemetery Foundation and the Bureau of Land Management to clean the site and install an iron fence. Representatives of the northern Nevada synagogues rededicated it in 2004.[33]

Reno Hebrew Cemetery

The two-acre Reno Hebrew Cemetery had a placid beginning on what is now Angel Street in 1877, but controversy punctuated its past fifty years. The cemetery accommodated Jewish funerals across northern Nevada through the reunion of Temple Beth Or with Temple Emanu-El in 1947. Thereafter, it became the site for bones of contention. Almost every old-timer had an example of a contested burial, and almost no one wanted the story attributed to them.

Some generalizations are possible. The rules of interment for Orthodox, Conservative, and Reform Jews differ, and committees from Reno's two synagogues were expected to work out guidelines. The differences of opinion and practice include the burial of cremated remains, whether Gentile spouses should be permitted in a family plot, and whether to use electronic probes to determine the presence of a bona fide grave—particularly under degraded wooden markers. Some say exceptions to the rules were made for wealthy families. Others noted strange requests, such as being buried with cans of a favorite soft drink or business files. One family wanted the deceased dressed in cowboy boots and costume, rather than in the traditional simple shroud.

Although volunteers have carried on the tradition of the *hevrah kadishah* for the most observant, many left the arrangements to a local funeral home. Mortician Silas Ross, the founder of Ross, Burke, and Knobel Funeral Home, claimed to have learned the procedure for preparation of Jewish bodies for burial from local merchant Sol Jacobs. Ross also observed that the cemetery was well kept.[34]

For more than fifty years, someone from the Garfinkle family cared for the cemetery grounds. The Reno Hebrew Cemetery was vandalized early in 1990. Markers were overturned, but nothing appeared to be stolen. It was all quickly restored and remained intact. The cemetery is nearly full, and the joint synagogue committee is exploring an alternate site.

Las Vegans' Burial Options

Unlike the settlers in most Nevada towns, Las Vegas Jews made no early provision for their own cemetery. Woodlawn Cemetery has been a public municipal grave site since at least 1910. Over the years, Jews were interred in what came to be called its "Jewish section." Temple Beth Sholom purchased that section in 2004, while the city was negotiating with a private firm to provide perpetual care. Some Jewish veterans were buried near the Woodlawn Jewish section, but most were to be found in the Veterans Cemetery of Southern Nevada at Boulder City. Other Las Vegas–area cemeteries with Jewish sections and scattered burials outside the section were Eden Vale (Bunker's Memorial Gardens), Davis Paradise Valley Cemetery, and three Palm cemeteries. The newest addition catering to the Jewish population, founded by Jay Poster, is the King David Memorial Chapel and Cemetery, which had its first Jewish funeral in spring 2001. It encompasses ten acres of lease-purchased land owned by Palm Mortuaries. The complex has separate sections for Reform, Conservative, and Orthodox burials. The amenities include arrangements for a *shomer* to keep vigil throughout the night and a sterile cleaning room for the *taharah*.[35]

Conclusion

Northern Nevada's Jewish support system was largely limited to programs and groups sponsored by the four congregations and Chabad. With the exception of some joint functions among the three Reform synagogues at Reno and Lake Tahoe, few programs crossed temple lines. The area lacked a completely kosher restaurant or delicatessen, though during Passover some of the major markets advertised kosher products. The Reno Chabad hoped to add a kosher eatery to its new facility. By contrast, Las Vegas blossomed with kosher eating opportunities. Although southern Nevada may have given the appearance of having a full range of support facilities, some gaping holes remained. There were only three K–8 Jewish day schools, no home for the elderly, and no brick-and-mortar JCCSN facility—unlike even smaller Jewish communities. Although the southern Nevada Jewish population increased by about six hundred people a month in 2005, many were retirees with little interest in funding schools and Jewish programs, which they may have generously supported earlier in their lives. Meanwhile, the synagogue affiliation of Las Vegas's Jews was one of the lowest in the nation.

Rabbi Sanford Akselrad made an impassioned plea to Las Vegas Jewry in 2005. Speculating that southern Nevada Jews numbered as high as one hundred thousand—between 7 percent and 10 percent of the total population—he asked where were the missing, and "what are they doing to affirm their Jewishness? Do they belong to a Jewish organization? . . . Does Judaism touch their lives beyond the holydays of Yom Kippur and Rosh Hashana? If we hired a religion detective to follow them for a month or more would that detective find in their lives clues that lead us to know that, yes, they are indeed Jewish?" He worried about those Jews who did not feel connected enough to worry about the future of Jewish identity. Having challenged the community's lukewarmness, Akselrad called for a renewed sense of peoplehood that would fill the synagogues, exceed *tzedakah* campaign goals, and build the facilities necessary to meet specifically Jewish needs, while fulfilling the social-justice goal of Judaism to perfect society.[36]

Walking the Walk

The characteristic of being "Jewish" might be observed in one's organizational affiliations, dress, or speech. However, Jewish values learned from childhood, such as *tzedakah* and *tikun olam,* inform the social consciences of religious adherents and those who have abandoned any external observance. These are matters of remembrance and intention. No substantive documentary evidence supports an explicit connection between religious belief and public persona during the first century of Nevada Jewish history. In recent times, it was possible to obtain some clues about the relationship of religion and life through interviews, which are subjective by nature. The ways in which Judaism, rearing, or exposure to Jewish culture affected the public lives of elected officials and community leaders proved as diverse as their expressions in the general population.

The Philanthropists: Beneficence and Competition

Tzedakah is the Hebrew word for charitable giving that encompasses everything from major philanthropy to pocket change in a poor box. The medieval Jewish scholar Maimonides wrote of *tzedakah*'s progression from the worst (grudgingly) to the best (anonymously).[1] Jews contributing to the present work recalled heavy-handed solicitation for one or another Jewish cause to which the donors, in the end, gave halfheartedly. Others proudly contributed with panache and flair, reportedly to encourage others to give. A few gave conditionally or to achieve some tangible benefit. Others gave without fanfare. Many benefactors of Judaism and of Jewish causes were not religious. Some recipients of this beneficence attributed it to loyalty to tradition; others suggested it was a way for nonobservant Jews to have someone else do the observing for them. Another view was that Jews measured each other not so much by a devotional religious standard but through philanthropy. If there is broad curiosity among Jews about the levels of *tzedakah,* it is a characteristic shared by Christian and nonreligious philanthropists.

Nevada casino owners were among the early high-profile contributors to Jewish causes, and a few chaired the United Jewish Appeal campaign. Few local agencies, programs, and congregations could have survived without regular donations from the rank and file and the occasional noteworthy bounty from a wealthy angel. Las Vegas medical facilities might not have been erected without the benefactions of Dalitz, Rudiak, Molasky, and Nate and Merv Adelson.[2]

Many Jewish philanthropists, such as Sol and Ella Savitt of Reno, were affiliated with no Jewish organization and directed most of their generosity to the University of Nevada's School of Medicine and the School of Journalism.[3] The Las Vegas area was studded with public schools named for those who had been generous with time and money in the interest of education. Eisenberg, Goldfarb, Greenspun, Hill, Katz, Mack, Molasky, Ober, Sedway, Wiener, Wolff, and Wynn were some of the Jewish surnames adorning the lintels of the area's schools. An alternative to the public school system was the Meadows School, founded and chaired by Carolyn Goodman. Nevada's only nonprofit, independent, κ–12 college-preparatory school, it attracts a number of Jewish students.[4]

Most wealthy Jews in Las Vegas and Reno were consistently generous in supporting Israel, international Jewish causes, the local synagogue with which they were affiliated, and pet Jewish programs or agencies in the area. The walls of every synagogue and adjacent meeting hall were filled with acknowledgments of support. The Las Vegas Jewish Federation publicly honored philanthropists at annual fund-raising galas, as did the Lubavitch Chabad, and the Milton I. Schwartz Hebrew Academy. Two of those honored by the federation in 2006 were Jayn and Art Marshall, who, like counterpart John Farahi in Reno, were bridge builders—forces of reconciliation—across denominational and political lines.[5]

Milton I. Schwartz's Future for Judaism in Nevada

Milton I. Schwartz was born in Brooklyn in 1921, of immigrant parents and raised in an Orthodox household. After serving in the U.S. Army Signal Corps he responded to an advertisement placed by Bugsy Siegel's Flamingo developers for "the best mechanic." He snagged the job in 1946, was paid well, and claimed never to have met the boss. Schwartz avoided the gambling business, saying, "Those were people you didn't want to be associated with. Maybe that wasn't the best move. I could've made a lot of money. Not that I did that bad though."[6] He became president of Valley Hospital, sold it in 1979, was involved in dozens of businesses, owned a cable television company in competition with Hank Greenspun's Prime Cable, and was part owner of the Yellow Checker Star Cab Company, which resisted unionization and promoted ecological responsibility by using propane for fuel. Greenspun went after his cable competitor by convincing authorities that Schwartz's propane tank was a threat to the community. The tank was moved, but Schwartz sued Greenspun and the *Las Vegas Sun* for defamation and lost the case. The two men, major supporters of Jewish causes and members of the same temple, were not friendly.[7]

With his accumulated wealth, Schwartz founded and endowed the Milton I. Schwartz Hebrew Academy in 1980. Originally located at the Oakey Boulevard Temple Beth Sholom, it later moved to the Summerlin area. Beth Sholom moved to Summerlin and started its own modest day school, which Schwartz considered in competition with the academy. He consequently moved his temple membership to Ner Tamid. Schwartz has said unabashedly that God was the biggest influence in his decision-making process and that he tried "very hard to live by the moral teachings I learned over my lifetime." He believed that Judaism's future in Nevada was with those who received an excellent education that included religion. Schwartz bemoaned the lack of a stand-alone Jewish Community Center, but saved his harshest criticism for Jews marrying out and losing the faith. "I believe we Jews are doing to ourselves what Hitler tried and failed to do," said Schwartz. "So I decided to bring Jewish children together . . . and hope to reduce the amount of intermarriage that is destroying our religion." That, he said, motivated founding the Hebrew Academy.[8] The vision has been shared by Toni and Victor Chaltiel as well as the Sheldon Adelsons, who are making the academy's location a magnet for future educational programs.

The Farahi Family's Atlantis

The erection of the MGM Hotel-Casino outside of downtown Reno led some to believe that the slow-growing area had reached its casino capacity. One who took a chance against the odds was David Farahi and his three sons, whom his wife, Parvin, nicknamed Abraham, Isaac, and Jacob, when they were celebrating Jewish festivals. Their real names were John, Bob (Bahram), and Ben (Behrouz).

Born in Teheran in 1948, John came to California to attend college. His father brought the remaining family to the United States in 1970 and purchased a property, managed by his sons, which became the Golden Road Motor Inn, Inc., D.B.A. Clarion Hotel Casino. The Clarion's first tower would have been impossible, said Farahi, without a gutsy real estate loan from Sidney Stern's Nevada First Thrift. When Stern sold this property, Bank of America accepted responsibility for all of his loans except that to the Farahis, which they never expected to be paid off. Two years later, the family went public under the holding company Monarch Casino and Resort, with John as chief executive officer. The multimillion-dollar Atlantis Casino Resort Spa was completed in 1999. Farahi attributed the success story first to his father, his brothers, and then Sid Stern, who also introduced him to the needs of the local and international Jewish communities.[9]

Although the Farahi families were not strictly Orthodox, they were observant and affiliated with the Conservative Temple Emanu-El. As their fortunes grew, they became financial lifelines for the congregation. John Farahi explicitly connected the families' charitable giving to the mitzvah of *tzedakah* in which they were raised as children. His commitment was long-standing as chair of the Northern Nevada United Jewish Community and the local branch of the American Israel Public Affairs Committee. Personally involved in soliciting donations, he acknowledged that although some Jews were initially reluctant to give, they felt good by the time they wrote the check. The motivation for some secular Jews who donated to AIPAC was that support of Israel as a homeland was up to all ethnic Jews.

The Farahi families also were among the major contributors to the building of Reno's only *mikveh,* located on the grounds of the Lubavitch Chabad. The Farahis' benevolence went beyond Jewish causes. Their Atlantis Hotel Casino contributed generously to local public charities. Many northern Nevadans saw John Farahi at the turn of the century as the area's most influential Jewish person and with his family among the foremost supporters of Jewish causes.[10]

Steve Wynn: "No One with a Greater Impact on Our Industry"

Michael Weinberg changed his name early in life, when he feared not getting a job from a reputedly antisemitic employer. Zelma and Mike (Weinberg)

Wynn lived in Utica, New York, where he ran a marginal bingo operation. Their son Stephen, born in 1942, was only ten when his father brought him to Las Vegas and opened a legal bingo parlor. Young Steve gained some experience in his father's several ventures before earning a degree in English literature at the University of Pennsylvania. He married Elaine Pascal and came to Las Vegas in 1967. He obtained a 3 percent interest in the Frontier Hotel and Casino, which he parlayed into a position as chief executive officer of the downtown Golden Nugget property. His Lake Tahoe neighbor Michael Milken arranged for the sale of high interest–bearing bonds, giving Wynn the leverage to be a visionary. Although Milken and an associate, Ivan Boesky, went to prison for felonious activities, Wynn used more "junk" bonds to bankroll the Las Vegas Mirage in 1989. Its cost of $611 million was greater than the combined cost of all previous hotel casinos. At the Mirage, Siegfried and Roy entertained with their white tigers, while sharks and dolphins cavorted in pools and a volcano exploded outside. The Mirage set a new standard for the industry and became a tourist attraction in itself. John Farahi credited Wynn with revolutionizing the gaming industry in Nevada. No one, he said, had made a greater impact. One of Wynn's biographers credited him with a charismatic leadership and creativity so profound that he had "no natural successor."[11]

The Wynns directed their philanthropy toward UNLV. Elaine became a leader in the university's foundation, whereas Steve's private foundation supported university president Robert Maxson and the athletic department. Much of this proved controversial, and eventually Maxson and basketball coach Rollie Massimino had to find new jobs. Untainted by it all, the Wynns continued their benefactions to the university and the arts community. Wynn followed the Mirage with Treasure Island, then built the Bellagio with its art museum, and in 2005 unveiled a spectacular resort and casino carrying only the name "Wynn."

The Wynns maintained a membership at Temple Beth Sholom. Wynn's daughter Kevyn (sometimes Kevin), who survived a kidnapping for ransom, married Daniel Friedman, the temple's cantor. The Wynns were very much a part of Las Vegas social life but not particularly prominent in local Jewish activities.[12]

Steve Wynn and Las Vegas newcomer Sheldon Adelson appeared to have much in common. Both were in the Forbes 500 in 2004, at approximately the same level of net worth, less than $2 billion. They had humble beginnings, went to college, built casinos in Las Vegas and in the Chinese gambling city of Macao, and were active in politics. There the similarities began to pale. The two also were continually in public competition, with Las Vegans on one or another side of their various disputes, some of which descended to name-calling and personal confrontations.[13]

Sheldon Adelson: Venetian Owner with Philanthropic Priorities

Born in Boston in 1933 of poor but observant parents, Sheldon Adelson (no relation to other Las Vegans Mervin and Nathan Adelson) created and brought to maturity fifty companies, including the computer trade show COMDEX. He purchased the Sands Hotel and Casino in Las Vegas in 1989, sold COMDEX in 1995, imploded the venerable Sands, and in its place built the $1.5 billion Venetian Resort and Casino. When he went public with Sands stock in December 2004, Adelson was suddenly worth $15.1 billion and one of the wealthiest persons in the world. He shared that good news with Lubavitch rabbi Shea Harlig, who quipped, "When do I get my cut?!"[14] Even before this windfall, Adelson was donating to Jewish causes in Las Vegas and elsewhere.

Lubavitchers in 2000 singled out Sheldon and Dr. Miriam Adelson for their substantial support for a drug-addiction clinic in Tel Aviv and the Chabad of Southern Nevada. Adelson claimed to "love the Chabad organization because they do for people who can't do for themselves. . . . What they preach is Judaism and they don't shove it down the secular throat."[15]

The Adelsons' benefactions included $15 million in 2005 to the multigenerational Hebrew Senior Life Center in Boston and, shortly thereafter, a $25 million pledge to build a Jewish high school and community center facilities on the campus of the Milton I. Schwartz Hebrew Academy. It was the largest single donation in the Las Vegas Jewish community's history.[16]

Adelson has publicly defended the Venetian's nonunion labor policy. He is quoted as claiming union policies border on socialism and their tactics are un-American because they discourage promotion on the basis of merit. The Venetian's base pay was competitive with union pay, and the employee benefits included paid sick days, a 401(k) retirement plan with matching funds from the company, child care, and an employee health club. Adelson complained about the personal harassment that he blamed on his successful barring of the Culinary Union from his hotel. According to printed sources, he received death threats, and, after a break-in to his home swimming pool area, someone scrawled "Dead Jew" on a cabana mirror. On the heels of this incident, Temple Beth Sholom chose to hold its fund-raising roast of Oscar Goodman at the Four Seasons, and Adelson terminated his membership.[17]

Some philanthropists have been influential in politics due to their generosity or by reason of their position. Milton Schwartz chaired the Clark County Republican Party in the late 1990s. Adelson served on the board of directors of the Republican Jewish Coalition and, together with his wife, contributed $500,000 to President Bush's 2005 inauguration. He has also been an active supporter of state and county Republican office seekers. Steve Wynn, though aligned nationally with the Republican cause, supported Democrats and competing candidates for the same local political office.[18] Neither Adelson nor Wynn was reported to have supported the congressional bid of Shelley Berkley, who had been Adelson's vice president for government and legal affairs. Berkley was unapologetically Jewish, pro-Israel, and pro-Union.

Women in New Roles

Karla Goldman concludes her sweeping study of women's role in nineteenth-century synagogues with the assessment that "the leaders of American synagogues and American Judaism still confront issues of gender as they try to strike a balance between the Jewish past and present."[19] Although this may be a subject of national debate, Nevada Jewish women have left only the most patriarchal with any doubt about their essential role in the synagogue and public life. The extraordinary participation of women in Nevada's human rights efforts was only a signal of what was to come.

Because of concessions to women across all three major Jewish movements, some outside Nevada feared a "feminizing" of the synagogue.[20] But the presence of women in traditionally male posts did not discourage Nevada men from also continuing to serve. Except in Orthodox congregations, Nevada women rose to the presidency of congregations in Reno and Las Vegas. The wives of rabbis (*rebbetzins*)—including the Orthodox—have been active as teachers, writers, and publicists.

Nevada's Hadassah chapters have long been a highly visible source of financial support for international Jewish causes. In the past, Sisterhoods and B'nai B'rith auxiliary organizations provided services and funds for local causes. More recently, women affiliated with the United Jewish Community/Jewish Federation of Las Vegas (UJC/JFLV) have become fund-raisers in their own name and sought out others to satisfy their "obligation of *tzedakah,* independently of husbands and families." The 2005 campaign, headed by the Women's Philanthropy Council chairwoman, comprised cocktail or luncheon events tiered to one's level of annual giving: from $136 to $5,000. The women's philanthropy group claimed to have added 252 new female donors to the UJC/JFLV annual campaign. Women were predicted to raise $1.7 million in the 2007 campaign.[21]

Jewish historian Jacob Rader Marcus recalls the Talmudic tradition according to which emancipation from Egyptian slavery owed everything to that generation's pious female activists. "Without them," he writes, "there would have been no Exodus and no salvation." Closer to home, Rabbi Isaac Meyer Wise shamed Nevada Jewish businessmen for being observers only of High Holidays and usually lacking a minyan for Sabbath worship. Consequently, he wrote, "the ladies uphold Judaism."[22] These words still resonate in Nevada, where Judaism and Jewish causes are very much in the hands of its activist women. Renoite Heidemarie Rochlin oversees the foundation her late husband's parents established. It has supported Jewish documentary films and the university's Center for Holocaust, Genocide, and Peace Studies. The Abraham and Sonia Rochlin Foundation also funds medical research at the Weizman Institute and Washoe Medical Center.

Rank-and-File Support for Israel and Jewish Causes

A survey of the Las Vegas Jewish community, sponsored by the Jewish Federation in 1966, generated data showing that almost half the population contributed to Jewish organizations, and more than 80 percent agreed that "caring about Israel is a very important part of my being Jewish." Philanthropy from Las Vegans at 54 percent fell below the national average and paled in comparison to Chicago's 76 percent and Louisville's 91 percent. Nevertheless, the low affiliation with synagogues (then at 15 percent) was not the measure of Las Vegas Jewry's support of Jewish causes.[23]

Being Jewish and a Public Servant

Tikun olam literally means "repairing the world." It is a concept taught to children and can extend from picking up litter on the playground to leading a social-service project. The relationship of this Jewish ideal to the public-policy positions of Nevada's Jewish elected officials challenged a generalization. Since statehood in 1864, Nevada's Jews have been well represented in elected office at the state and local levels. Of the eight Jewish state legislators from 1864 to 1885, all were Republican except Sen. Gabriel Cohn. Between 1887

and 1997, the following served one or more terms in the state senate or assembly: Hirsch Harris, Al Livingston, Sam Platt, Phil Jacobs, Herman Freudenthal, John Sinai, George Rudiak, Stan Irwin, Bud Garfinkle, Chic Hecht,
Flora Dungan, Bernard Posin, Eileen Brookman, William Hernstadt, Shelley
Berkley, Marvin Sedway, Myrna Williams, Lori Lipman Brown, David Goldwater, Merle Berman, and Valerie Wiener. Of these, four were Republican,
and the remainder were Democrat, Independent, Silverite, or Populist.[24] Milton Badt, David Zenoff, Nancy Becker, and Michael Cherry were among the
state's supreme court justices. The relationship of their political activity to
religious tradition awaits a comprehensive study.

Stormy, Savvy, and Colorful Marvin Sedway

Clark County elected Democrat Marvin Sedway in 1982 to the first of four
terms in the assembly. His priorities as Ways and Means Committee chair
were support of welfare mothers, aid to the elderly, children's rights, and
public education. Testifying before Sedway or even serving on his committee
was an experience requiring fortitude and forbearance. Democratic assemblyman Morse Arberry could not forget the times that Sedway called into
his office rookie legislators who had strayed from the party line to give them
what he remembered as "a Jewish blessing."[25] He was an irascible antagonist
who often peppered his remarks with obscenities, in both Yiddish and English. His appearance could be ferocious when he scowled or yelled through
his black scruffy beard. Sedway was a social liberal and a fiscal conservative,
which won him grudging bipartisan support.[26]

Born in New York, Sedway grew up in Las Vegas, where his father ran the
race book for uncle Moe Sedway at the Flamingo. Marvin earned a degree in
optometry at Pacific University in Portland, where he dealt cards in an illegal
club until it was raided. He was apologetic about neither his past nor that of
his relatives. He was his own man—in no one's shadow. He was a curmud-
geon who loved to argue for a cause he considered in the state's best interest.
One battle he lost was to cancer. Sedway smoked two packages of cigarettes a
day—even after losing one lung to the disease. At one of the several memorial
services after his death in 1990, he was remembered as having once set his
beard on fire while lighting a cigarette in the midst of an agitated conversation, and then quipped, "If I am going to die from smoking, I'd rather it be
from the inside than outside."[27]

He was a mentor to neophyte legislators in the art of getting legislation passed. "Marvin Sedway was my teacher," said Assemblywoman Jan Evans. "He was my rabbi." "Marvin Sedway is our conscience," echoed Chris Giunchigliani, "and he lives on in every one of us that worry about the underprivileged, the elderly, the children in this state."[28] Even those legislators who disagreed with Sedway's political positions acknowledged that he was what Republican John Carpenter of Elko called "a straight-up guy." Seven years after Sedway's death, state legislators on both sides of the aisle overwhelmingly passed a resolution to be sent to the Clark County School District honoring his commitment to education. The result, in 2002, was the Marvin M. Sedway Middle School in North Las Vegas. Several years earlier, a new state office building—commonly referred to even before it was built as the "SOB"— was appropriately named for the provocative and occasionally cantankerous Sedway.[29]

Although Sedway was not a perfect example of all the virtues of observant Judaism, he lived by its principles of social justice and wore his religion on his sleeve. At Hanukkah, Shelley Berkley remembered Sedway giving a bottle of Jewish wine to each of his colleagues in the legislature. In private conversation, he was most explicit and articulate about the correlation of his religious values and political positions. *Tikun olam* was Sedway's personal mantra. Because of his well-known advocacy for the less fortunate, the rabbi at Temple Beth Sholom commented at Sedway's funeral that his "sense of justice and righteousness was a beautiful expression of his sense of Jewishness."[30]

Jewish but Not Observant

Judith Eaton and Valerie Wiener both had a strong sense of being part of Jewish tradition. They were outspoken, assertive, and articulate, but neither was religiously observant. Judith Eaton explicitly stamped a Jewish heritage on her accomplishments. Less than a decade after receiving her doctorate at Wayne State University, Eaton became the first female and first Jewish president of a Nevada institution of higher learning. One of her earliest memories as a child in Trenton, New Jersey, was "being chased home from elementary school by some students who were screaming 'dirty Jew.'"

Born in 1942 and raised in a household that was "at times Reform and at times Conservative," Eaton went to Hebrew school but was never bat mitzvahed or, she wrote, "observant in my adult life." Yet she said that "of the important defining features of my life, being Jewish is vital." She grew up with what she called a typical Jewish heritage—"valuing the intellectual and analytic, self-responsibility, judicious concern for others, [and mental] discipline."

When Eaton assumed the presidency of Clark County Community College (now the College of Southern Nevada) in 1979, the institution was less than eight years old. During her four-year tenure, she was able to convince state legislators, donors, and regents of the school's desperate need to become a multicampus institution. Her success was marked by persistence. One female member of the University of Nevada Board of Regents, who was known for her own forthrightness, was heard to say that she was "taken aback" by Eaton's assertiveness.

She was, indeed, a fighter, which she directly connected to her Jewish heritage. "Because the history of the Jews is the history of survival against incredible odds," she wrote, "I admire courage and tenacity.... We Jews have always been exception-making and I am, by nature, perverse and pugnacious. . . . I am incredibly proud to be a Jew. I am very lucky."[31]

The young president confidently brought recognition to her small college, in part because she was "networked" (said one admirer) to generous Jewish supporters in Las Vegas. She was one of the many talented Jews who left Nevada but who stayed long enough to help build a growing and broadly appreciated institution. After leaving Nevada, she became chancellor of Minnesota State College and Universities and since 1997 has been president of the Council for Higher Education Accreditation.

Valerie Wiener, unlike Eaton, was a native of Las Vegas, born in 1948. Her grandparents Louis and Kitty Wiener were among Las Vegas's earliest permanent Jewish residents and part of the city's first worshiping Jewish community. Her father, Louis Wiener Jr., was exposed to Judaism as a child and absorbed its values. Louis was not particularly religious (he was confirmed but not bar mitzvahed) and married a Gentile woman after passing the Nevada Bar. He represented Moe Dalitz and Bugsy Siegel, among others, in the heyday of Jewish casino ownership. Not until her parents divorced did Valerie come to realize she was Jewish. Her mother and brother lived in Arizona, and she lived in Las Vegas with her father, who passed on to her the values—but not the practice—of Judaism. Putting other people first, being a community servant, trying to change society for the better, and giving generously to good causes (including the Anti-Defamation League) were all examples of Jewish *tzedakah* and *tikun olam*—though she would not have known these words. She was Jewish by osmosis.

Wiener described herself religiously and culturally as a "hybrid." Many, she said, did not think of her as Jewish, and others presumed it. As a Jewish practitioner of Religious Science, she considered herself in the best of both worlds. She experienced a freedom—which she attributed to her father's mentoring—to explore the universe without labels. Her father's best friend, Republican Jim Rogers, encouraged her to take her Jewish values and work ethic into politics. After serving as an aide to Senator Harry Reid, she won three terms in the state senate, where she was Democratic minority whip. Wiener was a communications specialist, owned her own company, and had enough legal education to give her an edge in the Senate Judiciary Committee.

Her relationship to the powerful Las Vegas Culinary Union was complex. As a legislator, she received regular visits from union representatives currying her favor for legislation. She routinely explained to them that "my family and your union have a very bad history." Her father once co-owned a restaurant whose employees received good benefits and competitive salaries. Regularly badgered to join the union, they consistently refused, and for nineteen years the Culinary Union picketed his Alpine Village restaurant. With that memory, Wiener put off union lobbyists with the noncommittal, "I'll vote my head and vote my heart and the best of both I hope."[32]

Nevada's First Jewish U.S. Senator

Mayer Jacob "Chic" Hecht was born of Russian immigrant parents who moved to Las Vegas in 1947. He served two years in the U.S. Army, married the former Gail Kahn, and owned several clothing stores before expanding into real estate and banking. Hecht entered politics as a staunch Republican and defeated Howard Cannon in the 1982 U.S. Senate race. According to some, Hecht was elected partly because he was related to the popular rabbi with the same surname, Mel Hecht. As the rabbi later stated, the relationship was "popular mythology" and absolutely untrue.[33] While he served in the Senate and was attending a Republican luncheon, a piece of apple lodged firmly in his throat. He stumbled out of the room and collapsed just as future Democratic presidential hopeful John Kerry stepped off an elevator. Kerry raced to his side, determined from a colleague that Hecht had been choking, and executed the Heimlich maneuver four times, saving Hecht's life.[34]

Liberal Jews considered Chic Hecht's senatorial term an embarrassment. In addition to standing aloof as the Republican-dominated Congress eyed Yucca Mountain for what Hecht inadvertently (but, some would say, accurately) called "a nuclear suppository," he took positions that enraged Jews from Israel to Las Vegas. He supported arms packages to Saudi Arabia and Jordan, and then opposed the "Yarmulke Bill," which would have permitted Jewish medics and military men to wear the religious cap under their medical or battle helmets. When he ran again for the Senate against then governor Richard Bryan, he received only a fraction of donations from pro-Israel political action committees compared to his non-Jewish challenger. Democrat Shelley Berkley, asked to generate money from the Jewish community for Bryan, had a dilemma. "How do I raise money against a Jew in the Jewish community?" she asked herself. It turned out to be easy. "The Jewish community supported Dick Bryan," she said, "because Mr. Hecht had such a mixed record on Jewish issues."[35]

What was not known at election time was that Hecht had been using his position to advance Jewish causes in the Soviet Union. He had earlier met Lubavitch rebbe Menachem Schneerson, who urged him to "use quiet diplomacy" to get Jews out of Russia. The Soviet Union's discriminatory emigration policy prevented the United States from extending to it "favored nation" status, but the Politburo had remained unwilling to budge on the Jewish issue. Hecht obtained a list of twelve hundred refuseniks from an in-law relative of his sister, who was connected to the Council of Soviet Jewry. The senator personally handed the list to President Reagan, asking that it be presented to Chairman Gorbachev at a forthcoming October 1986 arms summit in Reykjavik, Iceland. It was, said Hecht, a favor in return for his vote on the Saudi arms deal.

In the end, Gorbachev agreed to let the Jews emigrate quietly, as long as there was no publicity. When asked whether his refusal to speak openly of his role in the release of Soviet refuseniks could cost him reelection, he confided to his friend Art Marshall, "Even if I don't get elected, I'm doing the right thing." Only a few close friends and family knew the whole story, and he lost his 1988 reelection bid. One of the refuseniks released under the unpublicized Reagan-Gorbachev arrangement later chose to honor Hecht's intervention by getting married in a Jerusalem synagogue erected by the Hecht families.[36]

Despite bashing from Democrats, Hecht expressed pride in his political conservatism. He pointed, in particular, to cutting fat from welfare programs and opposing federal funding for education. Based on his party fealty and banking experience, George Bush Sr. appointed him ambassador to the Bahamas (1989–1993). Hecht returned to Las Vegas where he was active in Jewish affairs and a supporter of the Lubavitch Chabad. He died of cancer in May 2006.[37]

Unabashed Pro-Israel Congresswoman: Shelley Berkley

Like Marvin Sedway, for whom she had great affection, Shelley (née Levine) Berkley was born in New York and described her upbringing as "Jewish, but not strictly observant." Her family came across the country in 1962, stopped in Las Vegas, and never left. Her father became a waiter and active member of the Culinary Union. The family joined Temple Beth Sholom, where Shelley was confirmed.[38] Berkley's first major election success was as student body president at UNLV, where she earned a degree in political science. After finishing law school at the University of San Diego in 1976, she returned to Las Vegas, where she founded the Southern Nevada Association of Women Attorneys.

Berkley won one term in the assembly (1982–1984) and lost a state senate bid before Governor Bob Miller appointed her to the Board of Regents in 1990. She was an unapologetic supporter of UNLV's basketball team, its president Bob Maxson, and its new foundation leaders Steve and Elaine Wynn. Then all hell broke loose, and Berkley was in the midst of a donnybrook involving them all. The Wynn private foundation had provided the president with a number of perquisites that gave him some independence from the regents, who nevertheless signed his contract. When Maxson's administration approved the surreptitious closed-circuit taping of an illegal basketball practice that jeopardized Jerry Tarkanian's coaching job, Berkley was openly critical of the president. When she went public with her criticism, she reportedly received threatening telephone calls. In the upshot, it became clear to Berkley that the Wynns controlled the president. Tarkanian was fired and Rollie Massimino hired with a supplemental salary from the private foundation. The Nevada Commission on Ethics investigated in 1994, and Massimino and the foundation were found guilty of breaching the standards.[39] Maxson moved on to another university presidency, the Wynns were not implicated in the investigation because they were not state employees, and Berkley earned some enmity in the bargain. Nevertheless, she won two terms to the Board of Regents through 1998.

Often a springboard for persons seeking higher office, the board was a perfect platform for Berkley, who became the fifth Jewish woman member of Congress in 1998. How she got there and stayed there was, in part, a credit to her ability to pay her dues as a mother and as a member of the local Jewish community and Democratic organizations.

Berkley described a once-a-month meeting of Jewish Congress members with a rabbi who related the Torah or Talmud to a legislative issue they were addressing. On one occasion, they met (without the rabbi) to discuss a foreign-aid package, which included funds for Israel and Africa. "Everyone spoke eloquently on the issue." At the end of the discussion, the chair urged that the group come off unanimously on the same page, but when a straw vote was taken, "we were divided 1/3 across the board," the last third not sure. "We all laughed," she said. "It was so Jewish." Some were reticent to support the bill because there was not enough money for Africa. They thought that if they withheld their support, more money would be forthcoming for Africa. "That's a very Jewish way of approaching things. We take care of the world"—an explicit reference to *tikun olam.* Berkley voted for the package, some voted against, and "in the end we got what we needed."

Berkley had her eye on public life for a long time and has acknowledged that her heritage was a controlling factor. In her words: "I wanted not to be a public official who happened to be a Jew, but rather a Jew who happened to be a public official." She strongly supported Israel and earned the reputation for receiving more campaign money from national organizations than any other congressperson. Southern Nevada enjoyed substantial improvements resulting from federal funding, for which she claimed bragging rights. During her first term, Clark County received a five hundred thousand–dollar "After School Program," UNLV snagged one hundred thousand dollars for a children's literacy program, twenty-nine million dollars went for local flood control, and other multimillion-dollar projects went to Nellis Air Force Base and the North Las Vegas Airport.[40]

Although Berkley experienced no overt antisemitism in her elected posts, some opposed what she called "some of my 'Democratic' ideas which are rooted in my Judaism." Being truly Jewish, she repeatedly emphasized, meant to be humanitarian and charitable. Shelley Berkley wore her religion around her neck. It was a piece of jewelry worked into the Hebrew word *chai,* meaning "life." She said it was her way of publicly demonstrating that the principles of Judaism were basic to her political activities. "When Jewish people see it," she said, "they are proud of me and 'us.'" The open commitment to Israel, southern Nevada, and her Jewish heritage helped her win a fifth successive congressional term in 2006.

Educator and Critic: Regent Howard Rosenberg

Not all Nevada Jews retained a hospitable relationship with Judaism. One of the best-known and -recognized public figures in northern Nevada in the past half century, Howard Rosenberg, had a reputation as an enthusiastic, competent, demanding instructor and film critic for the local CBS affiliate. Rosenberg was born in Boston in 1934 to American-born parents. His father, Leo Louis Rosenberg, transported illegal alcohol for the Kennedys during Prohibition before owning a tavern and then a café. His mother, Rosalie Gertrude Pearlstein, did not keep a kosher kitchen (except for meat—though bacon could be a treat when her husband was not at home). Rosenberg's upbringing included Hebrew school, bar mitzvah, and parental injunctions to him and his sister to "never lie, be kind, always do what you say you are going to do," and marry a Jew. The latter was not to be, he said.[41]

After study at Harvard and a position at the University of Hawaii, he joined the University of Nevada Art Department in 1967. Temple Emanu-El sponsored some Rosenberg lectures, but he never joined the congregation. His widowed mother died in Reno, with a request to be cremated. The rabbi at Emanu-El was uncooperative, said Rosenberg, who turned to Rabbi Myra Soifer at Temple Sinai, who arranged for Rosalie's burial next to her husband at a Jewish cemetery in Massachusetts. The memorial and burial ceremony were about as close to Judaism as Rosenberg came in his adult years.

Faithful viewers who appreciated Rosenberg's witty reviews were shocked to learn of his firing after twenty-five years as a television film critic. Rosenberg explained that the station managers decided that his style was unappealing to a new audience. His viewers, students, and academic colleagues were even more surprised to learn he planned to run for the university's Board of Regents. People wondered how his penchant for outspokenness and occasional flamboyance would work in a context requiring diplomacy. Questions arose about whether he might have a conflict of interest as a faculty member and regent, and whether he could be objective about the system's other institutions. He was able to overcome these concerns to earn a second term as regent.

Like others before him, Rosenberg had become a secular Jew—neither denying nor flaunting his Jewish heritage. He did not customarily support specific Jewish causes, though he made an annual contribution to Temple Sinai in memory of his parents' and grandparents' *yahrzeits*. He also acknowledged that he continued to carry the traditional "Jewish guilt" about not being observant—it was a constant companion.[42]

"Happiest (Meanest?) Mayor in the World"

Oscar Baylin Goodman was born in 1939 and grew up in West Philadelphia. His grandfather was Orthodox, but Oscar's father raised him in Conservative Judaism. His mother kept a kosher-style kitchen, and to this day he claims never to have eaten pork or shellfish. Goodman considered becoming a rabbi and attended nearby Grantz College, a seminary, until he was about sixteen. He received an undergraduate degree at Haverford College and began dating his future wife, Carolyn Goldmark, a student at Bryn Mawr. She was from a family Oscar described as "Jewish people who hated being known as Jews."

The Goodmans married in 1962 and two years later moved to Las Vegas, where Oscar earned a national reputation as a defense attorney. Some of his clients, such as Chicago mobster Tony "the Ant" Spilotro, drug trafficker Jimmy Chagra, and Meyer Lansky (whom he never met personally), had unsavory reputations. In 1970, the FBI engaged in wholesale raids on bookmakers across the country, and Goodman successfully argued in many cases that the government's wiretaps were illegal. He became known as the Mob's lawyer, though he denied the existence of "the Mob" to anyone who would listen.[43]

Goodman defended his role as a defense attorney as an exercise in upholding the constitutional rights of all people. When asked whether his defense of such clients was in conflict with the Torah, he said:

> I always made sure the government proved its case beyond a reasonable doubt with lawfully obtained evidence. If they were able to do that, they were entitled to my client, but I can't remember a case where they did it. I saw my function as completely consistent with Jewish teachings. I was taking up the cause of the oppressed against the oppressor, which is what we are taught to do as Jews. Judas Maccabee [sic] was my hero when I was a kid. I even wrote a play about him when I was in the fourth or fifth grade.[44]

The Goodmans became members of Temple Beth Sholom, where he served as temple president from 1975 to 1977. It was a turbulent period in the synagogue's history. Goodman recalled having to mediate the "war zone" that characterized the relationship between Rabbi Phillip Schnairson and executive director Leo Wilner.[45] Twenty years later, he decided to run for mayor. He conducted a poll through UNLV to test his chances, and they turned up negative. His grown children initially opposed his candidacy, thinking those waiting to resurrect his defense of criminal clients would stigmatize him. According to Carolyn, he did not finally decide to run until the last filing day, March 4, 1999. With him at the hastily called press conference were Carolyn, Rabbi Felipe Goodman, and Lubavitch rabbi Shea Harlig. As preliminary signs indicated a victory on election day, he drove to the Chabad, wrapped his left arm and forehead with the tefillin, donned the *tallith* (prayer shawl), and davened with the minyan "to thank God," he later recalled, "that everything went nicely."[46] Goodman won by a two-to-one margin.

Harlig claimed some credit with his prayers for the election result, and on the feast of Purim informed the mayor he was coming to the office with his children. The banter between the two appeared contentious, but it was playful. "No no no, who let you in?" the mayor asked. "Be nice," countered Harlig, adding he had not seen the mayor at the Chabad shul since Election Day. "Because I go to another shul, because of the wickedness of you Haman," retorted the mayor (referring to the rabbi as the villain in the book of Esther, which Purim celebrates). The rabbi wanted to say a prayer and demanded that the mayor wear a yarmulke. None was at hand, so Goodman growled and put on a baseball cap. Harlig reminded the mayor that the rabbi's prayers vaulted him into office. The visit ended with Goodman half-grinning and commenting that the rabbi had brought only two dollars' worth of Purim candy. He wrote Harlig a check for nine hundred dollars.[47]

Goodman has been accused of being heartless toward Las Vegas's homeless people. The National Coalition for the Homeless ranked Las Vegas the "meanest" city in the United States in 2003. Goodman said he was "intolerant of those who don't follow the basic rules to get help, like leaving behind booze and drugs. We will help those who are mentally ill, those who need and want our help." However, his alleged references to specific homeless people as "cockroaches and dangerous" and his order for "sweeps" of the homeless downtown damaged his credibility with some. Nevertheless, Goodman won his second term handily in 2003 and received a commendation from U.S. Department of Housing and Urban Development for his regional approach to the homeless problem.[48]

Las Vegas Sun columnist Jon Ralston has been highly critical of the mayor, whom he accused of "moral relativism." Goodman considered Ralston an unfair media aggressor. According to the mayor, some commentators accused him of being "ethically challenged," with Ralston in the lead. The mayor picked and chose his interviews, but did not elect to banter with Ralston as he had with Harlig. ACLU executive director Gary Peck was also critical of the mayor's treatment of the homeless. Being Jewish was no guarantee of agreement on political or religious matters.[49]

Oscar Goodman was rumored as a candidate for governor in 2005, but he proclaimed himself "the happiest mayor in the world." Meanwhile, he told me, "Every morning I get up and thank God for allowing me to continue during the day, and every night I say my prayers and thank him for letting me do it."[50] Goodman's future will depend on his continuing to remake himself from Mob lawyer into a charismatic, visionary, and politically astute advocate for the homeless, the tourists, and the voters.

Conclusion

Nevada's Jewish public servants and philanthropists in the past quarter century represented the spectrum of affiliations with Jewish organizations across the state—from "strong" to "none." In Las Vegas, it was not for want of a program, agency, or synagogue with which to identify. The array of options to connect with Jewish tradition was compelling, though the level of participation was puny. The record of support for Jewish programs and agencies was mixed. Three of Las Vegas's most prominent supporters of Judaism—Milton Schwartz, Oscar Goodman, and Rabbi Felipe Goodman—agreed with Moe Dalitz that a problem with benevolence from Jews in Las Vegas was that everyone expected to be "comped."[51] Nevertheless, Nevada boasted some sterling examples of those for whom giving was more important than getting. On the outside—not looking in—were tens of thousands of Jews who appeared unconcerned.

The Past Need Not Be Prologue

When Isaac Cohn began his half-century residency in the shadow of the Comstock in 1850, few could have imagined the extent to which his fellow Jews would be instrumental in shaping Nevada's economic, social, and political landscape. They were among the first to arrive in Nevada's many isolated mining outposts. In those camps that became settled towns, Jews were among the chief merchants, taxpayers, officers of fraternal lodges, and respected city fathers. They constituted more than their slim percentage of the population as state and local elected officials. When the ore production played out and the state was desperate to diversify, Jews promoted boxing as a tourist attraction, which became the province of Bob Arum in Las Vegas a century later.[1] From 1931 forward, Nevada's gradual transition to a tourist economy based on gambling and entertainment reflected prominent Jewish involvement. In the intervening battle for desegregation of public facilities, Jewish men and women were among the leaders. Finally, major Jewish ownership and management of hotel-casinos in Las Vegas beginning in the 1950s was simply a prologue to the theme megaresorts introduced by Steve Wynn's Mirage and followed by Sheldon Adelson's Venetian.

The model of religious observance left by Nevada Jews was more tortuous and considerably less spectacular. Early on, Jewish merchants generally adapted to the Christian Sabbath and made still more accommodations to the exigencies of the Sinai-like desert environment. Isolation, itinerancy, and the fragility of the mining economy militated against a minyan of Jews doing much more than establishing a benevolent society and purchasing a burial ground. Forming a permanent congregation required an organizational miracle.

When Samuel Goldstone proudly announced the presence of one hundred Jews in Eureka in 1876, it was in the context of a focused community that had coalesced and determined to be part of official Reform Judaism. This starkly contrasted with Jacob Kaplan's description of Virginia City Jewry riven by petty disputes. The state of Nevada's Judaism was a mélange of dedicated commitment to Jewish ideals side by side with pockets of disagreement or, worse, indifference. Virginia City Jews could not agree on where and under whose auspices they might establish a Jewish library. Two competing B'nai B'rith lodges celebrated High Holidays in the earliest years of that city at two locations.

Though Virginia City Jews could not find common ground to establish a permanent congregation among their over four hundred coreligionists, they proudly celebrated their heritage by sponsoring popular Purim balls, which were open to all. The Olcovich boys candidly explained that their newspaper was thin around High Holidays because they were Jews and did not work on Yom Kippur. Newspapermen teased Jewish merchants about not taking off enough weight during the traditional fast. Being Jewish was not a mark of shame in small-town Nevada, and public demonstrations of antisemitism were a rarity until modern times.

The lack of fear about being Jewish did not slow the process of cultural adaptation that inexorably eroded Jewish identity. Perhaps because Nevada Jews were normally not on the defensive because of their religion or ethnicity, they more easily lost their sense of religious and cultural differences from the Gentile population. The history of Jewry—particularly in Europe—was of a chosen people singled out for discrimination, which had the salutary side effect of bonding "us against them." Nevada's Jewish men, women, and children interacted daily in stores and schools with Gentiles who provoked neither anxiety nor a fear of friendship. From there it was a short step for some to adopt the religion of these amicable Christians; for others, maintaining Jewish tradition was difficult.

Despite poor odds and attendant costs, Nevada Jews maintained a semblance of Judaism for seventy years. They imported rabbis to perform brises and weddings and, for a short time, to kosher their meat products. Communal Sabbath services were virtually nonexistent, but generally Passover, Rosh Hashanah, and Yom Kippur observance could be found in even the most remote locations. Laymen from B'nai B'rith or the local Hebrew Benevolent Society led worship, while laywomen in Eureka and Reno were the mainstays of small Hebrew schools. Out-migration after 1880 saved Judaism for some, whereas marriages to Gentiles routinely spelled the end of observance for those who stayed.

Judaism realized a fixed beachhead when Nevada's second permanent congregation formed at Reno in 1914 and built the first synagogue in 1921. It signaled a settled Jewish community, but not one that could yet afford a permanent rabbi or a Hebrew school. Temple Emanu-El was an Orthodox synagogue at its inception, but its congregants ran the spectrum of belief and practice. The seeds of dissidence germinated into open schism in 1939. While Reno Judaism was dividing, the Las Vegas Jewish community was uniting to form its first permanent Conservative congregation, Temple Beth Sholom. It also comprised people with various religious inclinations—some of whom left to start the Reform Temple Ner Tamid.

Thereafter, finding and keeping a rabbi with the right congregational fit was the exception rather than the rule in both Reno and Las Vegas. The reason for retaining or firing a rabbi often had as much to do with factionalism within the congregation as with the rabbi himself. Continuity of rabbinical leadership was a necessary condition for congregational growth, but the future of Judaism also depended on the education of children and financial support for facilities and auxiliary personnel.

At the turn of the twenty-first century, demographic studies revealed a declining Jewish population in the United States, low rates of synagogue affiliation, a rising median age of affiliated Jews, and the pestering problem of intermarriage. Another national trend was toward greater observance of traditional mitzvoth by the already affiliated. For example, requests for traditional burial rites increased, as did kosher observance and Conservative use of the *mikveh* for conversion rites. The liberal Reform Pittsburgh Platform of 1885, which had provoked the formation of American Conservative Judaism, was revised in 1999. It encouraged renewed consideration of traditional practices, learning Hebrew, studying the Torah, and even immigrating to Israel. Meanwhile, Conservative Judaism adopted some practices that were once Reform's exclusive domain, such as allowing the use of electricity and automobiles on the Sabbath (1950), counting women in a minyan (1973), and ordaining women rabbis (1977–1979). Contemporary Nevada reflected all of these negative and positive characteristics of American Judaism, with one exception. Southern Nevada's spectacular population growth gave the Las Vegas area an opportunity to reverse some of the negative national trends.

Greater Las Vegas counted more than 1.8 million people in 2006 and was the nation's fastest-growing metropolitan area. Of these, nearly 100,000 were

Jews, giving Las Vegas a larger Jewish population than all but eleven countries in the world.[2] The area's eighteen Jewish congregations spanned the broad diversity within Judaism. On the face of it, Las Vegas appeared to be beating the national odds.

There were, however, some troubling trends and statistics. The *American Jewish Year Book* in 2000 predicted that the U.S. Jewish population would shrink by one-third over the next eighty years and Israel's population would double. The two deciding factors were the birth rates and marrying within the faith. A ray of hope was visible nationally when in 2003 the National Jewish Population Survey retracted its former estimate of a 52 percent intermarriage rate, stating it was several points too high. It was small comfort to Nevadans. A 1996 study of Las Vegas Jews revealed that more than 70 percent of those married between 1980 and 1995 were in mixed or conversionary marriages.[3]

A serious problem was the rate of Jews affiliated with synagogues. In Phoenix, the Jewish community was shocked to discover that its synagogue affiliation rate had dropped to 29 percent—five points below the national average—and took immediate steps to lower financial barriers to synagogue membership. A sophisticated study of Las Vegas Jews concluded that the area's synagogue affiliation rate was 15 percent. Almost a decade later, in 2005, local rabbis estimated it between 7 percent and 10 percent. These low figures placed Nevada near the bottom of any ranking. Although the unaffiliated may have been religious or maintaining some Jewish traditions privately, the vast majority of them were presumed to be alienated or indifferent to religion but no less productive in works to heal the world. Some were hostile to institutional politics, others to what they considered a constant preoccupation with money. In the latter category were those who simply thought they could not afford to be affiliated with a synagogue.[4]

Mayor Oscar Goodman observed that younger people tended to be critical of the synagogue membership tradition requiring annual dues—even on a sliding scale. "How dare they charge me to go to a synagogue?" he has heard them complain, when they see Catholics and others with free membership and a passing of the plate. "We might be better off having a different form of fund raising or membership structure," Goodman suggested, "that would educate the people that they are paying for a 365 day a year sanctuary, not just 3 days a year."[5] This raised the issue of whether the charitable giving in Las Vegas was enough to support both synagogues and a cultural infrastructure.

The median age of Jewish migrants to Las Vegas was more than forty-nine in 1996 and rising. It was high by national standards and included those with the money and will to support Jewish life. According to both rabbinic and lay sources, many Las Vegas–area Jews preferred to say that they "gave at the office" or had "already paid our dues." A common belief was that a sliver of the Jewish population supported 95 percent of the state's Jewish causes.[6] Las Vegas alone had millionaires and billionaires who could collectively bankroll any Jewish program, synagogue, or agency. Dependence on the few may be necessary in times of emergency, but a mature and flourishing Jewry requires *tzedakah* from the many.

A recent arrival from San Francisco described the Las Vegas Jewish infrastructure as similar to what one would expect in a city with a Jewish population twenty times smaller. Such an appraisal came as a surprise to Las Vegas Jews who—despite apathy and accommodation—believed they were experiencing a cultural renaissance: regular Jewish film festivals, klezmer and Jewish classical musical programs, Jewish dancing, Hebrew courses at synagogues and at the university, Yiddish classes, a growing array of kosher eateries and outlets, and a bona fide Jewish high school.

Some scholarly observers noted that the trends toward decline *and* revitalization were operating simultaneously on the national scene and wondered which would prove more powerful amid a national debate about the best way to preserve Judaism. Some thought the answer lay in reaching out to those on the fringe; others chose to strengthen the observance of those active and affiliated.[7] Actually, both approaches were at work in Las Vegas. Synagogues nurtured their congregants and friends on the periphery, while organizations such as the Southern Nevada Jewish Community Center focused on programs that appealed both to the religiously committed and to those who wanted only to dabble in their Jewish heritage. The Lubavitch rabbis reached out as well to those they regarded as the dispossessed and the religiously tepid. Their emphasis was on regular prayer and Torah study, but included social programs.

"Las Vegas Jewry has been deeply divided," complained some members of its community. Although the autonomous congregations and organizations provide many options for affiliation, they can also encourage turf protection. Commenting on what he called the bifurcation of the Las Vegas Jewish community, the mayor observed that "everyone tries to get their own niche and is very protective of their territory." In 2004, the reorganization of the Jewish Federation upset many. The Jewish Family Service Agency and the Jewish Community Center disaffiliated from the federation, whereas the Hillel Foundation at UNLV stayed in, but had its board replaced by the federation. The politics were byzantine or simply interesting and unpredictable.[8] On the other hand, Jewry in northern Nevada was almost too small to be divided by anything more than the Reform, Conservative, and Chabad affiliations.

Another note of dissonance could be found among Las Vegas rabbis themselves. Those who received their education at nontraditional seminaries were excluded from official rabbinical group meetings, and the ultra-Orthodox Lubavitchers chose to exclude themselves.[9] The Jewish Federation and the *Las Vegas Israelite* recognized them all without comment. It is curious to some that rabbis across the religious spectrum can write columns in the shared pulpit of the *Las Vegas Israelite* yet not meet, speak jointly, or engage each other on an issue of common concern.

A discussion item in both northern and southern Nevada was the Hasidic Lubavitch Chabad presence. For some, it was a cause for alarm; for others, it signaled a return to ancient roots. Rabbi Shea Harlig and his colleagues established kosher opportunities in a city that only a generation ago had to travel to Los Angeles for seder food. Harlig was on the doorstep of the mayor, the philanthropists, and those who remembered a long-gone Orthodoxy. He encouraged them to pray at least once a week with the tefillin on their arms and head, in an effort to bring them back to the true fold as he envisioned it. In the end, Conservatives were moving closer to Reform practices, and both Conservative and Reform reclaimed traditional practices once abandoned in the name of modernity. All versions of institutional Judaism shared a renewed focus on education of children.

For seventy years, Nevada Judaism survived with makeshift worshiping arrangements in storefronts, Masonic temples, fraternal lodges, motels, dance studios, and Christian churches. It had, however, no continuous religious education program for children. If Judaism in Nevada were to prosper, providing for elementary Jewish education was essential. In 2007 the Reno Chabad organized a Jewish day school, and Las Vegas's recent growth allowed for the formation of several stand-alone day schools. As congregations planned to relocate and expand their synagogues, many were building in a K–6 educational component. The Conservative Midbar Kodesh Temple, which moved to Henderson, chose to build a school before a sanctuary. One result was a 50 percent increase in the number of temple memberships. The Reform Congregation Ner Tamid had similar plans. Rabbi Mel Hecht's Temple Beth Am moved west to the Summerlin area and envisioned a school to educate children through the sixth grade. The three Chabads in the Las Vegas area all had elementary schools, and the Jewish high school was to be completed in 2008.

Jews in Nevada have never been monolithic. They are as diverse politically, socially, religiously, and economically as the rest of the nation. Jews are wealthy and poor, gay and straight, Republican and Democrat, affiliated or not with a synagogue or Jewish organization. They are also as individualistic in their opinions about how to be Jewish as Jacob Rader Marcus's assessment that there are as many Judaisms as Jews.

Nevada Jews will not magically or suddenly achieve a unanimity of common purpose, but there is evidence of renewed commitment to tradition. For example, in northern Nevada there have been recent intradenominational trips to Israel facilitated by John Farahi. Ten Elko families use the services of rabbis from Reno and Salt Lake City for bar mitzvoth and maintain an active *havurah,* which has been coordinated by Pamela Zohar since 1992. And in West Wendover, on Nevada's remote eastern border, Chalom Copelan, raised as an Orthodox Jew, chose immigration to Israel ("make *aliyah*") rather than matriculation to an Ivy League school.[10]

In southern Nevada there are new signs of forbearance, leadership, and dialogue as formerly adversarial relationships are mellowing and old wounds healing. The Las Vegas Jewish Federation has provided direct financial support to Temple Beth Sholom's L'Dor V'Dor program for the elderly, which was once considered in competition with the federation's Senior Lifeline outreach program. It appeared to at least one observer that federation president Bodoff and Rabbi Felipe Goodman were on the verge of a "bear hug." Several funding agencies were responding to the widespread call for a Jewish Community Center facility. And at the groundbreaking for the new Jewish high school, staunch Democrat and union supporter Mayor Oscar Goodman enthusiastically proclaimed the day in honor of the school's benefactors, Dr. Miriam and Sheldon Adelson.[11]

Nevada has a chance to shape a revival of Jewish culture and religion in the West at a time when prophets of doom point only to national decline. Las Vegas's recent growth and expansion of a Jewish infrastructure and its ability to exert a supportive influence to northern Nevada will be the tipping points of success or failure. Proponents of a more robust Jewry in Nevada may be comforted or perplexed knowing that Las Vegas once had a Jewish mayor who prayed as well as he cursed and who, on the feast of Purim, may not have known the difference between the villain Haman and Mordechai the hero.

NOTES

Abbreviations for Frequently Cited Sources and Organizations

AI   *American Israelite* (Cincinnati)

AIPAC   American Israel Public Affairs Committee

AJA   American Jewish Archives, Jacob Rader Marcus Center, Cincinnati

CA   *Carson (Daily) Appeal*

DSR   *Daily State Register* (Virginia City)

EI   *Elko (Weekly) Independent*

EDL   *Eureka Daily Leader*

EDS   *Eureka (Daily) Sentinel*

GC   *Goldfield Chronicle*

GHN   *Gold Hill (Daily) News*

GN   *Goldfield News*

GWC   *Genoa Weekly Courier*

H   *Hebrew* (San Francisco)

HSSV   *Hebrew Sabbath School Visitor* (Cincinnati)

IOBB   International Order of B'nai B'rith

JP   *Jewish Progress* (San Francisco)

JR   *Jewish Reporter* (Las Vegas)

LVA   *Las Vegas Age*

LVI   *Las Vegas Israelite*

LVRJ   *Las Vegas Review-Journal*

LVS   *Las Vegas Sun*

MA   *Morning Appeal* (Carson City)

NHS   Nevada Historical Society, Reno

NSA   Nevada State Archives, Carson City

NSJ   *Nevada State Journal* (Reno)

PR   *Pioche (Daily) Record*

RC   *Reno Crescent*

REG   *Reno Evening Gazette*

RGJ   *Reno Gazette-Journal*

SA   *Silver Age* (Reno)

TE *Territorial Enterprise* (Carson City and Virginia City)
UNLVSC University of Nevada, Las Vegas, Lied Library, Special Collections
UNRSC University of Nevada, Reno, Getchell Library, Special Collections
VEB *Virginia Evening Bulletin*
WG *Weekly Gleaner* (San Francisco)
WJHC Western Jewish History Center, Judah Magnes Museum, Berkeley, California
WPN *White Pine (Daily) News*
WSJHQ *Western States Jewish Historical Quarterly* or *Western States Jewish History* (beginning 1983)
YR *Yerington Rustler*

Introduction: Celebrating Tradition and Resisting Assimilation

1. Leonard Dinnerstein, *Antisemitism in America,* xx. As explained more fully in the chapter on anti-Semitism, I have adopted Dinnerstein's unhyphenated spelling of the word *antisemitism.*

2. James Carroll, *Constantine's Sword: The Church and the Jews, a History,* 244, 254, 301–10.

3. Hugh Hastings, ed., *Ecclesiastical Records, State of New York* (Albany, 1901), 1:335–36, as quoted in Edwin S. Gaustad, *A Documentary History of Religion in America to the Civil War,* 86.

4. Dinnerstein, *Antisemitism in America,* 4–8, 9.

5. Hasia R. Diner, *A Time for Gathering: The Second Migration, 1820–1880,* 1, 4, 8–17. See also Jacob R. Marcus, *United States Jewry, 1776–1985,* 2:12–17.

6. John P. Marschall, "The House of Olcovich: A Pioneer Carson City Jewish Family," 173–74. For more detail on the plight of Jews in eastern Prussia, see Artur Eisenbach, *The Emancipation of the Jews of Poland, 1780–1870,* 92, 284, 286–93, 304, 340, 514.

7. Diner, *Time for Gathering,* 5.

8. U.S. Bureau of the Census, *U.S. Census Records, State of Nevada, 1880* (copy of original); Marschall, "House of Olcovich," 174–75.

9. Jonathan Sarna, *American Judaism: A History,* 470, 480, 482, index passim. Concerning opinions about "who is a Jew," see ibid., 367ff. See also "A Statement of Principles for Reform Judaism Adopted at the 1999 Pittsburgh Convention Central Conference of American Rabbis, May 1999," available online at http://www.ccarnet.org/platforms/principles. For further information, see the Web sites of the various groups for their own self-described place within Jewish history and their current claims and activities.

Chapter 1. Peddlers and Merchants, 1850–1863

1. Diner, *Time for Gathering*, 11, 28, 44, 48. For more on Jewish peddlers, see Harry Lewis Golden, *Forgotten Pioneers*, 20.

2. Robert E. Levinson, *The Jews in the California Gold Rush*, 4–5. The first Jewish woman credited with crossing the plains to California via Salt Lake City was Fanny (Bruck) Brooks in 1853. Brooks's daughter, Eveline, married Samuel Auerbach in 1879. Samuel and his brothers had earlier business in California and in Austin, Nevada, before moving east to Salt Lake City. See Ava F. Kahn, ed., *Jewish Voices of the California Gold Rush: A Documentary History, 1849–1880*, 105, 111, 117.

3. Myron Angel, ed., *History of Nevada, 1881, with Illustrations*, 30; S. Lissner to Henry Lissner, San Francisco, September 23, 1860, Box 549, Folder 1860 1X–23, AJA; Jacob R. Marcus, *Studies in American Jewish History: Studies and Addresses*, 161.

4. *Nevada City, Nevada, Journal*, November 20, 1857, 1, quoted in Levinson, *Jews in the California Gold Rush*, 26, 148–49; "Murder of Two Israelites," *H*, April 9, 1869, 4.

5. Henry J. Labatt, *Voice of Israel*, ca. November 1856, reprinted most recently in *WSJHQ* (April 1996): 177. See also John Livingston, introduction to *Jews of the American West*, 22; and Dinnerstein, *Antisemitism in America*, 51.

6. Norton B. Stern, "The Labatts' Attack in San Francisco and Los Angeles."

7. For a modern account of how the term *Jew* could be used by Jews and Gentiles, see Stella Suberman, *The Jew Store*, 3, 64.

8. J. Ross Browne, *A Peep at Washoe and Washoe Revisited*, 36–42.

9. William Perkins, *Three Years in California*, as quoted in Levinson, *Jews in the California Gold Rush*, 27.

10. Levinson, *Jews in the California Gold Rush*, 27–28; Leonard Dinnerstein and Mary Dale Palsson, eds., *Jews in the South*, 27–28, 135; Dinnerstein, *Antisemitism in America*, 27–30.

11. Helen S. Carlson, *Nevada Place Names: A Geographical Dictionary*, 93, 118. The Cohn obituary is in *Lyon County Times*, March 13, 1897, 3:3.

12. Sam P. Davis, *The History of Nevada*, 2:978–99; Angel, *History of Nevada*, 532. Curry is not known to have a Jewish heritage.

13. David Thompson, comp., *The Tennessee Letters: From Carson Valley, 1857–1860*, 61, 66. See also Andrew J. Marsh et al., eds. *Letters from Nevada Territory, 1861–1862*, 682n155.

14. Ronald M. James, *The Roar and the Silence: A History of Virginia City and the Comstock Lode*, 1–22.

15. Browne, *Peep at Washoe*, 54–57.

16. Ibid., 66, 68.

17. "Jewish News," *WG*, March 2, 1860, 2.

18. Thompson, *Tennessee Letters*, 75, 128.

19. Harriet Rochlin and Fred Rochlin, *Pioneer Jews: A New Life in the Far West*, 31, 32; Marcus, *United States Jewry*, 2:146–48.

20. One of the territorial senators representing Washoe Valley for two terms was rancher Solomon Geller, who served in the first Nevada Territorial Legislature. A review of his Ohio birth record at the Cincinnati Public Library revealed no evidence of a Jewish heritage. See also McDonald Legislative File, "Geller," NHS.

21. I[saac] J[oseph] Benjamin, *Three Years in America, 1859–1862*, 2:201, 206–7. Benjamin mysteriously noted that "only fifty Israelites are interested in mining." The census records for 1860 and J. Wells Kelly's 1862 *First Directory of Nevada Territory* reveal no more than ten certainly Jewish miners from Dayton to Virginia City during this period. For the most accurate Comstock population figures, see James, *Roar and the Silence*, 35, 245.

22. For biographical information on Klauber, see Lawrence M. Klauber, "Abraham Klauber: A Pioneer Merchant, 1831–1911." On Epstein, see Mark Twain's "Letter from Carson [City]," February 6, 1863, as cited in Henry Nash Smith, ed., *Mark Twain of the "Enterprise": Newspaper Articles and Other Documents, 1862–1864*, 59.

23. Kelly, *First Directory*, 213, 219; TE, November 11, 1876, 3:4, March 9, 1897, 3:3; *Lyon County Times*, March 13, 1897, 3:3. The possible Jewish lineage of Keller and Coleman is uncertain.

24. "Transcript of the Oral Memoirs of Mortimer and Janet C. Fleishhacker Concerning Family Business, and the San Francisco, California Community: San Francisco, Ag 6–My 31, 1974," copy in AJA. In Norton B. Stern, "Harriet Ashim Choynski: An 1850 Western Arrival," it is stated that the Ashims crossed the country by covered wagon (215). That notion is contradicted in Janet Fleishhacker's memoirs.

25. "Mortara Affair Mass Meeting, 1859," in Kahn, *Jewish Voices*, 466, 467.

26. Angel, *History of Nevada*, 422.

27. Isidor Choynski to Harriet Ashim Choynski, Aurora, May 17, 1863, reprinted in Kahn, *Jewish Voices*, 346.

28. Ashim's granddaughter Janet married Aaron Fleishhacker's grandson, who founded the Truckee River General Electric Company at the turn of the twentieth century. See AI, September 24, 1858, 92–93; and WG, April 6, 1860, 4.

29. Marcus, *United States Jewry*, 1:610–13, as quoted in Sarna, *American Judaism*, 46–47.

30. Jacob Klein, "Autobiographical Sketch," 1883, NHS; U.S. Bureau of the Census, U.S. Census Records, State of Nevada, 1860, 1870; H, June 18, 1869, 5, June 17, 1870, 5; Baptismal Record Book, St. Teresa of Avila Catholic Church, Carson City, 1865, p. 9. His two daughters memorialized him in a stained-glass window at St. Teresa of Avila Church. Gentiles John Wagner and August Berhauser were the other cofounders of the brewery.

31. Marcus, *United States Jewry*, 2:185.

32. Charles H. Meyer to Isaac Leeser, Carson City, November 13, 1862, "Trail Blazers of the Trans-Mississippi West." Leeser was the untitled head of traditional Orthodox Judaism and editor of the *Occident*.

Chapter 2. From Territory to Statehood, 1861–1865

1. Kelly, *First Directory*, cover, 141, 143; Marcus, *United States Jewry*, 2:124.

2. The third house built in the subdivision by attorney J. J. Musser later became the home of Rabbi and Pauline Sheyer at the corner of Fall and King Streets. Angel, *History of Nevada*, 551.

3. See Ormsby County Assessment Roll, lot 8, block 17, Proctor and Green subdivision, 9:272.

4. *SA*, October 2, 1862, 2:4.

5. Kelly, *First Directory*, 115–68; Norton B. Stern, "The Jewish Community of a Nevada Mining Town," 50–68; James, *Roar and the Silence*, 92.

6. *GHN*, May 5, 1864, 2:5.

7. "Epstein, Henry," McDonald Papers, NHS; Kelly, *First Directory*, 213–19.

8. The minister was Rev. H. O. Smeathman (*SA*, October 20, 1861, 2:5).

9. *SA*, October 2, 1862, 2:4.

10. C. H. Meyer to Rabbi Isaac Leeser, Carson City, November 13, 1862, "Trail Blazers of the Trans-Mississippi West," 105.

11. Benjamin, *Three Years in America*, 2:85.

12. Ormsby County Deeds, 1862–1863, 1:139. In addition to the "pioneer" Jews already noted above, the founding members of the Carson Hebrew Benevolent Society likely included the following 1862 residents: Samuel Cohn, Isaac Cohn, Charles Harris, and D. Barney Woolf.

13. *VEB*, August 4, 1863, 3:2; "City Sexton's Report" on cemetery internments in *VEB*, August 15, 1863, 2:4; 1958 record of grave inscriptions in the Virginia City Hebrew Cemetery by Verna Stumpf Patterson, available in Storey County Courthouse Records. For mention of the religious service, see Meyer to Leeser, "Trail Blazers." Nevada's B'nai B'rith records are held at the WJHC.

14. Hasia R. Diner, *The Jews of the United States, 1654–2000*, 134, 138–41. For a scholarly history of the organization, see Deborah Dash Moore, *B'nai B'rith and the Challenge of Ethnic Leadership*.

15. Marsh et al., *Letters from Nevada Territory*, 2, 115 (brackets in the original).

16. Ibid., 116, 129.

17. Ormsby County Assessment Roll, 1863; Marsh et al., *Letters from Nevada Territory*, 195, 238, 243.

18. Smith, *Mark Twain*, 9–13.

19. *H*, September 11, 18, 1868, 4; September 30, 1868, 1; December 4, 1868, 2; March 4, 11, 1870, 1. See also *Jewish Messenger*, June 10, 1859, 174, as cited in Adah Isaacs Menken, *Infelicia, and Other Writings*, 31n; Renee M. Sentilles, *Performing Menken:*

Adah Isaacs Menken and the Birth of American Celebrity, 193–97; and Marcus, *United States Jewry*, 2:115, 121.

20. See John P. Marschall, "Rabbi on the Comstock: The Irrepressible Herman Bien, 1864–1865," 167–71.

21. For Bien's background in San Francisco, see Reva Clar and William M. Kramer, "Julius Eckman and Herman Bien: The Battling Rabbis of San Francisco."

22. *GHN*, April 5, 1864, 3:2; "Nesop" (Jacob Kaplan) to *H*, October 21, 1864, 4:4.

23. For a summary of the Reform Movement in the mid-nineteenth century, see Arthur Hertzberg, *The Jews in America: Four Centuries of an Uneasy Encounter, a History*, 143–46 and passim. On the liberalism of reform advocates Isaac Mayer Wise and David Einhorn, see Sarna, *American Judaism*, 96–99.

24. Margaret G. Watson, *Silver Theatre: Amusements of the Mining Frontier in Early Nevada, 1850 to 1864*, 270; *VEB*, April 5, 1864, 3:1; April 6, 1864, 3:2; April 9, 1864, 2:4, as cited in Margaret G. Watson, *History of the Theatre of Virginia City, Nevada, from 1849–1865*, 124–25.

25. *AI*, June 24, 1864, 411:2; Richard E. Lingenfelter and Karen Rix Gash, *The Newspapers of Nevada: A History and Bibliography, 1854–1879*, 89. There are no extant copies of the *Nevada Staats Zeitung*.

26. *H*, October 21, 1864, 4:4.

27. *H*, August 5, 1864, 4:3.

28. *Virginia Daily Union*, October 18, 1864, 3:1; January 12, 1865, 2:7. Further evidence of Bien's popularity is in *GHN*, October 1, 1864, 3:1, which reported him representing the German Union Club (Verein) with a speech at a patriotic rally.

29. *TE*, November 8, 1863.

30. James, *Roar and the Silence*, 72. See Smith, *Mark Twain*, 17–19, for Mark Twain's alleged friendliness with secessionists.

31. December 1864 Assembly Records as cited in Angel, *History of Nevada*, 275; "Epstein, Henry," McDonald Papers, NHS.

32. "Rosenblatt, Meyer," McDonald Papers, NHS.

33. *GHN*, January 3, 1865, 2; January 9, 1865, 2.

34. *GHN*, January 12, 1865, 2; January 17, 1865, 2:2.

35. *Journal of the Assembly* (1864–1865), 253, 304–10; *Virginia Daily Union*, March 11, 1865, 2:1; March 30, 1865, 2:1.

36. *Journal of the Assembly* (1864–1865), 112–13, 337, 353.

37. *H*, February 17, 1865, 4:3.

38. *H*, March 17, 1865, 3:3; Rudolf Glanz, *The Jews of California: From the Discovery of Gold until 1880*, 140–43.

39. *H*, March 17, 1865, 3:4.

40. Bien also invented a rocking chair whose action operated a wafting fan. His last days were depressing, because he was unable to secure a permanent rabbinate

due to his age. He took his own life on April 22, 1895. See Marschall, "Rabbi on the Comstock," 186–87.

41. *H*, July 21, 1865, 3:5; October 4, 1865, 4; October 27, 1865, 4.

42. Russell R. Elliott with William D. Rowley, *History of Nevada*, 101–3; James W. Hulse, *The Silver State: Nevada's Heritage Reinterpreted*, 79; correspondence to *H*, Austin, N.T., March 18, 1864, reprinted in *H*, March 25, 1864, 4, in [Norton B. Stern], "The Rise and Fall of the Jewish Community of Austin, Nevada."

43. "Frederick H. Auerbach," in *Biographical Sketches* (Utah: Bancroft Library, n.d.), 9, as cited in Levinson, *Jews in the California Gold Rush*, 35, 152.

44. *H*, November 17, 1865, 4; Hynda L. Rudd, "The Mountain West as a Jewish Frontier."

45. *H*, March 25, 1864. The officers of the Hebrew Benevolent Society were listed as L. Wolf, president; S. J. Ehrlich, vice president; S. Goldstein, treasurer; J. Sichel, secretary; and A. E. Shannon, H. Aaron, E. Bornstein, S. Goldstein, and Victor Fernbach, trustees.

46. Angel, *History of Nevada*, 259, 261, 264. See also John P. Marschall, "Jews in Nevada, 1850–1900," 64; and *H*, November 17, 1865, 4.

47. See *AI*, April 21, 1871, 6, concerning the murder of Elias Asher, April 1, 1871, in Austin.

48. Ruth Rafael, interview by Mrs. Dorothy Coblentz, 1974, as cited in "Epstein, Henry," McDonald Papers, NHS.

Chapter 3. Riveted Jeans, Shopkeepers, and Ranchers in Railroad Towns, 1868–1880

1. Despite reports of Theodore Judah's Jewish lineage, there is no documentary evidence yet supporting his being part of a Jewish community or family.

2. John Townley, *Tough Little Town on the Truckee, 1868–1900*, 54, 189–92; Angel, *History of Nevada*, 272–80. Reno was named for Jesse Lee Reno, an army officer who served in the Mexican War and was killed in action during the Civil War.

3. Ed Cray, *Levi's*, 16–17, 19–20. The primary source for Jacob Davis's Nevada years is his sworn deposition of June 17, 1874, in *Levi Strauss et al. v. A. B. Elfelt et al.*, hereafter cited as "Davis Interrogatory." For references to the inventions, see "Deposition of William T. Frank," January 13, 1875, Reno, in "Davis Interrogatory."

4. Washoe County Deeds for January 20, 1870, show that Davis's shop and home had been owned by Abraham, David, and Samuel Haas, who did business in Virginia City as the Haas Brothers. There is some ambiguity in the documentation about whether Davis had a brother or brother-in-law who accompanied Packsher to Strauss's firm. See "Davis Interrogatory," 10.

5. "Davis Interrogatory," 3, 7.

6. Cray, *Levi's*, 20–21; "Davis Interrogatory," 22, 24–26; "Deposition of William T.

Frank," a Virginia City miner who returned to his trade as a druggist in Reno. The letter from Davis to Strauss is not extant. A typescript alleging to be a copy has been widely quoted but may be a remembered dialect version of the original, according to Levi Strauss authorities.

7. "Davis Interrogatory," 20.

8. Ibid., 16–19.

9. See http://www.levistrauss.com regarding the company's history and culture in the 1870s.

10. Cray, *Levi's*, 23; Guy Louis Rocha, assistant administrator for archives and records, Carson City, to Felvia Belaustegui, May 25, 2004, copy to the author.

11. *TE*, July 3, 1874, 2:4. See, for example, interrogatories of P. N. Norton of Cisco [Grove], Andrew Wright of Carson City, and George W. J. Wilson of Reno (taken between 1874 and 1875) in *Levi Strauss et al. v. A. B. Elfelt et al.* Concerning 1875 letters of patent, see "Subpoena," in *Strauss et al. v. B Greenbaum*, May 6, 1878, and subsequent judgment in favor of Strauss et al., July 8, 1878, Ninth Circuit Court, District of California, no. 1906.

12. Cray, *Levi's*, 33, 37. For more than a century, the myth of Levi Strauss having invented the copper-riveted jeans that bear his name has continued to overshadow Jacob Davis's enduring entrepreneurship. As recently as 1999, news stories out of San Francisco continued to credit Strauss as the man who "designed the riveted work pants for Gold Rush miners." Among those who got the story straight were Levi Strauss and Company archivist Lynn Downey; *Levi's* author, Ed Cray; and Alvin M. Josephy, "Those Pants That Levi Gave Us: From Workingman's Duds to Jet-Set Chic." For recent examples of the mythology exposed, see Guy Rocha, "Levi's 501 Jeans: A Riveting Story in Early Reno."

13. Angel, *History of Nevada*, 252; *H*, December 9, 1870, 5; *RC*, August 19, 1871, 3:2. A *ketubbah* (the Lachmans' Jewish marriage contract) was once on display in the Nevada State Archives and Library and noted the Hebrew date of the marriage as 21 Marcheschwan, 5631. For reasons unknown, Sheyer did not file the marriage record with the Washoe County Recorder's Office until February 10, 1871. The Lachmans had four children who survived infancy.

14. *RC*, August 19, 1871, 3:2; *NSJ*, October 5, 1872, and annually through October 10, 1875, 3:3; October 10, 1905, 2:3.

15. *NSJ*, January 26, 1882, 3:2. The Chebra B'rith Shalom society was not incorporated until April 1878. See Angel, *History of Nevada*, 641; and Philip I. Earl, "'A House to Offer Our Prayers . . .': A Brief History of Reno's Jewish Community and the Building of the Temple Emanu El," 47. Concerning the Sabbath school, see *AI*, January 3, 1879, 6, letter from Reno, December 11, 1878, noting as president Samuel Cahn and as secretary David Pechner and listing the female teachers and their assistants.

16. Angel, *History of Nevada*, 641. The Reno fire of 1879 also destroyed many Jew-

ish properties (*REG*, October 15, 1887, 3:2). Henrietta Lachman died in 1930, an active member of the Temple Emanu-El Sisterhood (*NSJ*, May 30, 1930, 8:2).

17. Carlson, *Nevada Place Names*, 247–48. For colorful early descriptions of the tumultuous beginnings of Humboldt County, see Davis, *The History of Nevada*, 2:888–921; and Angel, *History of Nevada*, 444–60.

18. Velma Stevens Truett, *On the Hoof in Nevada*, 263a; Angel, *History of Nevada*, 448, 459; *JP*, March 13, 1885, 4.

19. *Winnemucca Argent*, April 27, 1868, 2:6; Truett, *On the Hoof*, 231a, 242b, 301d, 496c; Angel, *History of Nevada*, 253. Other possible Humboldt County Jews in 1870 were rancher Frank Openheim and merchant M. Openheimer.

20. Hulse, *Silver State*, 125; Angel, *History of Nevada*, 384–401. Future researchers should be warned about inconsistencies in the following articles, because there were two Simon Reinharts—one elder and a younger nephew—and the names of the Winnemucca and Elko Reinhart stores were so similar that they were often confused by later historians. See "The Oldest Business in Elko, Nevada: Reinhart's in 1958." This reprint from the *Elko Free Press* of March 25, 1958, called attention to new "indisputable evidence" that the founding merchant in Elko was the father and not the sons, Simon and Benjamin. For other useful studies of the Reinhart family, see "E. Reinhart & Company of Winnemucca, Nevada: A 1911 Description," a reprint from the *Humboldt Star*, Humboldt County Development Edition, August 21, 1911, 23; "The Reinharts of Nevada: A Picture Story"; Edna B. Patterson, "Reinhart Family: Pioneer Nevada Merchants"; and Doris Cavanagh, "Winnemucca Firm," *NSJ*, October 20, 1968, 38. See also *EI*, January 2, 1875, as cited in Patterson, "Reinhart Family," 121.

21. *EI*, May 11, 1872, 3:1.

22. James W. Hulse, *The University of Nevada: A Centennial History*, 15–39.

23. Howard Hickson, "Hardly a High School: University of Nevada at Elko, 1874–1885," 6–7; Hulse, *University of Nevada*, 20.

24. *EI*, June 19, 1875, 5, as cited in Hulse, *University of Nevada*, 21.

25. *REG*, January 4, 1879, 2; Hulse, *University of Nevada*, 5, 21.

26. *EI*, February 12, 1875, 2:2, 3; February 16, 1875, 2:1; February 17, 1875, 2:2.

27. *EI*, January 23, 1875, 3:1, 2; March 13, 1875, 3:1.

28. Badt, *An Interview with Milton Badt*, 1–2.

29. *TE*, December 24, 1876, 2:7; Lester W. Mills, *A Sagebrush Saga*, 32.

30. Truett, *On the Hoof*, 99a, 275d. Cohns in Carson City numbered thirty who were interrelated, including some whose parents had Prussian Polish places of birth. For births of Gabriel Cohn's children, see Box 11, McDonald Papers, NHS.

31. Angel, *History of Nevada*, 276.

32. Elliott, *History of Nevada*, 158; Henry M. Yerington to A. N. Towne, San Francisco, January 11, 1879, Yerington Papers, vol. 2, as cited in Elliott, *History of Nevada*,

160; F. E. Fisk to "Dear Sirs," The Dalles, Oregon, April 12, 1881, in Angel, *History of Nevada*, 291. For a different version of the story, see Patterson, "Reinhart Family," 123, 125.

33. Norton B. Stern, "Abraham Mooser: First Businessman of Santa Monica, California," 123. In some Nevada sources, "Mooser" is spelled "Moser."

34. Samuel was also an officer in a second Elko Odd Fellows lodge, the Cornucopia, no. 29, in 1881. See U.S. Bureau of the Census, *U.S. Census Records, State of Nevada, Elko County, 1880;* and Angel, *History of Nevada*, 253.

35. Stern, "Abraham Mooser," 111. For other details not incorporated in the article, see Stern, "Report of an Interview with Mrs. Seymour (Carolyn Mooser) Wisekopf, Beverly Hills, California," October 30, 1967, Box 2802, "Report," AJA.

36. Truett, *On the Hoof,* 99a, 166a, 178c, 275d, 301c, 361b, 371c, 428a.

37. Badt, *Interview with Milton Badt,* 3–5; Gertrude N. Badt, "Milton Benjamin Badt, 1884–1966," 91–99.

Chapter 4. A Gunfighter, a Physician, an Alleged Arsonist, and a Reform Congregation, 1865–1885

1. On Pioche, see Hulse, *Silver State,* 111–12; Elliott, *History of Nevada,* 107–10; and Martha Lauritzen, "Pioche: Boom and Bust in the Most Violent Camp in Nevada and the History of Thompson's Opera House."

2. Angel, *History of Nevada,* 350; Davis, *The History of Nevada,* 2:940–41; Rochlin and Rochlin, *Pioneer Jews,* 171–72. "Levy" often appears as "Leavy."

3. Lauritzen, "Pioche," 4, 6.

4. Henry Bergstein, M.D., "Medical History," 1:610–11.

5. *PR,* January 17, 1873, 3:1; January 23, 1873, 3:3; April 10, 1873, 3:2.

6. *PR,* June 17, 1882, 3:4; November 18, 1882, 1:1.

7. Angel, *History of Nevada,* 479, 672.

8. The Cohn brothers served on the county grand jury. See *PR,* October 25, 1872, 1; September 24, 1872, 1:2; October 1, 1872, 3:2; September 12, 1874, 3:1; and Lauritzen, "Pioche," 7.

9. *PR,* June 28, 1873, 3:2.

10. *PR,* June 16, 1874, 2:4; June 30, 1874, 3:1; June 17, 1875, 3:4.

11. *PR,* September 8, 1874, 2:4; February 15, 1876, 3:1.

12. See, for example, *PR,* September 10, 1874, 3:1.

13. Bergstein, "Medical History," 1:613; Silas E. Ross, *Recollections of Life at Glendale, Nevada: Work at the University of Nevada and Western Funeral Practice,* 422.

14. *WPN,* July 12, 1873, 2:2; John P. Marschall, "The 1873 Fire at Hamilton: Finding the Culprit."

15. *WPN,* May 30, 1870, 1:3–5; June 21, 1873, 2:6; Elliott, *History of Nevada,* 104.

16. *WPN,* June 28, 1873, 2:1–2; *Reese River Reveille,* June 27, 1873, 2:3.

17. *State v. Cohn,* in *Reports of Cases Determined in the Supreme Court of the State*

of Nevada, during the Year 1873–74, 9:181, 186–7. Hereafter, this latter case will be referenced as *State v. Cohn* 9 Nev. (relevant page) (1874).

18. *PR*, October 24, 1873, 2:3; *State v. Cohn* 9 Nev. 186 (1874).

19. R. Sadler et al. to the Hon. Board of Pardons of the State of Nevada, n.d. (ca. May 1, 1876), Executive Branch Agencies, Pardons and Paroles, NSA.

20. Among the remaining signers were H. Mau, White Pine County commissioner in 1873; Dr. H. S. Herrich, superintendent of Schools; J. Liddle, county commissioner; H. Bush and P. Wagner, officers in Hamilton's Order of Odd Fellows; mining official Louis A. Hauck; Jerry Schooling, member of the Board of Regents; former Douglas County assemblyman Henry F. Dangberg; prominent Presbyterian trustee William H. Corbett; former Storey County assemblyman O. T. Barber; J. R. Mason, Ormsby County commissioner; Jacob Tobriner, Ormsby County assemblyman; George W. Kitzmeyer, prominent Carson City businessman; former state senator Israel Crawford; Charles Harris and Frank Boskowitz, Carson City Jewish merchants; and Carson City druggist O. P. Willis. See F. W. Cole et al., "To the Honorable, the Board of Pardons . . . ," June 11, 1877, NSA: and Ellis and King to the Honorable Board of Pardons (copy), September 29, 1877, followed by an October 9 notarization.

21. Prison Records, folio 47, Alexander Cohn, NSA; *EDS*, November 14, 1878, 3:3, quoting the *CA*.

22. *EDS*, May 14, 1876, 3:3, quoting the *WPN* (issue not extant); *EDS*, July 25, 1880, 3:1. There is no evidence of an "A. Cohn" residing or doing business in Eureka in that year.

23. There is a vast literature relating disasters to a scapegoat and scholarly treatments of the psychological need to place blame for calamities. See, for example, Tom Douglas, *Scapegoats: Transferring Blame.*

24. Eureka, April 1, 1879, Goldstone (signed "Quartz Rock"), to *Hebrew Observer* as reprinted in *HSSV*, May 2, 1879, 143. See also Hulse, *Silver State*, 109; Elliott, *History of Nevada*, 106; and Carlson, *Nevada Place Names*, 110. A dated but useful resource is Lambert Molinelli, *Eureka and Its Resources: A Complete History of Eureka County, Nevada, Containing the United States Mining Laws, the Mining Laws of the District, Bullion Product and Other Statistics for 1878, and a List of County Officers.*

25. Stern, "Jewish Community," 65.

26. *AI*, September 3, 1875, 5.

27. Stern, "Jewish Community," 51. Rudolf Glanz devotes an entire chapter to the hostility between "the Pollack and the Bavarian in California," writing, "the feelings seem to have been particularly strong" (*Jews of California*, 140).

28. *AI*, September 3, 1875, 6.

29. *AI*, August 25, 1876, 5:5.

30. *AI*, March 2, 1877, 6. See also Stern, "Jewish Community," 56. For incorporation data on October 29, 1877, see *EDS*, November 2, 1877, 2. Portland's Congregation Beth Israel affiliated with Wise's organization in 1865 but maintained traditional Or-

thodox rituals (William Toll, "The Origins of an Ethnic Middle Class: The Jews of Portland in the Nineteenth Century," in *European Immigrants in the American West: Community Histories,* edited by Frederick Luebke, 82).

31. *AI,* July 24, 1863, editorial page.

32. *AI,* May 4, 1855, 341, as cited in Clar and Kramer, "Julius Eckman and Herman Bien," pt. 1, p. 109.

33. *AI,* April 28, 1876, 6; May 26, 1876, 5; *EDS,* May 15, 1877, 3. The latter reported that Goldstone was to represent Eureka Jews at a meeting of Reform congregations in Cincinnati.

34. Glenn S. Dumke in William M. Kramer, ed., *The Western Journal of Isaac Mayer Wise, 1877,* vii. Wise originally published his journal in letter form in the *American Israelite* as his trip progressed. Citations in this work will be from the edited Kramer publication.

35. Ibid., 12, 20. Wise's description compares favorably to the 1880 description found in Angel, *History of Nevada,* 443. An E. B. Baum is listed as treasurer of the Palisade Odd Fellows Lodge no. 26 for 1880 in Angel, *History of Nevada,* 253.

36. Morris Rockman's given name was Moses, as noted in Stern, "Jewish Community," 65n76. In the U.S. Census for 1880, he appears as having been born in Poland in 1834.

37. Kramer, *Western Journal,* 21–22.

38. July 27, 1877, 2, as cited in Stern, "Jewish Community," 58.

39. *EDS,* January 13, 1878.

40. *EDS,* October 11, 1876, 3; *AI,* December 8, 1876, 2–3, as cited in Stern, "Jewish Community," 54.

41. *EDS,* April 19, 1876, 3; September 3, 1875, 3; April 25, 1876, 3; March 23, 1876, 3.

42. *EDS,* February 11, 1877, 3; February 13, 1877, 2; February 27, 1877, 3; March 7, 1879, as quoted in Stern, "Jewish Community," 62. On B'nai B'rith as more than a benevolent society, see *H,* December 4, 1868, 4:4.

43. *AI,* September 3, 1875, as cited in Stern, "Jewish Community," 63.

44. *AI,* September 3, 1875, 5; Angel, *History of Nevada,* 252, 254, 263, 428.

45. *EDS,* October 25, 1877, 3, as cited in Stern, "Jewish Community," 67.

46. *Eureka Daily Republican,* ca. May 16, 1877, with handwritten note of Goldstone's repurchase in Eureka County Courthouse scrapbook of sheriff's sales.

47. *Eureka Daily Republican,* ca. June 6, 1878, in Eureka County Courthouse scrapbook of sheriff's sales.

48. Eureka, April 1, 1879, "Quartz Rock" (Goldstone) to *Hebrew Observer,* as reprinted in *HSSV,* May 2, 1879, 143.

49. *EDL,* April 19, 1879, 2:1–2; *EDS,* January 21, 1879, 3:1; Stern, "Jewish Community," 70.

50. *EDS,* July 1, 1879, 1; advertisement of May 26, 1879; Eureka County Deeds, Book 8, 503.

51. Phillip I. Earl, "Nevada's Italian War," 60.

52. Brian Frehner, "Ethnicity and Class: The Italian Charcoal Burners' War, 1875–1885," 54. Bohemian-born Hausman was a gunsmith who converted to Judaism in 1877 to marry Evelyn Boas. Isaac Mayer Wise conducted the ceremony in the home of the Sol Ashims. See Stern, "Jewish Community," 57. For officers, see *EDL*, July 8, 1879, 3:2.

53. Earl, "Nevada's Italian War," 57–59.

54. Ibid., 70.

55. Nevada historian Phillip I. Earl has determined that the factual data do not clearly identify those responsible for the Fish Creek bloodshed. He concludes, however, that "the burners' version appeared most plausible and consistent, and the lawmen seemed to be in some disagreement with each other as to what happened" (*EDS*, September 26, 1879, 3:2, as cited in Earl, "Nevada's Italian War," 81, 83).

56. See Stern, "Jewish Community," 50, 75; and *EDL*, November 25, 1879, 5:1.

57. Angel, *History of Nevada*, 262, 439. William Rockman also appears in Eureka as a contributor to the Pacific Hebrew Orphan and Home Society (Stern, "Jewish Community," 61, 73n121).

58. Stern, "Jewish Community," 75.

59. *EDS*, November 25, 1879, 5:1.

60. Eureka County Deeds, Book 9, 12; *EDS*, August 6, 1880, 1:6; August 12, 1880, 3:1.

61. Angel, *History of Nevada*, 440–41. The Cohn store originally built by Sol Ashim is now a bar and restaurant on Eureka's walking tour of historic places.

62. *EDS*, March 5, 1880, 3; September 17, 1880, 3; Stern, "Jewish Community," 75.

63. *San Francisco City Directory, 1898*, 709–10; and *San Francisco City Directory, 1902*, 762, as cited in Stern, "Jewish Community," 76.

Chapter 5. Settling, Praying, Working, and Partying in the Halcyon Years, 1865–1880

1. Elliott, *History of Nevada*, 396–97; James, *Roar and the Silence*, 95, 142.

2. Dean L. May, "Fleeing Babylon: The English Mormon Migration to Alpine, Utah," 39; Dino Cinel, "Italians in San Francisco: Patterns of Settlement," 70.

3. *Carson Valley News*, October 27, 1876, 3; April 24, 1877, 3; July 2, 1880, 3; Klauber, "Abraham Klauber," 81–82.

4. Chinatown extended east of Fall Street to Valley Street between East Second and East Fourth Streets. See Guy Rocha, "Where Was Carson City's Chinatown Anyway?" *RGJ*, January 27, 2001, E1:7. See also James, *Roar and the Silence*, 98–99, 143, 149–50, 153. Basques did not arrive in significant numbers until after 1900.

5. Among the newer Polish arrivals were the Charles, Hirsch, Mark, and Benjamin Harris brothers from Poznán. The determination of Polish ethnicity here and elsewhere in this book is drawn, in part, from *Judische Gemeinde Kempen, 1825–1847* in

Poznán State Archives (listing of births, deaths, and marriages during this period for the city of Kempen/Kepno) and Prezydium Policji w Poznanin, Akta meste Poznenie, Archiwum Panstwowe w Poznaniu. Police Headquarters in Poznán, Acta of Poznán City, State Archives in Poznán (listing of persons emigrating from Posen/Poznán).

6. These conclusions have been drawn by checking residential addresses in the city's directory. I am grateful to members of the Carson City Preservation Coalition who, subsidized by a grant from Nevada Humanities, faithfully checked census records from 1860 to 1880 against all available Carson City directory listings.

7. *SA*, October 20, 1861, 2:5; October 2, 1862, 2:4; *VEB*, September 1, 1863, 2:4; *TE*, September 22, 1863, 3:1.

8. Ormsby County Assessment Roll, 1862–[1865], 194. *Ashim v. Ashim*, September 11, 1865, Ormsby County Court Records, shows Sheyer as purchaser of Lot 9, Block 6, and the highest bidder at four hundred dollars. Regarding Kempen immigrants in Marysville, see Susan Morris, *A Traveler's Guide to Pioneer Jewish Cemeteries of the California Gold Rush*, 66, 67; and Kahn, *Jewish Voices*, 321.

9. For example, he presided over the marriage of Lewis Hess (Virginia City) and Helena Epstein at Washoe City on December 15, 1869, (*RC*, December 18, 1869, 2:3), and of Samuel Rice to Fanny Mannheimer at Genoa in 1870 (*CA*, March 16, 1870, 3:2), and he performed the rite of circumcision on the son of David Lachman in Reno (*RC*, August 19, 1871, 3:2).

10. Emphasis added. *DSR*, September 26, 1871, 1:1; September, 15, 1871, 1:1; October 13, 1872, 4:1.

11. *DSR*, October 11, 1872, 4:2; *New Daily Appeal*, October 4, 1872, 4:2; *TE*, October 1, 1873, 1:1; Dinnerstein, *Antisemitism in America*, 35–38, 56–57.

12. *DSR*, November 10, 1872, 3:2.

13. *CA*, April 11, 1875, 2:1; June 11, 1875, 3:1. Sheyer's body was buried in Lone Mountain Cemetery's Jewish section and later moved to Reno Hebrew Cemetery in Reno, where Amelia and her daughter Rose Levy lived at the end of the century.

14. David A. D'Ancona and William M. Kramer, eds., *A California-Nevada Travel Diary of 1876*, 31. Although the parent group had been founded in New York in 1843 as a German-speaking organization, it had become cosmopolitan enough to embrace Jews of all language backgrounds. See Sarna, *American Judaism*, 89–90. Membership lists for Nevada's lodges are preserved at the WJHC.

15. *Nevada Tribune*, September 27, 1875, 2:1; September 30, 1875, 2:2.

16. *TE*, September 30, 1875, 3:2.

17. *TE*, October 9, 1875, 3:5; October 10, 1875, 3:2. Cohen listed his occupation to the 1870 census enumerator as a "gentleman of leisure." He was born in Germany in 1830 and was still unmarried at the age of forty. For Cohen's style and wit, see Wells Drury, *An Editor on the Comstock Lode*, 187–88; and Drury, "Journalism," 1:480.

18. *TE*, January 10, 1874, 3:2; James, *Roar and the Silence*, 95, 200–201.

19. *TE*, October 3, 1876, 3:4.

20. Kramer, *Western Journal*, 47, 74n114.

21. The most complete biography of Sutro is the dated but useful *Adolph Sutro: A Biography* by Robert E. Stewart Jr. and Mary Frances Stewart.

22. Ibid., 32; *Alta California*, April 20, 1860, as cited in Angel, *History of Nevada*, 505.

23. Kelly, *First Directory*, 219; Kahn, *Jewish Voices*, 442, 445–46.

24. Otis E. Young, "Philipp Deidesheimer, 1832–1916: Engineer of the Comstock," 361–65. Philipp Deidesheimer is referenced as a Jew in the 1942 edition of the *Universal Jewish Encyclopedia* under the authorship of Rabbi Hans Zucker of Temple Beth Or in Reno. Deidesheimer is also mentioned as presumably Jewish in Bernard Postal and Lionel Koppman's Nevada section of *A Jewish Tourist's Guide to the U.S.*, 294. There is, however, no solid linkage of this remarkable person to a Jewish lineage. Deidesheimer never patented his invention and died penniless. See Clark C. Spence, *Mining Engineers and the American West: The Lace-Boot Brigade, 1849–1933*, 9, 343, 366; and Miriam Michelson, *The Wonderlode of Silver and Gold*, 85, 262.

25. Angel, *History of Nevada*, 505.

26. Stewart and Stewart, *Adolph Sutro: A Biography*, 54.

27. James, *Roar and the Silence*, 88–89; Kahn, *Jewish Voices*, 441; Hulse, *Silver State*, 104–5; Elliott, *History of Nevada*, 164. Nevada historian William Rowley offers the notion that Sutro exploited the Yellow Jacket fire to foster his tunnel plan, just as power brokers used the memory of disasters to manipulate their projects ("Fire in the Mines: The Power of a Mining Disaster," paper read at Seventh Biennial Conference on Nevada History, Nevada Historical Society, May 26, 2004).

28. Angel, *History of Nevada*, 508–9. For a strong anti-Sutro editorial with no hint of antisemitism, see *PR*, September 12, 1874, 3:1.

29. Walter Van Tilburg Clark, ed., *The Journals of Alfred Doten, 1849–1903*, 2:xvi, 1222. Though editor Clark thought that Doten had "an unusual lack of racial and religious prejudice," he critically summarized his coverage of the meeting, noting Doten's outrageous siding with the anti-Sutro forces.

30. Ibid., 1226–28, 1234; Mark Twain, *Roughing It*, 382.

31. *AI*, May 30, 1879, 4:3.

32. James, *Roar and the Silence*, 58–59, 88–90, 238; Stewart and Stewart, *Adolph Sutro: A Biography*, 163.

33. Stewart and Stewart, *Adolph Sutro: A Biography*, 162, 165, 169–70, 175. Sutro's last will did not include Leah, but it provided a fifty thousand–dollar benefit to "Mrs. George Allen" in reparation for the "false and malicious" charge leveled at Virginia City in 1879. Allen predeceased Sutro and never received the money.

34. Elliott, *History of Nevada*, 165; Stewart and Stewart, *Adolph Sutro: A Biography*, 166–69.

35. Adolph Henrick Joseph Sutro. "Autobiography," marked as a dictation, typescript, H. H. Bancroft Collection, c-d 799:5, Bancroft Library, University of California at Berkeley, as cited in Kahn, *Jewish Voices*, 443–44.

36. *RC*, April 10, 1873, 2:4; Bergstein, "Medical History," 1:612.

37. Bergstein, "Medical History," 1:612.

38. Ross, *Recollections of Life*, 422.

39. Bergstein, "Medical History," 1:614.

40. *San Francisco Morning Call*, January 20, 1880, 4:6; U.S. Bureau of the Census, *U.S. Census Records, State of Nevada, Storey County, 1880.*

41. *Footlight*, December 15, 1880, 3:1; December 16, 1880, 3:2; *TE*, December 17, 1880, 3:3; December 18, 1880, 3:4; December 22, 1880, 3:3. For a brief assessment of Brown as a journalist, see Clark, *Journals of Doten*, 2:2255.

42. For a brief summary of medical care in Virginia City—including some examples of quackery—see James, *Roar and the Silence*, 197–98. Bergstein's medical, political, and marital involvements will be treated in a later chapter.

43. Wise judged the Jewish population to be "about forty to fifty" families plus a number of unmarried men in 1877 (Kramer, *Western Journal*, 45–47). My estimate is based on census data, city directories, B'nai B'rith rosters, and newspaper coverage of Jewish religious observances.

44. The past presidents were the famous jeweler and silver artisan M. M. Frederick, Adolph Wolfe, Louis Kaplan, Louis Guggenheim, Jake Goodfriend, W. Kierski, and L. Lobenstein (Kramer, *Western Journal*, 46, 47, 57).

45. Ibid., 46, 47.

46. Angel, *History of Nevada*, 571; *TE*, May 10, 1878, 2:7. For more on Strouse and his brief marriage to the wealthy and allegedly unfaithful Lillie Edgington, see Bernadette Francke, "The Neighborhood and Nineteenth Century Photographs: A Call to Locate Undocumented Historic Photographs of the Comstock Region," 4, 262–67.

47. Adolph Sutro to Rev. Dr. Wise, Sutro, August 12, 1877, *AJA*, I. M. Wise Manuscript Collection, 436 1/9, l-w, General.

48. Kramer, *Western Journal*, 47.

49. Ibid., 45, 47–48.

50. *Nevada Appeal*, July 21, 1878, 3:1. See also Bill Dolan, "Past Pages," *Nevada Appeal*, July 12, 1997, n.p.

51. *MA*, September 1, 1880, 2:4; September 10, 1880, 3:1.

52. Boskowitz died in 1930 at the San Francisco home of his physician son, George (*REG*, June 19, 1930, 12:4). For extended newspaper coverage of a legal conflict arising from Boskowitz's low rental price in the County Building, see *MA*, July 13, 1877, 3:3.

53. *TE*, October 22, 1870, 3:1; November 10, 1870, 3:1; November 11, 1870, 3:1; September 6, 1871, 3:2, September 9, 1871, 3:2; December 3, 1871, 3:2; December 8, 1871, 3:2; October 8, 1872, 23; October 21, 1872, 3:1; Davis, *The History of Nevada*, 1:445–47. The reference to Emperor Norton relates to a popular San Francisco Jewish eccentric

who considered himself emperor of the United States and protector of Mexico. He died in 1880 and was interred by Episcopalians rather than Jews, who were embarrassed by his antics, although many other San Franciscans tolerated and encouraged him. Thirty thousand people attended his funeral (Rochlin and Rochlin, *Pioneer Jews*, 169–70). On water issues in Virginia City, see James, *Roar and the Silence*, 59–60, 110–11. Herman Schussler, the engineer, who designed a way to bring water from Lake Tahoe to Virginia City in 1873, was not certainly Jewish.

54. *H*, April 7, 1865, 4:3; James, *Roar and the Silence*, 160.

55. *H*, February 17, 1865, 4:3 (bracketed material in original).

56. *H*, April 7, 1865, 4:3; June 6, 1865, 4:4.

57. *TE*, March 4, 1870, 3:1; Clark, *Journals of Doten*, 2:1211.

58. *TE*, October 12, 1876, 3:3; March 20, 1878, 3:2; March 11, 1879, 3:2; February 26, 1880, 3:2–3.

Chapter 6. Women, Their Children, and Their Occupations, 1860–1900

1. *PR*, June 30, 1874, 2:1; *TE*, May 1, 1879, 2:5. There is no indication that the two returned to Nevada. For announcement of the engagement and marriage in San Francisco of Theresa Harris and William Lewish, see *JP*, October 31, 1879, 4; and *AI*, February 6, 1880, 7.

2. Reprinted from the *New York Sun* in *JP*, March 28, 1879, 1:2–3.

3. For examples of infant mortality, see Morris, *Traveler's Guide*, 1, 19, 36.

4. *H*, February 17, 1865, 4:3.

5. James, *Roar and the Silence*, 192, 245. In Virginia City, the male Jewish population was estimated by Jewish observer, David D'Ancona, to be 100 in 1876. The total number of Virginia City Jewish inhabitants alone in 1876 is conservatively estimated to have been about 350 and the number of infants or children in school at 80 (U.S. Bureau of the Census, *U.S. Census Records, State of Nevada, 1870, 1880*; Virginia City, Gold Hill, and Silver City directories; D'Ancona and Kramer, *California-Nevada Travel Diary*, 42).

6. "Mortara Affair Mass Meeting, 1859," in Kahn, *Jewish Voices*, 465–67; *WG*, March 9, 1860, 2.

7. *H*, January 27, 1871, 4:3; Anne M. Butler, "Mission in the Mountains: The Daughters of Charity in Virginia City," 160.

8. Diner, *Time for Gathering*, 65, 219–21.

9. Concerning Jewish public school attendance and the conflicts with the Christian ideology in public education, see Diner, *Time for Gathering*, 152–53, 217, 275n26. It is reported that 85 percent of Storey County's eligible students attended school (James, *Roar and the Silence*, 169, 195, 198). For reports on the sad condition of Nevada's schools, see Angel, *History of Nevada*, 220–24.

10. William C. Miller, *Reports of the 1863 Constitutional Convention of the Territory of Nevada*, 235, 256.

11. Butler, "Mission in the Mountains," 160.

12. Carson City Library Circulation Records, 1895, 3–11, NSA.

13. Irwin Olcott (grandson of Hyman Olcovich), "Olcott Family History," two-page manuscript, courtesy of Irwin Olcott to the author; *Carson Daily Index*, February 2, 1886, 3:2–3; March 23, 1886, 3:3; May 1, 1886, 3:2; May 3, 1886, 3:3.

14. EDS, October 27, 1877, 3; June 29, 1878, 3, cited in Stern, "Jewish Community," 70; HSSV, November 11, 1881, 356, as noted in Stern, "Jewish Community," 72.

15. Dorothy Michelson Livingston, *The Master of Light: A Biography of Albert A. Michelson*, 12. Dorothy was Albert Michelson's daughter.

16. Fitch to Ulysses Grant, Hamilton, White Pine County, June 17, 1869, in D. Livingston, *Master of Light*, 25.

17. Ibid., 37, 118. For a vivid description of the brawl between Michelson and the gang, see Michelson, *Wonderlode of Silver and Gold*, 315–16.

18. D. Livingston, *Master of Light*, 177, 179, 180, 294. Albert Michelson posthumously received the Distinguished Nevadan Award from the University of Nevada, Reno, in 2003.

19. The divorce was unusually amicable. During their marriage, Bernhard had ceded to her full or joint ownership of the family residence on King Street, a jewelry store, and a half-dozen residential lots. After the divorce, Carrie quitclaimed to Bernhard all of the real estate for a token five dollars. The children's later move to Bernhard's San Francisco residence may have been due to the availability of good schools and proximity to their mother (Jim Jaffe, great-great-grandson of Bernhard and Carrie Olcovich, conversation with author, Carson City, July 24, 1998). There is pictorial evidence that some of the children were reconciled with their mother in later years. Bernhard, who moved to Los Angeles, never remarried.

20. *Weekly*, October 5, 1891, 1.

21. The *Ormsby County Ledger*, "published monthly by Olcovich Brothers," was an advertising vehicle for the store. Internal evidence places the publication in 1891. See Lingenfelter and Gash, *Newspapers of Nevada*, 45, 47, who estimated the date as after 1899 and attributed the publication to the two boys. It was evidently the work of the elder Olcovich brothers.

22. Benjamin, *Three Years in America*, 1:89.

23. GHN, October 13, 1863. (There is no evidence that Minerva Morris was related to any of the Jewish Morrises in Nevada.) For an elaboration on her comments, see Anita Ernst Watson, Jean E. Ford, and Linda White, "'The Advantages of Ladies' Society': The Public Sphere of Women on the Comstock," 179–81.

24. For background, see C. Elizabeth Raymond, "'I Am Afraid We Will Lose All We Have Made': Women's Lives in a Nineteenth-Century Mining Town," 14–16; and Ronald M. James and Kenneth H. Fliess, "Women of the Mining West, Virginia City Revisited," 17–39, appx. 3.

25. Janet I. Loverin and Robert A. Nylen, "Creating a Fashionable Society: Com-

stock Needleworkers from 1860 to 1880," 117, 122–23, 344n35; *TE*, July 20, 1861, 2; *SA*, July 13, 1861, 2:5; *VEB*, August 31, 1863, 2:4; September 28, 1863, 3:1. See also *GHN*, May 21, 1864, 2:2; January 3, 1865, 1:3.

26. *VEB*, August 10, 1863, 2:3; August 11, 1863, 3:1.

27. U.S. Bureau of the Census, *U.S. Census Records, State of California, San Jose Ward no. 2, 1870*, available online at http://www.rootsweb.com. The basis for assigning Jewish ethnicity and religion to the Loryeas is D'Ancona and Kramer, *California-Nevada Travel Diary*, 40; their affiliation with Congregation Bickur Cholim in the mid-1870s documented by Stephen D. Kinsey, "The Development of the Jewish Community of San Jose, California," 178–79; and their inclusion in Stern, "Jewish Community," 65n78.

28. In 1868, she advertised for the "Women's Rights Convention" (*TE*, March 31, 1868, 2, as noted in Loverin and Nylen, "Creating a Fashionable Society," 123, 125, 126). Sarah's husband served as president of B'nai B'rith Lodge no. 52 in 1876, was one of the founders of local Masonic Lodge no. 2, and was an officer in Nevada's Grand Lodge (Angel, *History of Nevada*, 237, 244). Census data, directories, and B'nai B'rith lists did not specify Jackson's first name.

29. The Mayers' Jewish identity is not certain, in part because the head of the household, Jacob, was not affiliated with the local B'nai B'rith organization. Since neither Jacob nor Fanny showed any assets in the census record, they simply may have been too needy to pay the B'nai B'rith dues. Fanny was Prussian-born (often meaning from the Duchy of Poznán), their three children had common Jewish first names, and they did live next door to the family of Annie and Isaac Goodfriend, who was affiliated with the local Jewish men's group (U.S. Bureau of the Census, *U.S. Census Records, State of Nevada, 1880*; B'nai B'rith records, 1870 to 1886).

30. *CA*, April 11, 1875, 3:1; *MA*, May 17, 1881; August 6, 1882, 2:2; *REG*, July 1, 1895.

31. Diner, *Time for Gathering*, 152.

32. Reva Clar and William M. Kramer, "The Girl Rabbi of the Golden West: The Adventurous Life of Ray Frank in Nevada, California, and the Northwest," 99–103.

33. *Daily Nevada Tribune*, March 6, 1895, 3; March 19, 1895, 3, as cited in Clar and Kramer, "Girl Rabbi," 101–2; Joe Arthur, *Broken Hills: The Story of Joe Arthur, Cowpuncher and Prospector Who Struck It Rich in Nevada*, 36.

34. Diner, *Time for Gathering*, 152; Rochlin and Rochlin, *Pioneer Jews*, 181–82; Angel, *History of Nevada*, 228; "Biographies," in "Nearprint Box," AJA.

35. D. Livingston, *Master of Light*, 118; Angel, *History of Nevada*, 228–29.

36. High school diploma, MS NC 27, Box 7, Folder 5, NHS; teaching credentials in NHS card file "Nevada Teachers"; newspaper clippings in MS NC 27, Box 2, Volume 1, NHS. Cohn's birth date was May 14, 1878, not 1884, as it often appears in contemporary and posthumous biographies.

37. William R. Gillis, comp., *The Nevada Directory for 1868–69*, 226; Kramer, *Western Journal*, 22; *EDS*, April 19, 1876, 3; September 3, 1875, 3.

38. U.S. Bureau of the Census, *U.S. Census Records, State of Nevada, 1870, 1880;* H, September 22, 1871, 5, reported the death of the Levanthals' infant daughter; EDS, September 3, 1875, 3; March 23, 1876, 3; April 19, 1876, 3.

39. Raymond, "'I Am Afraid,'" 6; James and Fliess, "Women of the Mining West," 21.

40. James and Fliess, "Women of the Mining West," appx. 3, 318; Sue Fawn Chung, "Their Changing World: Chinese Women on the Comstock, 1860–1910," 213. For a critique of Marion S. Goldman's enumeration of prostitutes on the Comstock in *Gold Diggers and Silver Miners: Prostitution and Social Life on the Comstock Lode,* see James and Fliess, "Women of the Mining West," 29–30.

41. Michelson, *Wonderlode of Silver and Gold,* 47, 218–20. According to U.S. Bureau of the Census, *U.S. Census Records, State of Nevada, Storey County, 1870,* Miriam (Mary) Michelson was born in California and grew up on A Street.

42. U.S. Bureau of the Census, *U.S. Census Records, State of Nevada, Storey County, 1870,* 425; Sharon Lowe, "The 'Secret Friend': Opium in Comstock Society, 1860–1887," 101–2.

43. Samuel Bowles, *Across the Continent: A Summer's Journey to the Rocky Mountains, the Mormons, and the Pacific States, with Speaker Colfax,* 142–43.

44. Kathryn Dunn Totten, "'They Are Doing So to a Liberal Extant Here Now': Women and Divorce on the Comstock, 1859–1880," 91. See also U.S. Bureau of the Census, *U.S. Census Records, State of Nevada, White Pine County, 1870,* 514, which annotates the residences of these women as adjacent.

45. Concerning Jewish prostitution rings in New York, see Gerald Sorin, *A Time for Building: The Third Migration, 1880–1920,* 84–85, 89, 216–17. Two Jewish prostitutes were identified in Butte, Montana, in the early decades of the twentieth century: "Jew Jess" who was a drug addict, and Madam Ida Levy, who had a reputation as an extraordinary Jewish cook. See Rochlin and Rochlin, *Pioneer Jews,* 171.

46. Sarna, *American Judaism,* 138–39.

47. Kramer, *Western Journal,* i, 45, 47, 61–62.

48. Jeffrey Shiovitz, ed., *B'kol Echad in One Voice,* 1–4.

49. The problem of low male participation in religious matters was not restricted to Jews. Louise Palmer, wife of a Comstock mining superintendent, complained of Christian religious observance performed "by proxy," by the wives of men who claimed the demands of business took precedence over religious matters. See Watson, Ford, and White, "'The Advantages of Ladies' Society,'" 186–87.

50. Stern, "Jewish Community," 60–62.

51. "Quartz Rock" (Goldstone) to editor, HSSV, May 2, 1879, 143.

52. Ibid. Mrs. Steler, born of Irish parents in New York in 1843, likely was a convert.

53. AI, January 3, 1879, 6; letter from Reno, December 11, 1878.

54. "One of the Harrises" to the editor, Carson City, AI, March 17, 1882, 301:4, 6.

55. *HSSV,* April 9, 1875, 2; February 2, 1883, 73.

56. G. Badt, "Milton Benjamin Badt," 101.

57. Ann Braude, "Women's History Is American Religious History," 90.

Chapter 7. Coping with Depression, 1880–1910

1. Patricia Nelson Limerick, *The Legacy of Conquest: The Unbroken Past of the American West,* 20–27; "Nevada Natural Resource Status Report," available online at http://dcnr.nv.gov/nrp01.

2. Letter from "B. O. Nanza," Virginia City, March 22, 1881, in *JP,* March 25, 1881, 4:3.

3. "Letter from Nevada," Virginia, Nevada, May 2, 1881, in *JP,* May 6, 1881, 4:2.

4. Choynsky (signed "Maftir," which could be translated as "the Last Word"), San Francisco, August 8, 1882, in *AI,* August 25, 1882, 58:2. For a brief sketch of Choynski, see "A Caustic Observer," in *Jewish Voices,* edited by Kahn, 192–94, 345–46.

5. Michelson, *Wonderlode of Silver and Gold,* 9–11. Joseph P. Goodman penned a similarly nostalgic piece years later. See Davis, *The History of Nevada,* 1:472. Goodman's putative Jewish ancestry has never been proved, but his comparison of the Comstock's jewel to Jerusalem through the eyes of an Israelite is curious.

6. Marschall, "House of Olcovich," 181–82.

7. *H,* March 25, 1864, 4; *AI,* April 21, 1871, 6; "Jay" to *American Hebrew* (New York), October 13, 1882, 103–4, as reprinted in *WSJHQ* 9:1, 88–90; Angel, *History of Nevada,* 254, 259, 260, 467.

8. *GHN,* July 20, 1868, 3:1.

9. Wilbur S. Shepperson, *Restless Strangers: Nevada's Immigrants and Their Interpreters,* 93.

10. Mary McNair Mathews, *Ten Years in Nevada; or, Life on the Pacific Coast,* 254.

11. Axel Nissen, *Bret Harte: Prince and Pauper,* 26–28.

12. Hart's "Plain Language from Truthful James" (1870) can be found online at http://www.assumption.edu/HTMLAcademic/history/.

13. Gary Scharnhorst, *Bret Harte: Opening the American Literary West,* 52–57.

14. Henry Nash Smith and William M. Gibson, eds., *Mark Twain–Howells Letters: The Correspondence of Samuel L. Clemens and William Dean Howells, 1872–1910,* 2:235. See also Charles Neider, ed., *Autobiography of Mark Twain,* 123–29, 294–302. For a discussion of Harte's sympathetic attitude toward Jews, see Nissen, *Bret Harte,* 27–30. Harte may have been the cousin (through a common grandfather, Bernard Hart) of Frederick H. Hart (1835–1897), who edited several Nevada newspapers and was best known for his humorous treatment of Austin's Sazerac Lying Club. See Drury, *Editor on the Comstock,* 187.

15. See Rudolf Glanz, "Jews and Chinese in America," which discusses the anti-Chinese bias of western Jews criticized by eastern Jews fearing legislation against

Jews similar to the Chinese Exclusion Act. For more on the divergent attitudes of California Jews toward the Chinese, see Reva Clar and William M. Kramer, "Chinese-Jewish Relations in the Far West, 1850–1950"; and Kahn, *Jewish Voices*, 309, 432–33, 457–60.

16. Kramer, *Western Journal*, 20, 21, 26, 27, 29–31, 33–35, 55, 76n146.

17. *WPN*, May 27, 1876, 3:2.

18. *Statutes of the State of Nevada Passed at the Eighteenth Session of the Legislature, 1897*, chap. 73, p. 81; Elliott, *History of Nevada*, 168–69.

19. *MA*, February 21, 1886, 3:3; February 24, 1886, 3:2; March 7, 1886, 3:2.

20. *Carson Daily Index*, April 2, 1886, p. 2, cols. 2–4; *MA*, February 20, 1886, 3:2; February 21, 1886, 3:3; February 24, 1886, 3:2. For the Chinese washhouse, see Ormsby County Assessment Roll, 1900, 26, 27.

21. Earl Pomeroy, "On Becoming a Westerner: Immigrants and Other Migrants," 201, 203; Dinnerstein and Palsson, *Jews in the South*, 13.

22. The Chinese presence in northern Nevada received a permanent memorial on October 31, 2003, near the center of Carson City's once bustling Chinatown.

23. *AI*, March 17, 1882, 301:6.

24. *MA*, March 19, 1899, 3:2.

25. Marschall, "House of Olcovich," 184–86, 190n56; Irwin Olcott to the author, Santa Rosa, December 28, 1998. See also Sylvia Gutstadt Olcott, *On the Sidewalk of the War: A Different Kind of Love Story*, 166, 203, 220–21.

26. *Weekly*, October 3, 1898; *MA*, January 25, 1900, 1.

27. *MA*, September 29, 1910, 1:1; *Carson City Directory*, 74. Clarence Rosenbrock was a bookkeeper at the State Printing Office. Morris Cohn's daughter, Bertha, was a stenographer at the Attorney General's Office; son Louis was registrar at the U.S. Land Office; Herbert was a physician and Felice a lawyer.

28. James Scrugham, ed., *Nevada: A Narrative of the Conquest of a Frontier Land, Comprising the Story of Her People from the Dawn of History to the Present Time*, 2:100–101.

29. *REG*, May 24, 1961, 15:1. Cohn's birth year has often been incorrectly cited as 1884.

30. See Marvin Cohodas, "Dat-So-La-Lee and the Degikup"; Anita Ernst Watson, *Into Their Own: Nevada Women Emerging into Public Life*, 139; "Carson City, Nevada, Patron of Dat-So-La-Lee"; and "Dat-So-La-Lee," in Scrugham, *Nevada*, 3:114.

31. Cohodas, "Dat-So-La-Lee," 127–28.

32. *CA*, January 29, 1934, 1:6; Maria Davis Denzler, "The Dat So La Lee Basket Mystery," 13.

33. *H*, March 7, 1879, 5.

34. See *NSJ*, September 19, 1880, 3:1; March 16, 1881, 3:2; October 15, 1883, 3:2; and *AI*, January 3, 1879, 6.

35. All material in this chapter relating to the benevolent society (except as noted)

is taken from "Reno Hebrew Benevolent Society, Minutes, 1879–1907," microfilm at UNRSC.

36. For other officers, see *NSJ*, December 4, 1895, 3:3.

37. *NSJ*, 3 December 1896, 3:2.

38. "Reno Nevada Hebrew Cemetery," p. 1, Small Collections, AJA; Washoe County Recorder, Real Estate Division, Book 32, p. 402.

39. *NSJ*, December 17, 1908, 8:1.

40. IOBB, Reno Lodge no. 759, minutes, WJHC; *NSJ*, April 4, 1911, 3:4. See *REG*, January 22, 1916, 8:4, for an example of charitable outreach to starving Polish Jews.

41. Sylvia and Lena Jacobs, interview by author, Reno, July 26, 1982; their relatives worked at the Scheeline Bank. See also Scrugham, *Nevada*, 2:115–17.

42. A Legislative Joint Committee called on Bergstein in 1887 to explain Reno's outbreak of typhus malarial fever. Bergstein analyzed that the cause was toxins from sawdust deposited into the Truckee River by upstream lumber mills. He noted there were no illnesses resulting from water powdered with fresh sawdust or from water pumped from wells (Bergstein, "Medical History," 1:614; letter to the editor on "Our State Insane," *TE*, May 8, 1878, 1:1; Anton Sohn, *The Healers of Nineteenth-Century Nevada*, 109).

43. Townley, *Tough Little Town*, 53, 151–52.

44. *Appendix to the Journals of the Eighteenth Session*, vol. 1, *Report of the Commissioners (1897)*, 13–14, as cited in Ellen Pillard, "Nevada's Treatment of the Mentally Ill, 1882–1961," 90.

45. Pillard, "Nevada's Treatment," 96n57, 97; State of Nevada, *Investigation of Charges against Dr. H. Bergstein: Testimony Taken and Proceedings Held before the Board of Commissioners for the Care of the Indigent Insane, Reno, Nevada, Monday, December 20, 1897*, 1.

46. May 17, 1899, Second Judicial District Court, 4270.

47. *REG*, October 4, 1898, 1:3; October 5, 1898, 2:1.

48. Clark, *Journals of Doten*, 2:2032.

49. The terms were that Pauline was to have custody of their three children and receive $100 per month in alimony and child support, two and a half lots in the I Block of the Powning addition—including a dwelling at Second and Chestnut (Arlington) with all its personal property (on which was a $3,000 mortgage)—and all their joint property at the state-owned residence on the grounds of the Nevada State Hospital. The three children were Lewis (fourteen), Marion L. (twelve), and Albert (eleven). Bergstein was also to pay $125 to Pauline for her counsel fees and court costs. The only exception to the decree was that if Bergstein wanted his eldest son to attend the University of Nevada, Bergstein would have to assume all costs (May 17, 1899, Second Judicial District Court, 4270).

50. *NSJ*, June 15, 1900, 3:4. Clare Poor Powning was the daughter of James Johnson Poor, of Reno, who had purchased acres of land west of what is now the center of

Reno. The family was of Congregationalist background. See *NSJ*, August 11, 1940, 5, for a history of Poor's family.

51. Henry Bergstein appears in the 1903 San Francisco telephone directory, living at 826 Sutter; however, there is a C. (Clare?) Bergstein residing at 1653 Post Street.

52. U.S. Bureau of the Census, *U.S. Census Records, State of Nevada, 1910*, shows Bergstein as a widower. See also *REG*, December 1, 1914, 8:3; November 12, 1915, 8:1; September 26, 1916, 8:1; and *NSJ*, June 8, 1915, 8:5.

53. The 1920 U.S. Census recorded Bergstein as "living alone," widowed, seventy-two years of age, and practicing medicine at 217 North Virginia Street. The 1921 Reno telephone directory did not include him. He was reported as dying in San Francisco in 1930 (*REG*, December 22, 1930, 14:2). Thirty years later, another Jewish physician, Dr. Sidney Tillim, became the State Mental Hospital's superintendent. As president of Reno's Temple Emanu-El, he had impeccable religious credentials. For a brief summary of Tillim's contributions to the hospital, see Pillard, "Nevada's Treatment," 93–94, 97–98.

Chapter 8. Dashed Hopes, New Discoveries, and the Goldfield Bubble, 1890–1920

1. Ephraim Deinard to John E. Jones, Philadelphia, August 12, 1897, in Sadler Papers, Box A-36, NHS. A longer version of the material in this section appeared in John P. Marschall, "Jewish Agricultural Experiment, Wellington, Nevada, 1896–1902: Epilogue to a Communal Failure." Permission has been granted by the University of California Press to reprint its published segments.

2. *Emanu-El*, November 12, 1897, 5, as cited in Norton B. Stern and William M. Kramer, "An American Zion in Nevada: The Rise and Fall of an Agricultural Colony," 131. Stern and Kramer's description of the Wellington experiment ends with the colony's sale in 1898.

3. *JP*, November 12, 1897, 4:1.

4. *GWC*, November 5, 1897, from the *San Francisco Post*.

5. The Dakota colony was north of "Painted Woods," a Jewish-immigrant agricultural commune underwritten by the Reverend J. Wechsler of St. Paul and Jacob Schiff of New York. See Ina H. Stiner et al., "Some Studies in Local History," manuscript, 1934, p. 221, Porterville Public Library, as cited in Norton B. Stern, "The Orangevale and Porterville, California, Jewish Farm Colonies," 164.

6. Estelle Moore, "Smith Valley Colony," 71; *JP*, November 12, 1897, 3:1. For reference to Cohn serving as *"shochet* and *mohel,"* see Eugene R. Nudelman, "The Family of Joseph Nudelman: A Biography as Related by His Sons Hyman, Robert, and Louis," 1969, p. 6, draft copy of unpublished manuscript courtesy of the author's family, hereafter cited as "Family History." In addition to the Katz family from North Dakota, there is another, Jacob Lloyd (Loged?), who is named in 1900 as a Jewish farmer accompanying Nudelman to Nevada. The *Reform Advocate* (Chicago), September 29,

1900, 144, as cited in Abraham R. Levy, "Central North Dakota's Jewish Farmers in 1903," 11n. Census records show Russian-born Jacob and Sophia Loged and three children as adjacent neighbors of the Nudelmans.

7. *GWC*, November 5, 1897, 2:1, 5:1 quoting *EI*, November 19, 1897, 6:4, quoting the *Carson City News*; Clark, *Journals of Doten*, 3:1970; *YR*, November 18, 1897, 4:3.

8. Lyon County Recorder, Book of Deeds, Book M, p. 541.

9. Nudelman, "Family History," 11; E. Moore, "Smith Valley Colony," 71.

10. *GWC*, January 28, 1898, 6:3; Nudelman, "Family History," 12.

11. *GWC*, February 18, 1898, 6:2; February 25, 1898, 2:3.

12. *GWC*, August 12, 1898, 3:2; September 16, 1898, 1:2; September 23, 1898, 2:1.

13. *GWC*, December 9, 1898, 3:2. The Lloyd (or Loged) family arrived sometime before 1900.

14. *Public Opinion* (San Francisco), August 14, 1898, 1, quoted in Stern and Kramer, "American Zion," 133; *AI*, October 13, 1898, 3:2.

15. *AI*, January 20, 1899, 3:1; *YR*, January 21, 1899, 1:1; Nudelman, "Family History," 13. See also Lyon County Recorder, Deeds, December 14, 1898, Book M, p. 681.

16. *GWC*, February 24, 1899; March 10, 1899. Not all legal documents describing Joseph Nudelman's gifts to relatives and friends have been uncovered. I wish to thank Leonard Acton of Specialized Real Estate Projects, Inc., of Yerington, Nevada, for his assistance.

17. *YR*, May 6, 1899, 2:3; *GWC*, May 26, 1899, 3:2. In September 1898 and June 1899, Bell and Schwartz were seen in Philadelphia, but there is no record of extradition or repayment. *GWC*, September 16, 1898, 3:2; June 2, 1899, 3:2. The *Genoa Weekly Courier* altered its name several times in this period.

18. *GWC*, November 11, 1900, 3:2, which misidentified the victim as Joseph's daughter. For a bogus claim against the properties, see *GWC*, March 1, 1901, 3:1; and March 29, 1901, 3:2.

19. Nudelman, "Family History," 13–16; Lyon County Recorder, Book of Deeds, Book N, p. 351. Joseph Nudelman became cofounder and president of Portland's Orthodox Congregation Shaarie Torah, opened a kosher meat market, and founded Portland's Jewish Old Men's Home. Nudelman descendants maintained a higher-than-average commitment to Judaism through four generations (Joseph Nudelman's grandson Harvey Fields, rabbi of Wilshire Boulevard Temple, conversation with author, July 18, 2000). Joseph Nudelman died in 1935 (Nudelman, "Family History," 20–22 of draft copy).

20. Cora Gage Sayre, *Memories of Smith Valley*, 34. The Isaac Cohns are not noted in the 1900 or 1910 census reports.

21. *American Jewish Year Book*, 2:624, as cited in Jacob R. Marcus, *To Count a People: American Jewish Population Data, 1585–1984*, 119.

22. *YR*, July 2, 1896, 2:4; U.S. Bureau of the Census, *U.S. Census Records, State of Nevada, 1900, 1910*. In 1913, Isidore Margolis, of the Jewish Farmers Protective As-

sociation of Pittsburgh, asked the president of the University of Nevada, Joseph E. Stubbs, for information concerning the possible purchase of twenty-five thousand acres that could be settled by Jewish farmers. Beleaguered by political infighting, Stubbs died suddenly in the spring of 1914. Nothing came of the request from Margolis (*Territorial Enterprise*, December 9, 1913, 4:4; Hulse, *University of Nevada*, 38–39).

23. During the same period, California received 4,162 and Utah 87 (Industrial Removal Office, *The Thirteenth Annual Report of the Industrial Removal Office for the Year Nineteen Thirteen*, 11). For a comprehensive study of the IRO, see Jack Glazier, *Dispersing the Ghetto: The Relocation of Jewish Immigrants across America*.

24. C. Aronson to IRO, July 11, 1906, Box 105, "Reno, Nevada," 1906, American Jewish Historical Society Archives. Prior correspondence is dated February 21, 1906, with response dated February 26, 1906, Box 76. Permission to quote granted by American Jewish Historical Society executive director Michael Feldberg, June 29, 2004.

25. Aronson to IRO, Reno, August 7, 1906; Clink and Aronson to IRO, Reno, February 19, 1907, Box 88, "Reno, Nevada," both in ibid.

26. Mrs. N. Raymond to IRO, Ely, June 20, 1912, Box 105, "Ely Nevada, 1912"; J. I. Star to IRO, Winnemucca, August 17, 1914, Box 76, "Winnemucca, Nevada," both in ibid.

27. Lester J. Hilp, *Reminiscences of a White Pine County Native, Reno Pharmacy Owner, and Civic Leader*, 3–4.

28. *WPN*, "Registered Voters," May 30, 1870, 1; October 22, 1892, 2; *REG*, January 4, 1915, 8; Christine Hilp Tweet to the author, Sparks, August 18, 2001. Tweet is a direct descendant of the Cincinnati Hilp family. For an anecdote involving Sol Hilp and his African American valet in Taylor, see *REG*, January 4, 1915, 8.

29. *WPN*, September 4, 1886, 2, 4; December 13, 1890, 4; July 16, 1893, 3. Concerning Emma Hilp, see *REG*, August 20, 1946, 18.

30. *WPN*, December 13, 1890, 4; July 16, 1892, 3; December 3, 1892, 1. Hilp twice ran unsuccessfully for state senator (*REG*, January 4, 1915, 8).

31. Tweet to the author; IOBB, Reno Lodge no. 759 and no. 450, member lists, WJHC; *Weekly Gazette and Stockman*, March 21, 28, 1899; *REG*, November 26, 1902, 5; October 6, 1914, 8; August 20, 1946, 18; *NSJ*, September 22, 1911, 2; October 7, 1917, 6. For other details, see B. F. Miller, "Nevada in the Making: Being Pioneer Stories of White Pine County and Elsewhere," 396–405, cited in McDonald Papers, NHS, Box 24.

32. *Lode*, June 13, 1899, as cited in James W. Hulse, *Lincoln County, Nevada, 1864–1909: History of a Mining Region*, 54–55, 59; *WPN*, November 6, 1910, 2. Bamberger died on October 6, 1926, and was interred in Salt Lake's B'nai Israel Cemetery (Juanita Brooks, *History of the Jews in Utah and Idaho*, 166, 174).

33. Thomas Wren, ed., *A History of the State of Nevada, Its Resources and People*, 437–38; U.S. Bureau of the Census, *U.S. Census Records, State of Nevada, 1900*. For Levy, see *Weekly*, February 15, 1892, 1:2.

34. Hulse, *Silver State*, 164–65; Elliott, *History of Nevada*, 211–13.

35. Rochlin and Rochlin, *Pioneer Jews*, 172–3; Jacob Rader Marcus, *The American Jewish Woman, 1654–1980*, 66. See also Guy Rocha in REG, October 20, 2002, B2:8.

36. Mrs. Hugh Brown, *Lady in Boomtown: Miners and Manners on the Nevada Frontier*, 49.

37. Davis, *The History of Nevada*, 2:1100. Louis Blumenthal does not appear in the 1910 census, but Charles Blumenthal does. He was likely a brother or relative of Louis, since both were born in Tennessee. Charles F. Wittenberg and his wife, Elizabeth Kopp, were both identified in the 1910 census as being born of Yiddish-speaking parents—he in Eureka, Nevada, and she in Ohio. There is no evidence, however, that either was identified as Jewish in their adult lives. The record may be in error, or the two converted to Christianity sometime between 1910 and 1920. Wittenberg invested heavily in mining and was president of the Gypsy Queen and Manhattan Dorris Companies. In 1939 and 1941, he served as state senator for Nye County. Charles's sister, Florence Butler, was buried from the Tonopah Episcopal Church. *Tonopah Times-Bonanza and Goldfield News*, December 1970, clipping copy to the author, courtesy of William Pettite. See also Davis, *The History of Nevada*, 2:1274.

38. Hulse, *Silver State*, 165, 181; Elliott, *History of Nevada*, 219, 224. Likely Jewish merchants in Tonopah between 1910 and 1920 were Harry Bergman, Max Blumberg, Leon Cohen, and Moses Cohn—slightly less than 2 percent of city's merchants. Fritz Taback was a tailor, and Abraham Elias Dobrin worked in a silver mine (U.S. Bureau of the Census, *U.S. Census Records, State of Nevada, Nye County, 1910, 1920*).

39. Elliott, *History of Nevada*, 210–13; Hulse, *Silver State*, 164. The gender ratio leveled out at about two to one. See Sally Zanjani, *Goldfield: The Last Gold Rush on the Western Frontier*.

40. The names and occupations of Jewish residents were established using *Directory of the City of Goldfield: Columbia, Diamondfield, Jumbo Town, Mill Town, Nevada, 1907–8*, Esmeralda County and Nye County records (including mining claims), newspaper advertisements, and U.S. Census data, which in 1910 and 1920 included the language of parents. Another source is Lena Hammond, "Memories of Austin, Bodie, and Goldfield, 1900–1910," 10. Jewish and Gentile population estimates are based on the *Directory of the City of Goldfield* and U.S. Bureau of the Census, *U.S. Census Records, State of Nevada, 1880, 1900, 1910, 1920*.

41. The elderly Louis Lobenstein was among the few identified as "peddling" in the U.S. Census for 1910. Others preferred to identify themselves as "travelling merchants" and are indistinguishable in census records from established Jewish merchants. Isaac Solomon was elected justice of the peace and served many years in that capacity, but his supposed Jewish lineage has not been established. Among those with registered mining claims in the area were G. D. Cohn (1912), Bernard Rosenbaum of Reno in partnership with Jake Goodfriend (a total of nine claims in 1912), M. Rosenthal (three claims in 1912), and Samuel Rosenberg (two claims in 1916).

42. U.S. Bureau of the Census, *U.S. Census Records, State of Nevada, 1910;* Sidney Flower, "Editorial Notes," *Goldfield Gossip,* May 18, 1907, 1. Flower may have had a Jewish heritage, but that has not yet been established.

43. *Goldfield Gossip,* May 18, 1907, 1.

44. Sparks to Rosenthal, Carson City, December 26, 1907; Rosenthal to Sparks, Goldfield, December 29, 1907, both in Governor John Sparks correspondence, file folder 068, Rosenthal, Benjamin, NSA. See also GC, May 23, 1908, 2:1–4. Sparks had an antisemitic strain, which may have been at work against Rosenthal. See later chapter on antisemitism.

45. GC, August 5, 1908, 1; October 14, 1908, 1, 2; October 16, 1908, 1.

46. GN, October 31, 1908, 4:1. Sheriff Ingalls was a Gentile.

47. C. Elizabeth Raymond, *George Wingfield: Owner and Operator of Nevada,* 77–79; Zanjani, *Goldfield,* 220–21, 227. For reference to Rosenthal's support of unions, see GN, November 11, 1908, 4:1.

48. Sally Zanjani, *The Glory Days in Goldfield, Nevada,* 114. The U.S. Census of 1910 shows him at age forty-four and also in a second marriage. See also Hammond, "Memories," 9.

49. GN, August 17, 1907, as cited in Zanjani, *Goldfield,* 171.

50. Hammond, "Memories," 10–13. Hammond's view of Goldfield's working girls fits a traditional literary genre portraying them as "soiled doves" or harlots "with hearts of gold." For a corrective, see Zanjani, *Goldfield,* 102–3, 104–8.

51. Hammond, "Memories," 13–15. A different version of this story places Meyer's "vacation" prior to the suicide. See Zanjani, *Goldfield,* 122. See also GC, May 8, 1908, as cited by Zanjani, indicating her name was Nana Young, at the Oriental Hotel, and her parents refusing to pay for the return of her body to her hometown. Max Meyer does not appear in the 1910 U.S Census for Nevada, but a twenty-three-year-old Max Meyer is enumerated for San Francisco in that year.

52. *Statutes of the State of Nevada Passed at the Twenty-first Session of the Legislature, 1903,* chap. 12, sec. 124, p. 34.

53. Davis, *The History of Nevada,* 2:1156; U.S. Bureau of the Census, *U.S. Census Records, State of Nevada.*

54. U.S. Bureau of the Census, *U.S. Census Records, State of Nevada, Esmeralda County, 1910,* 167; *Directory of the City of Goldfield.*

55. Zanjani, *Goldfield,* 144.

56. Ibid., 144–46. The citation for this statement is GN, September 24, 1904. The *News* was a weekly and in that year published on September 9, 16, and 23. No mention of the Jewish observance could be found in these issues. There is hearsay evidence that dry-goods merchant Harry Coffee was president of a temporary congregation set up for High Holidays in 1907 and that Sam Baylis served as cantor.

57. *Ironwood Daily Globe,* March 16, 1927, 9:2; *Directory of the City of Goldfield;* William Pettite to the author, Fair Oaks, Calif., July 25, 2001, November 2, 2005, in-

cluding newspaper clipping on Abelman's Saloon in 1897. See also Raymond, *George Wingfield*, 52–57.

58. Charlotte L. Nay (1877–1967) (sister of Harry Stimler) to William Pettite, Winnemucca, September 16, 1967, copy of handwritten letter provided to the author; *Tonopah Times-Bonanza and Goldfield News*, October 27, 1967, 1, 3; Esmeralda County Mining Records, registered by year, book, and page and indexed.

59. Fred Steen to Mrs. Florence Wittenberg Butler, Tonopah, n.d. (circa 1945), courtesy of William Pettite; Raymond, *George Wingfield*, 28–29, 28on9; Dwayne Kling, *The Rise of the Biggest Little City: An Encyclopedic History of Reno Gaming, 1931–1981*, 1, 57, 106; Pettite to the author, Fair Oaks, Calif., July 25, 2001, September 1, 2003.

60. Abelman's claims included camps at Weepah, Round Mountain, Manhattan, Bellehelen, and Gilbert as well as at Beatty and Rhyolite in the Bullfrog Mining District. Several other of his properties near Tolicha Peak (now in the heart of the Nellis Air Force Bombing and Gunnery Range) also proved profitable. See the indexed Nye and Esmeralda County Mining Records.

61. Charlotte L. Nay (née Stimler) to William Pettite, Winnemucca, September 16, 1967, copy courtesy of William Pettite; Shawn Hall, *Preserving the Glory Days: Ghost Towns and Mining Camps of Nye County, Nevada*, 32; *Tonopah Times-Bonanza* and *Goldfield News*, June 1, 2000, 1; Herman W. Albert, *Odyssey of a Desert Prospector*, 252–53; *NSJ*, December 16, 1951, 2:1. See also Albert Woods Moe, *Nevada's Golden Age of Gambling*, 96; and Pettite to the author (with a map of Abelman's holdings), Fair Oaks, Calif., received July 31, 2003. Charles F. Wittenberg, future Nye County state senator (1939 and 1941), was Abelman's mining partner.

62. Audrey Marie Porter's possible Jewish lineage is based solely on the names of her living relatives. Her siblings included Mrs. Sam Diamond and Mrs. Theo Sheidler of Seattle. Audrey Abelman died of pneumonia in Reno on December 7, 1932 (*REG*, December 7, 1932, 12:1). Her burial services were conducted by Baptist minister Brewster Adams.

63. *GN*, June 9, 1905, 3.

64. *Goldfield Daily Tribune*, August 15, 1907.

65. Hattie Baruch married Joseph Olcovich, brother to the Carson City merchants. See Marschall, "House of Olcovich," 179, 188n32.

66. Raymond, *George Wingfield*, 52–65, 81; Zanjani, *Goldfield*, 67. For an interested insider's view of the Baruch-Nixon-Wingfield partnership, see George Graham Rice (Jacob Simon Herzig), *My Adventures with Your Money*, 189–90, 196–98.

67. *Syracuse Evening Herald*, April 20, 1895, 1:5.

68. Rice, *My Adventures*, 1, 11–12, 53–56, 118–23.

69. *Rawhide Rustler*, October 24, 1908, 2:4.

70. Elliott, *History of Nevada*, 221.

71. *Rawhide Rustler*, October 24, 1908, 3:4, 4:2; *Rawhide Daily Press*, February

4, 1908, 4:6; November 6, 1908, 4:3, 6. Frieman had no permanent Nevada address, while getting an occasional visit from his wife. See *Rawhide Press Times*, May 6, 1910, 4:1; U.S. Bureau of the Census, *U.S. Census Records, State of Nevada, 1910, 1920*; and *Rawhide, Fallon, and Vicinity City Business Directory, 1908–1909*, 23, 36, 38, 44, 56.

72. Hulse, *Silver State*, 174–75; Elliott, *History of Nevada*, 225, 228–29.

73. U.S. Bureau of the Census, *U.S. Census Records, State of Nevada, 1910*. Concerning Sam Bernstein, see *NSJ*, September 20, 1924, 8:1. Milton Glick, interview by author, Reno, October 18, 2006. Bloom, wife Clara, and daughter Cora were not certainly Jewish.

74. U.S. Bureau of the Census, *U.S. Census Records, State of Nevada, 1920*; *WPN*, November 6, 1910, 2; *Nevada State Gazetteer and Business Directory, 1914–1915*, 112.

75. *NSJ*, November 29, 1924, 2:7; January 5, 1926, 1:3; January 11, 1926, 5.2.

76. The Bergman son was bar mitzvahed but became a Muslim. The remaining descendants are not religious (Betty Akert Brown, granddaughter of Ben and Sadie Bergman, conversations with author, Reno, November 17, 29, 2004).

77. Elliott, *History of Nevada*, 231. For Herzig/Rice's version, see Rice, *My Adventures*, 246–48.

78. *Engineering and Mining Journal*, July 30, 1921, as cited in Rice, *My Adventures*, 18, 19–22.

79. *Goldfield Daily Tribune*, as cited in Rice, *My Adventures*, 16.

Chapter 9. Building a Tourist Economy and a Permanent Synagogue, 1897–1946

1. *State of Nevada, Journal of the Senate, 1903*, 10, 146. For the complex politics of water, see Elliott, *History of Nevada*, 175–209. On prizefighting, see Allen Bodner, *When Boxing Was a Jewish Sport*, 7–9.

2. Kelly, *First Directory*, 57; Angel, *History of Nevada*, 258–59, 377; Wren, *History of the State*, 259. See *Ex Parte A. Livingston*.

3. Willa Oldham to Eileen Cohen, communicated to the author, July 1997.

4. Clark, *Journals of Doten*, 3:1946–47. See also Elliott, *History of Nevada*, 200; and *Statutes of the State of Nevada, 1897*, 2:12.

5. Elliott, *History of Nevada*, 175–77, 201–6; *Journal of the Senate of the Nineteenth Session of the Legislature of the State of Nevada, 1899*, 88, 94.

6. Guy Rocha and Eric Moody, "Marvin Hart vs. Jack Root: The Heavyweight Championship Fight That Time Forgot," 12–14; Elliott, *History of Nevada*, 200.

7. For a picture of Samuel Berger sparring with Jeffries at a Reno arena in 1910, see "A Western Picture Parade," 172. See also William D. Rowley, *Reno: Hub of the Washoe Country, an Illustrated History*, 37.

8. *REG*, May 2, 1940, 13:3; *NSJ*, May 3, 1940, 13:3.

9. For background on horse racing in northern Nevada, see Davis, *The History of Nevada*, 2:721–23.

10. *Journal of the Senate of the Twenty-seventh Session of the Legislature of the State of Nevada, 1915,* 64.

11. Rowley, *Reno,* 57; Elliott, *History of Nevada,* 285.

12. *Las Vegas Evening and Review Journal,* April 4, 1931, as cited in Elliott, *History of Nevada,* 282.

13. Rowley, *Reno,* 52–57.

14. Mella Rothwell Harmon, "Divorce and Economic Opportunity in Reno, Nevada, during the Great Depression," 84. Figures for the period are as follows: January 1, 1931–June 30, 1932, 7,123 total divorces in Nevada, 5,642 in Washoe County; July 1, 1932–June 30, 1934, 7,161 total, with 5,281 in Washoe County; and July 1, 1934–June 30, 1936, 8,515 and 6,102, respectively.

15. King Features, 1933, undated newspaper clipping in Felice Cohn Papers, Scrapbook, NHS.

16. John Sanford (no friend of Sam Platt), interview by author, Reno, December 29, 1981. Platt's clients included the Standard Oil Company of California, Bell Telephone Company, and the Reconstruction Finance Corporation, which raised his visibility as a potential divorce lawyer for the rich and famous. He and his partner's reputations for discretion and protection from unwanted attention led to their handling the divorce actions of Anna Roosevelt Dall and Rachel and Cornelius Vanderbilt Jr. (Sylvia Olcott, interview by author, Santa Rosa, August 14, 2001). For more on divorce issues, see Rowley, *Reno,* 36–39, 47; and Raymond, *George Wingfield,* 127–28, 130–31.

17. Sally Zanjani, *The Unspiked Rail: Memoir of a Nevada Rebel,* 246; Sylvia G. Olcott (Platt's niece) to the author, Santa Rosa, June 13, 1999; IOBB Lodge no. 760, "Minute Book Commencing January 1933 to September 27, 1951," entry June 14, 1944, WJHC. There are discrepancies concerning Helen Marks Faith Platt's birth date and cause of death (*NSJ*, June 8, 1934, 2; Olcott, interview; Maggie Tomoszyk, grandniece of Helen Platt, to the author, June 29, 2003).

18. *REG,* February 28, 1921; Works Progress Administration, Nevada, "Jewish Congregation of the Temple Emanu-El, 1921," Collection 206, Box 2/2, AJA. See also Julius Stein, *Synagogue Life in Northern Nevada,* 36–39.

19. For more detail on temple matters, see Earl, "'A House to Offer Our Prayers'" and Stein, *Synagogue Life,* 40–41, 46.

20. *NSJ,* September 2, 1922, 8:21; September 10, 1922, 2:1–2; "Temple Emanu-El Church, 1914 . . . ," Works Progress Administration report, 1935, AJA. See also Stein, *Synagogue Life,* 47.

21. Julius L. Jacobs, "Story of the Jacobs (Jacobowicz) Family," January 5, 1995, 7, typed copy to the author courtesy of Mervin Tarlow.

22. Mervin Tarlow to the author, Torrance, Calif., July 17, 2000, September 9, 2002; Mervin Tarlow, interview by author, Reno, August 19, 2002. There is evidence of a short-lived kosher delicatessen in 1958 at 26 West Second Street—a location sur-

rounded by Jewish establishments (Stein, *Synagogue Life*, 58). Pearl Tarlow's obituary credits her as being the "operator" of the Center Street guest house (*REG*, June 2, 1959, 11:2).

23. Mervin Israel Tarlow and wife Frances Tarlow, interview by author, Reno, August 19, 2002.

24. IOBB Lodge no. 760, "Minute Book," entries October 12, 1939, January 25, 1940, March 26, 1942, WJHC.

25. Sam Frank (mayor) to Rabbi Opochinsky [*sic*], Reno, February 2, 1934; William J. Kane, acting inspector in charge, U.S. Department of Labor, Immigration and Naturalization Service, to Rabbi H. A. Tarlow, Reno, April 25, 1939; August C. Frohlich (mayor) to Rabbi H. A. Tarlow, Reno, August 5, 1941; Moses A. Leavitt, secretary, American Jewish Distribution Committee, Inc., to Rabbi Harry A. Tarlow, New York, December 19, 1944, copies courtesy of Mervin Tarlow.

26. Mella Harmon to Susan James, Reno, April 25, 2001, copy to the author.

27. The original membership consisted of Olga and Don Berman, Leah and Bill Garell, Rowena and Leo Ginsburg, Ed and Laura Ginsburg, Bert Goldwater and his sister Sylvia Anapolsky, Abe and Rae Melner, Lilian and Paul Rubin, and Isobel and Jack Sloat (Ruth Dickens, "A History of Reform Judaism in Reno," *Temple Sinai Newsletter*, July 1993, 2).

28. Goldwater to Elwood H. Beemer, clerk, Reno, February 16, 1940, "Reno, Nev. Assoc. . . . ," Correspondence Box, AJA.

29. Ruth Dickens, interview by author, Reno, June 6, 1981.

30. *Passover Seder Service* (pamphlet), April 19, 1943; Arthur Berman to Rabbi Harry Tarlow, Los Angeles, October 15, 1943, copies to the author, courtesy of Mervin Tarlow.

31. Stein, *Synagogue Life*, 50–51.

32. Morgenstern to Samuelson, Cincinnati, February 19, 1946; Samuelson to Morgenstern, Reno, February 27, 1946, MS Collection no. 5, Box 21, Folder 10, AJA.

33. Morgenstern to Samuelson, Cincinnati, March 13, 1946; Morgenstern to Samuelson, Cincinnati, April 15, 1946; Samuelson to Morgenstern, Reno, April 20, 1946, in ibid.

34. Mrs. Frank died on November 14, 1931. See Scrugham, *Nevada*, 3:507–8; and *REG*, December 18, 1950, 13:5.

35. Eddie Ginsberg, interview by author, Reno, June 29, 1982; *REG*, June 28, 1937, 14:4–5.

36. Carol Coleman, "On the National Register of Historic Places: The El Cortez Hotel," 7; Kling, *Rise of the Biggest Little City*, 45–46; Scrugham, *Nevada*, 3:434; *REG*, December 30, 1949, 9:4; *NSJ*, April 4, 1951, 10:2.

37. *REG*, April 1, 1929, 10:6; *NSJ*, May 30, 1964, 8:4; Kling, *Rise of the Biggest Little City*, 46, 133, 172; Judge Bert Goldwater, interview by author, Reno, July 17, 2002; Mel

Gordon, interview by author, Reno, July 23, 2001; IOBB Lodge no. 760, "Minute Book," January 1933, first entry, WJHC.

38. Kling, *Rise of the Biggest Little City*, 1; Pettite to the author, Fair Oaks, Calif., December 1, 2000, July 13, 2003.

39. Raymond, *George Wingfield*, 166–67, 194–95.

40. Kling, *Rise of the Biggest Little City*, 149–50.

41. *REG*, December 7, 1932, 12:1; *NSJ*, December 10, 1932, 8; Pettite to the author, Fair Oaks, Calif., September 27, 2000.

42. Concerning Wingfield's financial woes from 1931 to 1935 and his subsequent full ownership of the ranch, see Raymond, *George Wingfield*, 231–37, 166–67. Concerning Abelman's purchase of the property (identified in the following only as the former E. E. Roberts ranch), see *REG*, August 19, 1935, 2:5. For Abelman's Riverside lease arrangements, see Kling, *Rise of the Biggest Little City*, 140; and Pettite to the author, January 20, 2007.

43. The previous two paragraphs are based on a half-dozen letters from Abelman's nephew William Pettite to the author. They are all cited elsewhere. For Abelman's obituary, see *NSJ*, December 16, 1951, 2:1.

44. Stacher was deported to Israel in 1960. Eric N. Moody, "The Early Years of Casino Gambling in Nevada, 1931–1945," 181, 186; Warren Nelson, *Always Bet on the Butcher: Warren Nelson and Casino Gaming, 1930s–1980s*, 63–64; Kling, *Rise of the Biggest Little City*, 57–58.

45. Kling, *Rise of the Biggest Little City*, 25–27, 179; Ginsberg, interview; Goldwater, interview.

46. Alan Balboni, *Beyond the Mafia: Italian Americans and the Development of Las Vegas*, 16; Kling, *Rise of the Biggest Little City*, 1, 27, 138; Eugene P. Moehring, *Resort City in the Sun Belt: Las Vegas, 1930–1970*, 48; *LVRJ*, June 4, 1948, 3.

47. Kling, *Rise of the Biggest Little City*, 104, 141, 174; Goldwater, interview.

48. Gordon, interview; Goldwater, interview; Kling, *Rise of the Biggest Little City*, 83, 125.

49. Kling, *Rise of the Biggest Little City*, 1, 83, 104, 174, 179.

Chapter 10. The Early Years of Las Vegas, 1905–1955

1. Carlson, *Nevada Place Names*, 152.

2. Solomon Nunes Carvalho, *Incidents of Travel and Adventure in the Far West*, chap. 35, p. 295.

3. Ibid., chap. 17, p. 170; chap. 18, p. 177; chap. 20, p. 189. One of the more accessible translations (though unpaginated) is available on the Internet at http://www.jewish-history.com/WildWest/carvalho.

4. Moehring, *Resort City*, 1.

5. Hulse, *Lincoln County*, 62; Moehring, *Resort City*, 2–4, 11; Carlson, *Nevada*

Place Names, 152. See also Eugene P. Moehring and Michael S. Green, *Las Vegas: A Centennial History,* 12–13.

6. *Rhyolite Herald,* December 28, 1906; July 7, 1905. See edition of October 13, 1905, for a reference to a tailor named Samuels and December 2, 1906. Cohen, Cohn, and Samuels were likely Jewish, but there is no evidence yet of their Jewish activity or affiliation in Rhyolite or elsewhere in Nevada. For Adolph Levy, see *LVA,* March 10, 1906, 1:2.

7. The quotes and biographical snapshot of Levy are based on U.S. Bureau of the Census, *U.S. Census Records, State of Nevada, 1910; LVA,* March 10, 1906, 1:2; March 24, 1906, 1:2; March 31, 1906, 1:2; April 7, 1906, 2:1; and April 14, 1906, 2:1. Las Vegas was not incorporated until 1909, when Clark County was carved out of Lincoln County, and Las Vegas became the county seat (Moehring, *Resort City,* 9; Moehring and Green, *Las Vegas,* 21, 36, 53).

8. Michael Green, "History of Las Vegas Jews Links Past and Present," *JR,* March 22, 2002, 4–5.

9. U.S. Bureau of the Census, *U.S. Census Records, State of Nevada, 1910; LVA,* April 26, 1913, 1:2; September 15, 1914, 6:6.

10. C[harles] P. Squires, "Clark County," in Davis, *The History of Nevada,* 2:802–3; Moehring and Green, *Las Vegas,* 60–61.

11. *LVA,* September 30, 1932, 1:6; Green, "History of Las Vegas Jews," 5; Charles Salton, interview by author, Las Vegas, May 8, 2001; U.S. Bureau of the Census, *U.S. Census Records, State of Nevada, 1910, 1920.*

12. Charles Salton, interview by author, Las Vegas, February 14, 2001; Ralph Denton with Michael S. Green and R. T. King, *A Liberal Conscience: Ralph Denton, Nevadan,* 8; Clifford C. Walton, "Capitol's Who's Who for Nevada," 271.

13. Moehring, *Resort City,* 16–18.

14. Salton, interviews.

15. Valerie Wiener, interview by author, Carson City, May 5, 2005; Salton, interview, February 14, 2001; *LVA,* November 29, 1932, 1:2, announcing Roberta Gordon's birth.

16. *LVS,* January 27, 1963, 4–5.

17. Balboni, *Beyond the Mafia,* 16, 140n65, in which he cites Mack's casino investments from 1947 to 1950; Melvin Moss to the author, San Diego, September 25, 2000.

18. Salton, interview, February 14, 2001. For more on Jewish linkages, see Green, "History of Las Vegas Jews," 5.

19. *LVA,* February 1, 1933, 6:4; September 12, 1933, 2:3–4; September 16, 1933, 1:3; March 1, 1935.

20. Wiener, interview. See also Sandy Mallin, dedication of Temple Beth Sholom, September 24, 2000, Jewish Emigration Archives, UNLVSC, copy to the author courtesy of Professor Michael Green; *LVA,* March 23, 1932, 2:4; September 30, 1932, 1:6;

Charles Salton, conversation with author, May 16, 2001; and Reba Saiger, telephone interview, October 8, 2001.

21. Moehring, *Resort City,* 8–13, 33–35.

22. Michael Green, "The Jews," 165; Deborah Dash Moore, *To the Golden Cities: Pursuing the American Jewish Dream in Miami and L.A.,* 13–19.

23. Salton, conversation.

24. Moss to the author, San Diego, September 25, 2003.

25. *LVS Sunday Magazine,* January 27, 1963, 4–5; Salton, interviews; Melvin Moss and David Zenoff, interview by author, San Diego, February 28, 2001. Mack included Hank Greenspun in his list of associates building the Jewish Community Center, but Greenspun did not arrive in Las Vegas until late 1946. Apparently, he meant to acknowledge Greenspun's financial help in building Temple Beth Sholom some years later.

26. Rudolph Glanz, *Jew and Italian: Historic Group Relations and the New Immigration, 1881–1924,* 137. The New York *Bollettino Della Sera* urged its readers, "Let us do as the Jews do. Do we not all see the giant strides which the Hebrew element is making in their growing influence in this country?" as cited in Glanz, *Jew and Italian,* 137–38; see also p, 148 for a more modern assessment of the Italians' views of Jewish successes.

27. Glanz, *Jew and Italian,* 9–10, 38, 85–88, 145; Sorin, *Time for Building,* 146.

28. For a recent study of the fire, see David Von Drehle, *Triangle: The Fire That Changed America.*

29. Heribert [*sic*] Jone and Urban Adelman, *Moral Theology,* 56–57, 206–7; Glanz, *Jew and Italian,* 74; Sorin, *Time for Building,* 80.

30. See, for example, Yanki Tauber, "The Purim Drunk," on the Lubavitch Chabad Internet home page at http://www.chabad.org/holidays/purim/article.asp?AID'2814.

31. Glanz, *Jew and Italian,* 78–80; Lindsay Denison, "The Black Hand," *Everybody's Magazine* 19 (September 1908): 292, 300, as noted in Glanz, *Jew and Italian,* 81.

32. Neil Cowan and Ruth S. Cowan, *Our Parents' Lives: The Americanization of East European Jews,* 66, as cited in Sorin, *Time for Building,* 81; Mike Gold, *Jews without Money,* 6, as quoted in Sorin, *Time for Building,* 85.

33. Moehring, *Resort City,* 52–54.

34. Beatrice Sedway, interview, May 23, 1992, as cited in W. R. Wilkerson III, *The Man Who Invented Las Vegas,* 51–52, 73. See also Green, "The Jews," 165; and Hal Rothman, *Neon Metropolis: How Las Vegas Started the Twenty-first Century,* 12, 127. Other local Jews investing in Siegel- and Sedway-controlled properties were Dr. Marty Bernstein with the Rex Club in 1946 and theater owner Art Brick, who owned part of the Golden Nugget before Siegel's Flamingo opened. See Balboni, *Beyond the Mafia,* 16.

35. Moehring and Green, *Las Vegas,* 111; Wilkerson, *Man Who Invented Las Vegas,* 49, 66.

36. Wilkerson, interview by Greg Bautzer, May 5, 1972, in Wilkerson, *Man Who Invented Las Vegas*, 62.

37. Jerry Hirsch, "An Exodus to Vegas," *Los Angeles Times Calendar*, May 13, 2003, E12; Moehring, *Resort City*, 49. See also the reminiscences of Arthur M. Smith Jr., *Let's Get Going: From Oral History Interviews with Arthur M. Smith Jr., a Narrative Interpretation, by R. T. King*, 90.

38. Balboni, *Beyond the Mafia*, 27; Balboni, "Southern Italians and Eastern European Jews: Cautious Cooperation in Las Vegas Casinos, 1940–1967," 153.

39. Moehring, *Resort City*, 70, 87; Dick Odessky, *Fly on the Wall: Recollections of Las Vegas' Good Old Bad Old Days*, 110–12; Alan Balboni, "Moe Dalitz: Controversial Founding Father of Modern Las Vegas," 30; Balboni, "Southern Italians," 160.

40. For a summary of the committee's emergence and opposition, see Sally Denton and Roger Morris, *The Money and the Power: The Making of Las Vegas and Its Hold on America, 1947–2000*, 79–85; and Moehring, *Resort City*, 52–54.

41. Dalitz's history of legal and illegal activities has been well chronicled. Two recent biographical sketches based on previously documented information are Balboni, "Moe Dalitz"; and John L. Smith, "Moe Dalitz and the Desert."

42. Balboni, "Moe Dalitz," 25–28; Denton and Morris, *Money and Power*, 46–47; Ed Reid and Ovid Demaris, *The Green Felt Jungle*, 54, as cited in Ronald A. Farrell and Carole Case, *The Black Book and the Mob: The Untold Story of the Control of Nevada's Casinos*, 25.

43. Moss and Zenoff, interview; Moehring, *Resort City*, 88–89; Denton and Morris, *Money and Power*, 107–9.

44. Cited from the record in Denton and Morris, *Money and Power*, 111.

45. John L. Smith, "Moe Dalitz and the Desert," 37; Denton and Morris, *Money and Power*, 113.

46. Ed Vogel, "First Gaming Regulator Looks Back," *LVRJ*, June 10, 1990, B7, as noted in Farrell and Case, *Black Book*, 26.

47. Farrell and Case, *Black Book*, 25. See also *LVRJ*, May 1, 1951, 1.

48. See Hank Greenspun with Alex Pelle, *Where I Stand: The Record of a Reckless Man*; Michael S. Green, "Hank Greenspun: Where He Stood," 74–95; Denton and Morris, *Money and Power*, 59–74.

49. "Pack everything, baby, and come on out! We won't be going back" was the much quoted invitation (Greenspun with Pelle, *Where I Stand*, 53, 68; Denton and Morris, *Money and Power*, 59–61; Green, "Hank Greenspun," 78).

50. Greenspun with Pelle, *Where I Stand*, 67, 71, 82–83.

51. Greenspun devoted almost a third of his autobiography to his involvement with Israel's security and his subsequent indictment (ibid., 80–181, 193ff).

52. Denton and Morris, *Money and Power*, 60, 64, 67–69; Green, "Hank Greenspun," 80–81, 87, 92, 95; Moehring, *Resort City*, 90.

53. Edward S. Shapiro, *A Time for Healing: American Jewry since World War II*, 63–64.

54. Gordon, interview. Gordon had a small used-merchandise store on Commercial Row across from the train station.

55. Odessky, *Fly on the Wall*, 112. The United Jewish Appeal in Reno during the same period was headed by Temple Emanu-El board members—none of whom were involved in the casino industry.

56. Moehring, *Resort City*, 76; Balboni, "Southern Italians," 160–61; Joel Fleekop, "Jews Wandering in the Desert: A History of the Jewish Community of Las Vegas," 45–46.

Chapter 11. Building a Temple, Keeping a Rabbi, and Schisms North and South, 1950–1980

1. Edythe Katz Yarchever, interviews by author, Las Vegas, February 14, April 5, 2001; Salton, interview, May 8, 2001.

2. Salton, interview, May 8, 2001; Moss and Zenoff, interview; "Temple Beth Sholom Files," UNLVSC.

3. Denton and Morris, *Money and Power*, 133; Farrell and Case, *Black Book*, 49.

4. Moss and Zenoff, interview; Yarchever interview, April 5, 2001.

5. Moss, interview; Moss, telephone conversation, March 11, 2001.

6. Moehring, *Resort City*, 78.

7. Melvin Moss, conversation with author, March 13, 2001.

8. Balboni, "Southern Italians," 161; Moss to the author, San Diego, March 17, 19, 2001.

9. Yarchever, interview, April 5, 2001. For an undocumented allegation that Entratter was a bagman for the Mob, see Rothman, *Neon Metropolis*, 13–15, 180, 311.

10. Yarchever, interviews, February 14, April 5, 2001, January 8, 2005; Charles Salton and Adele Baratz, interview by author, Las Vegas, May 8, 2001. See also Susan Berman, *Easy Street*, 32–34. The date of the Costello shooting was May 2, 1957.

11. *NSJ*, January 11, 1968, 3:7; Donald H. Harrison, "Golden Years: The Life and Times of Rabbi Aaron Gold," *San Diego Jewish Press-Heritage*, April 6, 2001, 1–11; Donald H. Harrison, "The Golden Touch: Rabbi Aaron Gold's Western Exodus Continues, from Las Vegas to San Diego," *San Diego Jewish Press-Heritage*, April 13, 2001, as reprinted in *LVI*, July 6, 2001, 40; Oscar Goodman, interview by author, Las Vegas, December 20, 2004.

12. The debacle contributed to Aaron Gold's divorce from his wife Rita, with whom he had four children. He remarried and secured a position at San Diego's Tifereth Israel Synagogue, where he served for eighteen years (*NSJ*, September 18, 1972, 10; September 16, 1977, 16; Moss and Zenoff, interview; Rabbi Mel Hecht, conversation

with author, January 3, 2005; Yarchever, conversation with author, Las Vegas, January 5, 2005; Harrison, "Golden Years," 1).

13. Moss and Zenoff, interview.

14. IOBB Lodge no. 760, "Minute Book," entry November 6, 1947, 241, WJHC. See also Frances Steiner Tarlow to the author, Torrance, Calif., July 15, 2003; Mervin Tarlow to the author, Torrance, Calif., January 27, 2005.

15. "Reno, Temple Emanu-El," AJA.

16. IOBB Lodge no. 760, "Minute Book," entry February 27, 1948, 247, WJHC.

17. Ibid., May 25, June 29, November 1, 1950.

18. Membership Meeting Bulletin and certificate, November 14, 1950, MSS Col. 244, AJA.

19. Harry Tarlow died in Los Angeles in 1986 (Frances Steiner Tarlow to the author, Torrance, Calif., July 15, 2003; Mervin Tarlow to the author, Torrance, Calif., January 27, 2005).

20. Stein, *Synagogue Life*, 56–59, 63.

21. Dickens, "History," September 1993, 6; Robert Dickens, interview by author, Reno, June 1, 2004. Other interviewees were both critical and supportive of Weinberg.

22. Dickens, "History," July 1993, 6; Stein, *Synagogue Life*, 59.

23. Dickens, "History," July 1993, 6; Ethel Jaffe, interview by author, Reno, September 16, 2003.

24. Ruth Dickens, interview.

25. *NSJ*, May 25, 1963, 3:3–4; September 8, 1963, 7:5; Dickens, "History," August 1993, 5.

26. Stein, *Synagogue Life*, 63–64.

27. John P. Marschall, "Nevada's First Synagogue: Temple Emanu-El, 1921," 5; Michael Melner, interview by author, Reno, April 28, 2005.

28. Stein, *Synagogue Life*, 68–69.

29. Rabbi Keller, conversation with author, Reno, n.d.; Dr. Leonard Shapiro, conversation with author, Reno, January 11, 2005; Gordon, interview; Stein, *Synagogue Life*, 67, 70–71. On Bovit, see *RGJ*, April 9, 2005, A3; and April 19, 2005, A7:5.

30. Janet Shapiro, "Temple Emanu-El," *RGJ*, April 19, 2005, A7.

31. Dickens, "History," September 1993, 4, 7; Stein, *Synagogue Life*, 61.

32. Robert Dickens, interview.

33. Jaffe, interview; Dickens, "History," December 1993, 2; Stein, *Synagogue Life*, 61. Feinberg's community contributions will be discussed in a later chapter.

34. *LVI*, May 27, 1966, 1; March 15, 1968, 1; May 5, 1972, 11; May 12, 1972, 5; November 8, 1974, 1; April 23, 1976, 23. All of these references are cited in Fleekop, "Jews Wandering," 72–73.

35. Yarchever, interviews, February 14, April 5, 2001; Salton, interview, February 15, 2001.

36. Harry Alter and David Shaw of Temple Ner Tamid authored two independent short institutional histories of the congregation. Shaw's work is "Congregation Ner Tamid: an Unofficial History." Alter's manuscript is untitled and will be cited as "Ner Tamid." Weisberg graduated from Brandeis University and the Hebrew College Institute of Religion. He was accompanied to Las Vegas by his wife, Devorah, and their four children (Alter, "Ner Tamid," 3).

37. Rabbi Mel Hecht, telephone conversation, January 3, 2005.

38. Denton and Morris, *Money and Power*, 331–44; Milton I. Schwartz, interview by author, Las Vegas, March 23, 2005; Yarchever, conversation with author, February 9, 2005; Green, "The Jews," 171.

Chapter 12. Antisemitism in the Twentieth Century

1. Throughout this book, I have chosen to use the term *antisemitism* rather than *anti-Semitism*. I agree with James Parkes, A. Roy Eckardt, and Leonard Dinnerstein that the latter term implies a hostility toward some imagined "Semitism." As used in this book, *antisemitism* means hostility to Jews simply because they are Jews. Accordingly, it is possible that Semitic groups, such as Arabs, could be antisemitic—but not "anti-Semitic." See James Parkes, *The Conflict of the Church and the Synagogue: A Study in the Origins of Antisemitism;* A. Roy Eckardt, *Your People, My People: The Meeting of Jews and Christians*, xi–xii; and Dinnerstein, *Antisemitism in America*, ix. Likewise, "anti-Judaism" is more properly a hostility toward the Jewish religion and therefore distinct from the prejudice against a people. For more on these distinctions, see Carroll, *Constantine's Sword*, 22, 28, 40, 274, 348, 382. Regarding Nevada's foreign-born population, see Elliott, *History of Nevada*, 382–33.

2. Henry Feingold, *A Time for Searching: Entering the Mainstream, 1920–1945,* 226–28, 295n1, for a brief bibliography on the debate over American Jewry's response to the Holocaust. A controversial work on the Holocaust is Peter Novick, *The Holocaust in American Life.* For a crushing rebuttal to Novick's thesis that the Holocaust was not publicly remembered until after 1967, see Hasia R. Diner, "Post–World War II American Jewry and the Confrontation with Catastrophe."

3. Sparks to Newlands, January 9, 1905, Newlands Papers, Box 11, NHS.

4. M. Badt, *Interview with Milton Badt*, 5–6.

5. Mark Twain, "Concerning the Jews," *Harper's*, March 1898, 531–32, 534–35, as cited in Dinnerstein, *Antisemitism in America*, 56–57.

6. Shapiro, *Time for Healing*, 15–16.

7. Feingold, *Time for Searching*, 11.

8. Goldwater, interview; Mervin and Frances Tarlow, interview by author, Reno, August 19, 2002.

9. *JP*, San Francisco, April 10, 1896, 4:1, as quoted in Stern and Kramer, "Anti-Semitism and the Jewish Image in the Early West," 105.

10. Lynn Dumenil, *Freemasonry and American Culture, 1880–1930*, 70.

11. Dinnerstein, *Antisemitism in America,* 81–82; William L. Fox, *Lodge of the Double-Headed Eagle: Two Centuries of Scottish Rite Freemasonry in America's Southern Jurisdiction,* 250.

12. The situation was similar in northern California. See Levinson, *Jews in California Gold Rush,* 64; and Tony Fels, "Religious Assimilation in a Fraternal Organization: Jews and Freemasonry in Gilded-Age San Francisco," *American Jewish History* 24 (June 1985): 376, 393, as cited in Pomeroy, "On Becoming a Westerner," 206n30; and Joseph Friedman, "Jewish Participation in California Gold Rush Era Freemasonry."

13. REG, October 13, 1921, as cited in Earl, "'A House to Offer Our Prayers,'" 52–53.

14. Olcott, interview; "Centennial Speech of Samuel Platt at the Anniversary Ceremonies of Carson Lodge, no. 1, F. & A.M.," February 13, 1962, p. 5, manuscript copy in possession of the author.

15. Craig F. Swallow, "The Ku Klux Klan in Nevada during the 1920s," 208–10.

16. Ibid., 217–19, on the Elko and Las Vegas Klaverns.

17. Zanjani, *Unspiked Rail,* 245. See Raymond, *George Wingfield,* 186, on Wingfield's later support.

18. Pete Petersen to Pat McCarran, October 25, 1940, as cited in Jerome E. Edwards, *Pat McCarran: Political Boss of Nevada,* 98.

19. NSJ, November 10, 1940, 1; Guy Rocha and Dennis Myers, "Pittman on Ice." See also Betty Glad, *Key Pittman: The Tragedy of a Senate Insider,* 55, 307.

20. NSJ, April 25, 1943, 13; Goldwater, interview by author, Reno, December 1, 2000; Sanford, interview; NSJ, November 1, 1940, 9:5–6; November 6, 1940, 8:1.

21. "The Personal Diary of Clel Georgetta," vol. 13, 1928, August 30–31, 1928, arranged by dates, in Washoe County Library, Downtown Reno Branch, Special Collections.

22. Ibid., vol. 25, 1940, entries for February 16, 17, 21, October 28, 1940.

23. Ibid., November 10, 1940.

24. *Political History of Nevada,* 185, 234, 301.

25. Tarlow, interview. See also Raymond, *George Wingfield,* 256–58; and Elliott, *History of Nevada,* 301–5.

26. Petersen to McCarran, January 6, 1950, as cited in Edwards, *Pat McCarran,* 139.

27. McCarran to Mrs. McCarran, October 20, 1952, as cited in Edwards, *Pat McCarran,* 180. For more on post–World War II antisemitism, see Shapiro, *Time for Healing,* 4–16.

28. A recent biographer of McCarran characterized his antisemitism as "casual"—and typical of the times (Michael J. Ybarra, *Washington Gone Crazy: Senator Pat McCarran and the Great American Communist Hunt,* 286, 697). Green, "Hank Greenspun," 81–86; Eddie Ginsberg, interview by author, Reno, June 15, 1982. Polish-born Mort Saiger was vice president of Temple Beth Sholom, casino greeter, and

one-time "Pony Express" carrier of the Last Frontier's mail to the post office (Saiger, *An Interview with Morton Saiger, Conducted by R. T. King*, vi, 1, 20, 30–31).

29. Robert M. Gorrell, *University Growing Up: Rambling Reminiscences of an English Professor and Administrator, 1945–1980*, 381–82; Robert M. Gorrell, conversation with author, March 12, 2004; Richard Siegel, conversation with author, March 2, 2004; George Herman, conversation with author, March 13, 2004. For more on discrimination against faculty elsewhere, see Dinnerstein, *Antisemitism in America*, 86–89, 158–62; and Shapiro, *Time for Healing*, 97–99.

30. Gorrell, *University Growing Up*, 381–32; UCCSN Board of Regents' Meeting Minutes, Reno, September 20–21, 1947, "Personnel, English #5."

31. Judy Nash to the author, Reno, June 16, 2004.

32. Novick, *Holocaust in American Life*, 113, 170; Shapiro, *Time for Healing*, 7–12, 18–21. See also Stephen J. Whitfield, *In Search of American Jewish Culture*, 2, 59, 65, 69–70, 158–59; and Pamela S. Nadell, "On Their Own Terms: America's Jewish Women, 1954–2004," 394.

33. For a study of the effects of papal directives concerning biblical studies on Catholicism worldwide, see Darrell Jodock, ed., *Catholicism Contending with Modernity: Roman Catholic Modernism and Anti-modernism in Historical Context*, 104–5, 199–203, 223–25.

34. *Nostra Aetate* [Declaration on the Relationship of the Church to Non-Christian Religions], sec. 4 in Walter M. Abbott, S.J., ed., *The Documents of Vatican II*, 665–68. For a description of Paul VI's opposition to the decree, see Michael Phayer, *The Catholic Church and the Holocaust, 1930–1965*, 208–15.

35. Hulse, *University of Nevada*, 213–14. Feinberg was a high-profile civil rights advocate whose accomplishments will be treated in a later chapter.

36. Eileen Brookman, interview by author, Las Vegas, May 6, 2001. Founded in 1927, the organization has since changed its name to the National Conference for Community and Justice.

37. Moss to the author, March 19, 2001.

38. John E. Linnan, C.S.V., to the author, Bourbonnais, January 15, 2004. See also A. Smith, *Let's Get Going*, 85.

39. *LVS*, July 12, 1970, 3.

40. "A Man Among Men," *LVI*, June 19, 1970.

41. *JR*, January 9, 2004, 5–7; January 23, 2004, 5; Msgr. Leo McFadden, interview by author, Reno, March 11, 2004; George Brookman, conversation with author, Las Vegas, March 23, 2004.

42. *JR*, March 12, 2004, 5.

43. Goldwater, interview, July 17, 2002; James Kidder, interviews by author, Reno, February 21, 2004, April 28, 2005; Dinnerstein, *Antisemitism in America*, 156–57. See also Marianne Sanua, *Going Greek: Jewish College Fraternities in the United States, 1895–1945*, 42–45, 83–86, 181.

44. Garfinkle became a local high school principal. Melner was a lieutenant general in the U.S. Army and deputy chairman of the NATO Committee in Belgium. Marmor became an internationally acclaimed orthopedic surgeon. Leonard Marmor to the author, Los Angeles, April 17, 200; Richard Trachok, conversation with author, Reno, February 17, 2004; Melner, interview.

45. Judi Havas Kosinski, interview by author, Reno, April 18, 2004.

46. Moehring, *Resort City*, 74–75, 80.

47. Moss and Zenoff, interview. Zenoff died near his home at La Costa, Calif., in October 2006.

48. Ibid.

49. Dr. David R. Wasserman, as cited in *JR*, March 12, 2004, 12.

50. Sydell Miller, interview by author, Las Vegas, October 20, 2001.

51. Thomas R. C. Wilson, interview by author, Reno, January 3, 2001.

52. Assembly Bill 426 in Nevada Legislature, 54th Session, Assembly, vol. 3, Bills 350–540, resolutions arranged by bill numbers; *LVRJ*, March 9, 1967, 4:3, "Trailblazer" edition; *LVS*, March 8, 1967, 6:1. Brookman was born in Denver in 1921 to Mary and Max Milstein, whose maternal grandparents were from Odessa. The family moved to southern California, where Eileen attended her rabbi grandfather's Hebrew school. She married George Brookman and moved to Las Vegas in 1953 (Brookman, interview).

53. *LVRJ*, October 11, 1988, B1, B3; October 13, 1988, B1; Moss, interview by author, San Diego, August 4, 2001. Engelstad was born in 1920 of Belgian-Norwegian descent and raised Catholic. He moved from North Dakota in the early sixties and became a housing developer before opening the Imperial Palace in 1979 (Jeff Burbank, *License to Steal: Nevada's Gaming Control System in the Megaresort Age*, 65–66).

54. *LVRJ*, October 14, 1988, B1, B5; Burbank, *License to Steal*, 57, 64–66, 78.

55. *LVRJ*, January 6, 2000, available online at http://www.reviewjournal.com/lvrj_home/2000/Jan-06-Thu-2000.

56. *LVRJ*, July 15, 2000, available online at http://www.reviewjournal.com/lvrj_home/2000/Jul-15-Sat-2000.

57. E-mail from Rabbi Jonathan Freirich to all congregants, South Lake Tahoe, January 7, 2004.

58. Joseph and Virginia Kempler, interview by author, Reno, April 30, 2001.

59. Herb Jaffe, "Las Vegas Holocaust Survivors Tell the Hard Truth," *JR*, November 21, December 4, 19, 2003, 4. Katz Yarchever's Holocaust education program is described later.

Chapter 13. Civil Rights and Uncommon Causes

1. Michael Lerner and Cornel West, *Jews and Blacks: Let the Healing Begin*, 1.

2. Sarna, *American Judaism*, 308–11; L. Sandy Maisel, ed., *Jews in American Politics*, 7–8, 100, 115–16; Shapiro, *Time for Healing*, 223.

3. The origin of the "Mississippi" epithet is disputed. Rothman traces it to the wartime strike at Basic Magnesium, Inc., which was broken by bringing in black workers to undermine the Congress of Industrial Organizations, better known as the CIO (*Neon Metropolis*, 129). Others claim it was a name applied by blacks to Nevada in the 1950s, when there was renewed opposition to racism. See James W. Hulse, *Forty Years in the Wilderness: Impressions of Nevada, 1940–1980*, 91. William F. "Bob" Bailey personally claimed authorship of the phrase. See "Interview of William F. (Bob) Bailey," in Elizabeth Nelson Patrick, "The Black Experience in Southern Nevada," 220.

4. Marc Dollinger, *Quest for Inclusion: Jews and Liberalism in Modern America*, 6–11, 20–21, 173–180.

5. Townley, *Tough Little Town*, 232; Elmer R. Rusco, *"Good Time Coming?": Black Nevadans in the Nineteenth Century*, 35–37, 207; Hulse, *Silver State*, 307.

6. Moehring, *Resort City*, 173–79. On the NAACP, see Joseph Crowley, "Race and Residence: The Politics of Open Housing in Nevada," 119n1.

7. Elmer Rusco, interview by Ruth Dickens, Reno, February 25, 1993, Box CR 10, p. 8, Rusco Papers, NHS.

8. Charlotte Hunter Arley, interview by author, Reno, July 15, 2001.

9. Rusco, interview by Dickens, February 25, 1993, 8–10.

10. Dr. James B. McMillan, Gary E. Elliott, and R. T. King, *Fighting Back: A Life in the Struggle for Civil Rights*, 74, 79, 140; Woodrow Wilson, *Race, Community, and Politics in Las Vegas, 1940s–1980s*, 80, 84; Saiger, *Interview with Saiger*, 23. See also Moehring, *Resort City*, 182; and Hulse, *Forty Years in the Wilderness*, 91

11. Lubertha Johnson, *Civil Rights Efforts in Las Vegas, 1940s–1960s*, 38. A Julius F. Fox appears in the 1910 U.S. Census as Russian-born, of Polish-speaking parents, married ten years, forty-nine years old, and farming on First Street in Las Vegas. Florence McClure, a Las Vegas citizen since 1967 and author of a column titled "Herstory," names Abe Fox as the owner of Foxy's Firehouse restaurants, which were integrated (*LVRJ*, February 2, 1997, E3).

12. *LVRJ*, January 22, 1997, B1; October 9, 1944, 6; Dorothy Eisenberg to the author, April 15, 2004. Lloyd Katz was born in New York in 1919, son of Polish-born Benjamin Katz (b. 1878), who immigrated to New York in 1897 and shortly afterward married his wife, Bertha ("Lloyd Katz," Scrapbook, UNLVSC). Ira Goldring, one of Las Vegas's earliest permanent Jewish settlers, was the building contractor for the Huntridge theater. See also Green, "The Jews," 171.

13. Wanderer moved to Las Vegas in 1946 and became a civil rights activist. Her son, John, commented that her accomplishments were not easy for a Jewish woman in those days (*LVRJ*, March 4, 2005, available online at http://www.reviewjournal.com/lvrj_home/2005.

14. Kathleen M. Coles, ed., *Charlotte Hunter Arley*, 48–54, 69, 78, 80–81. Arley died in 2006.

15. *LVRJ*, February 19, 1953, 3:3.

16. *NSJ*, March 17, 1953, 2:3.

17. *LVRJ*, May 30, 1954, 19.

18. Wilson, *Race, Community, and Politics*, 80.

19. Rudiak has been credited with being the first chairman of the Nevada Equal Rights Commission. In fact, he was the third chairman, elected by commission members after his appointment in 1965. See Records of the Secretary of State, SEC-state 1038, Nevada State Library and Archives. Martha Gould stated that she resigned from the ACLU board because she could not "handle" Rudiak's abrasiveness (interview by author, Reno, March 5, 2004). See also Denton with Green and King, *Liberal Conscience*, 100, 178–79.

20. Earnest N. Bracey, "The Moulin Rouge Mystique: Blacks and Equal Rights in Las Vegas," 274.

21. Moehring, *Resort City*, 76, 182–83.

22. Gary Elliott, "James B. McMillan: The Pursuit of Equality," in Davies, *Maverick Spirit*, 53–54; McMillan, Elliott, and King, *Fighting Back*, 97–98; Moehring, *Resort City*, 184–85.

23. Sheila Goodman to the author, Golden Valley, Ariz., January 21, 2001; Moehring, *Resort City*, 186.

24. Elmer R. Rusco, "The Civil Rights Movement in Nevada," 76–77.

25. Goldwater, conversation with author, Reno, April 23, 2004. Goldwater was born in 1915. He was appointed a U.S. bankruptcy judge in 1979 from which he resigned to practice law until 1992. He was recalled by the U.S. Court of Appeals for the Ninth Circuit to serve as a U.S. bankruptcy judge on a year-to-year basis, which he did until his death in 2006 (see *RGJ*, May 6, 2006, C11). For Sawyer's opinion of Goldwater, see Grant Sawyer, *Hang Tough! Grant Sawyer, an Activist in the Governor's Mansion*, 149. See Records of the Secretary of State, SECstate 1038, and Governor Grant Sawyer Correspondence, GOV-0338, Equal Rights Commission, July 1, 1961, Nevada State Library and Archives; and Leslie B. Gray, "Nevada Beginnings in Civil Rights: A Memoir," 87–88.

26. Brookman, interview.

27. Rusco, "Civil Rights Movement," 79.

28. Goodman to the author, Golden Valley, Ariz., January 21, 2001; Katherine (Goodman) Selinsky to the author, Las Vegas, March 4, 2004; Moehring, *Resort City*, 199, 292n57.

29. Eleanore Bushnell, "Reapportionment and Responsibility," in *Sagebrush and Neon: Studies in Nevada Politics,* by Bushnell, 104–6, 116.

30. Goodman to the author, Golden Valley, Ariz., January 21, 2001; Rusco, "Civil Rights Movement," 78.

31. Crowley, "Race and Residence," 66–76; "Voting Records of Assembly and Senate: Nevada State Legislature, 1971"; Brookman, interview; McMillan, Elliott, and King, *Fighting Back*, 87–89; Moehring, *Resort City*, 199.

32. Marcus, *American Jewish Woman*, 157. For more detail on the early days of Jewish women's ordination, see Sarna, *American Judaism*, 338–44. For Betty Friedan's impact on Jewish women's groups, see Karla Goldman, *Beyond the Synagogue Gallery: Finding a Place for Women in American Judaism*, 213–15.

33. Blu Greenberg, *On Women and Judaism: A View from Tradition*, 27–28.

34. In 1868, Jackson advertised for the "Women's Rights Convention," *TE*, March 31, 1868, 2, as noted in Loverin and Nylen, "Creating a Fashionable Society," 125. Jean Ford and James W. Hulse, "The First Battle for Woman Suffrage in Nevada: Correcting and Expanding the Record, 1869–1871"; A. Watson, *Into Their Own*, 77–79.

35. Renee Diamond to the author, Las Vegas, April 19, 2004, 2; Marcus, *American Jewish Woman*, 158.

36. Nevadans for ERA, Inc., *Newsletter*, September 1978, edited by Beverly Funk and Barbara Blythin; Kimble to Barbara Weinberg, AAUW, Reno, March 8, 1974, Women's Political Caucus Papers, Box 86–26/IV/3, UNRSC.

37. "Remarks from the Floor," concerning Senate Joint Resolution no. 5 (Equal Rights Amendment), February 11, 1977, "Nevadans for ERA," Box 92–46, UNRSC.

38. Diamond to the author, April 19, 2004.

39. Dorothy Eisenberg to Barbara Weinberg, Las Vegas, April 4, 2004, copy to the author; Hulse, *Forty Years in the Wilderness*, 100.

40. Mylan Hawkins, interview by author, Reno, May 21, 2004. Hawkins was born Mylan Barin (formerly Baringoltz) in 1938 in Chicago and raised in the Reform tradition at Chicago's Temple Sholom from which she earned a scholarship to the Orthodox Yeshiva (Hebrew Theological College), which as a woman she was barred from attending. She received a degree from the University of Chicago and was a Hebrew religious-school teacher in Reno.

41. Deborah Achtenberg, interview by author, Reno, April 21, 2004. Achtenberg was born in Kansas, City, Missouri, in 1951. Her parents were Reform Jews active in Jewish and human rights organizations. She was a regular attendee at Jewish religious school. In Reno, Achtenberg also served on the board of the Stonewall Democrats of Northern Nevada (a gay political club).

42. Samuel Walker, *In Defense of American Liberties: A History of the ACLU*, 219–20, 304–6, 323–29; Richard Siegel, interviews by author, Reno, March 2, April 13, 2004; Shapiro, *Time for Healing*, 221.

43. Sari Aizley, "The Southern Nevada ACLU: Strategies and Tactics," 52.

44. Elmer R. Rusco and Richard Siegel, "The ACLU in Nevada," 47–48. Michael Melner estimated that 50 percent of Nevada's ACLU membership were Jewish (conversation with author, Reno, April 29, 2005).

45. Rusco and Siegel, "The ACLU in Nevada," 48–49.

46. All quotations and paraphrases are drawn from Siegel, interviews by author, Reno, December 11, 2000, March 2, 14, April 14, 2004.

47. See Rusco and Siegel, "The ACLU in Nevada," 51; Siegel, conversation with au-

thor, Reno, May 7, 2004. For a profile of Gary Peck, see *Life & Style: The Las Vegas Jewish Magazine* (May 2005): 14–15.

48. Patricia Blanchard (wife of Feinberg), interview by author, Reno, May 11, 2004; Victoria Berry, "Abe Feinberg, the Radical Rabbi," 22; Abraham L. Feinberg, "An Invitation from Ho Chi Minh to LBJ," *Globe and Mail*, February 4, 1967, 9; *Montreal Gazette*, May 31, 1969, 4.

49. Hawkins, interview.

50. Michael Hanlon, "Abe Feinberg: A Radical Rabbi Working as Fast as He Can," *Toronto Star*, May 17, 1986, M1; Blanchard, interview.

51. Gayle J. Hardy, *American Women Civil Rights Activists: Biobibliographies of 68 Leaders, 1825–1992*, 26, 40, 55, 57, 64.

52. Marcus, *American Jewish Women*, 153–54.

53. Diamond to the author, Las Vegas, April 19, 2004.

54. Judi Kosinski to the author, Reno, April 18, 2004.

55. NOW Northern Nevada Chapter, "Guestbook," Box 97–31, UNRSC; Barbara Weinberg, telephone conversation, April 2, 2004. Weinberg had been active with the American Association of University Women in Sacramento before coming to Reno in 1974. She later was elected president of Reno's Temple Sinai. See also Gould, interview. Gould was raised in an observant household in New Hampshire and attributed to her eastern European grandparents the Jewish lesson to "give something back." She earned a graduate degree in library science, married, came to Reno in 1972, and was active in Temple Sinai's Hebrew school. She was named Civil Libertarian of the Year by the ACLU in 1988, ran unsuccessfully for mayor of Reno, and has served on several national library commissions.

56. Goldwater to the author, Reno, April 24, 2004; Marcus, *American Jewish Women*, 183.

57. Sarna, *American Judaism*, 309–10.

58. This conclusion is based on the interviews for this work, in which all were asked a question about the relationship of Judaism to their public lives. It is also corroborated for women nationally in Marcus, *American Jewish Woman*, 181.

Chapter 14. The Varieties of Religious Observance, 1974–2005

1. G. Badt, "Milton Benjamin Badt"; Nancy Badt Drake, conversation with author, Fair Haven, N.J., January 7, 2005.

2. Zenoff to the author, Carlsbad, Calif., March 16, 2001. See also "Badt," in McDonald Papers, NHS.

3. Allen Silver, telephone interview, December 6, 2004.

4. For some of this information and for other kindnesses, I am grateful to several former members of Chai Sierra Havurah who have asked to remain anonymous.

5. Notes taken at the meeting of July 21, 2000, Carson City.

6. Judith Greenspan, telephone conversation, December 6, 2004; Silver, telephone interview.

7. Richard J. and Gloria L. Novack, "History of Jewish Community in North Lake Tahoe, 1979–2002," 2002, available online at http://www.recognos.net/nthc/home.

8. Jon Miller, "President's Message" (to North Tahoe Hebrew Congregation), June 2004, available online at ibid.

9. Jaffe, interview. Jaffe was born in Vermont in 1915, moved to Reno with her husband and children in 1957, originally affiliated with the Conservative Temple Emanu-El, and later became a member of Temple Sinai.

10. Myra Soifer, interview by author, Reno, August 3, 2001. Soifer was ordained in 1978 at Hebrew Union College, Jewish Institute of Religion in Cincinnati, Ohio. Before accepting her post at Reno in 1984, Soifer served as assistant rabbi at Temple Sinai in New Orleans.

11. Soifer, conversation with author, Reno, October 17, 2002; Gordon, interview.

12. Soifer, conversation with author, Reno, January 18, 2005.

13. The statistics for Jews come from many quarters and are all estimates. According to some sources, the numbers are deflated to reduce expectations of revenue from national fund-raising agencies. See Maisel, *Jews in American Politics,* 474; *American Jewish Year Book* 62 (1961): 58; 71 (1970): 350; 81 (1981): 178; 85 (1985): 180; Stephen J. Dubner, "Orthodox in an Unorthodox Place," 46–48; and Felipe Goodman, interview by author, Las Vegas, December 20, 2004. For Israeli foreign-born, see Nevada State Data Center, Nevada State Library and Archives. The obituary survey is an Excel file in the author's papers.

14. Sanford Akselrad to the author, Las Vegas, December 28, 2004; Shaarei Tefilla's Web site, http://www.Shaarei-Tefilla.org.

15. Nancy Katz, "X-Odus from Israel," 18.

16. *LVS,* June 21, 2000, B1:1, 8; August 24, 2001, B1:1, 7.

17. Mel Hecht, "An Open Letter from Rabbi Mel Hecht," *LVI,* August 31, 1984, 30:1; Mel Hecht, telephone conversation, January 3, 2005.

18. Lola Rivera, formerly with Beth Am and Adat Ari El, became the new Temple Sinai's cantor, and Kenneth Segal was named its full-time pulpit rabbi. See Akselrad to the author, Las Vegas, December 28, 2004; *LVI,* April 15, 2005, 16; July 13, 2007, 1; August 31, 2007, 5; and the congregation's Web site, http://www.templesinailv.org.

19. Miller, interviews, October 20, 2001, December 11, 2004; Lubavitch rabbi Shea Harlig, interview by author, Las Vegas, December 19, 2004.

20. Akselrad to the author, December 28, 2004; *LVI,* November 25, 2005, 3:8. Akselrad has served on many community boards, including the Humana Hospital Pastoral Advisory Board, the Jewish Federation of Las Vegas, and the National Conference of Community and Justice. Akselrad is currently a board member of the Anti-Defamation League in Las Vegas and a member of the Governor's Council on Holocaust

Education. He was appointed to serve on the National Commission on Jewish Living, Worship, and Music for the Union of Reform Judaism. See "Brief History" at the congregation's Web site, http:///www.lvnertamid.org. Akselrad consecrated the Greenspun Campus for Jewish Life and Spiritual Renewal on February 24, 2007.

21. See *UNLV Magazine* 12, no. 1 (Spring 2004); Charles Salton, conversation with author, May 9, 2001; "Dedication of Temple Beth Sholom," September 24, 2000, Jewish Emigration Archives, UNLVSC.

22. F. Goodman, interview; background information at the congregation's Web site, http://www.bethsholomlv.org.

23. The account of this incident and its ramifications is based on an article by Mike Zapler, *LVRJ,* December 27, 1999, B1; O. Goodman, interview; Art Marshall, telephone conversations, December 20, 2005, January 8, 2006; subsequent e-mail correspondence editing the substance of these conversations by Marshall; and corroborating testimony from several people who requested anonymity.

24. Background information available at http://www.bethsholomlv.org; F. Goodman, interview, at which the incident with Adelson was not mentioned.

25. Ruth Goldfarb, telephone interview, December 22, 2004.

26. Rothman, *Neon Metropolis,* 309, 312–13. See also information available at the congregation's Web site, http://www.midbarkodesh.org. According to one interviewee, who asked to remain anonymous, the Greenspun property in Green Valley had earlier been offered to Temple Beth Sholom for its new facility, but the offer was declined in favor of the Summerlin area.

27. Dubner, "Orthodox," 47; F. Goodman, interview; Akselrad to the author, December 28, 2004.

28. Lubavitch was the Belorussian village where the early Hasidic rebbes lived. "Chabad" is an acronym composed of the Hebrew words *chochmah, binah,* and *daat* (wisdom, knowledge, and understanding), which refer to three intellectual harnesses of divine emanations *(sephiros).* Harlig, interview.

29. Samuel G. Freedman, *Jew vs. Jew: The Struggle for the Soul of American Jewry,* 77.

30. Shea Harlig, telephone conversation, December 5, 2004; Harlig, interview. See also Dubner, "Orthodox," 50.

31. *Chabad Times* 13, no. 2; F. Goodman, interview; Akselrad to the author, Las Vegas, December 28, 2004; Harlig, interview.

32. Rabbi Mendel Cunin, interview by author, Reno, December 8, 18, 2004.

33. *RGJ,* August 19, 2004, B1–4. Reno donors for the *mikveh* were the Shapiro and several Farahi families.

34. Dubner, "Orthodox," 50–51.

Chapter 15. *Yiddishkeit,* or Ways of Being Jewish, 1931–2005

1. Blanchard, interviews, May 11, 2004, April 10, 2007; Carli Cutchin, "Joy of the Dance," *Reno News and Review,* September 26, 2002, available online at http://www. newsreview.com/issues/reno/2002–09–26/pulse.asp.>

2. *LVI,* January 13, 1984, 7.

3. Rabbi Shea Harlig, telephone interview, December 19, 2004; Hugh Jaffe, "Kosher Las Vegas, Nu?" *JR,* March 26, 2004, 4–5.

4. For a humorous romp through Yiddish-inspired English, see Leo Rosten, *Hooray for Yiddish: A Book about English.*

5. Hugh Jaffe, "Yiddishkeit: Keeping a Dying Language Alive," *JR,* May 28, 2004, 4.

6. Fleekop, "Jews Wandering," 6, 73.

7. Lingenfelter and Gash, *Newspapers of Nevada,* 22, 119; Jake Highton, *Nevada Newspaper Days: A History of Journalism in the Silver State,* 147–48. For more on Zenoff, see *LVRJ,* April 12, 1996, B2.

8. For example, see *LVI,* March 29, 1968, 1; and April 15, 2005, 24–38.

9. Fleekop, "Jews Wandering," 75, based on *LVI,* May 8, 1970, 4; January 18, 1974, 5; and June 18, 1976, 7.

10. *Life & Style: The Las Vegas Jewish Magazine,* July–August 2004, 3–5.

11. Donald Feldstein, "The Jewish Federation: The First Hundred Years," 62–75; Sarna, *American Judaism,* 200–201, 433.

12. *REG,* May 24, 1982, C10.

13. Leonard Shapiro, conversation with author, Reno, April 6, 2004, January 11, 2005; Siegel, interviews, December 11, 2000, April 14, 2004. In 2004, the Reno-Tahoe Jewish Community Council formed as a bridge across religious groups. It sponsored a trip to Israel for members of four congregations (*REG,* June 18, 2005, A8:1).

14. "Temple Beth Sholom" and "Jerome D. Mack" files in UNLVSP.

15. Doug Unger, interview by author, Las Vegas, May 8, 2001.

16. *JR,* May 23, 2003, 4–5.

17. *JR,* October 10, 2003, 4–5; November 26, 2004, 4–5.

18. *JR,* September 26, 2003, 4–5; December 5, 2003, 6.

19. Sarna, *American Judaism,* 249.

20. Jewish Community Center Web site, http://www.jccsn.org.

21. Eric Goldstein of the JCCSN, telephone conversations, January 14, 2005; Joyce Scheinman, interview by author, Las Vegas, January 17, 2005.

22. Mitchell S. Gilbert, "Never Alone," 32.

23. Mitchell S. Gilbert, director of the JFSA, conversation with author, Las Vegas, January 28, 2005.

24. *JR,* March 16, 2001, 4–5; May 10, 2002, 4–5; April 16, 2004, 30; Yarchever, interviews.

25. Minutes of the Nevada Legislative Assembly Committee on Ways and Means, Seventieth Session, Carson City, March 3, 1999; *JR*, April 28, 2000, 4–5.

26. *RGJ*, April 14, 2001; Judy and Ron Mack (originally Makovsky), conversation with author, Las Vegas, May 6, 2001. Judith Szrut Mack, born about 1938, came from Germany in 1949 with her grandmother to San Francisco. She and her husband moved to Reno in 1959 and then to Las Vegas in 1990 with their three children.

27. Edythe Katz Yarchever was born in Boston in 1920 to Gertrude and Hyman Sperling. She married Lloyd Katz in May 1948. They came via San Francisco to Las Vegas in 1951, where he managed movie theaters leased by Edythe's family. After Lloyd's death, Edythe married Judge Gil Yarchever, father of Regina, who once served as cantor for Ner Tamid (Yarchever, interview, April 5, 2001; *LVI*, February 11, 2005, 23; *JR*, April 22, 2005, 29).

28. *JR*, April 16, 2004, 33; Ruth Dickens, interview; Ethyl Jaffe, conversation with author, Reno, June 10, 2004; *JR*, March 2, 2007, 43.

29. On the relationship between AIPAC, Israel, and the U.S. Congress, see Nathan Guttman, "AIPAC and Israel," in *Moment: Jewish Culture, Politics, and Religion for the Twenty-first Century*, 40–45, 60–64. On the influence of AIPAC, see Michael Massing, "The Israel Lobby."

30. Society president Charlotte Showel, conversation with author, Las Vegas, June 6, 2006. Michael Brenner was president in 2007. See Jewish Organizational Directory in *JR*, March 2, 2007, 43.

31. Sarna, *American Judaism*, 9–10, 173–74.

32. Gordon, interview; Cunin, interview, December 8, 2004; Larry Sigurdson, "Chevrah Kedesha: As He Came, So Shall He Go." Born in Boston in 1934, Gordon (née Cohen) came to Reno in the late 1950s and was active in Temple Emanu-El. He was murdered on September 25, 2002, in his home. The case is unsolved.

33. Jewish visitors to Virginia City complained to authorities about the unholy condition of the cemetery. See unsigned correspondence Alfred Barnston, Sutro, and Company, San Francisco, August 19, 1963, Collection "Cemeteries/Correspondence," AJA; and Dr. Leslie Malkin to the author, Roseville, October 24, 2001.

34. Ross, *Recollections of Life*, 550–61. Examples of unusual cemetery arrangements were communicated to the author on condition the source be anonymous.

35. F. Goodman, interview; Erin Auerbach, "First Jewish Cemetery, Mortuary Opens."

36. *JR*, March 18, 2005, 36.

Chapter 16. Walking the Walk, 1970–2005

1. Joyce Eisenberg and Ellen Scolnic, *The JPS Dictionary of Jewish Words*, 168.

2. John L. Smith, "Moe Dalitz and the Desert," 42–44; Moehring, *Resort City*, 243; Yarchever, interview, April 5, 2001.

3. Sol Savitt (1896–1988) and his wife, Ella (1903–2004), founded the Reno News

Company (Professor James Ellis [friend of the Savitt Family], conversation with author, Reno, January 28, 2005).

4. For a profile of Goodman's educational philosophy, see Kate Hausbeck, "Classical Education for Postmodern City: Wise and Feisty Words from Carolyn Goodman," 11.

5. *JR*, January 13, 2006, 4. The Hebrew Academy feted Toni and Victor Chaltiel, who joined a long list of Las Vegas Jewish benefactors.

6. Schwartz, interview; Brian Sodoma, "Cab Company Owner Rides Way to Success."

7. Schwartz, interview; *LVRJ*, July 18, 1999; Steve Kanigher and Mary Manning, "Coverage Helps Expose Abuses of Power."

8. Schwartz, interview. Schwartz died August 9, 2007.

9. Relatives of the Farahi family, Isaac Poura, and Houshang Saraf, from 1976 to 1979 were owners of the Reef Hotel and Casino in Reno (John Farahi, interview by author, Reno, January 29, 2005; and Kling, *Rise of the Biggest Little City*, 136–37).

10. Farahi, interviews by author, Reno, December 17, 2004, January 29, 2005; "John Farahi Biography" supplied by the Atlantis Casino Resort; Cunin, interview; Blanchard, interview; Gould, interview.

11. Farahi, interview, January 29, 2005; Moehring, *Resort City*, 267; John L. Smith, *Running Scared: The Life and Treacherous Times of Las Vegas Casino King Steve Wynn*, 31, 35, 194; William N. Thompson, "Steve Wynn: 'I Got the Message,'" 209. Through his public relations office, Steve Wynn declined to be interviewed for this study.

12. W. Thompson, "Steve Wynn," 205–6; J. Smith, *Running Scared*, 308–11; Sue Fishkoff, "Out with the Gangsters, in with the Orthodox."

13. See, for example, Matthew Miller, "The Gambler."

14. Shea Harlig, conversation with author, December 19, 2004.

15. Deana Di Dio, "Newsmakers," *LVRJ*, December 26, 2000, available online at http://www.lvrj.com.

16. Jewish Community Center of Southern Nevada, *The Inside Scoop*, July 1, 2005, 1; *JR*, August 19, 2005, 4–5; Fishkoff, "Out with the Gangsters," 5.

17. *LVRJ*, November 30, 1998, 1–2, available online at http://www.lvrj.com; M. Miller, "The Gambler," 2; *LVRJ*, December 27, 1999, B1.

18. Jon Ralston, *The Anointed One: An Inside Look at Nevada Politics*, 128, 135, 181, 200.

19. Goldman, *Synagogue Gallery*, 215.

20. See, for example, Sylvia Barack Fishman, "Comparative Reflections on Modern Orthodoxy and Women's Issues," 5, available online at http://www.edah.org.

21. *JR*, December 24, 2004, 4–5; April 22, 2005, 26; October 20, 2006, 4–5.

22. Marcus, *American Jewish Woman*, 187; Kramer, *Western Journal*, 45.

23. Gary A. Tobin et al., *Jewish Federation of Las Vegas Community Study, 1996*, 83, 95, 113.

24. *Political History of Nevada*, 158–217, 220–23.

25. *Journal of the Assembly of the Sixty-sixth Session of the Legislature of the State of Nevada, 1991*, 480.

26. "Sedway," McDonald Papers, NHS.

27. *LVRJ*, July 10, 1990, B1:8; *Journal of the Assembly, 1991*, 478.

28. *Journal of the Assembly, 1991*, 480–81.

29. Ibid., 483; *Journal of the Assembly, 1997*, 1553–55.

30. *LVRJ*, July 8, 1990, A1:5. When I interviewed Sedway on June 20, 1983, he testified to the direct relationship of Judaism to his public-policy positions. The Sedway interview audiotape was accidentally demagnetized, but others have corroborated his motivation.

31. Judith Eaton to the author, October 23, 2004; University of Nevada faculty member who requested anonymity.

32. Wiener, interview. Among her proudest achievements were gold medals won in the Nevada Senior Olympics.

33. *RGJ*, March 6, 1983, A1:2–4; Mel Hecht, telephone conversation.

34. *LVS*, February 6, 2004, available online at http://www.lasvegassun.com/.

35. Congresswoman Shelley Berkley, interview by author, Las Vegas, June 2, 2001.

36. Mel Hecht, telephone conversations, December 22, 2004, December 21, 2005; Art Marshall, conversation with author, Las Vegas, December 20, 2005; Donald H. Harrison, "Hecht Synagogue," *San Diego Jewish Press-Heritage*, May 7, 1999, as cited online at http://www.jewishsightseeing.com/ and link to Donald H. Harrison stories on the date May 7, 1999.

37. *RGJ*, February 19, 1984, C7:3, 4; *LVS*, May 15, 2006, 1.

38. All succeeding quotations were taken from Berkley, interview.

39. J. Smith, *Running Scared*, 308–11.

40. *LVRJ*, December 13, 1999; Berkley, interview.

41. Howard Rosenberg, interview by author, Reno, February 17, 2001. According to Rosenberg, he secretly married his high school sweetheart in 1960 in New York, where she was at Julliard. She was Lutheran, and they went through three ceremonies: Jewish, Lutheran, and civil. The marriage was kept secret from all parents, said Rosenberg. She died of liver cancer in 1963.

42. Ibid. Because no tape recorder was used in the interview, I have avoided using quotation marks based on my notes. The substance, however, is as reviewed and corrected by Rosenberg.

43. John L. Smith, *Of Rats and Men: Oscar Goodman's Life from Mob Mouthpiece to Mayor of Las Vegas*, 12–16, 79. Carolyn was related through her mother to the Seligman family, which had mining interests in White Pine County in the 1880s. Seligman, Nevada, founded in 1886, was likely named after the family (Stephen Birmingham, *"Our Crowd": The Great Jewish Families of New York*, 224–26; Carlson, *Nevada Place Names*, 212).

44. Robert Mirisch, "Interview with Our Jewish Mayor Oscar Goodman," 44.

45. Ibid., 17.

46. J. Smith, *Of Rats and Men*, 316; O. Goodman, interview; *People*, June 28, 1999, 114, which includes a picture of the mayor at prayer.

47. O. Goodman, interview; Dubner, "Orthodox," 46–48.

48. *LVRJ*, September 26, 2003, available online at http://www.lvrj.com.

49. "Columnist Jon Ralston: Lack of Ethics Lamentable," *LVS*, December 17, 2004, available online at http://www.lasvegassun.com; O. Goodman, interview. Ralston is distantly related to Nevada's first rabbi on the Comstock, Herman Bien.

50. O. Goodman, interview.

51. Schwartz, interview; O. Goodman, interview; F. Goodman, interview.

Conclusion: The Past Need Not Be Prologue

1. For a biography of Arum, see http://en.wikipedia.org/wiki/Bob_Arum. For Chabad's celebration of his community service, see Nevada newsletter, retrieved online at http://www.chabadlv.org/dinner2002.

2. "The Jewish Population of the World," in Jewish Virtual Library, a Division of the American-Israeli Cooperative Enterprise, retrieved online at http://www.jewish-virtuallibrary.org, January 2, 2005.

3. Nacha Cattan, "New Population Survey Retracts Intermarriage Figure," *Forward*, September 12, 2003, available online at http://www.forward.com/issues/2003; Tobin et al., *Jewish Federation*, 16.

4. "Closet Jews: Reaching the Unaffiliated Majority in Las Vegas," 26, 39; Tobin et al., *Jewish Federation*, 95–97; Sanford Akselrad, "One Rabbi's Impassioned Plea for Community," *JR*, March 18, 2005.

5. Mirisch, "Oscar Goodman," 44.

6. Tobin et al., *Jewish Federation*, 31–32; F. Goodman, interview; O. Goodman, interview; Schwartz, interview.

7. Newsletter of the National Foundation for Jewish Culture, January 29, 2005, available online at http://www.jewishculture.org.

8. Caroline Orzes, "A House Divided: The Breakup of the Jewish Federation of Las Vegas," 14–15, 36; Mirisch, "Oscar Goodman," 17.

9. Fishkoff, "Out with the Gangsters," 6.

10. *Jewish Life and Style: Las Vegas*, October 2005, 16.

11. *Jewish Community Today* (*Las Vegas Israelite* insert) 1, no. 4 (October–December 2006): 1; *Jewish Life and Style: Las Vegas*, December 2005, 6; *LVI*, December 15, 2006, 20; *JR*, February 16, 2007, 6.

GLOSSARY

In the text, words that appear in the *Merriam-Webster's Collegiate Dictionary*, 11th edition, are set in roman type. Those not in the dictionary are treated as foreign words and italicized. Except as noted, all spellings are from *The JPS Dictionary of Jewish Words*, the work of Joyce Eisenberg and Ellen Scolnic.

bar mitzvah: A ceremony for thirteen year old boys or older, initiating them into the adult Jewish community

bat mitzvah: A ceremony for twelve year old or older girls, initiating them into the adult Jewish community

bimah: Raised platform in a synagogue from which services are led

challah: Braided bread usually prepared for the Sabbath

Hanukkah: Often called the Festival of Lights, it celebrates the rededication of the Second Temple in 165 BCE

havurah: Informal Jewish fellowship group

hazzan: The cantor who chants prayers and in the absence of a rabbi leads services

hevrah kadishah: Lay organization devoted to ancient burial rites

huppah: ritual canopy

Kabbalah: Jewish mystical tradition

kaddish: Prayer of praise to Yahweh, customarily recited by someone mourning the dead

kashruth: Dietary laws determining whether food is "kosher"

kehillah: Originally, autonomous Polish communities of Jews governing themselves

masgiach: Overseer of kosher laws

mezuzah: doorpost Torah scroll

mikveh: Ritual bath, often used in conversion services

minhag: Custom or ritual

minyan: Ten people needed for a communal religious service

Mishnah: Section of the Talmud that deals with oral prescriptions passed down over time

mitzvah: Commonly, a deed of kindness or avoidance of a proscribed action (plural, **mitzvoth**)

mohel: One certified to perform a ritual circumcision

Purim: Celebration of the Jews' salvation from oppression as described in the book of Esther

rebbetzin: wife of a rabbi

Rosh Hashanah: Jewish New Year

seder: Ceremonial dinner on Passover (Pesach)

sefer Torah: A handwritten parchment scroll of the Torah

shivah: Seven days of mourning after burial

shochet: One certified in the rules of kosher slaughtering of animals

shomer: Guardian of a body awaiting internment

shul: Synagogue

sofer: scribe

taharah: Washing of the body for burial

tallit: fringed prayer shawl

tefillin: Black leather pouches containing Torah parchments, worn during prayer

Tikun olam: Literally, "repairing the world," such as social-service projects

Torah: The first five books of the Hebrew Bible

tzedakah: Literally, "righteousness," commonly connoted as charitable giving

yahrzeit: Annual commemoration of someone's death

yarmulke: small, round head covering worn as a symbol of religious respect; it is often called a *kippah*

Yom Kippur: Day of fasting and asking forgiveness for past misdeeds

SELECTED BIBLIOGRAPHY

This bibliography is limited to works cited in this book and to a few others that have been central to its interpretations.

Manuscript Collections

American Jewish Archives, Jacob Rader Marcus Center, Cincinnati
American Jewish Historical Society, New York
Judah Magnes Museum, Berkeley, California
National Archives Federal Records Center, San Bruno, California
Nevada Historical Society, Reno
Nevada State Library and Archives, Carson City
University of Nevada, Las Vegas Library, Special Collections
University of Nevada, Reno Library, Special Collections
Washoe County Public Library, Special Collections

Government Documents and Publications

Census of the Inhabitants of the State of Nevada, 1875. Vols. 1 and 2. In *Appendix to the Journals of the Senate and Assembly of the Eighth Session of the Legislature of the State of Nevada.* Vols. 2 and 3. Carson City: State Printer, 1877.

Ex Parte A. Livingston. No. 1304, *Reports of Cases Determined in the Supreme Court of the State of Nevada during the Year 1887, 1888, 1889, 1890.* Vol. 20, April [no day], 282–89. Carson City: State Printing Office, 1890.

Journal of the Assembly during the First Session of the Legislature of the State of Nevada, 1864–1865. Carson City: John Church, State Printer, 1865.

Journal of the Assembly of the Sixty-sixth Session of the Legislature of the State of Nevada, 1991. Carson City: State Printing Office, 1992.

Journal of the Assembly of the Sixty-ninth Session of the Legislature of the State of Nevada, 1997. Carson City: State Printing Office, 1998.

Journal of the Senate of the Nineteenth Session of the Legislature of the State of Nevada, 1899. Carson City: State Printing Office, 1899.

Journal of the Senate of the Twenty-first Session of the Legislature of the State of Nevada, 1903. Carson City: State Printing Office, 1903.

Journal of the Senate of the Twenty-seventh Session of the Legislature of the State of Nevada, 1915. Carson City: State Printing Office, 1915.

Judische Gemeinde Kempen, 1825–1847. Listing of births, deaths, and marriages during this period for the city of Kempen/Kepno. Poznán [Poland] State Archives.

Levi Strauss et al v. A. B. Elfelt et al. U.S. Ninth Circuit Court, District of California, Case no. 1211 at San Bruno, California, Federal Archives RA/4545/I.

Mining Claim Records. Esmeralda County, Goldfield.

Mining Claim Records. Nye County, Tonopah.

Nevada Territorial and State Censuses, 1861, 1863, 1875, 1880, 1900, 1920.

Ormsby County Assessment Roll, 1862–[1865], 1900. Nevada State Library and Archives, Carson City.

Prezydium Policji w Poznanin. *Akta meste Poznenie, Archiwum Panstwowe w Poznaniu* [Listing of Persons Emigrating from Posen/Poznán]. Poznán Police Headquarters, Acta of Poznán City, State Archives in Poznán, Poland.

Prison Records. Folio 47, "Alexander Cohn." Nevada State Archives, Carson City.

[Proceedings], May 17, 1899. Second Judicial District Court (Washoe County), 4270.

Records of the Secretary of State, SECstate 1038, and Governor Grant Sawyer Correspondence, GOV-0338, Equal Rights Commission, July 1, 1961, Nevada State Library and Archives, Carson City.

Reports of Cases Determined in the Supreme Court of the State of Nevada, during the Year 1873–74. Vol. 9. San Francisco: Frank Eastman, Printer, 1874.

State of Nevada. *Investigation of Charges against Dr. H. Bergstein: Testimony Taken and Proceedings Held before the Board of Commissioners for the Care of the Indigent Insane, Reno, Nevada, Monday, December 20, 1897.* Carson City: State Printing Office, 1898.

State v. Cohn. In *Reports of Cases Determined in the Supreme Court of the State of Nevada, during the Year 1873–74.* Vol. 9. San Francisco: Frank Eastman, Printer, 1874.

Statutes of the State of Nevada Passed at the First Session of the Legislature, 1864–1865. Carson City: John Church, State Printer, 1865.

Statutes of the State of Nevada Passed at the Sixteenth Session of the Legislature, 1893. Carson City: State Printing Office, 1893.

Statutes of the State of Nevada Passed at the Eighteenth Session of the Legislature, 1897. Carson City: State Printing Office, 1897.

Statutes of the State of Nevada Passed at the Twenty-first Session of the Legislature, 1903. Carson City: State Printing Office, 1903.

U.S. Bureau of the Census. *Religious Bodies, 1906.* Pt. 2, *Separate Denominations: History, Description, and Statistics.* Washington, D.C.: Government Printing Office, 1910.

———. *U.S. Census Reports, State of Nevada, 1860, 1870, 1880, 1900, 1910, 1920, 1930.*

"Voting Records of Assembly and Senate: Nevada State Legislature, 1971." Manuscript in Getchell Library, Governmental Records, University of Nevada, Reno.

Washoe County Recorder, Real Estate Division, Reno.

Other Sources

Abbott, Walter M., S.J., ed. *The Documents of Vatican II.* New York: America Press, 1966.

Aizley, Sari. "The Southern Nevada ACLU: Strategies and Tactics." *Nevada Public Affairs Review,* no. 2 (1990): 52–53.

Albert, Herman W. *Odyssey of a Desert Prospector.* Norman: University of Oklahoma Press, 1967.

Alter, Harry. "Ner Tamid." 7 typed pages. Copy courtesy of the author.

Angel, Myron, ed. *History of Nevada, 1881, with Illustrations.* Introduction by David Myrick. 1881. Reprint, Berkeley: Howell-North, 1958.

Arnold, Emmett L. *Gold Camp Drifter, 1906–1910.* Reno: University of Nevada Press, 1973.

Arthur, Joe. *Broken Hills: The Story of Joe Arthur, Cowpuncher and Prospector Who Struck It Rich in Nevada.* New York: Vantage Press, 1958.

Auerbach, Erin. "First Jewish Cemetery, Mortuary Opens." *View,* June 27, 2001. Available online at http://www.viewnews.com.

Badt, Gertrude N. "Milton Benjamin Badt, 1884–1966." *Northern Nevada Historical Society Quarterly* 78 (Summer 1978): 91–104.

Badt, Milton B. *An Interview with Milton Badt.* Edited by May Ellen Glass. Reno: Oral History Project Center for Western North American Studies, University of Nevada, 1965.

Balboni, Alan. *Beyond the Mafia: Italian Americans and the Development of Las Vegas.* Reno: University of Nevada Press, 1996.

———. "Moe Dalitz: Controversial Founding Father of Modern Las Vegas." In *The Maverick Spirit: Building the New Nevada,* edited by Richard O. Davies, 24–43. Reno: University of Nevada Press, 1998.

———. "Southern Italians and Eastern European Jews: Cautious Cooperation in Las Vegas Casinos, 1940–1967." *Nevada Historical Society Quarterly* 38, no. 3 (1995): 153–73.

Benjamin, I[saac] J[oseph]. *Three Years in America, 1859–1862.* Translated by Charles Reznikoff. Vols. 1 and 2. New York: Arno Press, 1975.

Bergstein, Henry, M.D. "Medical History." In *History of Nevada,* edited by Sam P. Davis, 1:610–23. Reno and Los Angeles: Elms Publishing, 1913.

Berman, Susan. *Easy Street.* New York: Dial Press, 1981.

Berry, Victoria. "Abe Feinberg, the Radical Rabbi." *Reno,* October 1980.

Birmingham, Stephen. *"Our Crowd": The Great Jewish Families of New York.* New York: Harper and Row, 1967.

Bodner, Allen. *When Boxing Was a Jewish Sport.* Westport, Conn.: Praeger, 1997.

Bowles, Samuel. *Across the Continent: A Summer's Journey to the Rocky Mountains, the Mormons, and the Pacific States, with Speaker Colfax.* Springfield, Mass.: Samuel Bowles, 1865.

Bracey, Earnest N. "The Moulin Rouge Mystique: Blacks and Equal Rights in Las Vegas." *Nevada Historical Society Quarterly* 39, no. 4 (1996): 272–88.

Braude, Ann. "Women's History Is American Religious History." In *Retelling U.S. Religious History,* edited by Thomas A. Tweed, 87–107. Berkeley and Los Angeles: University of California Press, 1997.

Brooks, Juanita. *History of the Jews in Utah and Idaho.* Salt Lake City: Western Epics, 1973.

Brown, Mrs. Hugh. *Lady in Boomtown: Miners and Manners on the Nevada Frontier.* Reno: University of Nevada Press, 1991.

Browne, J. Ross. *A Peep at Washoe and Washoe Revisited.* Balboa Island, Calif.: Paisano Press, 1959.

Burbank, Jeff. *License to Steal: Nevada's Gaming Control System in the Megaresort Age.* Reno: University of Nevada Press, 2000.

Bushnell, Eleanore. *Sagebrush and Neon: Studies in Nevada Politics.* Reno: Bureau of Governmental Research, University of Nevada, 1976.

Butler, Anne M. "Mission in the Mountains: The Daughters of Charity in Virginia City." In *Comstock Women: The Making of a Mining Community,* edited by Ronald M. James and C. Elizabeth Raymond, 142–64. Reno: University of Nevada Press, 1998.

Cahlan, John F. *Fifty Years in Journalism and Community Development.* Reno: University of Nevada Oral History Program, 1989.

Carlson, Helen S. *Nevada Place Names: A Geographical Dictionary.* Reno: University of Nevada Press, 1974.

Carroll, James. *Constantine's Sword: The Church and the Jews, a History.* Boston: Houghton Mifflin, 2001.

"Carson City, Nevada, Patron of Dat-So-La-Lee." *Western States Jewish History* 15, no. 4 (July 1983): 291–97.

Carson City Directory. [Carson City: Nevada Press, 1907.]

Carvalho, Solomon Nunes. *Incidents of Travel and Adventure in the Far West.* 1954/5715. Reprint, New York: Kraus Reprint Company, 1971.

Chung, Sue Fawn. "Their Changing World: Chinese Women on the Comstock, 1860–1910." In *Comstock Women: The Making of a Mining Community,* edited by Ronald M. James and C. Elizabeth Raymond, 203–28. Reno: University of Nevada Press, 1998.

Cinel, Dino. "Italians in San Francisco: Patterns of Settlement." In *European Immi-*

grants in the American West, edited by Frederick C. Luebke, 65–74. Albuquerque: University of New Mexico Press, 1998.

Clar, Reva, and William M. Kramer. "Chinese-Jewish Relations in the Far West, 1850–1950." Pts. 1 and 2. *Western States Jewish History* 21, no. 1 (1988): 12–35; no. 2 (1989): 132–53.

——. "The Girl Rabbi of the Golden West: The Adventurous Life of Ray Frank in Nevada, California, and the Northwest." *Western States Jewish History* 18, no. 2 (1986): 99–111.

——. "Julius Eckman and Herman Bien: The Battling Rabbis of San Francisco." 3 pts. *Western States Jewish History* 15, nos. 2–4 (January–July 1983): 107–30, 232–53, 341–59.

Clark, Walter Van Tilburg, ed. *The Journals of Alfred Doten, 1849–1903.* 3 vols. Reno: University of Nevada Press, 1973.

"Closet Jews: Reaching the Unaffiliated Majority in Las Vegas." *Life & Style: The Las Vegas Jewish Magazine,* November–December 2004.

Cohodas, Marvin. "Dat-So-La-Lee and the Degikup." In *Halcyon, 1982: A Journal of the Humanities,* 119–40. Reno: Nevada Humanities Committee, 1982.

Coleman, Carol. "On the National Register of Historic Places: The El Cortez Hotel." *Footprints* 7, no. 1 (2004): 7.

Coles, Kathleen M., ed. *Charlotte Hunter Arley.* Reno: University of Nevada Oral History Program, 2001.

Collins, Charles, comp. *Mercantile Guide and Directory for Virginia City, Gold Hill, Silver City, and American City.* San Francisco: Agnew and Deffebach, 1864–1865.

Cowan, Neil, and Ruth S. Cowan. *Our Parents' Lives: The Americanization of East European Jews.* New York: Basic Books, 1989.

Cray, Ed. *Levi's.* Boston: Houghton Mifflin, 1978.

Crowley, Joseph. "Race and Residence: The Politics of Open Housing in Nevada." In *Sagebrush and Neon: Studies in Nevada Politics,* edited by Eleanor Bushnell, 59–79. Reno: Bureau of Governmental Research, University of Nevada, 1976.

D'Ancona, David A., and William M. Kramer, eds. *A California-Nevada Travel Diary of 1876.* Santa Monica: Norton B. Stern, 1955.

Dangberg, Grace. *Carson Valley: Historical Sketches of Nevada's First Settlement.* Reno: Carson Valley Historical Society, 1972.

Davies, Richard O., ed. *The Maverick Spirit: Building the New Nevada.* Reno: University of Nevada Press, 1999.

Davis, Sam P., ed. *The History of Nevada.* 2 vols. Reno and Los Angeles: Elms Publishing, 1913.

Denton, Ralph, with Michael S. Green and R. T. King. *A Liberal Conscience: Ralph Denton, Nevadan.* Reno: University of Nevada Oral History Program, 2001.

Denton, Sally, and Roger Morris. *The Money and the Power: The Making of Las Vegas and Its Hold on America, 1947–2000.* New York: Alfred A. Knopf, 2001.

Denzler, Maria Davis. "The Dat So La Lee Basket Mystery." *Nevada Magazine,* November–December 2002, 12–15.

Dickens, Ruth. "History of Reform Judaism." In *Temple Sinai Newsletter,* 1993 (various months).

Diner, Hasia R. *The Jews of the United States, 1654–2000.* Berkeley and Los Angeles: University of California Press, 2004.

———. "Post-World-War-II American Jewry and the Confrontation with Catastrophe." *American Jewish History* 91, nos. 3–4 (2003): 439–67.

———. *A Time for Gathering: The Second Migration, 1820–1880.* Baltimore: Johns Hopkins University Press, 1992.

Dinnerstein, Leonard. *Antisemitism in America.* New York: Oxford University Press, 1994.

Dinnerstein, Leonard, and Mary Dale Palsson, eds. *Jews in the South.* Baton Rouge: Louisiana State University Press, 1973.

Directory of the City of Goldfield: Columbia, Diamondfield, Jumbo Town, Mill Town, Nevada, 1907–8. New York: National Directory, 1907.

Directory of the City of Reno and Sparks, Nev., 1904–1907. Reno: Haley and Durley, 1904–1907.

Dollinger, Marc. *Quest for Inclusion: Jews and Liberalism in Modern America.* Princeton: Princeton University Press, 2000.

Douglas, Tom. *Scapegoats: Transferring Blame.* London: Routledge, 1995.

Douglass, William A. "The Mining Camp as Community." In *Social Approaches to an Industrial Past,* edited by A. Bernard Knapp, Vincent C. Pigott, and Eugenia W. Herbert, 97–108. London: Routledge, 1998.

Drury, Wells. *An Editor on the Comstock Lode.* Reno: University of Nevada Press, 1984.

———. "Journalism." In *History of Nevada,* edited by Sam P. Davis, 1:459–502. Reno and Los Angeles: Elms Publishing, 1913.

Dubner, Stephen J. "Orthodox in an Unorthodox Place." *Las Vegas Life* 3, no. 11 (2000): 46–53.

Dumenil, Lynn. *Freemasonry and American Culture, 1880–1930.* Princeton: Princeton University Press, 1984.

"E. Reinhart & Company of Winnemucca, Nevada." *Western States Jewish History* 24, no. 4 (1992): 297–98.

Earl, Phillip I. "'A House to Offer Our Prayers . . .' : A Brief History of Reno's Jewish Community and the Building of the Temple Emanu El." *Washoe Rambler* 2, no. 2 (1978): 47–55.

———. "Nevada's Italian War." *Nevada Historical Society Quarterly* 12, no. 2 (1969): 46–87.

Eckardt, A. Roy. *Your People, My People: The Meeting of Jews and Christians.* New York: Quadrangle, New York Times Book Company, 1974.

Edwards, Jerome E. "The Americanization of Nevada Gambling." In *Halcyon, 1992: A Journal of the Humanities,* 14:201–16. Reno: Nevada Humanities Committee and University of Nevada Press, 1992.

———. *Pat McCarran: Political Boss of Nevada.* Reno: University of Nevada Press, 1982.

Eisenbach, Artur. *The Emancipation of the Jews in Poland, 1780–1870.* Cambridge: Blackwell, 1991.

Eisenberg, Joyce, and Ellen Scolnic. *The JPS Dictionary of Jewish Words.* Philadelphia: Jewish Publication Society, 2001.

Elliott, Russell R. *History of Nevada.* Lincoln: University of Nebraska Press, 1973.

Elliott, Russell R., with William D. Rowley. *History of Nevada.* 2d rev. ed. Lincoln: University of Nebraska Press, 1987.

Farrell, Ronald A., and Carole Case. *The Black Book and the Mob: The Untold Story of the Control of Nevada's Casinos.* Madison: University of Wisconsin Press, 1995.

Feingold, Henry L. *A Time for Searching: Entering the Mainstream, 1920–1945.* Baltimore: Johns Hopkins University Press, 1992.

Feldstein, Donald. "The Jewish Federation: The First Hundred Years." In *A Portrait of the American Jewish Community,* edited by Norman Linzer, David J. Schnall, and Jerome A. Chanes, 62–75. Westport, Conn.: Praeger, 1998.

Fishkoff, Sue. "Out with the Gangsters, in with the Orthodox." *Jerusalem Post,* March 27, 2002. http://www.jpost.com.

Fishman, Sylvia Barack. "Comparative Reflections on Modern Orthodoxy and Women's Issues." *Edah Journal: Halakhic Possibilities for Women* 5. Available online at http://www.edah.org.

Fleekop, Joel. "Jews Wandering in the Desert: A History of the Jewish Community of Las Vegas." Senior honors thesis, Brandeis University, 2000.

Ford, Jean, and James W. Hulse. "The First Battle for Woman Suffrage in Nevada: Correcting and Expanding the Record, 1869–1871." *Nevada Historical Society Quarterly* 38, no. 3 (Fall 1995): 174–77.

Fox, William L. *Lodge of the Double-Headed Eagle: Two Centuries of Scottish Rite Freemasonry in America's Southern Jurisdiction.* Fayetteville: University of Arkansas Press, 1997.

Francke, Bernadette. "The Neighborhood and Nineteenth Century Photographs: A Call to Locate Undocumented Historic Photographs of the Comstock Region." *Nevada Historical Society Quarterly* 35 (1992).

Freedman, Abraham Kep. "The 'Jewish' Gold Rush, 1850–Onward: Marysville, Yuba County, California, Gateway to the Northern Gold Fields." Manuscript loaned to the author by Freedman.

Freedman, Samuel G. *Jew vs. Jew: The Struggle for the Soul of American Jewry.* New York: Simon and Schuster, 2000.

Frehner, Brian. "Ethnicity and Class: The Italian Charcoal Burners' War, 1875–1885." *Nevada Historical Society Quarterly* 39, no. 1 (1996): 43–62.

Friedman, Joseph. "Jewish Participation in California Gold Rush Era Freemasonry." *Western States Jewish History* 16, no. 4 (July 1984): 291–302.

Gaustad, Edwin S. *A Documentary History of Religion in America to the Civil War.* Grand Rapids: William B. Eerdmans Publishing, 1982.

Georgetta, Clel Evan. "The Personal Diary of Clel Georgetta." Vols. 19–38 (1934–1938) at Washoe County Library, Downtown Reno Branch, Special Collections. Vol. 20, Box 5–10 (1920s–1940s) at UNR Special Collections.

Gilbert, Mitchell S. "Never Alone." *Life & Style: The Las Vegas Jewish Magazine,* July–August 2004.

Gillis, William R., comp. *The Nevada Directory for 1868–69.* San Francisco: M. D. Carr, 1868.

Glad, Betty. *Key Pittman: The Tragedy of a Senate Insider.* New York: Columbia University Press, 1986.

Glanz, Rudolph. *Jew and Italian: Historic Group Relations and the New Immigration, 1881–1924.* New York: Shulsinger Brothers, 1972.

———. "Jews and Chinese in America." *Western States Jewish History* 38, no. 2 (2006): 112–32. First published in *Jewish Social Studies, a Quarterly Journal* 36, no. 3 (1954).

———. *The Jews of California: From the Discovery of Gold until 1880.* New York: Waldon Press, 1960.

Glazier, Ira A., and P. Willin Fiby, eds. *Germans to America: List of Passengers Arriving at U.S. Ports.* Wilmington, Del.: S. R. Scholarly Resources, 1990.

Glazier, Jack. *Dispersing the Ghetto: The Relocation of Jewish Immigrants across America.* Ithaca: Cornell University Press, 1998.

Gold, Mike. *Jews without Money.* New York: Avon, 1965.

Goldberg, Robert A. "Zion in Utah: The Clarion Colony and Jewish Agrarianism." In *Jews of the American West,* edited by Moses Rischin and John Livingston, 66–91. Detroit: Wayne State University Press, 1979.

Golden, Harry Lewis. *Forgotten Pioneers.* Cleveland and New York: World Publishing, 1963.

Goldman, Karla. *Beyond the Synagogue Gallery: Finding a Place for Women in American Judaism.* Cambridge: Harvard University Press, 2000.

Goldman, Marion S. *Gold Diggers and Silver Miners: Prostitution and Social Life on the Comstock Lode.* Ann Arbor: University of Michigan Press, 1981.

Gorrell, Robert M. *University Growing Up: Rambling Reminiscences of an English Professor and Administrator, 1945–1980.* Reno: University of Nevada Oral History Program, 1983.

Gray, Leslie B. "Nevada Beginnings in Civil Rights: A Memoir." *Nevada Public Affairs Review,* no. 2 (1987): 87–88.

Green, Michael S. "Hank Greenspun: Where He Stood." In *The Maverick Spirit: Building the New Nevada,* edited by Richard O. Davies, 74–95. Reno: University of Nevada Press, 1998.

———. "The Jews." In *The Peoples of Las Vegas: One City, Many Faces,* edited by Jerry L. Simich and Thomas C. Wright, 164–83. Reno: University of Nevada Press, 2005.

Green, Michael S., and Gary E. Elliott, eds. *Nevada: Readings and Perspectives.* Reno: Nevada Historical Society, 1997.

Greenberg, Blu. *On Women and Judaism: A View from Tradition.* Philadelphia: Jewish Publication Society of America, 1981.

Greenspun, Hank, with Alex Pelle. *Where I Stand: The Record of a Reckless Man.* New York: D. McKay, 1966.

Guttman, Nathan. "AIPAC and Israel." *Moment: Jewish Culture, Politics, and Religion for the 21st Century* 31, no. 3 (2006): 40–45, 60–64.

Hall, Shawn. *Preserving the Glory Days: Ghost Towns and Mining Camps of Nye County, Nevada.* Reno: University of Nevada Press, 1981.

———. *Romancing Nevada's Past: Ghost Towns and Historic Sites of Eureka, Lander, and White Pine Counties.* Reno: University of Nevada Press, 1994.

Hammond, Lena. "Memories of Austin, Bodie, and Goldfield, 1900–1910." In *Women, Children, and Family Life in the Nevada Interior, 1900–1930s,* edited by R. T. King, 1–17. Reno: University of Nevada Oral History Program, 1987.

Hardy, Gayle J. *American Women Civil Rights Activists: Biobibliographies of 68 Leaders, 1825–1992.* Jefferson, N.C.: McFarland, 1993.

Harmon, Mella Rothwell. "Divorce and Economic Opportunity in Reno, Nevada, during the Great Depression." Master's thesis, University of Nevada, Reno, 1998.

Hausbeck, Kate. "Classical Education for Postmodern City: Wise and Feisty Words from Carolyn Goodman." *Jewish Life and Style: Las Vegas,* August 2005, 10–11.

Hertzberg, Arthur. *The Jews in America: Four Centuries of an Uneasy Encounter, a History.* New York: Simon and Schuster, 1989.

Hickson, Howard. "Hardly a High School: University of Nevada at Elko, 1874–1885." *Northeastern Nevada Historical Society Quarterly* 4, no. 3 (1974): 3–9.

Highton, Jake. *Nevada Newspaper Days: A History of Journalism in the Silver State.* Stockton: Heritage West Books, 1990.

Hilp, Lester J. *Reminiscences of a White Pine County Native, Reno Pharmacy Owner, and Civic Leader.* Reno: University of Nevada Oral History Program, 1968.

Howard, Anne Bail. *The Long Campaign: A Biography of Anne Martin.* Reno: University of Nevada Press, 1985.

Hulse, James W. *Forty Years in the Wilderness: Impressions of Nevada, 1940–1980.* Reno: University of Nevada Press, 1986.

———. *Lincoln County, Nevada, 1864–1909: History of a Mining Region.* Reno: University of Nevada Press, 1971.

————. *The Silver State: Nevada's Heritage Reinterpreted.* 2d ed. Reno: University of Nevada Press, 1998.

————. *The University of Nevada: A Centennial History.* Reno: University of Nevada Press, 1974.

Hyman, Paula E., and Deborah Dash Moore, eds. *Jewish Women in America: An Historical Encyclopedia.* London: Routledge, 1997.

Industrial Removal Office. *Thirteenth Annual Report of the Industrial Removal Office for the Year Nineteen Thirteen.* New York: Industrial Removal Office, 1914.

Jacobs, Julius L. "Story of the Jacobs (Jacobowicz) Family." January 1995. Copy courtesy of Mervin Tarlow.

James, Ronald M. "Erin's Daughters on the Comstock: Building Community." In *Comstock Women: The Making of a Mining Community,* edited by Ronald M. James and C. Elizabeth Raymond, 246–62. Reno: University of Nevada Press, 1998.

————. *The Roar and the Silence: A History of Virginia City and the Comstock Lode.* Reno: University of Nevada Press, 1998.

James, Ronald M., and Kenneth H. Fliess. "Women of the Mining West: Virginia City Revisited." In *Comstock Women: The Making of a Mining Community,* edited by Ronald M. James and C. Elizabeth Raymond, 17–39. Reno: University of Nevada Press, 1998.

James, Ronald M., and C. Elizabeth Raymond, eds., *Comstock Women: The Making of a Mining Community.* Reno: University of Nevada Press, 1998.

Jodock, Darrell, ed. *Catholicism Contending with Modernity: Roman Catholic Modernism and Anti-modernism in Historical Context.* Cambridge: Cambridge University Press, 2000.

Johnson, Lubertha. *Civil Rights Efforts in Las Vegas, 1940s–1960s.* Reno: University of Nevada Oral History Program, 1988.

Jone, Heribert [sic], and Urban Adelman. *Moral Theology.* Westminster, Md.: Newman Press, 1958.

Josephy, Alvin M. "Those Pants That Levi Gave Us: From Workingman's Duds to Jet-Set Chic." *American West* (July–August 1985): 30–37.

Kahn, Ava F., ed. *Jewish Life in the American West: Perspectives on Migration, Settlement, and Community.* Seattle: University of Washington Press, 2002.

————. *Jewish Voices of the California Gold Rush: A Documentary History, 1849–1880.* Detroit: Wayne State University Press, 2002.

Kahn, Ava F., and Marc Dollinger, eds. *California Jews.* Hanover, N.H.: University Press of New England, 2003.

Kanigher, Steve, and Mary Manning. "Coverage Helps Expose Abuses of Power." *Las Vegas Sun,* July 1, 2000. Available online at http://www.lasvegassun.com.

Katz, Nancy. "X-Odus from Israel." *Life & Style: The Las Vegas Jewish Magazine,* July–August 2004, 18.

Kelly, J. Wells. *First Directory of Nevada Territory.* 1862. Reprint, Los Gatos, Calif.: Talisman Press, 1962.

———. *Second Directory of the Nevada Territory.* Virginia City: Valentien, 1863.

Kinsey, Stephen D. "The Development of the Jewish Community of San Jose, California." *Western States Jewish Historical Quarterly* 7, no. 2 (1975): 163–81.

Klauber, Lawrence M. "Abraham Klauber: A Pioneer Merchant, 1831–1911." *Western States Jewish Historical Quarterly* 2, no. 2 (1970): 67–90.

Klein, Jacob. "Autobiographical Sketch." 1883. 2 pages. Nevada Historical Society, Reno.

Kling, Dwayne. *The Rise of the Biggest Little City: An Encyclopedic History of Reno Gaming, 1931–1981.* Reno: University of Nevada Press, 2000.

Kramer, William M. *Emperor Norton of San Francisco.* Santa Monica: Norton B. Stern, 1974.

———, ed. *Sephardic Jews in the West Coast States.* Vol. 1, *The San Francisco Grandees.* Los Angeles: Western States Jewish History Association, 1996.

———. *The Western Journal of Isaac Mayer Wise, 1877.* Berkeley: Western Jewish History Center, Magnes Museum, 1974.

Kramer, William M., and Norton B. Stern. "Polish Preeminence in Nineteenth Century Jewish Immigration: A Review Essay." *Western States Jewish History* 17, no. 2 (1985): 151–55.

Langley, Henry G. *The Pacific Coast Business Directory for 1867.* San Francisco: Henry G. Langley, 1867.

———. *The Pacific Coast Business Directory for 1871–73.* 2d ed. San Francisco: Henry G. Langley, 1871.

Lauritzen, Martha. "Pioche: Boom and Bust in the Most Violent Camp in Nevada and the History of Thompson's Opera House." Duplicated manuscript. Reno: Nevada Historical Society, 1999.

Lerner, Michael, and Cornel West. *Jews and Blacks: Let the Healing Begin.* New York: G. P. Putnam's Sons, 1995.

Lescott, John, and Shelly Lescott, eds. *High Hopes and Gold Dust West! True Accounts of Early Twentieth-Century Life in Nevada.* Reno: Nevada Academic Press, [1979].

Levinson, Robert E. *The Jews in the California Gold Rush.* New York: KTAV Publishing House, 1978.

Levy, Abraham R. "Central North Dakota's Jewish Farmers in 1903." *Western States Jewish Historical Quarterly* 11, no. 1 (1978): 11.

Lilliard, Richard G. *Desert Challenge: An Interpretation of Nevada.* Lincoln: University of Nebraska Press, 1942.

Limerick, Patricia Nelson. *The Legacy of Conquest: The Unbroken Past of the American West.* New York: W. W. Norton, 1988.

Lingenfelter, Richard E., and Karen Rix Gash. *The Newspapers of Nevada: A History and Bibliography, 1854–1879.* Reno: University of Nevada, 1984.

Linzer, Norman, David J. Schnall, and Jerome A. Chanes, eds. *A Portrait of the American Jewish Community.* Westport, Conn.: Praeger, 1998.

Livingston, Dorothy Michelson. *The Master of Light.* New York: Charles Scribner's Sons, 1973.

Livingston, John. Introduction to *Jews of the American West,* edited by Moses Rischin and John Livingston, 15–25. Detroit: Wayne State University Press, 1991.

Loverin, Janet I., and Robert A. Nylen. "Creating a Fashionable Society: Comstock Needleworkers from 1860 to 1880." In *Comstock Women: The Making of a Mining Community,* edited by Ronald M. James and C. Elizabeth Raymond, 115–41. Reno: University of Nevada Press, 1998.

Lowe, Sharon. "The 'Secret Friend': Opium in Comstock Society, 1860–1887." In *Comstock Women: The Making of a Mining Community,* edited by Ronald M. James and C. Elizabeth Raymond, 95–112. Reno: University of Nevada Press, 1998.

Lowenstein, Steven. *The Jews of Oregon, 1850–1950.* Portland: Jewish Historical Society of Oregon, 1987.

Luebke, Frederick, ed. *European Immigrants in the American West: Community Histories.* Albuquerque: University of New Mexico Press, 1998.

Maisel, L. Sandy, ed. *Jews in American Politics.* Boulder: Rowman and Littlefield, 2001.

Marcus, Jacob R. *The American Jewish Woman, 1654–1980.* New York: KTAV Publishing House, 1981.

———. *Studies in American Jewish History: Studies and Addresses.* Cincinnati: Hebrew Union College Press, 1969.

———. *To Count a People: American Jewish Population Data, 1585–1984.* Lanham, Md.: University Press of America, 1990.

———. *United States Jewry, 1776–1985.* Vols. 1–3. Detroit: Wayne State University Press, 1989–1993.

Marschall, John P. "The 1873 Fire at Hamilton: Finding the Culprit." *Nevada Historical Society Quarterly* 44, no. 4 (2001): 333–52.

———. "The House of Olcovich: A Pioneer Carson City Jewish Family." *Nevada Historical Society Quarterly* 41, no. 3 (1998): 169–90.

———. "Jewish Agricultural Experiment, Wellington, Nevada, 1896–1902: Epilogue to a Communal Failure." *Agricultural History* 76, no. 2 (2002): 244–59.

———. "Jews in Nevada, 1850–1900." *Journal of the West* 23, no. 1 (1984): 62–72.

———. "Nevada's First Synagogue: Temple Emanu-El, 1921." *Footprints* 7, no. 4 (2004): 5.

———. "Rabbi on the Comstock: The Irrepressible Herman Bien, 1864–1865." *Nevada Historical Society Quarterly* 47, no. 3 (2004): 167–92.

Marsh, Andrew J. *Letters from Nevada Territory, 1861–1862.* Edited by William C. Miller, Russell W. McDonald, and Ann Rollins. Carson City: Legislative Counsel Bureau, State of Nevada, 1972.

Massing, Michael. "The Israel Lobby." *Nation,* June 10, 2002. Available online at http://www.webcom.com/hrin/magazine/israellobby.html.

Mathews, Mary McNair. *Ten Years in Nevada; or, Life on the Pacific Coast.* 1880. Reprint, Lincoln: University of Nebraska Press, 1985.

May, Dean L. "Fleeing Babylon: The English Mormon Migration to Alpine, Utah." In *European Immigrants in the American West,* edited by Frederick C. Luebke, 33–48. Albuquerque: University of New Mexico Press, 1998.

McMillan, James B., Gary E. Elliott, and R. T. King. *Fighting Back: A Life in the Struggle for Civil Rights.* Reno: University of Nevada Oral History Program, 1997.

Menken, Adah Isaacs. *Infelicia, and Other Writings.* Edited by Gregory Eiselein. Orchard Park, N.Y.: Broadview Press, 2002.

Meyer, Charles, to Isaac Leeser, Carson City, November 13, 1862. "Trail Blazers of the Trans-Mississippi West." *American Jewish Archives* 8, no. 2 (1956): 105.

Michelson, Miriam. *The Wonderlode of Silver and Gold.* Boston: Stratford, 1934.

Miller, Mary Ann. *Southern Lyon County, 1893.* Smith, Nev.: Double M Book, 1986.

Miller, Matthew. "The Gambler." *Forbes,* March 28, 2005. Available online at http://www.forbes.com.

Miller, William C. *Reports of the 1863 Constitutional Convention of the Territory of Nevada.* [Carson City]: Legislative Counsel Bureau, State of Nevada, [1972].

Mills, Lester W. *A Sagebrush Saga.* Springville, Utah: Art City Publishing, 1956.

Mirisch, Robert. "Interview with Our Jewish Mayor Oscar Goodman." *Life & Style: The Las Vegas Jewish Magazine,* July–August 2004.

Moe, Albert Woods. *Nevada's Golden Age of Gambling.* [Angel Fire, N.M.]: Puget Sound Books, 2001.

Moehring, Eugene P. *Resort City in the Sunbelt: Las Vegas, 1930–1970.* Reno: University of Nevada Press, 1989.

Moehring, Eugene P., and Michael S. Green. *Las Vegas: A Centennial History.* Reno: University of Nevada Press, 2005.

Molinelli, Lambert. *Eureka and Its Resources: A Complete History of Eureka County, Nevada, Containing the United States Mining Laws, the Mining Laws of the District, Bullion Product and Other Statistics for 1878, and a List of County Officers.* 1879. Reprint, Reno: University of Nevada Press, 1982.

Moody, Eric N. "The Early Years of Casino Gambling in Nevada, 1931–1945." Ph.D. diss., University of Nevada, Reno, 1997.

Moore, Deborah Dash. *B'nai B'rith and the Challenge of Ethnic Leadership.* Albany: SUNY Press, 1981.

———. *To the Golden Cities: Pursuing the American Jewish Dream in Miami and L.A.* New York: Free Press, 1994.

Moore, Estelle. "Smith Valley Colony." In *Nevada Official Bicentennial Book,* edited by Stanley W. Paher, 71. Las Vegas: Nevada Publications, 1976.

Morawska, Ewa. *Insecure Prosperity: Small Town Jews in Industrial America, 1890–1940.* Princeton: Princeton University Press, 1998.

Morris, Susan. *A Traveler's Guide to Pioneer Jewish Cemeteries of the California Gold Rush.* Berkeley: Judah Magnes Museum, 1996.

Nadell, Pamela S. "On Their Own Terms: America's Jewish Women, 1954–2004." *American Jewish History* 91, nos. 3–4 (2003): 389–404.

Neider, Charles, ed. *Autobiography of Mark Twain.* New York: Harper and Brothers, 1959.

Nelson, Warren. *Always Bet on the Butcher: Warren Nelson and Casino Gambling, 1930s–1980s.* Reno: University of Nevada Oral History Program, 1994.

Neusner, Jacob. "The Religion, Judaism, in America: What Has Happened in Three Hundred and Fifty Years." *American Jewish History* 91, nos. 3–4 (2003): 361–69.

Nevada-California States Gazetteer and Business Directory, 1905. San Francisco: Suits-Shuman, 1905.

Nevada State Gazetteer and Business Directory, 1914–1915. Salt Lake, Seattle, and Oakland: R. L. Polk, 1914.

Nissen, Axel. *Bret Harte: Prince and Pauper.* Jackson: University Press of Mississippi, 2000.

Novick, Peter. *The Holocaust in American Life.* Boston: Houghton Mifflin, 1999.

Nudelman, Eugene R. "The Family of Joseph Nudelman: A Biography as Related by His Sons Hyman, Robert and Louis." Draft copy of manuscript courtesy of Eugene Nudelman Jr.

Odessky, Dick. *Fly on the Wall: Recollections of Las Vegas' Good Old Bad Old Days.* Las Vegas: Huntington Press, 1999.

Olcott, Irwin. "Olcott Family History." 2 pages. Copy to the author.

Olcott, Sylvia Gutstadt. *On the Sidewalk of the War: A Different Kind of Love Story.* New York, Lincoln, and Shanghai: iUniverse, 2004.

"The Oldest Business in Elko, Nevada: Reinhart's in 1958." *Western States Jewish History* 24, no. 2 (1992): 99–101.

Orzes, Caroline. "A House Divided: The Breakup of the Jewish Federation of Las Vegas." *Life & Style: The Las Vegas Jewish Magazine,* July–August 2004.

Parkes, James. *The Conflict of the Church and the Synagogue: A Study in the Origins of Antisemitism.* Cleveland: World Publishing, 1961.

Patrick, Elizabeth Nelson. "The Black Experience in Southern Nevada." Pt. 2. *Nevada Historical Society Quarterly* 22, no. 3 (1979): 209–20.

Patterson, Edna B. "Reinhart Family: Pioneer Nevada Merchants." *Northeastern Nevada Historical Society Quarterly* 14, no. 4 (1984): 120–34.

Phayer, Michael. *The Catholic Church and the Holocaust, 1930–1965.* Bloomington: Indiana University Press, 2000.

Pillard, Ellen. "Nevada's Treatment of the Mentally Ill, 1882–1961." *Nevada Historical Society Quarterly* 22, no. 2 (Summer 1979): 83–99.

Political History of Nevada. 10th ed. Carson City: Office of the Secretary of State, 1996.

Polk's Reno City, Washoe County, and Carson City Directory. Seattle: R. L. Polk, 1920–1930.

Pomeroy, Earl. "On Becoming a Westerner: Immigrants and Other Migrants." In *Jews of the American West,* edited by Moses Rischin and John Livingston, 190–212. Detroit: Wayne State University Press, 1991.

Postal, Bernard, and Lionel Koppman. *American Jewish Landmarks: A Travel Guide and History.* New York: Fleet Press, 1970.

———. *A Jewish Tourist's Guide to the U.S.* Philadelphia: Jewish Publication Society of America, 1954/5715.

Poulton, Helen J. *Index to History of Nevada, 1881, Thompson and West.* Reno: University of Nevada Press, 1966.

R. L. Polk and Co.'s Reno, Sparks, and Washoe County Directory. Salt Lake City: R. L. Polk, 1913–1917.

Rafael, Ruth. *Western Jewish History Center: Guide to Archival and Oral History Collections.* Berkeley: Western Jewish History Center, 1980.

Ralston, Jon. *The Anointed One: An Inside Look at Nevada Politics.* Las Vegas: Huntington Press, 2000.

Raphael, Marc Lee. "Beyond New York: The Challenge to Local History." In *Jews of the American West,* edited by Moses Rischin and John Livingston, 48–65. Detroit: Wayne State University Press, 1979.

Rawhide, Fallon, and Vicinity City Business Mining Directory, 1908–1909. Reno: P. and C. Nevada Directory, [1909?].

Raymond, C. Elizabeth. *George Wingfield: Owner and Operator of Nevada.* Reno: University of Nevada Press, 1992.

———. "'I Am Afraid We Will Lose All We Have Made:' Women's Lives in a Nineteenth-Century Mining Town." In *Comstock Women: The Making of a Mining Community,* edited by Ronald M. James and C. Elizabeth Raymond, 3–16. Reno: University of Nevada Press, 1998.

Reid, Ed, and Ovid Demaris. *The Green Felt Jungle.* New York: Trident Press, 1963.

"The Reinharts of Nevada: A Picture Story." *Western States Jewish History* (January 1987): 115–20.

Rice, George Graham [Jacob Simon Herzig]. *My Adventures with Your Money.* 1913. Reprint, Las Vegas: Nevada Publications, 1986.

Rischin, Moses. *The Promised City: New York's Jews, 1870–1914.* Cambridge: Harvard University Press, 1977.

———, ed. *The Jews of the West: The Metropolitan Years.* Berkeley and Los Angeles: University of California Press, 1979.

Rischin, Moses, and John Livingston, eds. *Jews of the American West.* Detroit: Wayne State University Press, 1979.

Rocha, Guy. "Levi's 501 Jeans: A Riveting Story in Early Reno." Historical Myth a Month, no. 38. Nevada State Library and Archives, Carson City.

Rocha, Guy, and Eric Moody. "Marvin Hart vs. Jack Root: The Heavyweight Championship Fight That Time Forgot." *Hank Kaplan's World Wide Boxing Digest* (September 1980): 12–14.

Rocha, Guy, and Dennis Myers. "Pittman on Ice." *Sierra Sage* (Carson City/Carson Valley), March 1996.

Rochlin, Harriet, and Fred Rochlin. *Pioneer Jews: A New Life in the Far West.* Boston: Houghton Mifflin, 1984.

Rockaway, Robert A. *But He Was Good to His Mother: The Lives and Crimes of Jewish Gangsters.* Jerusalem: Gefen Publishing House, 2000.

———. "Hoodlum Hero: The Jewish Gangster as Defender of His People, 1919–1949." *American Jewish History* 82, no. 1 (1994): 215–35.

Ross, Silas E. *Recollections of Life at Glendale, Nevada: Work at the University of Nevada and Western Funeral Practice.* Reno: University of Nevada Oral History Program, 1970.

Rosten, Leo. *Hooray for Yiddish: A Book about English.* New York: Galahad Books, 1982.

Rothman, Hal. *Neon Metropolis: How Las Vegas Started the Twenty-first Century.* New York: Routledge, 2002.

Rowley, William D. *Reno: Hub of the Washoe Country, an Illustrated History.* Woodland Hills, Calif.: Windsor Publications, 1984.

Rudd, Hynda L. "The Mountain West as a Jewish Frontier." *Western States Jewish Historical Quarterly* 13, no. 3 (April 1981): 241–56.

———. *Mountain West Pioneer Jewry: An Historical and Genealogical Source Book from Origins to 1885.* Los Angeles: Western American Studies Series, 1980.

Rusco, Elmer R. "The Civil Rights Movement in Nevada." *Nevada Public Affairs Review,* no. 2 (1987): 75–81.

———. *"Good Time Coming?" Black Nevadans in the Nineteenth Century.* Westport, Conn.: Greenwood Press, 1975.

———. "Nevada Law and Race." *Nevada Public Affairs Review,* no. 2 (1987): 71–74.

Rusco, Elmer R., and Richard Siegel. "The ACLU in Nevada." *Nevada Public Affairs Review,* no. 2 (1990): 47–51.

Saiger, Morton. *An Interview with Morton Saiger, Conducted by R. T. King.* Reno: University of Nevada Oral History Program, 1985.

Sanua, Marianne R. *Going Greek: Jewish College Fraternities in the United States, 1895–1945.* Detroit: Wayne State University Press, 2003.

Sarna, Jonathan. *American Judaism: A History.* New Haven: Yale University Press, 2004.

Sawyer, Grant. *Hang Tough! Grant Sawyer, an Activist in the Governor's Mansion.* Interviews conducted by Gary E. Elliott. Narrative composed by R. T. King. Reno: University of Nevada Oral History Program, 1993.

Sayre, Cora Gage. *Memories of Smith Valley.* Reno: University of Nevada Oral History Program, 1977.

Scharnhorst, Gary. *Bret Harte: Opening the American Literary West.* Norman: University of Oklahoma Press, 2000.

Schlissel, Lillian. *Women's Diaries of the Westward Journey.* New York: Schocken Books, 1992.

Scrugham, James, ed. *Nevada: A Narrative of the Conquest of a Frontier Land, Comprising the Story of Her People from the Dawn of History to the Present Time.* 3 vols. Chicago: American Historical Society, 1935.

Sentilles, Renee M. *Performing Menken: Adah Isaacs Menken and the Birth of American Celebrity.* New York: Cambridge University Press, 2003.

Shapiro, Edward S. *A Time for Healing: American Jewry since World War II.* Baltimore: Johns Hopkins University Press, 1992.

Shaw, David. "Congregation Ner Tamid: An Unofficial History." 5 typed pages. Copy courtesy of the author.

Sheehan, Jack, ed. *The Players: The Men Who Made Las Vegas.* Reno: University of Nevada Press, 1997.

Shepperson, Wilbur S. *Restless Strangers: Nevada's Immigrants and Their Interpreters.* Reno: University of Nevada Press, 1970.

Shiovitz, Jeffrey, ed. *B'kol Echad in One Voice.* N.p.: United Synagogue of Conservative Judaism, n.d.

Shpall, Leo. "Jewish Agricultural Colonies in the United States." *Agricultural History* 24, no. 3 (1950): 120–46.

Siegel, Richard L. "The Jews of Western Nevada." *Nevada Public Affairs Review,* no. 2 (1987): 64–65.

Sigurdson, Larry. "Chevrah Kedesha: As He Came, So Shall He Go." *Life & Style: The Las Vegas Jewish Magazine,* January–February 2005, 22.

Simich, Jerry L., and Thomas C. Wright, eds. *The Peoples of Las Vegas: One City, Many Faces.* Reno: University of Nevada Press, 2005.

Smith, Arthur M., Jr. *Let's Get Going: From Oral History Interviews with Arthur M. Smith Jr., a Narrative Interpretation, by R. T. King.* Reno: University of Nevada Oral History Program, 1996.

Smith, Henry Nash, ed. *Mark Twain of the "Enterprise": Newspaper Articles and Other Documents, 1862–1864.* Berkeley and Los Angeles: University of California Press, 1957.

Smith, Henry Nash, and William M. Gibson, eds. *Mark Twain–Howells Letters: The Correspondence of Samuel L. Clemens and William Dean Howells, 1872–1910.* Vols. 1–2. Cambridge: Harvard University Press, Belknap Press, 1960.

Smith, John L. "The Ghost of Ben Siegel." In *The Players: The Men Who Made Las Vegas*, edited by Jack Sheehan, 81–91. Reno: University of Nevada Press, 1997.

———. "Moe Dalitz and the Desert." In *The Players: The Men Who Made Las Vegas*, edited by Jack Sheehan, 35–47. Reno: University of Nevada Press, 1997.

———. *Of Rats and Men: Oscar Goodman's Life from Mob Mouthpiece to Mayor of Las Vegas*. Las Vegas: Huntington Press, 2003.

———. *Running Scared: The Life and Treacherous Times of Las Vegas Casino King Steve Wynn*. New York: Barricade Books, 1995.

Sodoma, Brian. "Cab Company Owner Rides Way to Success." *Las Vegas Business Press*, April 28, 2003, 6.

Sohn, Anton. *The Healers of Nineteenth-Century Nevada*. Reno: Greasewood Press, 1997.

Sorin, Gerald. *A Time for Building: The Third Migration, 1880–1920*. Baltimore: Johns Hopkins University Press, 1992.

Spence, Clark C. *Mining Engineers and the American West: The Lace-Boot Brigade, 1849–1933*. New Haven: Yale University Press, 1970.

Stein, Julius. *Synagogue Life in Northern Nevada*. Reno: Western Book/Journal Press, 1996.

Stern, Norton B. "Abraham Mooser: First Businessman of Santa Monica, California." *Western States Jewish Historical Quarterly* 1, no. 2 (1969): 109–27.

———. "Harriet Ashim Choynski: An 1850 Western Arrival." *Western States Jewish History* 24, no. 3 (April 1992).

———. "The Jewish Community of a Nevada Mining Town." *Western States Jewish Historical Quarterly* 15, no. 1 (1982): 48–78.

———. "The Labatts' Attack in San Francisco and Los Angeles." *Western States Jewish History* (April 1996): 179–88.

———. "The Orangevale and Porterville, California, Jewish Farm Colonies." *Western States Jewish Historical Quarterly* 10, no. 2 (1978): 159–67.

———. "Report of an Interview with Mrs. Seymour (Carolyn Mooser) Wisekopf, Beverly Hills, California, October 30, 1967." Box 2802, American Jewish Archives, Cincinnati.

———. "The Rise and Fall of the Jewish Community of Austin, Nevada." *Western States Jewish Historical Quarterly* 9 (October 1976): 87–88.

Stern, Norton B., and William M. Kramer. "An American Zion in Nevada: The Rise and Fall of an Agricultural Colony." *Western States Jewish Historical Quarterly* 13, no. 2 (1981): 130–34.

Stewart, Robert E., Jr., and Mary Frances Stewart. *Adolph Sutro: A Biography*. Berkeley: Howell-North, 1962.

Stone, Eillen Hallett. *A Homeland in the West: Utah Jews Remember*. Salt Lake City: University of Utah Press, 2001.

Suberman, Stella. *The Jew Store*. Chapel Hill: Algonquin Books, 1998.

Swallow, Craig F. "The Ku Klux Klan in Nevada during the 1920s." *Nevada Historical Society Quarterly* 24, no. 3 (1981): 203–21.

Szasz, Ferenc Morton. *Religion in the Modern American West.* Tucson: University of Arizona Press, 2000.

Tarkington, Elizabeth Murray. "The Story of Sam Platt." *Sunset Magazine,* November 1921, 27, 70–71.

Thompson, David, comp. *The Tennessee Letters: From Carson Valley, 1857–1860.* Reno: Grace Dangberg Foundation, 1983.

Thompson, William N. "Steve Wynn: 'I Got the Message.'" In *The Maverick Spirit: Building the New Nevada,* edited by Richard O. Davies, 194–211. Reno: University of Nevada Press, 1998.

Tobias, Henry J., *A History of the Jews in New Mexico.* Albuquerque: University of New Mexico Press, 1990.

Tobin, Gary A., et al. *Jewish Federation of Las Vegas Community Study, 1996.* Las Vegas: Foundation of the Jewish Federation of Las Vegas, 1996.

Totten, Kathryn Dunn. "'They Are Doing So to a Liberal Extent Here Now': Women and Divorce on the Comstock, 1859–1880." In *Comstock Women: The Making of a Mining Community,* edited by Ronald M. James and C. Elizabeth Raymond, 68–94. Reno: University of Nevada Press, 1998.

Townley, John. *Tough Little Town on the Truckee, 1868–1900.* Reno: Jamison Station Press, 1983.

Truett, Velma Stevens. *On the Hoof in Nevada.* Los Angeles: Gehrett-Truett-Hall, 1950.

Twain, Mark. *Roughing It.* New York: Oxford University Press, 1996.

Tweed, Thomas A., ed. *Retelling U.S. Religious History.* Berkeley and Los Angeles: University of California Press, 1997.

Union of American Hebrew Congregations. *Statistics of the Jews of the United States.* Philadelphia: Union of American Hebrew Congregations, 1880.

Von Drehle, David. *Triangle: The Fire That Changed America.* New York: Atlantic Monthly Press, 2003.

Vorspan, Max, and Lloyd P. Gartner. *History of the Jews of Los Angeles.* Philadelphia: Jewish Publication Society of America, 1970.

Walker, Samuel. *In Defense of American Liberties: A History of the ACLU.* 2d ed. Carbondale: Southern Illinois University Press, 1999.

Walton, Clifford C. "Capitol's Who's Who for Nevada." In *Nevada Today: A Pictorial Volume of the State's Activities.* Portland, Ore.: Capital Publishing, 1949.

Watson, Anita Ernst. *Into Their Own: Nevada Women Emerging into Public Life.* [Reno]: Nevada Humanities Committee, 2000.

Watson, Anita Ernst, Jean E. Ford, and Linda White. "'The Advantages of Ladies' Society': The Public Sphere of Women on the Comstock." In *Comstock Women:*

The Making of a Mining Community, edited by Ronald M. James and C. Elizabeth Raymond, 179–99. Reno: University of Nevada Press.

Watson, Margaret G. "History of the Theatre of Virginia City, Nevada, from 1849–1865." Master's thesis, University of Nevada, Reno, 1940.

———. *Silver Theatre: Amusements of the Mining Frontier in Early Nevada, 1850 to 1864.* Glendale, Calif.: Arthur H. Clark, 1964.

Watters, Leon L. *The Pioneer Jews of Utah.* New York: American Jewish Historical Society, 1952.

"A Western Picture Parade." *Western States Jewish History* 17, no. 2 (January 1985).

Whitfield, Stephen J. *In Search of American Jewish Culture.* Hanover, N.H.: Brandeis University Press, 1999.

Wilkerson, W. R., III. *The Man Who Invented Las Vegas.* N.p.: Ciro's Books, 2000.

Wilson, Woodrow. *Race, Community, and Politics in Las Vegas, 1940s–1980s.* Reno: University of Nevada Oral History Program, 1990.

Wren, Thomas, ed. *A History of the State of Nevada, Its Resources and People.* New York: Lewis Publishing, 1904.

Ybarra, Michael J. *Washington Gone Crazy: Senator Pat McCarran and the Great American Communist Hunt.* Hanover, N.H.: Steerforth Press, 2004.

Young, Otis E. "Philipp Deidesheimer, 1832–1916: Engineer of the Comstock." *Southern California Quarterly* 57, no. 4 (1975): 361–70.

Zanjani, Sally. *Goldfield: The Last Gold Rush on the Western Frontier.* Athens: Ohio University Press, Swallow Press, 1992.

———. *The Glory Days in Goldfield, Nevada.* Reno: University of Nevada Press, 2002.

———. *The Unspiked Rail: Memoir of a Nevada Rebel.* Reno: University of Nevada Press, 1981.

Zwerin, Kenneth C., and Norton B. Stern. "Jacob Voorsanger: From Cantor to Rabbi." *Western States Jewish History* 25, no. 3 (1983): 195–202.

Newspapers

American Israelite (Cincinnati)
Carson City News
Carson (Daily) Appeal (Carson City)
Carson Daily Index (Carson City)
Carson Weekly (Carson City)
Daily State Register (Virginia City)
Elko (Daily) Free Press
Elko (Weekly) Independent
Eureka Daily Leader
Eureka Daily Republican
Eureka (Daily) Sentinel
Footlight (Virginia City)

Genoa Weekly Courier
Goldfield Chronicle
Goldfield (Daily) Tribune
Goldfield Gossip
Goldfield News
Gold Hill (Daily) News
Hebrew (San Francisco)
Hebrew Sabbath School Visitor (Cincinnati)
Jewish Progress (San Francisco)
Jewish Reporter (Las Vegas)
Jewish Tribune (San Francisco)
Las Vegas Age
Las Vegas Israelite
Las Vegas Review-Journal
Las Vegas Sun
Lyon County Times (Dayton, Nev.)
Morning Appeal (Carson City)
Nevada Appeal (Carson City)
Nevada State Journal (Reno)
Nevada Tribune (Carson City)
Pioche (Daily) Record
Rawhide Daily Press
Rawhide Press Times
Rawhide Rustler
Reno Crescent
Reno Evening Gazette
Reno Gazette-Journal
Rhyolite Herald
Sacramento Bee
Silver Age (Reno)
Syracuse Evening Herald
Territorial Enterprise (Carson City and Virginia City, Nev.)
Tonopah Times Bonanza and Goldfield News
Virginia Daily Union (Virginia City)
Virginia Evening Bulletin (Virginia City)
Weekly (Carson City)
Weekly Gazette and Stockman (Reno)
Weekly Gleaner (San Francisco)
White Pine (Daily) News (Hamilton and later Ely, Nev.)
Winnemucca Argent
Yerington Rustler

Selected Bibliography

Interviews

The author interviewed the following either in person or by telephone. Only those who released their comments for possible publication are listed. The asterisks signify those who are deceased.

Deborah Achtenberg
Sanford Akselrad
Charlotte Arley*
Adele Baratz
Shelley Berkley
Patricia Blanshard
Eileen Brookman*
Mendel Cunin
Renee Diamond
Robert Dickens
Ruth Dickens*
Nancy Badt Drake
John Farahi
Mitchell Gilbert
Eddie Ginsberg*
Milton Glick
Ruth Goldfarb
Eric Goldstein
Bert Goldwater*
Felipe Goodman
Oscar Goodman
Sheila Goodman*
Mel Gordon*
Robert Gorell
Martha Gould
Shea Harlig
Mylan Hawkins
Chic Hecht*
Mel Hecht
George Herman*
James Hulse
Lena Jacobs*
Sylvia Jacobs*
Ethel Jaffe
Joseph Kempler

[368]

James Kidder
Judy Kosinski
Leonard Marmour
Art Marshall
Leo McFadden
Michael Melner
Sydell Miller
Melvin Moss
Judy Nash
Sylvia Olcott*
William Pettite
Doris Rosenberg*
Howard Rosenberg
Charles Salton*
Doug Samuelson
John Sanford*
Joyce Scheinman
Milton Schwartz*
Leonard Shapiro
Richard Siegel
Allen Silver
Myra Soifer
Mervin Tarlow
Madge Tillim*
Christine Hilp Tweet
Douglas Unger
Valerie Wiener
Thomas R. C. Wilson
Edythe Katz Yarchever
David Zenoff*

INDEX

Page numbers in italics refer to maps and tables.

Flamingo Hotel and Casino, 171–72, 173, 177
Fleishhacker, Aaron, 21, 22
Fleishhacker, Janet, 17
Flower, Sydney, 133
food: kosher, 81–82, 248–49, 262
food pantries, 257
Footlight (newspaper), 80
Ford, Henry, 198
Fox, Abe, 333n11
Fox, Julius, 162, 217, 333n11
Foxman, Abraham, 242
Foxy's delicatessen, 217
Foxy's Firehouse restaurants, 333n11
Frank, Benjamin, 153
Frank, Esther, 96
Frank, Rachel "Ray," 96–97
Frank, Sam, 153
Frank, William T., 41, 297–98n6
Frankel, Rabbi Jack, 188–89, 206
Franklin, Max, 68
fraternal organizations: in Eureka, 64; Jewish presence in, 197–98. *See also individual organizations*
fraternities: Jewish membership and, 208
Frederick, Isaac, 43
Frederick, Leah, 101
Frederick, M. M., 306n44
freedom of religion, 205
Freeman, Merrill, 46
Freemasonry, 197–98. *See also* Masonic Lodges
freight rates, 49
Freirich, Rabbi Jonathan, 233
Frémont, John C., 160
French Canadians, 71
Freudenthal, Herman, 142, 145, 161, 272
Friedan, Betty, 223
Friedenthal, Henrietta Olcovich, 111
Friedman, Daniel, 268
Friedman, Ephraim, 125
Friedman, Frank, 131
Friedman, Louis, 166
Friedman, Sam, 165
Frontier Hotel and Casino, 268
funerals. *See* burials

Gallagher, Fr. Hugh, 19
Gambarana, Eddie, 182, 206
gambling: Jews in Las Vegas and, 171–73; legalization of, 146; notions of temperance and, 170. *See also* casinos; illegal gambling
Gancharov, Morris and Lottie, 218
Gang, Bobbie, 226
gangs, 170
Gann, Milton, 235
Gans, Joe, 138
Gardner, Alan, 204
Garfield, John, 204

Garfinkle, Bud, 272
Garfinkle, Buddy, 208, 332n44
Garfinkle, Jake, 187, 190
Garfinkle, Julius, 204
Garfinkle, Mary, 187
Garfinkle family, 261
garment unions, 169–70
Gass, Octavius Decatur, 161
gay rights, 225–26
Geller, Solomon, 294n20
Generation to Generation program, 243
Genoa, 12, 16
Gentlemen's Agreement (film), 204
Georgetta, Clel, 200–201
"Germanic" immigrants, 4–6
Gershwin, George, 204
Ghermaizian, Eskander, 247
Gibralter North Exchange, 137
gift shops, 169
Gilbert, Mitchell, 257
gin rummy tournament, 181
Ginsberg, Eddie, 203
Ginsburg, Gerald, 204
Giunchigliani, Chris, 273
Glanz, Rudolph, 169
Glaser, Rabbi Joseph, 187
Glick, Gene and Ruth, 225
Glick, Milton, 140
Glick, Morris and Esther, 140
Goddard, Paulette, 204
Goffstein, Ben, 173, 181
Golbart, Rabbi Gary, 238, 244, 251
Gold, Rabbi Aaron, 183–84, 207, 327n12
Gold, Rita, 327n12
Gold and Philippson's, 21
Goldberg, Arthur, 251
Golden, Augusta, 130
Golden Nugget Hotel and Casino, 268, 325n34
Golden Road Motor Inn, 267
Goldfarb, Ruth, 243
Goldfield: famous Jewish citizens, 130, 132–34, 136–37; famous Jewish visitors, 137–39; growth of, 131; illegal gambling in, 135; Jewish merchants and occupations, 131–32; prostitution in, 134; religious practice in, 135–36; restaurants and saloons, 134–35; stock exchange, 134
Goldfield Consolidated Mines Company, 138
Goldfield Mining District, 131
Goldfield News, 133
Goldfield Stock and Exchange Board, 134
Gold Hill News (newspaper), 94
Goldmark, Carolyn, 280
Goldring, Ira, 168, 333n12
gold rushes. *See* mining
Goldsmith, L., 42
Goldstein, A. B., 55
Goldstein, Eric, 257

periodicals: Jewish children and, 102
Perkins, William, 11
Perske, Betty, 204
Peter (saint), 1–2
Petersen, Peter, 200, 202
Pettite, June, 155
Petuchowski, Erin, 191
Peyser, Louis, 90
philanthropy: Sheldon Anderson, 269–70; Farahi family, 266–67; rank-and-file contributions and, 271; Milton Schwartz, 265–66; types of Nevada philanthropists, 265; *tzedakah*, 264–65; United Jewish Appeal, 178; women and, 270–71; Steve Wynn, 267–69
Phillips, Fred, 148
Phillips, Pauline Esther Friedman, 204–5
"Phillips & Ashim," 18
Phoenix, 286
Pinschower, Jacob, 84, 89
Pinschower, Mark, 84
Pinschower, Rose, 89
Pioche, 54–57
Pioneer Auction and Commission House, 21
Pioneer Jewish Ladies, 116
Pittman, Key, 200
Pittsburgh Platform of 1885, 285
Platt, Joseph, 23, 109, 112
Platt, Samuel: biographical overview of, 112; celebrities and, 147; criticism of Henry Ford, 198; fund raising and, 148; law career, 321n16; Masonry and, 148; music and, 92; politics and, 199–200, 201, 272; teaching and, 97
Platt family, 72
Poland: emigration from, 5
Pony Canyon, 36
Porter, Audrey Marie, 137, 319n62
Posener, Lina, 51
Posin, Bernard, 272
Postrel, Rabbi Oren, 233, 234
Powning, Christopher Columbus "C. C.," 117, 118
Powning, Clare Poor, 119, 313n50
Powning, James Johnson, 313–14n50
Poznán, Duchy of, 5, 9
Prell, Milton, 173
Prescott, A., 43
Prescott, J., 43
Prescott, Sophia, 101
Price, Samuel, 21, 22
prizefighting, 142–44. *See also* boxing
pro-choice movement, 225
Procter, Frank M., 12
Prohibition, 171
Prospectors' Club, 208, 221
prostitution, 98–100, 134, 310n45
Protestantism: ecumenical movement and, 205; notions of temperance in, 170. *See also* Christian churches

Protocols of the Elders of Zion, 198
Prussia: emigration from, 4–6
Purim: temperance and, 170
Purim balls, 63–64, 68, 86–87
Purple Gang, 174

Rabbinical Assembly, 7
rabbis: divisions between, 288; issues of continuity in leadership, 285; with nontraditional training, 244
Rabbit Creek, 36
racial discrimination: anti-Chinese sentiment, 107–10; in Las Vegas, 216, 217–18; in Nevada, 110; in Reno, 216–17
racial integration: of casinos, 220–21
Raggio, William, 225
Ragtown, 161
railroads: freight rates, 49; map of, *48*
Ralston, Jon, 281–82, 343n49
Rappaport, Ethyl, 166
Raum, Edward, 58
Raymond, Rae, 134
"Raymond & Ely/Pioche Phoenix Fight," 55
Reagan, Ronald, 276
real estate stock market, 23–24
reapportionment, 222
"Rebbe." *See* Schneerson, Rabbi Menachem Mendel "the Rebbe"
rebbetzins, 270
Reconstructionist Judaism, 7–8, 244
Reese, Michael, 77
Reese River Mining District, 36
Reese River Pioneers, 37
Reform Judaism: in Eureka, 60–62; on gay and lesbian unions, 225–26; ordination of women and, 223; origin of, 29; overview of, 6–7; Pittsburgh Platform of 1885, 285. *See also* Temple Ner Tamid; Temple Sinai (Reno); Temple Sinai (Summerlin)
Reform Union of American Hebrew Congregations, 60
refuseniks, 276
Reid, Harry, 275
Reinhart, Eli, 49
Reinhart, Samuel, 299n20
Reinhart, Simon, 46
Reinhart Brothers store, 45
Reinhart family, 45, 49
religion: ecumenical movement, 205; freedom of, 205; interfaith cooperation, 206–8
religious education, 101–2, 288–89
religious observance and practice: in Carson City, 74, 111–12; among Christians, 310n49; during the depression years, 105, 106; in early Nevada, 18–19, 71, 283–84; in Las Vegas, 162–63, 166–67; in Pioche, 55–57; Rabbi Jacob Sheyer and,